The Routledge Reader in Early Childhood Education

Early childhood education is integral to social policies in developed and developing countries, reflecting the significance of high quality education and care to children's immediate and future lives.

Issues about 'the nature of the child', and the purposes of early childhood education have remained open to debate and controversy in light of recent social, economic and political changes across the globe. These changes have had a profound impact on educational provision and on related services in health, social welfare, and family support. The carefully selected readings in this book have been chosen to exemplify contrasting theoretical, methodological, and epistemological orientations in research and scholarship, key conceptual shifts, and contemporary policy directions in early childhood education.

The purpose of this Reader is to examine change, transformation and continuity, and to present indicative scholarship in relation to five key themes:

- theoretical perspectives on learning
- curriculum and pedagogy
- play
- policy
- professionalism and research methods.

Within each theme, the readings have been chosen to exemplify national and international perspectives and trends. This is not to present a homogenised view of early childhood provision and services across cultural contexts; rather the intention is to take a critical perspective on past, present and future directions, and to map some of the challenges, dilemmas and contradictions posed in research and scholarship. This Reader will be invaluable to all undergraduate and postgraduate students of Early Childhood Education.

Elizabeth Wood is Professor of Education at the University of Exeter.

The Routledge Reader in Early Childhood Education

Edited by
Elizabeth Wood

Routledge
Taylor & Francis Group

LONDON AND NEW YORK

First published 2008
by Routledge
2 Park Square, Milton Park, Abingdon, Oxon OX14 4RN

Simultaneously published in the USA and Canada
by Routledge
270 Madison Ave, New York, NY 10016

*Routledge is an imprint of the Taylor & Francis Group,
an informa business*

Typeset in Garamond by Keyword Group Ltd
Printed and bound in Great Britain by MPG Books Ltd,
Bodmin, Cornwall

British Library Cataloguing in Publication Data
A catalogue record for this book is available from the British Library

Library of Congress Cataloging in Publication Data
The Routledge reader in early childhood education / [compiled by]
  Elizabeth Wood.
    p. cm.
  Includes bibliographical references.
  ISBN-13: 978-0-415-45151-2 (hardback)
  ISBN-13: 978-0-415-45152-9 (pbk.)
  ISBN-13: 978-0-203-93302-2 (ebook)
  ISBN-10: 0-415-45151-5 (hbk.)
  [etc.]
  1. Early childhood education. I. Wood, Elizabeth, 1955–
LB1139.23.R68 2008
372.21—dc22
2007027721

ISBN10: 0-415-45151-5 (hbk)
ISBN10: 0-415-45152-3 (pbk)
ISBN10: 0-203-93302-8 (ebk)

ISBN13: 978-0-415-45151-2 (hbk)
ISBN13: 978-0-415-45152-9 (pbk)
ISBN13: 978-0-203-93302-2 (ebk)

Contents

Sources

Theme I. Theoretical perspectives on learning, curriculum and pedagogy

Chapter 1. Introduction, *'Play in the Infants' School'*, E. R. Boyce, Methuen, 1946.

Chapter 2. Fleer, M. (2006) The cultural construction of child development: Creating institutional and cultural intersubjectivity, *International Journal of Early Years Education*, 14(2), 127–140.

Chapter 3. Soler, J. and Miller, L. (2003) The struggle for early childhood curricula: A comparison of the English Foundation Stage Curriculum, *Te Whāriki* and Reggio Emilia, *The International Journal of Early Years Education*, Vol.11, No. 1 (Taylor & Francis).

Chapter 4. Brooker, L. (2003) Learning how to learn: Parental ethnotheories and young children's preparation for school, *The International Journal of Early Years Education*, Vol. 11, No. 1 (Taylor & Francis).

Theme II. Play: Advances in theory and practice

Chapter 5. Holzman, L. and Newman, F. (1993) Playing in/with the ZPD, *Lev Vygotsky: Revolutionary Scientist* (Routledge).

Chapter 6. Janson, U. (2001) Togetherness and diversity in pre-school play, *The International Journal of Early Years Education*, Vol. 9, No. 2 (Taylor & Francis).

Chapter 7. Marsh, J. (2000) 'But I want to fly too!': Girls and superhero play in the infant classroom, *Gender and Education*, Vol. 12, No. 2 (Taylor & Francis).

Chapter 8. Sawyers, J. and Carrick, N. (2003) Symbolic play through the eyes and words of children, *Play and Educational Theory and Practice*, Ed. Lytle, D. (Ablex Publishing Corporation, U.S.).

Theme III. Policy generation and implementation

Chapter 9. Neuman, M. (2005) Governance of early childhood education and care: Recent developments in OECD countries, *Early Years*, Vol. 25, No. 2 (Taylor & Francis).

Chapter 10. Sylva, K. and Pugh, G. (2005) Transforming the early years in England, *Oxford Review of Education*, Vol. 31, No. 1 (Taylor & Francis).

Chapter 11. Ball, S. and Vincent, C. (2005) The 'childcare champion'? New Labour, social justice and the childcare market, *British Educational Research Journal*, Vol. 31, No. 5 (Taylor & Francis).

Chapter 12. Rosemberg, F. (2005) Childhood and social inequality in Brazil, in H. Penn, Ed., *Unequal Childhoods: Young Children's Lives in Poor Countries*, Chapter 8, pp. 142–70 (Routledge).

Theme IV. Professionalism and professionalisation

Chapter 13. Duncan, J. (2004) Misplacing the teacher? New Zealand early childhood teachers and early childhood education policy reforms, 1984–96, *Contemporary Issues in Early Childhood Education*, Vol. 5, No. 2 (Symposium Journals).

Chapter 14. Osgood, J. (2006) Professionalism and performativity: The feminist challenge facing early years practitioners, *Early Years*, Vol. 26, No. 2 (Taylor & Francis).

Theme V. Research methods: Agency and voice

Chapter 15. Sumsion, J. (1999) Critical reflections on the experiences of a male early childhood worker, *Gender and Education*, Vol. 11, No. 4 (Routledge).

Chapter 16. Farrell, A. Tayler, C. and Tennent, L. (2004) Building social capital in early childhood education and care: An Australian study, *British Educational Research Journal*, Vol. 30. No. 5 (Taylor & Francis).

Chapter 17. Montgomery, H. (2005) Gendered childhoods: A cross-disciplinary overview, *Gender and Education*, Vol. 17, No. 5 (Routledge).

Figures

Tables

Contributors

Elizabeth Wood is Professor of Education at the University of Exeter.

E. R. Boyce was a teacher at Raleigh Infants' School, Stepney, London.

Marilyn Fleer is at the Faculty of Education, Monash University, Australia.

Janet Soler and Linda Miller are at the Faculty of Education, The Open University, Milton Keynes.

Liz Brooker is at the School of Early Childhood and Primary Education, Institute of Education, University of London.

Lois Holzman and Fred Newman are authors of the book *Lev Vygotsky: Revolutionary Scientist*.

Ulf Janson is at Stockholm University, Sweden.

Jackie Marsh is at the Department of Educational Studies, University of Sheffield.

Janet K. Sawyers and Nathalie Carrick are contributors to the book *Play and Educational Theory and Pratice*.

Michelle J. Neuman is at Columbia University, New York, USA.

Kathy Sylva and Gillian Pugh are at the Department of Educational Studies, University of Oxford and Coram Family, London, respectively.

Stephen J. Ball and Carol Vincent are at The Institute of Education, University of London.

Fúlvia Rosemberg is a senior researcher with the Carlos Chagas Foundation and a full professor of social psychology at the PUC-SP, Brazil.

Contestation, transformation and re-conceptualisation in early childhood education

Elizabeth Wood

> At the heart of the educational process lies the child. No advances in policy, no acquisitions of new equipment have their desired effect unless they are in harmony with the nature of the child [.]
>
> (CACE, 1967, Para 9)

I have chosen to introduce this reader with one of the most famous quotations from the report of the Central Advisory Council for Education (1967), which was set up to review Primary education (ages 4–11) in England, and became widely known as the Plowden Report, after its chairperson, Lady Plowden. This quotation distilled the prevailing beliefs, values, theories and philosophies that reified a commitment to child-centred approaches in educational theory and practice. These approaches were grounded in the work of philosophers, psychologists and educationalists from the nineteenth and twentieth centuries, and from contrasting cultures and continents (Wood and Attfield, 2005). Their work created an eclectic theoretical framework that transcended international boundaries (Krogh and Slentz, 2001; May, 1997), and informed educational provision and services.

From a contemporary standpoint, this quotation indicates how decisions about early childhood education and care are informed by policy makers, and by multiple perspectives about children and childhood, including theories about early learning and development, and how young children might best be educated and cared for in home, pre-school and school contexts. In the last twenty years incremental policy interventions in young children's lives have been driven by concerns for their education, care and health, and by wider cultural, socio-political, economic and technological changes. Contemporary scholars focus on the role of government policies in shaping provision and services, wider issues of ethics and politics, and transformational processes in early childhood education. In recent trends towards re-conceptualising early childhood education, the focus has shifted from essentialist views of 'the nature of the child' towards broader theoretical frameworks that explore social, political and cultural constructions of childhood. Contemporary theorists are more likely to draw on the work of Foucault and Derrida than Froebel and Dewey (Dahlberg and Moss, 2005; MacNaughton, 2000, 2005). As Woodhead (2000) argues, in developed and developing countries education is generally regarded as one of the most powerful tools for enhancing children's quality of life, their achievements, aspirations and life chances. Whether contemporary trends are 'in harmony' with twenty-first century children remains open to debate, not least because Western views of early childhood education are being contested from theoretical, disciplinary and ethical perspectives. Furthermore, the challenge of ensuring that education is 'in harmony' with twenty-first century children necessitates critical understanding of global, national and local perspectives. Accordingly, the readings in this book have been selected to exemplify contrasting theoretical, methodological, and epistemological orientations, key conceptual shifts, and contemporary policy directions.

The purpose of this reader is to examine change, transformation and continuity, and to present indicative scholarship in relation to five key themes: theoretical perspectives on learning, curriculum and pedagogy; play; policy; professionalism and research methods. Originally I identified equity and diversity as a sixth theme, but as I chose the readings, issues of gender, ethnicity, culture, social class, ability/disability and sexuality were embedded throughout the five themes. I decided not to position diversity as deviance from established norms, or difference from dominant groups. Within each theme, the readings have been chosen to exemplify national (UK) and international perspectives, to take a critical perspective on past, present and future directions, and to identify some of the challenges posed in research and scholarship. Contemporary scholars consider children and childhoods in the context of social and cultural diversity, using different 'lenses' through which to examine structural positions, power relations and the construction of knowledge and meaning within an increasingly commodified and globalised world (Cannella and Viruru, 2004; Dahlberg and Moss, 2005; S. Edwards, 2003; R. Edwards and Usher, 2000; MacNaughton, 2000, 2005; Ryan and Grieshaber, 2005; Yelland, 2002). Therefore it is appropriate to address issues of equity and diversity not as 'bolt-on' extras, but as integral to the ethics, politics and practices of early childhood education.

Early childhood education has always provoked passionate feelings amongst stakeholders, which has arisen from the perceived need to defend and protect young children from inappropriate demands, to advocate children's rights, and to lobby local and national policy makers for improved services and provision. Whilst such passion is recognised as a valid response to decades of underfunding and poorly coordinated policies, it has also perpetuated taken for granted assumptions, masked conceptual weaknesses, and constrained critical engagement with broader social, cultural and political issues, and the ways in which these impact on the field. The rationale for this selection therefore reflects a deliberate intention to go beyond the emotive, and to focus on significant theoretical and conceptual advances that are transforming provision and practices.

This introductory chapter provides an overview of the five key themes, and links the selected readings with related research and policy frameworks for children from birth to eight years. This reflects the inclusion of children from birth to three years in national education policy frameworks (e.g. in England and New Zealand), and the varying ages (five, six or seven years) at which compulsory schooling begins. From historical and post-modern per-spectives, childhood is a cultural invention (Cunningham, 2006; Dahlberg and Moss, 2005), as are the institutions, policies, texts and discourses that define and regulate early childhood education and care. For many children, especially in developing countries, early childhood is not a discrete or tran-sitional phase, but a progressive continuum of activity and participation, in which they take on authentic work in their families and communities, with or without the benefit of formal schooling (Montgomery, 2005; Montgomery *et al.*, 2003; Rogoff, 2003). Therefore developing policies and practices that reflect such diversity raises challenging issues that are addressed through the readings.

THEME I

Theoretical perspectives on learning, curriculum and pedagogy

The first reading by Boyce (1946) provides a historical perspective from which many contemporary developments can be traced. Boyce was the head teacher of the Raleigh Infants School, in Stepney, East London, from 1933 to 1936. She wrote a detailed account of the aims, methods and outcomes of the school's child-centred experimental practices, which were based on the developmental and psychoanalytical theories of Susan Isaacs, and the advice of psychologists in the new Child Guidance Clinics. Although this reading can be approached as an historical account, readers will find it more productive to take a critical perspective and interrogate the ways in which prevailing theories, beliefs and ideologies influenced provision and practice. Whilst pro-moting child-centred approaches, Boyce describes the structures and routines that were used to regulate the children in order that they may benefit from the provision. Boyce also reveals the values, interests and power relations that influenced this experiment such as the concern with health, hygiene and 'habit training', and with addressing the problems in children's home lives such as the 'poverty of ideas and experience' (1946:6). Observing and recording children's interactions and activities were integral to child-centred approaches as the staff built the curriculum around observed needs and inter-ests. As a pedagogical tool, and as a research tool, observation remains central to understanding children's knowledge, meanings, perspectives and intentions, especially within adult-dominated worlds, as evidenced in the readings by Marsh (2000), Sawyers and Carrick (2003) and Farrell *et al.* (2004).

The other readings in Theme I indicate change and continuity in conceptualising learning, curriculum and pedagogy. Fleer (2006) charts significant transformations that have challenged predominantly Western theories and scientific methods for determining universal laws of human development. The view of education as promoting individual development has been contested, because of the ways in which developmental discourses normalise and regulate children, by proposing generic milestones, expectations or educational goals that define the 'normally' or 'abnormally' developing child. Contemporary scholars highlight the conceptual limitations of developmental theories, and the ways in which these have impacted on institutional structures and practices (Anning *et al.*, 2004; Dahlberg *et al.*, 1999; S. Edwards, 2003; Grieshaber and Cannella, 2001; Soto and Swadener, 2002; Yelland, 2005). Fleer (2006) summarises key theoretical advances, and presents a socio-cultural model of learning and development that recognises the diversity of children's cultural experiences, and the ways in which cultural practices change over time. Drawing on the work of Rogoff (2003) and Vygotsky (1978), Fleer argues that development can be seen as the transformation of participation in cultural activities. Learning is not merely evolutionary, but revolutionary, a theory which is extended by Newman and Holzman (1993) in Theme II (Play). Thus the image of the 'naturally developing child' gives way to the image of the socially, culturally and politically constructed child (see also Rosemberg [2005] and Montgomery [2005] in Theme V).

Soler and Miller (2003) explore the ways in which theoretical positions impact on the design of curriculum policies at national and local levels. They argue that curricula can be seen as sites of struggle between ideas and visions about what early childhood education is for, and what are appropriate content and contexts for learning and development. In comparing curricula in England, New Zealand and Northern Italy, they identify ongoing tensions between liberal, progressive traditions, and vocational and instrumental influences. In common with Fleer (2006) they identify the challenges that teachers and practitioners face in developing curricula that are grounded in socio-cultural theories and in contemporary images of children as possessing rights, and being active co-constructors of knowledge and competent social actors. The issue of curriculum design and content remains a contentious area in early childhood education. Placing the child at the heart of the education process, which is a central tenet of early childhood ideology (as evidenced in the Plowden report), challenged the formal approaches of the Primary and Elementary schools of the nineteenth and early twentieth centuries, and the 'top-down' pressures to prepare children for the next stage of schooling and for adulthood. The flexible 'play-based' approaches, derived from a developmental model of learning, propose that the curriculum can be built around children's needs and interests, as evidenced in their free play and self-initiated activities. In contrast, structured curricula define essential skills, knowledge and dispositions, to support learning and development, and to prepare children for compulsory schooling (Nuttall, 2003; Wood and Bennett, 2006). In reality, elements of both approaches can be seen in national policy frameworks in countries as diverse as England, New Zealand, Thailand and Saudi Arabia, but with different emphases on pedagogical approaches and curriculum content. The struggle to integrate learner-centred approaches with curriculum-centred approaches presents practical challenges regardless of whether the curriculum goals or outcomes are descriptive (as in the New Zealand early childhood curriculum) or definitive (as in the English Foundation Stage and National Curriculum) (Hedges and Cullen, 2005; Wood and Bennett, 2006).

Understanding learning cultures in children's homes, and in pre-school and statutory school contexts is a site for theoretical progress. Although Boyce (1946) was concerned with the 'poverty of ideas and experience' within children's home lives, she also documented the imaginative qualities of their play, and the richness of their mathematical knowledge, which were based on their everyday 'home and street experiences'. The reading by Brooker (2003) exemplifies the tensions between home and school cultures, and portrays the complex ways in which children negotiate these spaces through their talk, play, friendships and activities, and how they build their identities as learners and as individuals. Brooker (2003) problematises cultural assumptions in the English education system, and juxtaposes these with the home-based cultural practices of 16 children as they make the transition from home to a Reception class (age 4–5 years) in a Primary school (see Brooker [2002] for a full account of this study). Focusing on the ethnotheories of the parents, Brooker reveals how family beliefs and practices influence the children's home experiences, their orientations to play, and their participation and achievement in school. Brooker also demonstrates that whilst cultural constructions of learning and development can be conceptualised at broad theoretical levels (Cannella, 2005; Fleer, 2006), these need to be contextualised within local communities and contexts (Gutiérrez and Rogoff, 2003). Further research on the home-school interface, identity and diversity can be found in Gregory *et al.* (2004), and Grieshaber and Canella (2001). With regard to the implications for early childhood education, such theoretical shifts require that institutional structures and practices are informed by knowledge and understanding of cultural and linguistic diversity, which is situated in local communities.

. On the basis of these readings, it can be argued that significant sites for theoretical progress in early childhood education include synthesising individual and socio-cultural accounts of learning, and utilising this knowledge to inform pedagogy and curriculum design. These issues are further explored in Theme II, with a specific focus on play.

THEME II

Play: advances in theory and practice

The commitment to play constitutes one of the most enduring discourses in early childhood education, which has generated powerful professional allegiances. This commitment encompasses play as development, play as education, play-based learning and play-based curriculum, all of which are considered to be in harmony with the nature of the child. Play allows children to 'be themselves' because they can follow their needs and interests through free choice, discovery and exploration. Therefore the image of the 'naturally developing child', which is central to developmental theories, finds its clearest expression within free play activities. However, the commitment to play in education settings has always been strong on ideology and rhetoric and weak, or at least problematic, in practice (Bennett *et al.*, 1997). This in part reflects tensions between play as natural developmental activity, and play as intentional educational activity (Frost *et al.*, 2005; Sutton-Smith, 1997; Van Hoorn *et al.*, 2002). Furthermore, assumptions about the universal value of play are derived from Euro-American ideologies and developmental theories. Such assumptions sit uneasily within contemporary educational settings in the UK in light of increasing cultural and ethnic diversity, and where global perspectives provide contrasting views of play in childhood (Cannella and Viruru, 2004; Penn, 2005).

In terms of validating play in education settings, there is sustained empirical evidence that young children learn through play, which is related to the developmental domains and to the subject disciplines (Johnson *et al.*, 2005; Wood and Attfield, 2005). Play is also progressive: play choices and activities change, and children's play skills develop with age and experience, typically resulting in more sustained, complex forms of play and extended repertoires of activity and participation (Broadhead, 2004; Johnson *et al.*, 2005; Sutton-Smith, 1997). Play activities are socially and symbolically complex, and involve social reciprocity, which drives affective and personality development. Evidence about the role of teachers, and other adults, is more contentious, in terms of what roles (if any) they should take in children's play; whether play can (or should) be used for educational purposes, whose purposes and intentions are paramount, and what are the modes, intentions and outcomes of adult intervention (Wood, 2008).

Play has been studied from different theoretical perspectives often with the intention of developing explanatory theories for play forms, behaviours, purposes and outcomes. In contrast, the readings in Theme II exemplify theoretical and methodological directions in play scholarship, alongside post-modern concerns with power, equity, identity and voice. Newman and Holzman (1993) interpret Vygotksy's theories as a challenge to established developmental orientations, particularly Piaget's 'ages and stages' approaches to play.

Vygotsky's concept of the zone of proximal development (ZPD) has been widely adopted as a metaphor for describing how adults can support and extend children's learning. However, this concept has often been used uncritically (Ortega, 2003; Wood and Bennett, 2006), with an emphasis on the adult (or more knowledgeable other) controlling activities and interactions within the ZPD. The notion of learning as revolutionary activity and play as revolutionary activity requires that researchers and educators pay attention to the socially and culturally situated nature of learning and development, to children's individual and collaborative motivations, activities, choices, and meanings, and to the transformational processes that occur in children's minds. Contemporary theories support the view that participation in activities promotes learning, and that learning changes the nature of participation. Thus the development *of* play, and children's learning and development *in* play can best be understood in light of cultural contexts, tools, activities and practices which are created *by* children, and not just *for* children (Wood, 2004).

The readings by Janson (2001) and Marsh (2000) exemplify these theoretical issues, and challenge some taken for granted assumptions about the universal value of play. Janson problematises the nature of interaction and participation in social play, based on observations of blind and sighted children in Swedish pre-schools. The findings raise issues about relative power and agency in play. Togetherness (or social reciprocity) is hampered by differences in players' cognitive representations, their ability to co-ordinate perspectives and meanings, and to resolve conflicts. However, Janson emphasises *difference* rather than *disability,* which presents a more challenging conceptualisation of achieving equal and full participation in play for children with special or additional needs.

Marsh (2000) continues the theme of participation from the perspective of girls and superhero play in an English Year 2 classroom (age 6–7 years). Marsh draws on cultural and gender theory to explore the impact of popular culture on young children's play lives, and the dramatic appeal of warrior hero and superhero figures (see also Marsh, 2005; Marsh and Millard, 2000). Marsh contrasts versions of femininity and masculinity, and the ways in which these are enacted and reified through play narratives and wider hegemonic discourses in school and society. Play activities and narratives can reinforce the gendered positioning of young children, leading to negative stereotypes that may limit choice and agency. As Marsh notes, violence and sexism are inherent in warrior/superhero discourses, just as racism and xenophobia are endemic in children's popular culture. Contemporary scholars argue that such discourses need to be open to scrutiny and contestation in order to provoke changes in practice (Browne, 2004; MacNaughton, 2000, 2005; Reay, 2001). Marsh's research also portrays the power of narrative approaches for representing social action, and for inviting readers to reflect on its meaning and connection to their own lives and experiences.

Sawyers and Carrick (2003) present a small-scale study of symbolic play through the eyes and words of two children, age 5–6 years, exemplifying trends towards involving children as research participants, and seeing them as competent reporters of their own perspectives and experiences (Christensen and James, 2000; Farrell, 2005; Lewis and Lindsay, 2000). Such small-scale studies have benefits and limitations: whilst generalisations cannot be made, they can be valuable in exploring theoretical and methodological frameworks, and stimulating concerns about the ethics and politics of researching children's play. Sawyers and Carrick take an individual/cognitive perspective on understanding the children's construction of pretence. In contrast, Broadhead (2004) argues that play activities can best be understood in their social and cultural context, including the ways in which children cooperate towards building sustained sequences of play.

The contrasting theoretical perspectives used in contemporary play scholarship contest the notion of the naturally developing and the naturally playing child (see also Montgomery [2005] in Theme V). Sutton-Smith (1997) argues that the emphasis on play as development and progress has tended to obscure the ways in which children use play for their own affairs of power, how they construct personal and shared meaning, and how they establish multiple roles and identities. Children's play is not a neutral, space but rather a political and negotiated terrain (Ryan, 2005). Children utilise multiple discourses that are drawn from their social and cultural worlds; they build identities, express interests and enact choices that reflect differential positions and power relations between peer groups, and between children and adults (Grieshaber and Cannella, 2001; Ryan, 2005). Brooker (2002) argues that free choice and play-based approaches do not benefit all children, especially where these are not consistent with culturally situated child-rearing practices in homes and communities. In contrast, Gregory (2005) has demonstrated the importance of playful talk and activities for bilingual and monolingual children in bridging home and school discourses, and the assistance provided by family members in constructing those bridges.

A key challenge to established ideologies is that play-based approaches may constrain equality of opportunity and equal access to curriculum provision (MacNaughton, 2000; Yelland, 2005). Whilst building a curriculum around children's choices, needs and interests is ideologically seductive to early childhood practitioners, it is conceptually weak in practice (Wood, 2007). Needs and interests may be fleeting or sustained, trivial or purposeful. They may be shared with others in the community, or may be highly individual and idiosyncratic. Individual or group interests may be based on choices that are biased in terms of culture, social class, gender and ability/disability. In light of post-modern and post-structuralist theories such choices may result in unequal power relations and potentially detrimental power effects of free choice. Ryan (2005) argues that instead of choice being conceptualised as freedom from adult authority, adults' interactions should focus on helping children to understand the choices offered by different classroom discourses and the power effects of such choices. However, such a conceptual shift requires that play is examined from critical perspectives, and that researchers and practitioners are prepared to challenge assumptions about the universal efficacy of play, and the limitations of interpreting play in relation to curriculum goals and objectives.

THEME III

Policy generation and implementation

The political status of early childhood education and care has strengthened in the last forty years, as evidenced in extensive policy frameworks that operate at national and international levels. In contemporary policy studies, policy is construed as a multi-faceted, multi-dimensional social and political phenomenon (Farrell, 2001), which involves state regulation, monitoring and control as well as processes of change and transformation (Ball, 1997). This involves a range of stakeholders, who have different interests, perspectives and positions, and varying degrees of power and control. Thus the readings in Theme III reflect trends towards state regulation of early childhood education, including quality assurance processes, inspection regimes, and varying levels of prescription in curriculum, pedagogy and standards for professional training. The readings reflect profound transformations that have been driven by unprecedented policy interventions, ranging from the global perspective of the United Nations Convention on the Rights of the Child, to national frameworks within which regional and local developments take place. The education and care of young children is no longer dichotomised as a private or a public responsibility, but as a shared endeavour, in which provision and services are targeted towards children, their families and caregivers. For example, in the UK, children's centres and primary schools provide 'wrap-around' care and education for young people in order to support working parents. In England, 'Every Child Matters' (DfES, 2004) provides guidance for all service providers on matters of health, education, care and well-being. These policy aspirations encompass multiple objectives, such as improving the quality of education and care, tackling social exclusion, promoting early intervention for children at risk and in need, enhancing life chances for children and their families, and improving progression and continuity from home to pre-school and into primary education. Thus education policies are increasingly aligned with a social justice agenda.

Trends towards structuring pre-school and primary school curricula and improving provision and services, can be seen in developed and developing countries (Montgomery et al., 2003; Olmsted, 2000; Penn, 2000, 2005). The reading by Neuman (2005) provides an overview of international directions towards developing more coherent and coordinated policies in OECD countries. Neuman situates debates about the governance of early childhood education and care within wider policy frameworks and political structures. Her analysis draws together some of the issues raised in previous readings, such as the influence of the dominant culture of the primary school system; the challenges of integrating and coordinating provision and services across health, care and education; and the tensions between national frameworks, and the need for local flexibility in responding to children and their families in diverse cultures and contexts.

In the UK, there have been radical transformations in pre-school education from *ad hoc* provision to the full involvement of government across the maintained, private, voluntary and independent sectors. This marks a significant shift from the days of the experimental Raleigh School (Theme I). Boyce (1946) described a dual ethic of care and education, with an emphasis on rescue and restoration for children with physical disabilities, illness and developmental delay, which were often caused by poverty and low standards of living. Their provision was limited by the lack of wider social policy support systems: despite many successes Boyce noted that 'we were powerless against the conditions of their life out of school'. In contrast, the reading by Sylva and Pugh (2005) shows how contemporary policy aspirations (e.g. Every Child Matters) encompass multiple objectives within a broad social justice agenda. This reading charts the rationale for the intensification of policy initiatives, drawing on international evidence which demonstrates that high quality provision has positive and lasting effects on children's educational and social development (see also Wylie and Thompson [2003] for similar research in New Zealand). However, 'high quality' is associated with high costs, high levels of intervention by related service providers, and high levels of expertise in the workforce.

Sylva and Pugh present some of the persuasive evidence regarding the relationship between high quality inputs and outcomes, based on the British government-funded study of Effective Provision of Pre-school Education (EPPE) (for full details of the study see www.ioe.ac.uk/projects/eppe). Findings from the study are influencing policy directives on education and care (Siraj-Blatchford and Sylva, 2004; Siraj-Blatchford et al., 2006). However, a critical issue in this direct relationship between government-sponsored research and government-directed guidance is that curriculum and pedagogy may become constrained by apparent certainties based on a 'what works' perspective. Dahlberg and Moss (2005) contest the concept of quality in UK policy frameworks, and argue that educational practice within and beyond early childhood is driven by a crude effectiveness and performativity agenda. The drive to reify 'what works' is linked to the efficient governing of children, teachers and practitioners, as well as families and caregivers (since the latter are often required to support the educational objectives of schools). As discussed in Theme I, contemporary critiques have highlighted an over-reliance on outdated ideologies and theories. However, the fact that recent policy interventions claim the legitimacy of being evidence-based runs the risk of creating a different set of orthodoxies that may be equally constraining to development and innovation.

Whilst Sylva and Pugh are optimistic about policy directions, they chart the shifting landscape of provision as some services close, whilst others flourish, leaving parents with the task of navigating the 'maze' of different providers and services. As the EPPE study has shown, although high quality provision has positive social, educational and motivational impacts on children, not all settings are equal in terms of quality, resulting in unequal outcomes for children. In the next reading, Ball and Vincent (2005) question the extent to which the social justice policy agenda can be achieved through early childhood provision and services. Their policy analysis proposes that increasing provision is a necessary but not a sufficient approach to making meaningful choice in childcare available to all. They argue that social justice in childcare is understood to be primarily a matter of access, overlooking issues of form and content. Thus existing services and provision may reflect existing inequalities, rather than actively challenge them. These concerns are exemplified further by Vincent and Ball (2001) and Vincent *et al.* (2004) in detailed analyses of the ways in which gender and social class impact on parental choice, and the quality of children's experiences. Whilst investment in early childhood education does have the potential to deliver positive benefits to children, their families and society, this should not be seen as a panacea for entrenched social problems.

In the next reading Rosemberg (2005) explores similar issues, focusing on social inequality in Brazil, and the particular challenges of developing early childhood education and care. Rosemberg's analysis serves as a potent reminder that social inequality is nested within a wide range of influences, including the impact of globalisation, and the limitations of international agencies (however well-intentioned) in promulgating the 'best' ways to develop early childhood education and care. Instead of proposing a universal view of 'best practices' in addressing inequality, Rosemberg outlines the 'twenty cardinal sins' of multilateral organisations, and the ways in which external and internal agencies operate to perpetuate inequality through inappropriate policies. These 'twenty sins' offer some interesting concepts for discussion and analysis in comparing trajectories of progress in developed and developing countries, and the continued dominance of Euro-American ideas.

The readings in Theme III exemplify how early childhood education needs to be understood within wider political, social, economic and cultural influences. For students and scholars in the field, undertaking comparative analyses of international trends in policy and practice requires consideration of institutional structures and processes, the ideas that underpin them, the goals to which they aspire, and the cultural relevance of those aspirations. These issues are developed in Theme IV in relation to the professional status of the early childhood workforce.

THEME IV

Professionalism and professionalisation

Government interventions in policy and practice have impacted on the nature of professionalism in early childhood education, and have raised questions about the future qualifications and status of the workforce. The readings in Theme IV exemplify these tensions in the context of national educational reforms and their impact on early childhood teachers in New Zealand, Australia and England. Duncan (2004) follows the changes in the personal and professional lives of eight kindergarten teachers during a period of educational review and reform in New Zealand. Drawing on post-modern theories, Duncan argues that policy documents may contain differing discourses and practices from their initial conceptualisation, to their implementation. By eliciting the voices of the teachers, Duncan juxtaposes official versions of policy texts with the everyday realities of policy implementation, and the impact such innovations have on wider professional identities and activities.

Osgood (2006) presents a critical analysis of the nature of professionalism amongst early childhood practitioners using feminist poststructural theories to interpret the masculinist nature of managerialist discourses in education reforms. Osgood proposes the concept of a 'new agency' to help practitioners reposition themselves and develop alternative forms of professionalism that are not wholly dictated by these discourses. Whilst it must be acknowledged that the early childhood (and primary education) workforce is predominantly female, the next reading by Sumsion (1999) reveals how female hegemony may create barriers for men wishing to enter the profession. Women are considered to be naturally caring, nurturing and maternal; whilst this is a limited and limiting professional identity, it serves to make teaching in early childhood a socially sanctioned career choice. Osgood questions the idea of a 'new agency', and the extent to which this includes and accepts males in early childhood settings, as well as challenging social, political and institutional norms. Warin (2006) presents a similar study of a male early childhood worker, Ian, in an English nursery school. In contrast to James, Ian has more success in exploiting his 'scarcity value' as a male, and eventually fast tracks to a position of expertise and greater responsibility. These studies highlight the significance of gender politics in early childhood education, and contest policy-centred assumptions about the nature of professionalism being determined by externally imposed standards and skills.

Whilst these readings focus on qualified teachers in early childhood settings, the modern workforce in the UK includes adults with a range of qualifications and experiences. Therefore ongoing debates about professional knowledge, identity and professionalisation need to take account of this diversity, alongside policy drivers to improve the training and qualifications of the workforce.

THEME V

Research methods: agency and voice

Just as contemporary theories and discourses position children as competent social actors, they are also seen as competent reporters and interpreters of their knowledge and experiences. In terms of methodological advances, the tradition of using child observation as a research and pedagogical tool has been extended by participatory methods that integrate children's voices and perspectives on their lives in and out of school (Browne, 2004; Christensen and James, 2000; Farrell, 2005; Greig and Taylor, 1999; Wood, 2005). Such advances have posed ethical challenges to the research community, alongside concerns that children's voices and knowledge should be used to improve the social condition of childhood (see also Pollard and Filer, 1996, 1999; Triggs and Pollard, 2000). Several readings (Brooker, 2003, Marsh, 2000) illustrate respectful methods for listening to children, including commentaries on their ways of knowing and understanding, as evidenced in their work and play. These readings challenge established notions of children as active learners, where activity is equated with 'hands-on' experiences, discovery, exploration, enquiry and problem-solving. Children should be also seen as actively constructing knowledge and meaning, and actively maintaining identities within complex socio-cultural contexts.

The reading by Farrell *et al.* (2004) draws conceptually on the sociology of childhood, and uses the construct of social capital to interpret the impact of early childhood education and care on children and their families in Queensland, Australia. This study demonstrates that early childhood education takes place in and out of pre-school and school settings, and involves more than socially constructed and legitimised curricula, pedagogical approaches, and institutionalised norms and values. The research conversations with the children, although informal, were structured by the questions posed by the research team. In contrast, some researchers have used flexible, open-ended research conversations to explore children's knowledge and understand their own agendas.

In the final reading, Montgomery (2005) situates education within the broader theoretical framework of contemporary childhood studies, and examines the contribution of different disciplinary perspectives. For Montgomery the concepts of voice and agency extend to the social and economic activities in which young people participate in their homes and communities, thus providing a contrasting perspective to the institutionalised child-rearing and educational practices discussed in earlier readings. This reading proposes that agency can be constrained by gendered positioning within communities, a theme that is woven throughout this book from the perspectives of children, parents and early childhood professionals. Montgomery examines childhood as an age-related experience, as a culturally situated experience, and as a gendered experience, and provokes wider questions about where children are educated, who makes decisions about the form and content of provision, and the purposes that early childhood education serves.

HOW TO USE THIS READER

These readings offer contrasting perspectives that contest established assumptions about early childhood education and care, drawing on theory, policy and practice. Each reading is intended to provide a 'trail' for further research, which will enable students to engage more fully with the themes, and to extend their own searches of related literature. Whilst books can provide an in-depth focus on specific research projects or themes, journals provide useful overviews or syntheses of current research in national and international contexts. In addition, many of the issues identified in this collection connect with the readers in the Routledge/Falmer series. Therefore reference to this series will enable readers to situate issues in early childhood within wider debates about educational theory, policy and practice.

Inevitably this selection of readings is influenced (probably biased) by my own experiences, interests and perspectives, and is therefore limited. However, students should use this book to challenge their own ideas and ways of thinking, and understand how perspectives shift and change over time. The book can be used strategically to focus on a particular issue, or on one of the key themes. The readings can be understood at different levels, from gaining knowledge and understanding to engaging critically with the issues, trends and theories. Being a critical reader involves teasing out the assumptions, perspectives and values of the authors, and subjecting these to scrutiny against related research and scholarship. Critical readers also acknowledge and reflect on their personal perceptions, beliefs and prejudices, and are open to change and consideration of contrasting (and sometimes contradictory) explanations. By adopting critical perspectives, this reader will help students to challenge dominant discourses and practices, contest taken for granted assumptions, and consider the ways in which children and adults are positioned within different discourses.

Reflecting on the introductory quotation from the Plowden report, children are still at the heart of the educational process. However, advances in policy must be in harmony with twenty-first century children, with the complexity of their lives, and with local cultures, values and belief systems. Furthermore, much greater emphasis is placed on the educative role of professionals, families and communities, and greater collaboration across agencies and service providers. As the twenty-first century progresses, students of early childhood education will view the field in very different ways from the developmental certainties and ideological orientations of the previous century. Theories and practices in the field are now seen in relation to much broader processes of cultural, social, political, economic and technological change. However, whether such change processes sustain conformity or enable transformation remains open to debate. As a contribution to transformation and re-conceptualisation in early childhood education, this book aims to stimulate critical engagement with these debates, and to inspire further reading and research.

References

Anning, A., Cullen, J. and Fleer, M. (Eds.) (2004) *Early Childhood Education: Society and Culture.* London: Sage.

Ball, S. J. (1997) Policy sociology and critical social research: a personal view of recent education policy and policy research. *British Educational Research Journal,* 23(3): 257–274.

Ball, S. and Vincent, C. (2005) The 'childcare champion'? New Labour, social justice and the childcare market. *British Educational Research Journal,* 31(5): 557–570.

Bennett, N., Wood, E. and Rogers, S. (1997) *Teaching Through Play: Reception Teachers' Theories and Practice.* Buckingham: Open University Press.

Boyce, E. R. (1946) *Play in the Infants' School.* London: Methuen (2nd edition).

Broadhead, P. (2004) *Early years play and learning: Developing social skills and cooperation.* London: Routledge Falmer.

Brooker, L. (2002) *Starting school – young children learning cultures.* Buckingham: Open University Press.

Brooker, L. (2003) Learning how to learn: parental ethnotheories and young children's preparation for school. *International Journal of Early Years Education,* 11(2): 177–128.

Browne, N. (2004) *Gender Equity in the Early Years.* Maidenhead: Open University Press.

Cannella, G. S. (2005) Reconceptualizing the field (of early care and education): if 'western' child development is a problem, then what do we do? In Yelland, N (Ed.) *Critical Issues in Early Childhood.* Maidenhead: Open University Press, pp. 17–39.

Cannella, G. S. and Viruru, R. (2004) *Childhood and Postcolonisation.* London: Routledge Falmer.

Central Advisory Council for Education (England) (1967) *Children and their Primary Schools* (Plowden Report). London: HMSO.

Christensen, P. and James, A. (2000) *Research with Children: Perspectives and Practices.* London: Falmer.

Cunningham, H. (2006) *The Invention of Childhood.* London: BBC Books.

Dahlberg, G., Moss, P. and Pence, A. (1999) *Beyond Quality in Early Childhood Education and Care: Postmodern Perspectives.* London: Falmer Press.

Dahlberg, G. and Moss, P. (2005) *Ethics and Politics in Early Childhood Education.* London: RoutledgeFalmer Press.

Department for Education and Skills (2004) *Every Child Matters: Change for Children in Schools.* London: HMSO.

Duncan, J. (2004) Misplacing the teacher? New Zealand early childhood teachers and early childhood education policy reforms, 1984–96. *Contemporary Issues in Early Childhood,* Vol 5, 2004, pp. 160–177.

Edwards, R. and Usher, R. (2000) *Globalisation and Pedagogy: Space, Place and Identity.* London: Routledge.

Edwards, S. (2003) New Directions: charting the paths for the role of sociocultural theory in early childhood education and curriculum. *Contemporary Issues in Early Childhood*, 4(3): 251–266.

Effective Provision for Preschool Education (EPPE). www.ioe.ac.uk/projects/eppe.

Farrell, A. (2001) Policy Research. In MacNaughton, G., Rolfe, S. and Siraj-Blatchford, I. (Eds.) *Doing Early Childhood Research: International Perspectives on Theory and Practice*. Buckingham: Open University Press, pp. 240–253.

Farrell, A. (2005) *Ethical Research with Children*. Maidenhead: Open University Press.

Farrell, A., Tayler, C. and Tennent, L. (2004) Building social capital in early education and care: an Australian study. *British Educational Research Journal*, 30(5): 623–632.

Fleer, M. (2006) The cultural construction of child development: creating institutional and cultural intersubjectivity. *International Journal of Early Years Education*, 14(2): 127–140.

Frost, J., Wortham, S. C. and Reifel, S. (2005) *Play and Child Development*. New Jersey: Merrill/Prentice Hall.

Gregory, E. (2005) Playful talk: the interspace between home and school discourse. *Early Years*, 25(3): 223–235.

Gregory, E., Long, S. and Volk, D. (2004) *Many Pathways to Literacy: Young Children Learning with Siblings, Peers, Grandparents and Communities*. London: Routledge Falmer.

Greig, A. and Taylor, J. (1999) *Doing Research With Children*. London: Sage Publications.

Grieshaber, S. and Cannella, G. S. (2001) *Embracing Identities in Early Childhood Education*. New York: Teachers' College Press.

Guttiérez, K. D. and Rogoff, B. (2003) Cultural ways of learning: individual traits or repertoires of practice. *Educational Researcher*, 32(5): 19–25.

Hedges, H. and Cullen, J. (2005) Subject knowledge in early childhood curriculum and pedagogy: beliefs and practices. *Contemporary Issues in Early Childhood*, 6(1): 38–66.

Janson, U. (2001) Togetherness and diversity in pre-school play. *Intenational Journal of Early Years Education*, 9(2): 135–143.

Johnson, J. E., Christie, J. F. and Wardle, F. (2005) *Play, Development and Early Education*. Boston, MA: Pearson Education.

Krogh, S. L. and Slentz, K. L. (2001) *Early Childhood Education Yesterday, Today and Tomorrow*. Mahwah, NJ: Lawrence Erlbaum Associates.

Lewis, A. and Lindsay, G. (2000) *Researching Children's Perspectives*. Buckingham: Open University Press.

MacNaughton, G. (2000) *Rethinking Gender in Early Childhood Education*. Buckingham: Open University Press.

MacNaughton, G. (2005) *Doing Foucault in Early Childhood Studies: Applying Poststructural Ideas*. London: RoutledgeFalmer.

Marsh, J. (2000) 'But I want to fly too!': girls and superhero play in the infant classroom. *Gender and Education*, 12(2): 209–220.

Marsh, J. (2005) *Popular culture, new media and digital literacy in early childhood*. London: RoutledgeFalmer.

Marsh, J. and Millard, E. (2000) *Literacy and Popular Culture: Using Children's Culture in the Classroom*. London: Paul Chapman.

Montgomery, H. (2005) Gendered childhoods: a cross-disciplinary overview. *Gender and Education*, 17(5): 471–482.

Montgomery, H., Burr, R. and Woodhead, M. (2003) *Changing Childhoods: Local and Global*. Buckingham: Wiley/Open University Press.

Neuman, M. J. (2005) Governance of early childhood education and care: recent developments in OECD countries. *Early Years*, 25(2): 129–141.

Newman, F. and Holzman, L. (1993) *Lev Vygotsky – Revolutionary Scientist*. London: Routledge.

Nuttall, J. (2003) (Ed.) *Weaving Te Whāriki: Aotearoa New Zealand's Early Childhood Curriculum Document in Theory and Practice*. Wellington: New Zealand Council for Educational Research.

Olmsted, P. (2000). Early childhood education throughout the world. In Brown, S. Moon, R. and Ben-Peretz, M. (Eds.) *International Companion to Education*. London: Routledge, pp. 575–601.

Ortega, R. (2003). Play, activity and thought, reflections on Piaget's and Vygotsky's theories. In Lytle, D.E. (Ed.) *Play and Educational Theory and Practice*. Westport, Conn.: Praeger, pp. 99–116.

Osgood, J. (2006) Professionalism and performativity: the feminist challenge facing early years practitioners. *Early Years*, 26(2): 187–199.

Penn, H. (2000) *Early Childhood Services: Theory, Policy and Practice*. Buckingham: Open University Press.

Penn, H. (2005) *Unequal Childhoods: Young Children's Lives in Poor Countries*. London: Routledge.

Pollard, A. and Filer, A. (1996) *The Social World of Pupil Learning*. London: Cassell.

Pollard, A. and Filer, A. (1999) *The Social World of Pupil Career*. London: Cassell.

Reay, D. (2001) 'Spice girls', 'Nice Girls', 'Girlies' and 'Tomboys': gender discourses, girls' cultures and femininities in the primary classroom. *Gender and Education*, 13(2): 153–166.

Rogoff, B. (2003) *The Cultural Nature of Human Development*. Oxford: Oxford University Press.

Rosemberg, F. (2005) Childhood and social inequality in Brazil. In Penn, H. (Ed.) *Unequal Childhoods: Young Children's Lives in Poor Countries*. London: Routledge.

Ryan, S. (2005) Freedom to choose: examining children's experiences in choice time. In Yelland, N. (Ed.) *Critical Issues in Early Childhood*. Maidenhead: Open University Press, pp. 99–114.

Ryan, S. and Grieshaber, S. (2005) Shifting from developmental to postmodern practices in early childhood teacher education. *Journal of Teacher Education,* 56(1): 34–45.

Sawyers, J. K. and Carrick, N. (2003) Symbolic play through the eyes and words of children. In Lytle, D. E. (Ed.) *Play and Educational Theory and Practice*. Play and Culture Studies, Vol 5, Praeger, Wesport CT, pp. 159–182.

Siraj-Blatchford, I. and Sylva, K. (2004) Researching pedagogy in English pre-schools. *British Educational Research Journal,* 30(5): 713–730.

Siraj-Blatchford, I., Sammons, P., Taggart, B., Sylva, K. and Melhuish, E. (2006) Educational research and evidence-based policy: the mixed-method approach of the EPPE project. *Evaluation and Research in Education,* 19(2): 63–82.

Soler, J. and Miller, L. (2003) The struggle for early childhood curricula: a comparison of the English Foundation Stage Curriculum, *Te Whāriki* and Reggio Emilia, *International Journal of Early Years Education,* 11(1): 57–67.

Soto, L. D. and Swadener, B. B. (2002) Toward a liberatory early childhood theory, research and praxis: decolonialising a field. *Contemporary Issues in Early Childhood,* 3(1): 38–66.

Sumsion, J. (1999) Critical reflections on the experiences of a male early childhood worker. *Gender and Education,* 11(4): 455–468.

Sutton-Smith, B. (1997) *The Ambiguity of Play.* Cambridge, MA: Harvard University Press.

Sylva, K. and Pugh, G. (2005) Transforming the early years in England. *Oxford Review of Education,* 31(1):11–27.

Triggs, P., Pollard, A., Broadfoot, P., McNess, E. and Osborn, M. (2000) *What Pupils Say: Changing Policy and Practice in Primary Education.* London: Continuum.

Van Hoorn, J., Nourot, P., Scales, B., and Alward, K. (2002) *Play at the Center of the Curriculum* (3rd edn). New York: Macmillan.

Vincent, C. and Ball, S. J. (2001) A Market In Love? Choosing Pre-school Childcare. *British Educational Research Journal,* 27(5): 633–651.

Vincent, C., Ball, S. J. and Kemp, S. (2004) The social geography of childcare: making up a middle class child. *British Journal of Sociology of Education,* 25(2): 229–244.

Vygotsky, L. S. (1978) *Mind in Society.* Cambridge, MA:Harvard University Press.

Warin, J. (2006) Heavy-metal Humpty Dumpty: dissonant masculinities within the context of the nursery. *Gender and Education,* 18(5): 523–537.

Wood, E. (2004). Developing a pedagogy of play for the 21 st century. In Anning, A., Cullen, J. and Fleer, M. (Eds.) *Early Childhood Education: Society and Culture.* London: Sage, pp. 17–30.

Wood, E. (2005) Young Children's Voices and Perspectives in Research: methodological and ethical considerations, *Journal of Equity and Innovation in Early Childhood.* University of Melbourne, 3(2): 64–76.

Wood, E. (2007) Re-conceptualising child-centred education: contemporary directions in policy, theory, and practice in early childhood. *Forum,* 49(1), Spring 2007, 121–136.

Wood, E. (2008) Conceptualising a Pedagogy of Play: international perspectives from theory, policy and practice. In Kuschner, D. (Ed.) *Play and Culture Studies*, Vol. 8. Westport, CT: Ablex.

Wood, E. and Attfield, J. (2005) *Play, Learning and the Early Childhood Curriculum* (2nd edn). London: Paul Chapman.

Wood, E. and Bennett, N. (2006) Curriculum, pedagogy and learning in early childhood: sites for struggle-sites for progress. In Verschaffel, L. Dochy, F. Boekarts, M. and S. Vosniadou (Eds.) *Instructional Psychology: Past, Present and Future Trends. Essays in Honour of Erik de Corte. Advances in Learning and Instruction.* Netherlands: Amsterdam Elsevier, pp. 3–18.

Woodhead, M. (2000) Towards a global paradigm for research into early childhood. In Penn, H. (2000) *Early Childhood Services: Theory, Policy and Practice.* Buckingham: Open University Press, pp. 15–35.

Wylie, C. and Thompson, J. (2003) The long-term contribution of early childhood education to children's performance-evidence from New Zealand. *International Journal of Early Years Education,* 11(1): 69–78.

Yelland, N. (Ed.) (2005) *Critical Issues in Early Childhood.* Maidenhead: Open University Press.

Theoretical perspectives on learning, curriculum and pedagogy

Chapter 1

Play in the Infants' School

An account of an educational experiment at the Raleigh Infants' School, Stepney, London, E.I. January 1933–April 1936

E. R. Boyce

Source: *E. R. Boyce, Introduction, Play in the Infants' School: An Account of an Educational Experiment at the Raleigh Infants' School, Stepney, London, E.I. January 1933–April 1936. London: Methuen, 1946.*

Aims

My previous experience had taught me that when children are free from the dictatorship of adults, their achievements and development surpass that of children whose school lives are domineered by the time-table, by syllabus, examination, and inspection. I had already conducted an experiment when teaching a class of children from five to eight years old, along lines similar to the Project Method, and inspired by the books of Decroly, Kilpatrick, and Dewey. This group of children had gained a good background of general knowledge and could talk freely and behave naturally in school, yet I felt that the work and play had been over-organized, and that the social behaviour of the children, apparently co-operating so whole-heartedly and for so long, had been forced. The continuity of the experiment had also been disturbed by over-anxiety about results in reading, writing, and number.

When, therefore, I had an opportunity of teaching another group of fifty-four children, between four and five years old, I tried to find a more satisfactory approach to their education. Obviously, this was no age for the project method. A study of modern educational theory had convinced me that the usual practice of providing a 'sense-training' period together with routine in habit training, and some music and stories did not give either the necessary freedom or the adequate equipment for intellectual and social development. I believe that it is impossible to separate off the experience of the senses and to train them without reference to the child's wishes, phantasies and needs. Learning necessarily involves feelings and proceeds by way of the experiences of life. The possibility that these children might develop more satisfactorily through self-education in a stimulating environment with the minimum of interference by teachers was suggested to me by the two books of Dr. Susan Isaacs': *Intellectual Growth of children* and *The Social Development of children*. I therefore arranged to give them freedom for half their school days (two-and-a-half hours) with selected materials and toys and with the minimum of interference. They played in their own way, according to the need of each individual, and as problems presented themselves, they were solved by teacher and children together.

These previous experiences, together with the further observation of children outside school, strongly indicated that unorganized play should have a prominent place in the design for the development of the children who were now to be in my care for the next few years at the Raleigh Infants' School. The current general interest in play among psychologists and the prominence it had already achieved as a technique in child Guidance Clinics, gave me still more confidence.

At the first meeting of the Raleigh Infant School staff, we agreed to work for a 'child-centred school', the development of the individual being our first concern. We decided that the artificialities of the school machine should invariably give way to the needs of the children. We looked forward to their development socially, but determined to allow this to grow spontaneously in the atmosphere we should provide. Organization of large groups with set purposes was to be avoided. We hoped also that reading, writing, and number, with other knowledge of the world around, would arise as interests from problems encountered during play, and from the practical necessities of self-chosen pursuits.

We knew already that if there is to be freedom for long periods each day, the rest of the school régime cannot be formal or over-directed. Our problem was to decide how much freedom could be allowed in a restricted space to children whose lives had no routine or security and who knew nothing of self-discipline. In Chapter III [of Boyce's book] the solution is fully discussed, but I may say at once that the more freedom we gave, the richer became the personalities of the children and the more they responded to the environment which we had provided. From the beginning, we realized that certain restrictions were necessary and although these were modified from time to time, a few rules were always in existence and the children were happier for them. They dealt with such points as care of school furniture, and a certain part of the garden, the orderliness of materials, and bullying. These restrictions were fully discussed with the children and no change was made without good warning. The teachers were the recognized authorities on arbitrary questions, although none of the children was afraid to argue, and there were always leaders in each class who directed a good many of the play activities.

Although each class had a simple time-table (*see* Chapter I [of Boyce's book]) the teachers were free to alter them if necessary. Unexpected events, expeditions, birthdays, and dramatic happenings on the 'Nature Table' interrupted the daily rhythm; itself planned to provide a background of routine otherwise unknown to the children.

The principle of activity as a means of learning guided the efforts of the staff to foster the development of each child. Whatever they could undertake without too heavy a responsibility was given into their care. Throughout this account, the reader will find references to the many 'jobs' which were performed by the children in the ordinary school routine. Nature Study was entirely a matter of doing; number knowledge was result of daily experiences in and out of school. Reading and writing interests were levered from the post-office play and picture books. Knowledge of the world was gained through first-hand observation supplemented by the teachers' answers to their questions. Experiment was encouraged and led to discussion and further investigation. Most of the information needed was given at moments when some incident had aroused the curiosity of a group. There were, of course, stories, verse readings, and group teaching during formal instruction. During these periods when the teacher was active, there were no more concentrated listeners than our children. If possible, their attention was even closer when a group of their companions were acting or when one child was speaking alone.

Besides creative activity in play; dancing, making rhymes and tunes; painting and dramatics were profoundly expressive and some children found their chief outlet in one particular line, and continued the interest all through the school.

All these activities were considered real school-life; there was no antithesis between work and play. In fact, no one quite understood which was which. Bill, aged seven, was seen at 9.45 a.m. collecting tools for some woodwork, and a teacher asked him a trifle suspiciously: 'Have you finished your work?' 'Can't you see I am just going to begin?' he replied. The adult's notion of work was the three R's; Bill's was *the shop* he was making. Reading and writing were often chosen as play by the older children during free periods.

One important consideration determined the principles underlying the work. Going from room to room, watching the sick, immobile children and listening to their inarticulate voices, the new head teacher recognized the need for a school planned for these particular children and their disabilities. The ordinary standards in the ordinary Infants' School could not be applied here. Thinking of their congested home conditions, of their lack of free movements, of their poverty of ideas and experience and the irritability which ill-health brings with it, I felt convinced that this school had to provide what life had hitherto denied, and that intellectual attainment as such would have to be ignored, at least until happy, talkative, confident children filled the classrooms. From the beginning, our plans were strictly to avoid assessing the children in the ordinary school attainments and to give each one the encouragement needed for confidence. We wanted the children to feel, at any rate, 'At school I can do the right thing'.

Their poor physical condition and the lack of habit training in the homes caused us to use Nursery School methods as far as space and opportunity allowed. We did not, however, cease to care for these matters with the children over five. Every child in the school had its own towel and washed when necessary; every meal was arranged decently and as much outdoor activity as possible was allowed.

Records

Most of the material of this account had accumulated in volumes of records of individual children, kept by each teacher, and in diaries which reviewed the main interests, activities, and events of the preceeding week. Group efforts, suggestions from children, conversations, and questions were emphasized and were often noted on the same day. Many teachers forecast their work for a week but we could only do this for our physical training, music, and some stories. The rest depended upon questions, and interest of the moment, and so had to be recorded rather than forecast. The diaries are extremely illuminating but too voluminous to publish. The following extracts serve to show the sort of valuable information contained in them: the first indicates when the first writing interest of a group of six-year-olds occurred.

> *Feb.25th, 1935*
> 'A little group is really intrigued with writing, they asked how to do "cat". I wrote it for them and they copied it and thought it a good game. They then asked for one or two other words and I wrote down some of their names. Some of them form the letters well at once and others ask to be shown but go on practicing them until they can do them well'.

This note is followed up during the next few weeks and describes how the new skill developed and how reading soon followed the writing enthusiasm.

Here is quite a different extract from a diary dated June 28th, 1935, and dealing with the social development of a group of seven-year-olds.

> 'The dominant feature of the week's work had been the development of the story of the *Sleeping Princess* into a play. The four scenes, roughly planned last week, have now been filled out. Rosie, the wicked fairy, is the leader and stimulates everybody else. She has been ready with plans and suggestions and has introduced a fiendish chuckle which enthralls the class. The first time she did it, "ha-HA-HA", there were cries of "Do it again, Rosie, do it again". This appreciation of one another's work is growing rapidly. A new property-box has been made and more clothes with additional crowns and wands. There have been many private rehearsals, little groups have been practising at any time in the afternoon. The post office has been finished by Bert and Bill: the latter found an old wooden box, already divided into partitions, which he nailed on to the side of the post office to hold stamps and stationery. Joe is making a clock. There

have been groups cutting out stamps, sorting and making envelopes and post-cards.

'Programmes, posters, and bills announcing forthcoming events in the theatre have been made and the café supplied with cakes and jam tarts each day by a "cookery-group".

'Jim has kept the accounts for the pets. May and Rene have managed the "Little Wonder"(school shop) ... and so on'.

This is an extract from October 23rd, 1935, and deals with a group of four-year-olds.

'Jimmy, Lennie, and Albert painted aeroplanes. The only paint available was an uninteresting dark blue. They said that would do. Then Jim found a brush from a yellow pot and dipped it into the blue without washing it.

"Look, it's coming green. That's just what we wanted". Then the yellow ceased and he saw blue again. "Have you any yellow to pour in this blue tin, then we'll stir it up with a stick and it will be green?" This last remark was from Albert.

'There have been more offers to help each other. John is the only one who can tie bows and he has been wrestling with bootlaces and aprons. Joyce puts Margaret's coat on for her. Frank showed Ted how to use the dustpan, and Florrie spent seven minutes untying Arthur's boots. Several boys have washed up but they get tired after ten plates'.

It must be noted here that each teacher kept most of her group from the time they entered school until they left for the Junior Department. Change of teacher did occur occasionally and this was generally to give a child a fresh beginning or to put her with a more suitable age group.

Individual records

A weekly record, under headings, was kept for each child. These were simplified from time to time to make them more comprehensive or to save time. They chiefly concerned the undirected work of the children and the development noticed by the teacher during the free activity period. It was impossible either to notice all that went on or to record every detail. Actually, they indicated the outstanding features and general trend of a child's activity during each week. Sometimes a teacher overlooked a few of her large group and discovered this when she came to fill in their records. Of course, they were given attention the next week. Record keeping was also useful in indicating the general development of the individual and the deviations from the normal. As difficulties were noticed, we tried to help the child over his problems, whether these concerned his relation with other children, a lack of initiative, or incapacity to choose, or to settle to any occupation.

Figure 1.1 is an example of the record used for the three- to five-year-olds.

Materials used	Alone or with group	Part played in group	Suggested by	Solitary play
Sand	Group	Helped to heap up sand for castles.	Entirely own initiative	Drawing slow and careful.
Bricks	Group and alone	Dug hard when making pond.		Painted whole sheets of colour.
Chalk	Alone	Joined in tea-party with girls.		Poured dry sand through sieve.
Paint	"	Helped to make houses with bricks. Spent long time talking.		Indefinite play with bricks; no construction, concentration throughout.
Measures	"			
House	Group			

Figure 1.1 Individual record for Joe Durrell.   Date of birth 25.10.1929. Week ending 12.11.1934.

The children's own records

When a child became interested in reading and writing, he kept a book about himself. These were usually illustrated and the written material varied a great deal. They do, however, provide a delightful method of recalling their many and varied interests as well as the personalities of the young writers.

John was the most intelligent child we had in the school. He was able to read earlier than most of the children and could speak fluently. He wrote his first record at the age of 5¾ years and illustrated it with dashing pencil sketches.

> *Page I.*
>   I played a joke on my seeds one did not have any water one did not have any air and one did not have any warm and one did not have any sun.
>
> *Page 2 (illustrated by a drawing of a pea in a jar).*
>   This is a pea. this one groows proper he grows alright.
>
> *Page 3 (illustrated by a pea in a jar of water).*
>   This one had not any air he got drowned and did not grow.
>
> *Page 4 (illustrated by a pea in a jar of cotton wool).*
>   This is dry cotton wool this has not any water his coat got all wrinkled he did not grow.

Figure 1.2 is a sample of the six-and seven-year-old record.

Date	Materials used	Imaginative part in group play	Constructive part in group play	Contribution to discussion	Responsibility undertaken	Solitary play
22.3.34	Wood Paint Clay Cardboard	Porter at 'Covent Garden'	Counter for shop Fruit for shop	That paper bags must be made	Care of nature table	Writing book of poems, letters. Library.

Figure 1.2 A sample of the 6 and 7 year old record, Harry Applegate.   Date of birth 15.12.27.

Page 5 (another pea in a jar).
I put him in the cupboard in the dark he grew very long and tall (another drawing).

Page 6 (with a similar illustration).
I put him in the washhouse in the cold he did not grow it was too cold he will grow if you give him some water and some air but he will not grow if it is cold.

An older child, Jim, wrote about his new friend.

May 17th.
'I have a mate Fred P., and every play time he plays with me'.

May 29th.
I am going with Fred P. round to his house to play cowboys with Fred P. He comes round the corner. I jump on him.

Nellie was able to write her plans for the afternoon free period.

'I am going to make something for the farmhouse, I am going to make a table for downstairs and a chair for downstairs. Lilly S. is making some dolls out of raffia. I don't know how to make dolls, I know how to make a table I think. How to make dolls is like this. We get some raffia, we make it long, put some raffia round for its head and for its arms and body and legs'.

Charlie gives some out-of-school information.

May 27th.
'I am going to see the pictures to see Buck Jones and the serial of Bob Still and Micky Mouse. I like it because it is a laughing picture and its funny'.

May 31st.
'I am going to see the pictures to see Tom Tyler and Tim McCoy for a penny'.

June 8th.
'I went to the Penny Pictures and I saw Tom Tyler and Micky Mouse and the serial of the Wolf Dog the wolf dog saw the crooks run away from the Wolf Dog, this wolf dog was a biter'.

Jane records on a Monday:

'I went the hospital and our mother and our rose went to and we went to see our dad he is in hospital and we all went to see our dad and our dad gave my mother sixpence to have a drink'.

I have also some hundreds of letters written by the children and sent through the School post office. They were quite spontaneous efforts and reveal joys and anxieties as well as many interests and activities. The rest of the staff have similar recollections.

Billy, six years old, wanted an electric battery. He also wanted to show how well he could speak his part of the new play. Here is his way of mentioning these things:

'Dear Miss Boyce,
    'Did you give Miss E. that Battery and will you send me a letter have you seen Act 5 the King of the Golden River if you have not tell me if you have not asked Miss S. if we could act it for you. With love from Billy'.

Joan, aged six, reveals something of home life.

'Dear Miss Boyce,
    'Our baby is coming home and our dad is going to by a doll and she is going to let me hold it and she will not let our Doris hold it and we are going to have a birthday party and my Jeannie is going to sleep with me. With love from Joan'.

Nellie, aged six, wrote:

'Dear Miss Boyce,
    'I have not got enough match boxes and will you ask all the children to get some and all the match boxes you get will you give them to me from Nellie'.

The following are examples of children's first letters just before or after they had begun to learn to read and write. Many more were scribbled and interpreted by the teachers.

Dear Miss Boyce,
    'now our baby is getting some more teeth from Mary'.

'Dear Miss Boyce,
    'you havent answered my letter yet from Anna'.

'Dear Miss boyce who can read the best from Hilda'.

'Dear Miss boyce,
    'Eileen said if you dont believe in Father Christmas he will put coke in your stocking, from George'.

Mary, aged seven, in thanking a friend for the gift of a brown baby doll, mixes up phantasy and the talk she has heard about the trouble between Italy and Abyssinia. The doll was called Koffee.

'Dear miss W.
    'Koffee is ill and he has got his hand bandaged up because he got hurt in his Hand and his house got Bombed in the war in Africa and there was a war in Africa because Italy wanted to take some of their land. Because they wanted more than they had got. From Mary'.

Original poems and many pictures have also accumulated and are referred to in the following pages.

Organization and curricula

In January 1933, there were six classes arranged approximately in age groups. These remained during the next three years but a small additional class was organized each Spring and Summer term for the most delicate children and for some who, owing to mental and emotional instability, needed special attention. This class was held in the playground; an open shelter being used in bad weather.

There was a small central hall with one classroom leading from it. Two corridors led from the hall in opposite directions to the playground and the rest of the rooms led from these. Unfortunately, two rooms had been allocated for the use of the Senior Schools and were not available for our own use during the first part of the experiment. Cloakrooms, a line of low bowls and one deep sink were arranged at each end of the school, near the exit. In one corner of a lobby was an old copper heated by gas, our only supply of hot water.

The younger children were given two classrooms and the use of a fairly wide corridor where big toys could be used in wet weather. The three-year-olds had the larger room, which was known as the 'Big Nursery' and the four-year-olds lived in the 'Little Nursery'. The five-year-olds changed their room several times and we finally found that their best place was the room leading straight from the hall. It was small and square but the children had the advantage of overflowing into the hall each morning for play. Building, transport play, families, and workmen games usually went on here between 9 and 10 a.m.; while puzzles, modelling, painting, etc., took place in the classroom. The seven-year-olds used the room next to the senior girls, as we hoped that they would be quieter than the other classes. The older fives had a slightly larger room and the sixes a smaller one near the nurseries. Both fives and sixes changed their rooms during the three years but the sevens and the nurseries remained the same.

From the beginning, these was need for a quiet place for the few children who were worried by noise during the activity periods. It was also necessary to have other places besides classrooms for some of the play in order to give more space and opportunity for large construction and co-operative work. A corner of the hall was therefore screened off and furnished with gay book shelves, cosy deck chairs and cushions, little chairs and tables and rungs and plenty of picture books. The children came here freely. We asked them to mention to us that they were going and we sent a messenger to warn them of the conclusion of free periods. After a time, it became the custom to wash before using the books, and there was always a rule that voices were lowered in this place. Later on, the rooms used by the seniors were returned to us and we were able to have a whole room for quiet work with puzzles and books and pencils and paper. When the quiet games were put into this room, the children were asked to remember that when they were finished with them they had to go back in the right place. A knowing little Cockney observed: 'You mean really that we are not to nick (steal) anything'. That was just what we did mean!

We were able to have a school theatre when another room became vacant. We could not call it a 'theatre' as this was an entirely foreign concept to the children and there was no way of showing them a real theatre in action. They did, however, know all about the Cinema and we explained it as 'the Pictures where children act instead of Tom Mix and Laurel and Hardy' (who were great favourites at that time). We left them to decide on the name, and when a box of periwinkles came from the country they chose this name which sounded so fascinating to them. After the manner of the East End, it was soon shortened from 'The Periwinkle' to 'The Peri'. Parents and staff adopted the shorter name too.

During one term we were fortunate in having another vacant room and this was known as the 'Activity Room'. Here the equipment consisted of a long, low table for cooking, another for modelling, and a woodwork bench. Tools and materials for each activity were stored within easy reach of the children and the middle of the floor was left free for any work which required extra space. At other times the two benches were kept and used in corridors.

As the teachers usually spent their time in the rooms where the majority of the children were, those using the extra rooms were unsupervised except when one of us could look in to see that all was well. Sometimes the main part of the class was left for a short time whilst the teacher showed a special group how to use a tool or taught some simple technique in modelling or cooking.

The playground was used as much as possible and in the summer term, stories, dramatics, and discussions were often carried on in the open air. Light mats were provided so that building, target games, and puzzles could be enjoyed outside. The large sand trays were made on wheels so that they could be moved into the playground.

Syllabus of work

No class had a work syllabus, but at the beginning of each term the teachers considered and wrote down the aims of teaching in their particular group at that time. These were never used twice although they might resemble each other from term to term. The important point was that they were thought out for the particular group under consideration. For instance, these were the aims of the garden class in 1935 (age four and a half to seven and a half years).

1   To improve the mental and physical health of the children.
2   To provide materials for suitable activities, including gardening, care of animals, sand play, modelling, painting, and drawing, building, water play, woodwork, sewing, and dolls play, family, transport, and shop play.
3   To provide opportunities for creative expression through music, acting, and poetry speaking.
4   To improve speech and vocabulary.
5   To give instruction in reading and numbers to those over six, allowing each one to proceed at his own rate. (No formal lessons.)
6   To give as much happiness and security as possible.

The aims of the teacher of the Big Nursery were:

1   To encourage independence and confidence and the following habits: good speech, cleanliness, decent feeding, courtesy, and tidiness.
2   To provide suitable playthings.
3   To give children a healthy, happy, and secure environment.

After deciding upon aims, there followed a written plan of the way in which these aims were to be carried out. There were many staff meetings when general principles and details of practice were discussed.

The usual records of achievement in the three R's were kept after the children had begun formal work, but these were never displayed as wall lists and there were no examinations.

Time-tables

A certain amount of experiment resulted in several conclusions about time-tables. One was the necessity for a daily period of musical work with the piano or percussion band instruments. (Rhythmic movement, singing, and games were taken together in one period.) Singing had no place of its own on the time-tables, but the children knew many songs and sang naturally and happily when occasion arose. Whenever we wanted to sing, we sang. The music period did a great deal to help physical control and the concentrated efforts of the slower children, and the joy they found in the large, rhythmical movement, helped their development considerably.

We also decided that the daily assembly for the older children was impossible at the usual hour of 9 a.m. Most of them slept in crowded and badly ventilated rooms for far too short a time and had been roughly awakened for a quick wash and brush up and a piece of bread and margarine with a cup of tea just before 9 a.m. Some of them entered the school gates still munching a crust, other were bad tempered and sullen or only half-awake. Little wonder that on Monday mornings, no one answered the cheerful greetings of the staff, or that when they assembled at 9 a.m. nobody wanted to sing or talk but only to push any one who came too near. We, therefore, had the school ready with toys and materials displayed at about 8.30 a.m. The children entered just as they were ready; a few had jobs to do and the rest chose their occupations and settled down, gradually working off their sleepy, non-social feelings in their material and becoming chatty and cheerful during the next half-hour. Free work went on until 10 a.m. and then the older ones assembled together for a community effort which is described in Chapter XIII [of Boyce's book].

Experiment convinced us that one hour's free unorganized activity was the ideal period. Anything less did not give sufficient time to finish large constructions and if longer they became tired and quarrelsome. As the reader will see from the time-tables, it was not always possible to give as long as this, but as far as we could, we set aside periods of an hour for self-chosen, *undirected* activity.

Scripture stories were told to the children as they sat in groups on mats round the teacher at the end of the morning session. Sometimes they were dramatized. At the end of afternoon session, the older children had a period known as 'English'. Stories, poems, dramatic work, and speech-training games were taken during this time, the teacher using it in the way most valuable for her group.

The older the children, the more formal became the time-table, as the Primary Subjects had to be considered and because the children themselves were ready for more collective efforts.

The time-tables in use during 1937 are given here, but it must be emphasized again that they were altered or ignored according to the interests and purpose of the children. We insisted that the children should not be made to fit into any school machinery, but that the machinery could be altered to fit them.

Time-table in the nurseries

N.B. The actual times are approximate, the teacher used her judgment in shortening or lengthening period.

8.50 a.m. to 10.10 a.m.
Arrivals, putting on overalls, play and clearing up room at end of period.

10.00 a.m. to 11.a.m.
Washing, preparation of mid-morning meal, sing-song, lunch, washing up, sweeping. If a child did not help in these jobs, he played with quiet toys which were kept for the purpose.

11 a.m. to 11.25a.m.
Music and speech-training games.

11.25 a.m. to 11.45 a.m.
Play out of doors with big toys, balls, ropes, hoops, etc.

11.45 a.m. to noon
Preparation for home and school.

Afternoon

Sleep and play.

Note.   The little nursery had music earlier as they took less time to tidy after lunch. Their speech training was held in the classroom and longer time was spent on it, as they liked to act. Otherwise the two programmes were similar. They went into the open air whenever possible; rain was the only deterrent. If really too bad, they used the hall.

Time-table for five-year-olds

8.50 a.m. to 10 a.m.
Free activities, which as some of the children became interested in writing and reading, included some reading games and voluntary individual work. Time was allowed for tidying the room.

10 a.m. to 10.15 a.m.
School assembly.

10.15 a.m. to 10.30 a.m.
Play time.

10.30 a.m. to 10.50 a.m.
Washing and lunch.

10.50 a.m. to 11.20 a.m. (approx.).
Discussion which, when children wanted to write about themselves, was followed by drawing, scribbling, or writing in books. (*See* Chapter II [of Boyce's book])

11.20 a.m. to 11.35 a.m.
Physical training.

11.35 a.m. to 11.55 a.m.
Scripture story.

Afternoon

2 p.m. to 3 p.m.
Free activities with a period for music. (When the children had just come from the nurseries, they slept during this time; gradually the numbers needing sleep diminished, but some had a rest all through this year.)

3 p.m. to 3.15 p.m.
Play time.

3.15 p.m. to 3.30 p.m.
Play time had to be early to enable us to have the space to ourselves so the tidying up was left until now to give as long as possible for free work.

3.30 p.m. to 4 p.m.
English.

Time-tables for sixes and sevens

8.50 a.m. to 10 a.m.
Practice in the three R's, and free activities (this is explained in Chapter XII [of Boyce's book].)

10 a.m. to 10.45 a.m.
School assembly, play time, washing and lunch.

10.45 a.m. to 11 a.m.
Any necessary drills. (*See* Chapter XII [of Boyce's book].)

11 a.m. to 11.15 a.m.
Physical training.

11.15 a.m. to 11.35 a.m.

Discussion and, for some children, recording in books, wall-notices, letters, and poems.

11.35 a.m. to 12 noon.

Scripture story.

Afternoon

2 p.m. to 3 p.m.

Free activities with a music period.

3 p.m. to 3.15 p.m.

Play time. (Clearing away was done during this period by groups of volunteers who changed each week.)

3.15 p.m. to 4 p.m.

English.

Note.   The two physical training periods did not coincide. In the case of one group, it occurred between the discussion and the scripture story.

Chapter 2

The cultural construction of child development

Creating institutional and cultural intersubjectivity

Marilyn Fleer

Source: *M. Fleer, International Journal of Early Years Education, 14(2), 127–140, 2006.*

Since its inception in the early nineteenth century, early childhood education has moved beyond European communities and become institutionalized in countries such as Australia, India, Malaysia, New Zealand and Singapore. At the same time, many European countries have experienced migration, and now have broadly based culturally and linguistically diverse communities. Although early education has continued to evolve over time, some fundamental principles about the nature of learning have remained static. In drawing upon cultural–historical theory, this paper seeks to make visible early childhood institutional practices that may no longer be relevant, particularly when western theory and middle-class practices are not representative of the culturally and linguistically diverse communities they serve. In this paper, an alternative model of child development is offered that takes into account and values the diversity of children's cultural experiences.

Introduction

Educational systems are constructed on the basis of theories and values about children and childhood. Upbringing and education is directed towards ideals of where to bring the children through the educational system.

(Hedegaard, 2005, p. 8)

Early childhood education in most European heritage countries has been built upon a strong tradition of a materially rich and active play-based pedagogy and environment (e.g. Bruce, 1997; Dockett & Fleer, 1999; Einarsdottir, 1998; Michalopoulou, 2001). Support for this approach can also be seen in policy and curriculum implementation literature within many industrialized societies (Lubeck, 1996, 1998; Dahlberg *et al.*, 1999; Edwards, 2001;

Chan & Mellor, 2002). Yet the selection of materials, the organization of learning, and the beliefs that underpin centre-based environments remain largely uncontested. This is problematic, as many of these original communities, and those which have since appropriated western early childhood education, are culturally and linguistically diverse.

Early childhood education within many English-speaking countries has evolved routines, practices, rituals, artefacts, symbols, conventions, stories and histories (Siraj-Blatchford & Clarke, 2000; Siraj-Blatchford, 2004). In effect, our practices have become traditions which have been named and reified (Lave & Wenger, 1991; Wenger, 1998) evolving a specialist discourse. Yet what has become valued within the profession of early childhood education is essentially a western view of childhood (James & Prout, 1997; James *et al.*, 1998; Dahlberg *et al.*, 1999; Mayall, 2002; Fleer, 2003) and development (see Rogoff, 2003; Edwards, 2004).

Rogoff *et al.* (2003, p. 81) locate western learning within a child-centred pedagogy, arguing that 'These specialized child-focused situations – especially schooling, but also pre-school lessons and child-focused conversations in families – often employ instructional practices and a concept of learning that were heavily influenced by the organization of factories'. A particular social need at a particular point in western history creates a particular institutional structure. The legacy of the institution remains, but is largely uncontested. This paper seeks to examine the cultural–historical construction of early childhood education within the context of institutionalized taken-for-granted practices, such as child development.

Theoretical problem

Living in a particular community of practice will afford particular types of activity and learning, evolving community-specific cultural tools. Wertsch (1998) suggests that:

> ... we usually do not operate by choice. Instead, we inherently appropriate the terministic screens, affordances, constraints, and so forth associated with the cultural tools we employ. Unlike Lewis Carroll's Humpty Dumpty, then, speakers are not in a position to assert that 'When I use a word, it means whatever I want it to mean'
>
> (Carroll, 1872, p. 189; Wertsch, 1998, p. 55)

As a result, we appropriate the conceptual tools and discourses available to us. In the context of early childhood education within European heritage communities, it can be argued that we become enculturated into that practice, as it is enacted within our community. We use these existing cultural tools to inform us and guide us in our enactment of early childhood education. Yet examining some of these taken-for-granted cultural practices requires a broad cultural–historical analysis. In the past, critiques of early childhood education have been successfully undertaken (e.g. Dahlberg *et al.*, 1999), with some highlighting the cultural context as a resource (see Burman, 2001, cited in Edwards, 2004). Edwards (2004) argues that 'early education would be better served by a version of psychology which takes context seriously and allows us to see how it is more than a phenomenon to be ana- lyzed for clues about the individual, but is something that shapes and is shaped by those who participate in it' (p. 86). Edwards (2004) also sug- gests that we need to understand how adults contribute to and shape the cultural world of the child. She argues that whilst significant work has been done on identifying new forms of pedagogy and curricula, insuffi- cient attention has been paid to finding alternatives to individually oriented versions of developmental psychology for informing professional practice. Edwards (2004) has put forward the view that a new theoretical basis for early education practice is needed, and that any new alternative psychology should place 'culture at the centre of [our] interactions and our being in the world' (p. 86).

Culturally specific theories of child development – broadening our assumptions

Contemporary early childhood education in many European heritage coun- tries foregrounds the importance of educators' child development knowledge, the implementation of a play-based pedagogy (e.g. Bruce, 1997; Einarsdottir, 1998; Dockett & Fleer, 1999; Michalopoulou, 2001), with a corresponding environment based on learning centres, a child-centred philosophy, the need to work with children's interest, and their families, and for educators to build educational programmes based on close observations of children (Dockett & Fleer, 1999). Yet many European heritage communities that have appropriated these pedagogical practices are culturally and linguistically diverse. Schieffelin and Ochs (1998) suggest that 'the extent to which we are developing cul- turally specific theories of development (and therefore practice) needs to be considered' (p. 61).

Child development has traditionally been conceptualized as observable age- related stages of behaviour, which are universal for all children at roughly the same age. Physical milestones such as crawling and walking, or psychological milestones such as stranger anxiety or object permanence are reported in many child development texts and courses. Corresponding programming for young children is usually based upon these child development expectations. Child development viewed in this way not only forms the basic fabric of early child- hood education practice but is also the benchmark upon which all children are metaphorically compared. Yet developmental psychology, as it has been tradi- tionally applied to early childhood education, is but one cultural construction of development (Dahlberg *et al.*, 1999).

Woodhead *et al.* (1998, p. 2) argue that although all children develop emotional attachments, learn language and develop reasoning, 'they take place within culturally regulated social relationships, and are mediated by cultural practices'. Woodhead *et al.* (1998) argue that these 'practices are in turn shaped by knowledge and beliefs about what is normal and desirable'. Indeed, 'comparative material can lead us to reinterpret behaviours as cultural that we have assumed to be natural' (Schieffelin & Ochs, 1998, p. 50).

Cross-cultural research has provided evidence of many other constructions of development. For example, 'stranger anxiety' in western Kenya has been shown to be related to social niche rather than developmental norms (Super & Harkness, 1998), language acquisition in some villages in Papua New Guinea is related to social embeddedness of infants rather than disembedded practices where language lessons are introduced (Schieffelin & Ochs, 1998), and variations in sleeping patterns of infants (USA, 8 hours longest period of sleep; western Kenya, 4½ hours longest period of sleep) is significantly different across cultures (Super & Harkness, 1998).

Cross-cultural diversity in relation to how adults and children interact, and the subsequent communication strengths exhibited in different cultures, has profound consequences on assumed 'instructional styles'. For instance, Rogoff *et al.* (1998) suggest that when infants are separated out from the everyday activities of their community then a need for distal forms of communication is necessary, such as vocalizing. They argue that 'children who are constantly in the company of their caregivers may rely more on non-verbal cues, such as direction of gaze or facial expression' (p. 233) and infants who are in 'almost constant skin-to-skin contact with their mothers may manage effective communication through tactile contact in squirming and postal changes' (p. 233).

Expectations surrounding appropriate ways of interacting with infants have also been noted by Schieffelin and Ochs (1998). They found that in Kaluli families (Papua New Guinea) caregivers and infants do not gaze into each others' eyes, but rather face their babies outwards to the social group. In this way, infants interact with the social group earlier than in communities where infants predominantly are faced towards their caregivers. For example, 'older children greet and address the infant and, in response to this, the mother, while moving the baby, speaks in a high-pitched voice "for" the baby' (Schieffelin & Ochs, 1998, p. 54).

Examining cultural practices from within one's own culture is much more challenging than when looking cross-culturally. Expectations shape the data gathered and analyzed by researchers, including developmental psychologists. Schieffelin and Ochs (1998) suggest that:

> We are able to apply without effort the cultural framework for interpreting the behavior of caregivers and young children in our own social group; indeed as members of a white middle-class society, we are socialized to do this very work, that is interpreting behaviors, attributing motives,

and so on. The paradox is that in spite of this ease of effort, *we cannot easily isolate and make explicit these cultural principles.*

(Schieffelin & Ochs, 1998, p. 49; my emphasis)

Rogoff (2003) argues that when one learns more about another culture, one also learns more about one's own. Cross-cultural research provides us with other beliefs surrounding expectations in children's development. In some parts of West Africa child development is viewed as a social rather than a biological construct (Nsamenang & Lamb, 1998). Children are given different roles and responsibilities based on their perceived level of social competence rather than their age. Yet in many industrialized nations the age of children underpins the way we organize preschool, childcare and schools. Before the 1800s, age was not a criterion for organizing people. Generally, people were unaware of their age, and age-related practices were not the norm. Rogoff (2003) argues that industrialization saw the systemization of people into specialized institutions according to age. She states that 'Developmental psychology and paediatrics began at this time, along with old-age institutions and age-graded schools' (p. 8).

Child development as presently conceptualized and enacted within many European heritage communities has become normalized and institutionalized within early childhood education. Ages and stages underpin this particular taken-for-granted practice, and the expectations within stages focus on those appropriate for western communities. This particular cultural belief about children is relevant for children from European or North American backgrounds (given that this is the research base used) from a time period in which industrialization was an important cultural practice. However, the legacy of this cultural belief and assumption about how children develop in all contemporary societies is in need of review.

Other views on child development

We already know that the child's chronological age cannot serve as a reliable criterion for establishing the actual level of his [*sic*] development.

(Vygotsky, 1998, p. 199)

Vygotsky (1998, vol. 5) provides a powerful critique of child (developmental) psychology. He suggests that traditionally there have been two important conceptions of child development. First, 'development is nothing other than realization, modification, and combination of deposits; Nothing new develops here – only a growth, branching, and regrouping of those factors that were already present at the very beginning' (Vygotsky, 1998, p. 190). In contrast, the second perspective states that 'development is a continuous process of self-propulsion characterized primarily by the continuous appearance and formation of the new which did not exist at previous stages' (Vygotsky, 1998, p. 190).

The latter perspective has dominated psychology and early childhood education for the past century. The perspective taken by a caregiver or educator shapes how they respond to, think about, and plan for children. Vygotsky (1998) has argued that both perspectives highlight a linear path where deviating from 'the normal path' can be considered as '"diseases" of development' (p. 191). Educators look for and expect particular behaviours; when they are not forthcoming concern is expressed about the individual. An evolutionary view of child development is embedded within the institutionalized thinking of early childhood education in most European heritage countries.

Vygotsky (1998) argues for a different perspective of child development. He puts forward a dialectical process 'in which a transition from one stage to another is accomplished not along an evolutionary, but along a revolutionary path' (p. 193). Vygotsky (1998) argues that a dialectical approach to development invites the pedagogue to be continually projecting learning beyond the child's current capacities, but will do so in ways which connect with the child's growing sense of themselves within their communities/institutions. This particular perspective encourages teachers to examine context as well as the children's zones of proximal development when making judgements about children and when planning for learning.

In the context of early childhood education, teachers who have an evolutionary rather than revolutionary gaze on the children they teach will enact a pedagogy that is static and not dialectical. Vygotsky (1998) argues that an evolutionary gaze by the teacher sees the child becoming 'relatively difficult' when 'the pedagogical system applied to the child does not' match the child's projected developmental pathway (Vygosky, 1998, pp. 193–194).

On the other hand, a revolutionary gaze by the teachers foregrounds the cultural context, the institutional context, and the specific child's lived experience. Western heritage communities have tended to utilize an evolutionary perspective in their early childhood education institutions. A revolutionary gaze provides an alternative conceptual framework for early childhood educators, and helps practitioners move beyond the present developmental conceptual framework.

Having a revolutionary perspective allows teachers to foreground the social situation of development. For example, in many European heritage communities verbal language is privileged. However, in other communities, such as Mexican heritage communities, non-verbal competence is mastered much earlier and represents an important mode of communication (see Rogoff *et al.*, 2003). These different communication trajectories highlight the social nature of development, and foreground how cultural communities shape development by what they value and need.

> The social situation of development represents the initial moment for all dynamic changes that occur in development during the given period. It determines wholly and completely the forms and the path along which

the child will acquire ever newer personality characteristics, drawing them from the social reality as from the basic source of development, the path along which the social becomes the individual. Thus, the first question we must answer in studying the dynamics of any age is to explain the social situation of development.

(Vygotsky, 1998, p. 198)

The social situation of a child is determined by the society and cultural context in which the child is embedded. Two eminent scholars of cultural–historical theory – Barbara Rogoff and Mariane Hedegaard – have elaborated upon Vygotsky's seminal work and have provided further research and explanations of child development in the context of the social situation of the child.

In drawing upon a large corpus of cross-cultural research, Barbara Rogoff (1990, 1998, 2003) has argued that '*development can be understood only in light of the cultural practices and circumstances of their communities – which also change*' (Rogoff, 2003, pp. 3–4; original emphasis). In essence, culture determines not only the principles for defining development but also frames the contexts in which the development of children is supported. Rogoff (2003) argues that development can be viewed as a transformation of participation in cultural activities. Through this transformation, individual roles change and developmental transitions in communities become evident. Transformation through participation of individuals means not only that individuals change but also that they change the communities in which they live.

Assuming universal views on child development positions some children from some families in deficit. As suggested by Rogoff *et al.* (1998), we need to begin to understand 'the development of children in the context of their own communities' and this requires the 'study of the local goals and means of approaching life' (p. 228):

... the sociohistorical approach assumes that individual development must be understood in (and cannot be separated from) the social context.

(Rogoff *et al.*, 1998, p. 227)

Through this new view of development, traditional western lenses of social, emotional, cognitive and physical development are problematized, as noted by Woodhead *et al.* (1998):

Studying child development in social and cultural contexts cuts through the conventional demarcation between cognitive, social and emotional development researchers.

(Woodhead *et al.*, 1998, p. 1)

In many European heritage communities, a significant amount of programme support material available to early childhood teachers has been developed on a child development model in which social, emotional, physical and cognitive development are privileged. Of significance is the assumption that this model of child development should underpin quality-assurance and government regulations, particularly in relation to observing, assessing and planning for children's learning. In effect, an evolutionary model of child development has become normalized as the dominant approach within the institution of early childhood education. For early childhood professionals to reframe their thinking and to adopt a new conceptual framework, further examination of the institutional nature of early childhood education is needed.

Hedegaard (2004) has researched the construction of childhood and development within the framework of the institution, society and the individual. Her work is particularly powerful in that it draws extensively upon Vygotsky's (1998) seminal critique of child development, but specifically examines contemporary contexts, where cultural and linguistic diversity feature. In line with Vygotsky's work on the dialectical approach to development, and the social situation of development, Hedegaard (2004) views development as the relationship between the child and society. Development is not something that exists within the child but rather takes place as the child interacts with her/his cultural community. She argues that when development does not proceed it is not the fault of the child but rather the relationship between the child and society. As such the problem lies not in the child but in the institution. When an institution foregrounds only one view of development (e.g. western), then teachers expect and accept one developmental trajectory. This is problematic for culturally and linguistically diverse communities.

In drawing upon Vygotsky's writings on development, Hedegaard (2005) states that:

> Children develop through participating in everyday activities in societal institutions, but neither society nor its institution (i.e. families, kindergarten, school, youth clubs, etc.) are static but change over time in dynamic interaction between persons' activity, institutional traditions for practice, societal discourse and material conditions. Children's life and development is influenced by several types of institutional practice in a child's actual social situation. But at the same time children's development can be seen as socio-cultural tracks through different institutions. Children's development is marked by crises, which are created through change in the child's social situation.
>
> (Hedegaard, 20, p. 3)

In Hedegaard's (2005) research she identifies crisis points in children lives, which she believes provide the context for development. Hedegaard (2005) argues that when children enter a new societal or institutional context, where expectations and practices are unfamiliar, children experience a crisis situation. In researching adolescent boys who came from refugee camps in Lebanon and war-torn areas in Palestine before attending regular Danish schools and later an alternative school in Denmark, she was able to document three perspectives for development:

- the school's perspective;
- the child's perspective;
- the societal perspective.

In drawing upon her own research findings, Hedegaard (2005) has argued that because the children had not gained the literacy and numeracy skills expected of them, that they were deemed 'learning disabled children' (p. 4). Similarly, the protective and caring behaviours developed and valued in the adolescents' communities prior to integration into Danish society positioned these adolescents as being involved in gang activity against authority. Hedegaard (2005) argues that the adolescents' 'competencies were not seen as age adequate' and their 'social motive of caring for friends was not seen as positive' (p. 4). In essence, school expectations were normed against particular developmental milestones. Their behaviours were normed against societal expectations. Hedegaard (2005) found that from the adolescents' perspective, *their problem was not a learning problem, but a problem of finding strategies to survive in a new societal context'* (p. 4; original emphasis). Their behaviours were thought appropriate for those who they cared about. From a societal perspective, adolescents who end up as young criminals would be deemed as having *'inadequate development … {when they} cannot read and write Danish, and when they transgress the laws of society'* (p. 5; original emphasis).

Hedegaard (2005) argues that '[W]e need a developmental theory that can handle societal and institutional change and integrate this with the child's perspective' (p. 6). Rather than focusing on biological maturation, the concept of development should be constructed more broadly. Hedegaard's (2005) research focuses attention beyond just the child, and on to society and the institution. Of significance is the institutional nature of early childhood education, and the way developmental theory has framed how professionals work and think. Hedegaard's (2005) research further problematizes the way early childhood education has taken on, without question, an evolutionary universal developmental trajectory and institutionalized this perspective as the only way of conceptualizing teaching and learning.

If we consider Hedegaard's (2004) proposition of child development as being about the relationship between the child and society or institution, rather than simply something that occurs within the child, then we must closely scrutinize the institutions in which the child learns.

Hedegaard (2004) has put forward a model (see Figure 2.1) to illustrate child development as located within institutions. She argues that the theory of development gives conditions for how to realize the values held by a society. Hence the different cultural traditions of families and their interface with schools and

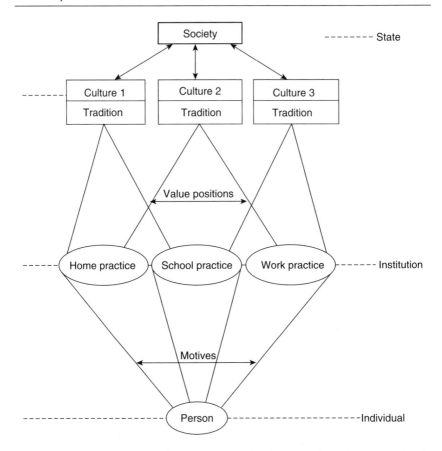

Figure 2.1 A model of children's learning and development through participation in institutional practice (Hedegaard, 2004, 2005).

community practice are shown (see Culture 1 Tradition; Culture 2 Tradition; and Culture 3 Tradition). The model begins to make visible the multifaceted nature of development and how a single universal view of development is problematic.

Here, Hedegaard (2004) highlights three cultural institutions that may or may not be aligned for a particular child in a particular society, namely home practice, school practice, and work practice. In more culturally homogeneous communities the values that are seen in relation to a society and what is deemed to be a 'good life' are also supported in the school and family. However, in more culturally and linguistically diverse communities a societal institution such as an early childhood centre does not always represent, or is not reflective of, *all* family values. When educators use an evolutionary model for child development, and focus on milestones that are representative of one culture (namely western heritage communities), the institution privileges this culture and silences other cultural groups. Hedegaard's (2004) research is important for early childhood professionals in that it draws to our attention the significance of the conceptual framework adopted for child development and the central place it holds within the institution, in western heritage communities.

Taken together, the diversity of cultural practice outlined in the previous section and the resultant expressions of child development detailed above illustrate that one universal view of child development as normalized within early childhood education is problematic. How our educational institutions take account of cultural variations has generally not been foregrounded in early childhood beliefs and practices within culturally and linguistically diverse communities.

Institutional values – institutional and cultural intersubjectivities

What is needed is a new model for re-forming early childhood education within communities that are culturally and linguistically diverse. A new model would need to be conceptualized in ways that bring together the values of culturally and linguistically diverse families. In drawing upon the literature discussed in the previous parts of this paper, what becomes apparent is the need for a cultural and institutional form of intersubjectivity for shaping early childhood education.

Much has been written about intersubjectivity, and the ability to read and be in tune with children and their families (e.g. Göncü, 1998). However, the cross-cultural studies introduced in this paper are examples of the diversity of cultural practices that can be found, and, as such, they demonstrate that the fundamentals of human worldviews and community practices sit outside the institutional practice of early childhood education. For instance, cultural beliefs that are not western in their origin are still 'added on' to mainstream fundamental early childhood education (see Figure 2.2). This is also relevant for European communities that have recently experienced an influx of migration. Social 'add-on' theory introduced by Rogoff (2003) best describes the way in which early childhood education theory and practice have taken account of culturally and linguistically diverse communities. In essence, we have mainstream early childhood education, with only some reference to cultural diversity. Culture is bolted on as something to be considered, but different views of development are not necessarily applied. We have not as yet seriously disrupted the western developmental perspectives as the main and only view of early childhood education. We have also not taken account of the linguistic and interactional patterns that feature among many cultures outside the western world. Similarly, we have not problematized dominant cultural assumptions about what happens in the home among families before and during the pre-school years. What prevails is the

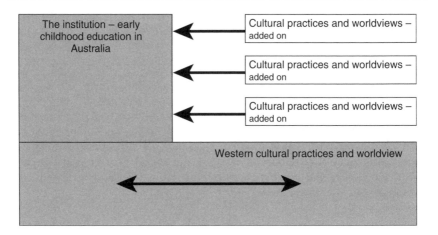

Figure 2.2 Institutional and western intersubjectivity.

institutional practice of western early childhood education, where intersubjectivity between the institution and families of western origin fits snugly (as shown in Figure 2.2).

When educators consider institutional intersubjectivity, the lens moves towards how the culture of the institution fits with the culturally and linguistically diverse communities which it serves. Intersubjectivity between the early childhood institution and the different cultural communities is urgently needed. Rather than different cultural groups being simply 'added on' to the institutional culture of early childhood education, institutional intersubjectivity problematizes a dominant worldview and practice.

A model that could reflect a new view of early childhood education could be described as shown in Figure 2.3. Here, the different cultural groups found within a community are carefully woven into a new form of early childhood education. In this new model, assumptions about 'child development' transform into the cultural nature of development (Rogoff, 2003), the social situation of development (Vygotsky, 1998) or the state, institutions and individual nature of development (Hedegaard, 2004). This new worldview invites educators to seek out the diversity of 'interactional patterns', 'beliefs and practices in relation to language acquisition', 'complexity and sophistication in non-verbal communication' and the central or disembedded place of children in everyday activities within communities. However, many other taken-for-granted practices need to be examined, and a new repertoire of cultural practices unearthed and made visible to the early childhood profession. A model of this kind does not allow one view of child development to dominate early childhood pedagogy.

In calling for new and different perspectives on child development, it is possible not only to change the way we think about children and how they

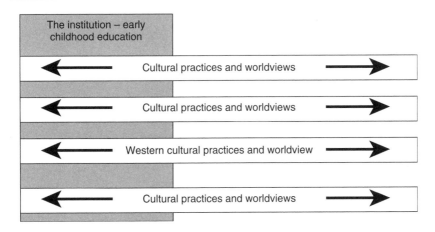

Figure 2.3 Institutional and cultural intersubjectivities.

learn but also to change the nature of the early childhood institution. For instance, Hedegaard and Chaiklin (2005) suggest that in homes and communities children's knowledge is presented informally 'and often not formulated explicitly' (p. 40). However, 'knowledge presented in school is dominated by the societal aspects of practice and is formulated through demands for activity in school and at examinations' (p. 40). For instance, teaching professionals are expected to teach children to read and write, and many governments shape how this will be assessed and monitored. However, how this plays out in practice can and does vary. Yet in many western heritage communities we find early childhood centres where staff expect developmental milestones and plan their programmes accordingly. Institutionalized learning becomes a form of cultural practice, which is taken for granted as the way one 'does school' or 'does early childhood education'.

Making these values and assumptions explicit is important in contesting their privileged and monocultural status within culturally and linguistically diverse communities. Through normalizing difference rather than recognizing only one cultural developmental trajectory, expectations in relation to development can be problematized immediately. Building institutional and cultural intersubjectivity gives teachers permission to move away from an evolutionary model of development and towards a revolutionary model, thus eliminating the perspective that any difference to normalized western development would be constituted as a 'disease' of normal child development (Vygotsky, 1998, p. 191). The model in Figure 2.3 is supportive of Hedegaard and Chaiklin's (2005) position that in making visible the different value sets that are working within the school or early childhood setting and the home it is possible to 'understand differences in the forms of practice that dominate at home and in school' (p. 39) and to value children's cultural development as valid and normal. Through this process, the foundations for constructing localized views on development can be put in place.

Conclusion

This theoretical paper has problematized the universal perspective on what constitutes an early childhood learning environment. The position put forward suggests that a cultural–historical critique of early childhood education can create a dialogical space (Moll & Greenberg, 1990) in which tradition and culture can generate new thinking and practices. As Wertsch (1998) suggests, the 'task of a sociocultural approach is to explicate the relationship between human *action*, on the one hand, and the cultural, institutional, and historical contexts in which this action occurs, on the other' (Wertsch, 1998, p. 24). Clearly, more research needs to be undertaken in rethinking the cultural construction of early childhood education as enacted within many communities and to build greater intersubjectivity between the early childhood institution and the culturally and linguistically diverse communities it serves. As suggested by Singer (1998), the claim to superiority of a western view of child development must be relinquished. 'Psychologists must explicate their own values and standards, and place themselves at the service of formally authorized upbringers (usually parents) and their children' (p. 75). As a community of early childhood professionals we must begin work on new 'context-bound theories that offer an insight into the developmental processes under the new pedagogic conditions of shared care of children' (Singer, 1998, p. 75) within a culturally and linguistically diverse community. Cultural and institutional intersubjectivity offers one way forward.

References

Bruce, T. (1997) Adults and children developing play together, *European Early Childhood Education Research Journal,* 5(1), 89–99.

Chan, L. K. S. & Mellor, E. J. (2002) *International developments in early childhood services* (New York, Peter Lang).

Dahlberg, G., Moss, P. & Pence, A. (1999) Beyond quality in early childhood education and care, in: *Postmodern perspectives* (London, Falmer Press).

Dockett, S. & Fleer, M. (1999) *Pedagogy and play in early childhood education: bending the rules* (Sydney, Harcourt Brace).

Edwards, A. (2001) Researching pedagogy: a sociocultural agenda, *Pedagogy, Culture and Society,* 9(2), 161–186.

Edwards, E. (2004) Understanding context, understanding practice in early education, *European Early Childhood Education Research Journal,* 12(1), 85–102.

Einarsdottir, J. (1998) The role of adults in children's dramatic play in Icelandic preschools, *European Early Childhood Education Research Journal,* 6(2), 87–106.

Fleer, M. (2003) Early childhood education as an evolving 'community of practice' or as lived 'social reproduction': researching the 'taken-for-granted', *Contemporary Issues in Early Childhood Education,* 4(1), 64–79.

Göncü, A. (1998) Development of intersubjectivity in social pretend play, in: M. Woodhead, D. Faulkner & K. Littleton (Eds) *Cultural worlds of early childhood* (London, Routledge), 117–132.

Hedegaard, M. (2004) A cultural-historical approach to learning in classrooms, paper presented at the *International Society for Cultural and Activity Research, Regional Conference,* University of Wollongong, 12–13 July.

Hedegaard, M. (2005) Child development from a cultural-historical approach: children's activity in everyday local settings as foundation for their development, paper presented at the triennial conference of the *International Society for Culture and Activity Research,* Seville, Spain, 12–17 September.

Hedegaard, M. & Chaiklin, S. (2005) *Radical-local teaching and learning* (Aarhus, Aarhus University Press).

James, A., Jenks, C. & Prout, A. (1998) *Theorizing childhood* (Cambridge, Polity Press).

James, A. & Prout, A. (Eds) (1997) *Constructing and reconstructing childhood. Contemporary issues in the sociological study of childhood* (2nd edn) (London, Falmer Press).

Lave, J. & Wenger, E. (1991) *Situated learning: legitimate peripheral participation* (Cambridge, Cambridge University Press).

Lubeck, S. (1996) Deconstructing 'child development knowledge' and 'teacher preparation', *Early Education and Development,* 2(2), 138–164.

Lubeck, S. (1998) Is developmentally appropriate practice for everyone?, *Childhood Education,* 74(5), 283–298.

Mayall, B. (2002) *Towards a sociology for childhood. Thinking from children's lives.* (Buckingham, Open University Press).

Michalopoulou, A. (2001) A spatio-pedagogical approach to symbolic play as kindergarten activity in early childhood, *European Early Childhood Education Research Journal,* 9(2), 59–68.

Moll, L. C. & Greenberg, J. B. (1990) Creating zones of possibilities: combining social contexts for instruction, in: L. C. Moll (Ed.) *Vygotsky and education: instructional implications and applications of sociohistorical psychology* (Cambridge, Cambridge University Press), 319–348.

Nsamenang, A. B. & Lamb, M. E. (1998) Socialization of Nso children in the Bamenda Grassfields of Northwest Cameroon, in: M. Woodhead, D. Faulkner & K. Littleton (Eds) *Cultural worlds of early childhood* (London, Routledge), 250–260.

Rogoff, B. (1990) *Apprenticeship in thinking: cognitive development in social context* (New York, Oxford University Press).

Rogoff, B. (1998) Cognition as a collaborative process, in: W. Damon (Chief Ed.) and D. Kuhn & R. S. Siegler (vol. Eds) *Cognition, perceptions and language* (5th edn) *Handbook of Child Psychology* (New York, John Wiley), 679–744.

Rogoff, B. (2003) *The cultural nature of human development* (Oxford, Oxford University Press).

Rogoff, B., Mosier, C., Mistry, J. & Göncü, A. (1998) Toddlers' guided participation with their caregivers in cultural activity, in: M. Woodhead, D. Faulkner & K. Littleton (Eds) *Cultural worlds of early childhood* (London, Routledge), 225–249.

Rogoff, B., Paradise, R., Arauz, R., Correa-Chávez, M. & Angelillo C. (2003) Firsthand learning through intent participation, *Annual Review of Psychology,* 54, 175–203.

Schieffelin, B. B. & Ochs, E. (1998) A cultural perspective on the transition from prelinguistic to linguistic communication, in: M. Woodhead, D. Faulkner & K. Littleton (Eds) *Cultural worlds of early childhood* (London, Routledge), 48–63.

Singer, E. (1998) Shared care for children, in: M. Woodhead, D. Faulkner & K. Littleton (Eds) *Cultural worlds of early childhood* (London, Routledge), 64–84.

Siraj-Blatchford, I. (2004) Educational disadvantage in the early years: how do we overcome it? Some lessons from research, *European Early Childhood Research Journal*, 12(2), 5–20.

Siraj-Blatchford, I. & Clarke, P. (2000) *Supporting identity, diversity and language in the early years* (Buckingham, Open University Press).

Super, C. M. & Harkness, S. (1998) The development of affect in infancy and early childhood, in: M. Woodhead, D. Faulkner & K. Littleton (Eds) *Cultural worlds of early childhood* (London, Routledge), 34–47.

Vygotsky, L. S. (1998) *The collected works of L.S. Vygotsky*, vol. 5: *Child psychology* (M. J. Hall, Trans.; R. W. Rieber, Ed. of the English translation) (New York, Kluwer Academic/Plenum).

Wenger, E. (1998) *Communities of practice. Learning, meaning and identity* (Cambridge, Cambridge University Press).

Wertsch, J. V. (1998) *Mind as action* (New York, Oxford University Press).

Woodhead, M., Faulkner, D. & Littleton, K. (Eds) (1998) *Cultural worlds of early childhood* (London, Routledge).

Chapter 3

The struggle for early childhood curricula

A comparison of the English Foundation Stage Curriculum, Te Whāriki and Reggio Emilia

Janet Soler and Linda Miller

Source: *J. Soler and L. Miller, International Journal of Early Years Education, 11(1), 57–67, 2003.*

Abstract

Parents, teachers, researchers and politicians often have strong and conflicting views about what is right for young children in the years before school. Curricula can become 'sites of struggle' between ideas about what early childhood education is for, and what are appropriate content and contexts for learning and development in early childhood. This paper focuses upon the way visions for early childhood are expressed through the curricula offered in three very different contexts – in England, New Zealand and Reggio Emilia in Northern Italy. These three examples of early childhood curricula are compared in order to explore how a growing pressure from vocational and instrumental influences can impact on progressive and socioculturally inspired early childhood curricula and approaches. A comparison of these examples also reveals how early childhood curricula and educational systems are often forged amidst differing contexts in relation to national and local control of early childhood curricula and approaches. These differing contexts can also give rise to differing conceptualisations of knowledge, learning and pedagogy.

Introduction

This paper examines three differing examples of contemporary early childhood curricula and approaches. In choosing these particular examples we aim to identify, compare and contrast specific visions, beliefs and ideas about children that underpin these different approaches to early childhood curricula and pedagogy. In our exploration and discussion we will investigate the ways in which different visions of childhood can be embedded in these curricula.

Instrumental views of the curriculum put an emphasis upon its serving an extrinsic aim or external purposes such as producing citizens who will benefit society. This can be contrasted with the view that the curriculum should serve the intrinsic aim of providing a value in its own right, so that it is seen as self-fulfilling and providing experiences that are worthwhile. Vocationalism is a particular subset of the instrumental view of the curriculum. Those that promote this view argue that the curriculum should be designed to prepare children for the world of work.

The views which have emerged in relation to the aims of the curricula and approaches examined in this paper can be placed on a continuum. At one end are the progressive views of the curriculum which emphasise the individual child and the decentring of adult authority. At the other end of the continuum are the vocational and instrumental views of education, which stress the authority of the adult over the child, and the needs of society rather than the individual.

Progressive ideals and the rise of instrumental views

While there is a cluster of progressive views of the curriculum, they are all usually characterised by a downplaying of the role of authority and a decentring of the power of the teacher so that the teacher is often seen as a facilitator rather than controller of curriculum activities (see Silcock, 1999, for a recent discussion of progressivism and new progressivism). They also emphasise the individual child as the centre of curriculum activities. Progressive and child-centred views of the curricula have been the most influential in early childhood curricula over the past two centuries. This came about through the initial influence of Rousseau who influenced later progressivists such as Robert Owen, Froebel, Pestalozzi, and Montessori in Europe and Dewey in the USA (see May, 1997).

The progressive curriculum ideas derived from Rousseau stressed that children should be enabled to learn what they wish to learn when they are ready to do so, and stressed play enriched by unobtrusive guidance from a teacher/facilitator. Froebel, who was constructing his ideas in the early nineteenth century, is seen as the creator of the pedagogy and practice of a specialist early childhood curriculum and was the first to envisage play as a key element (May, 1997). By the twentieth century, progressive ideas of early childhood education had come to be characterised by ideas such as the central role of play and movement and the adult as guide and moderator, through the influence of John Dewey (see, for example, Dewey, 1900, 1916, 1938, 1939) and other educators such as Stanley Hall (see, for example, Hall, 1883, 1895, 1901) and Maria Montessori (1912).

The work of these educators led to an emphasis upon the need to understand and explore pupils' experience of the curriculum. Froebel felt that a child possesses a 'divine essence' which is in need of cultivation and protection rather than interference (Froebel, 1887, p. 4). Hall and others in the child study movement drew upon this romantic notion of respecting and truly listening to children. They argued for a curriculum that would stress the child's real interests, needs and learning patterns (Kliebard, 1987, p. 28). John Dewey, whose name would come to be associated with 'progressive education' and curricular reform, also argued that pupil learning is not a static one-way process. Dewey's work stressed the way in which the pupil contributes to the construction of his/her learning environment and conditions, which in turn shape his/her learning experiences (Dewey, 1963 [1938], pp. 43, 45).

During the early part of the twentieth century, educators also became aware of the importance of the sociocultural context of learning (e.g. Vygotsky, 1978). Both progressive and sociocultural perspectives drew attention to how the pupil engages with the setting in which the curriculum is being presented. This gave rise to concerns with: what is present in that curriculum setting, what the children can see and hear, how children interact within the setting and how children speak and interact with other pupils, artefacts, and the teacher.

If early childhood educators accept this view of learning as being related to pupil experience, background and needs, it becomes impossible to view the teacher as agent and the pupil as the recipient of knowledge. Pupils are not merely absorbing abstract knowledge and facts, because they bring previous experiences into their setting and are constructing profoundly different lived experiences of what they encounter in their educational setting. This view also implies that measures of pupil learning by testing, administered after the pupils have been exposed to a particular curricular activity, will not reveal the kinds and qualities of experiences pupils have had during the course of learning.

The curricula we are investigating in this paper are set in societies where mass education and compulsory schooling have shaped the curriculum and children's experiences of schooling. Compulsory mass education has also tended to stress the homogenising of the curriculum and the need to compare one student with another. In the 1980s and 1990s many countries, which have a well-developed compulsory education system, have implemented National Curricula frameworks and have emphasised standardised testing, effective teaching and effective management. This paper will explore the impact of an instrumental/vocationally based trend in education upon three particular examples of early childhood curricula. These examples have adopted progressive and socioculturally based educational ideals to varying degrees.

The impact of these recent trends towards homogenisation, standardised testing, effective management and other aspects of what can be characterised as a 'social efficiency' movement (Kliebard, 1987) has, therefore, often resulted in struggles and compromises in order to address the tensions between progressive/sociocultural and instrumental/vocational views of the curriculum.

The first example examined in this paper is the recently developed English Foundation Stage Curriculum Guidance for early childhood settings in England. This national early childhood curriculum has largely been underpinned by a resurgence in instrumental beliefs, as it aims to provide guidance to early childhood practitioners and teachers so that children can be prepared for the next stage of schooling.

The second example, *Te Whāriki*, is the National Curriculum for the early childhood sector in New Zealand. This curriculum framework can be seen to have been inspired by progressive and sociocultural theories and beliefs. It also aims to take account of and promote the particular cultural influences that arise through cultural diversity and biculturalism.

The final example is based in Reggio Emilia, a prosperous region in Northern Italy. This approach provides the strongest contrast with instrumental/vocationally based views of education. The Reggio Emilia approach, unlike the Foundation Stage Curriculum in England and *Te Whāriki*, does not adhere to a National Curriculum framework or formalised curriculum policy. It represents a localised, learner-centred approach as an alternative to national centralised, uniform curricula. This context enables the Reggio Emilia approach to espouse progressive and sociocultural views of the child, without strong pressures from instrumental and vocationally oriented views of curriculum, learning and pedagogy. In this approach the child is viewed as: possessing rights, an active constructor of knowledge and a social being, and the instructor is viewed as a collaborator and co-learner with the child, whose role is to guide, facilitate and encourage research.

The Foundation Stage Curriculum in England

The introduction of a National Curriculum Framework in England in 1988 for primary and secondary schooling resulted in the first centrally defined National Curriculum based on a subject model of learning for English schools (DfEE, 1999). This centralisation has also impacted upon early childhood education in England. It has resulted in a struggle between upholding the progressive ideals held by many early childhood educators and the desire of recent governments and policy makers to create a more cohesive, centralised system of early childhood education with coherent links to the National Curriculum in primary schools.

Shortly after the introduction of a National Curriculum for primary schools, a group of expert early childhood practitioners, the Early Years Curriculum

Group (Early Years Curriculum Group, 1989, p. 3) asserted the view that 'Early childhood is valid in itself not simply a preparation for work, or for the next stage of education'. These claims were countered in the early to mid-1990s by Edwards and Knight (1994, p. 40), who argued that in the past the early childhood curriculum in many settings had been neither 'explicit, planned long term, nor coherent'. Underpinning this argument was a view that young children were entitled to a curriculum that would offer a sound basis from which they can develop into literate and numerate adults.

In 1996, a document entitled 'Desirable Outcomes for Children's Learning on Entering Compulsory Education' (SCAA, 1996) was introduced to all English early childhood settings with 4 year olds on their roll by the then Conservative government. Although it was claimed that the contents 'do not specify a curriculum' (SCAA, 1997, p. 5), the document described learning outcomes to be achieved by the age of 5. It was seen by many as an attempt by government to rationalise the early childhood curriculum across a diverse range of settings. As part of the process of creating a cohesive, centralised system, a national inspection scheme for early childhood settings was introduced and linked to funding. A formalised, centralised system of assessment was also introduced (QCA, 1998).

These centralised features added to the pressures felt by practitioners in early childhood settings, as many found that it conflicted with their views of childhood and how the early childhood curricula should be conducted. This in turn led to considerable criticism from the early childhood community regarding the prescriptive nature of the learning outcomes. It also resulted in pressure to make links with the National Curriculum in primary schools. Many early childhood educators saw these centralised features as inappropriate in relation to the ways in which young children learn (Anning & Edwards, 1999; David & Nurse, 1999). These changes were also perceived to be shaping the early childhood curriculum from the outside rather than from within the early childhood community. It was also seen to place a 'downward pressure' on those in charge of its implementation.

In 1999, new curriculum guidance was introduced which built upon the previous document. The new document entitled 'Early Learning Goals' (QCA, 1999) outlined goals to be achieved by children aged from 3 to 6, as they entered the first stage of the National Curriculum. There was an emphasis on literacy and numeracy, in line with government targets, in order to raise standards in these areas. Knowledge was presented as compartmentalised into six areas of learning, rather than integrated and holistic as in the later case studies. However, the reference to key principles and play were compatible with most early childhood practitioners' views about what is appropriate for early childhood education.

Following the protests by the early childhood community, further guidance was developed, namely 'Curriculum Guidance for the Foundation Stage'

(QCA, 2000). This document was constructed in consultation with a wide range of representatives from the early childhood community. Although the goals for learning were retained, there was a change in emphasis to a focus on describing learning opportunities and experiences considered to be appropriate for young children, rather than on the achievement of outcomes. This made the document more acceptable to the early childhood community (Anning, 2001).

The English early childhood curriculum that was in place by 2000 embraced a stepped sequential approach to learning. It is organised through externally imposed 'learning areas' linked to the subject areas of the National Curriculum. These learning areas are in turn organised into 'stepping stones' towards the early learning goals which are loosely related to age. The view of children's development underlying this model is that learning takes place in a straightforward sequential manner, which can be assessed and itemised at predetermined levels. In structuring the curriculum and its assessment in this manner, the policy makers have made assumptions about where the levels begin and end for all children. They have also determined what specific skills and knowledge can be learnt (Miller *et al.*, 2003).

Policy makers viewed this step model as helpful to practitioners because it provided clear guidance as to how the early learning goals could be implemented consistently across all early childhood settings (Staggs, 2000). From the early childhood community's viewpoint, the guidance for early childhood stems from a model that has been framed by people who stand outside of children's experiences and the teaching process. They are seen to be concerned more about what education is for rather than what the experience of education might entail (Miller *et al.*, 2003).

Despite the intervention of the early childhood community and subsequent collaboration with government agencies, the early learning goals were shaped by the need for pupils to attain clearly prescribed outcomes. Supporters of the early learning goals argue that they lay secure foundations for future achievement and therefore give children the best possible start in their life long learners (Staggs, 2000, p. 23). These goals are, therefore, based upon the need for schools to provide a curriculum that will equip children with the knowledge, skills and understandings that they will need for adult life and employment. This approach can be viewed as elitist, non-egalitarian and non-democratic because of the need to link with subsequent curricula that focus upon commercial and economic considerations. Some critics see this approach as ultimately driven by economic needs and an emphasis on commercial competitiveness (Kelly, 1994; Anning & Edwards, 1999). Although it is meant to be an inclusive curriculum which encompasses the needs of all children (Staggs, 2000), such a model can also be seen to prioritise competitiveness. It supports the notion that the main goal is to support those who can succeed and reach skills-based attainment targets rather than cater for individuality and access for all children.

Te Whāriki

New Zealand has developed a National Curriculum framework for early childhood, *Te Whāriki* (Ministry of Education, 1996). The developers of the New Zealand early childhood curriculum were working in similar contexts to those involved in the development of the early childhood curriculum in England (Miller, 2001) in that the curriculum was linked to the National Curriculum in primary schools. Despite this constraint, the developers of *Te Whāriki* developed a framework that has implemented a bicultural perspective, an anti-racist approach and reciprocal relationships with the Māori community in New Zealand (Smith, 1999, p. 6).

Margaret Carr, Helen May and Tilly Reedy, who were responsible for co-coordinating the development of the New Zealand early childhood curriculum, wished to incorporate 'equitable educational opportunities and quality early childhood policies and practices' into the framework (Carr & May, 2000, p. 53). Diverse groups of practitioners and representatives from different types of early childhood services were involved in consultations, as were people with nationally recognised expertise. Māori perspectives were a separate but integrally related framework and the document is written in both English and Māori (Smith, 1999, p. 6). From its very beginning *Te Whāriki* took into account the foundational principles assessed from Māori epistemology, via Tilly Reedy, to create a bicultural document (Carr, 2001).

The initiators were also aware of accounts of national and international views expressed in recent literature and research into early childhood. The underpinning vision drew upon a sociocultural view of curriculum and childhood derived from Vygotsky. Smith notes that the sociocultural emphasis of the New Zealand early childhood curriculum is expressed in the introductory statement in the *Te Whāriki* curriculum document (Smith, 1999, p. 6). This link to sociocultural theory fits the concern with developing a bicultural document and is drawn upon by Carr to argue that the early childhood curriculum can be conceived of as a cultural site involving the construction of social reality which leads to the construction of communicative interactions between teachers and students (Smith, 1999, p. 6).

The New Zealand early childhood curriculum is usually referred to by its shortened title of *Te Whāriki* (see Ministry of Education, 1993, 1996). *Te Whāriki*, as is often the case within Māori language, conveys multiple metaphoric meanings. This title draws upon real-life experiences of flax weaving a central area of learning within traditional Māori culture. 'Whāriki' refers to a woven mat, on which everyone can stand, yet which interweaves central principles and goals into different patterns or programmes which individual centres can develop to address their own particular learning situations (Ministry of Education, 1996; May & Carr, 1997; Carr & May, 2000). This can be seen to contrast with the 'step model' of the curriculum which underpins the Foundation Stage Curriculum in England.

Another metaphoric meaning conveyed in the title is the notion of a 'spider web' model of curriculum. May and Carr saw the notion of a web as a key feature of the conceptualisation of the curriculum document. Thus, *Te Whāriki* in name and content implies a move away from the 'step' model of curriculum assessed by measurable outcomes. The *Te Whāriki* model envisages the curriculum as a web or woven mat rather than a set of stairs:

> Eisener (1985, p. 143) contrasts a 'step model' of the curriculum with a 'spider web' model. The 'step' or 'staircase' model, conjures up the image of a series of independent steps that lead to a platform from which the child exits and at which point measurable outcomes can be identified. Whilst acknowledging that many skills and concepts have a sequence, Te Whāriki emphasises a model of knowledge and understanding for young children as a tapestry of increasing complexity and richness. The weaving model of learning conceptualises the child's development as a series of increasingly intricate patterns of linked experience and meaning, centred on cultural and individual purpose.
>
> (Carr & May, 1996, p. 102)

Thus, *Te Whāriki* views the curriculum as a complex and rich experiential process arising out of the child's interactions with the physical and social environment. It is divided into age groups, i.e. 'infants', 'toddlers' and the 'young child'. In their development of *Te Whāriki*, Reedy, May and Carr linked local cultural views of learning in New Zealand communities to the views in recent international and child development literature, which stresses varying viewpoints rather than a universal view of child development. It has adopted a 'holistic' approach which takes into account a sociocultural view of the child expressed by Vygotsky. The 'spider web' conceptualisation of the curriculum incorporated in the weaving metaphor implicit in *Te Whāriki* is the key to understanding the linking of a child-centred, sociocultural, bicultural vision of the New Zealand child which underpins this curriculum (see Carr & May, 1993, 2000).

May and Carr acknowledged that the 1980s development of Mäori and Pacific Island pre-school and primary school programmes necessitated the development of curricula which acknowledged the dual heritage of New Zealand people. These initiatives drew the attention of New Zealand educators of young children to the importance of a vision that incorporated links between culture, language and learning (McNaughton, 1996; Carr & May, 2000).

Te Whāriki represents a conscious modification of an initial government-driven, instrumental vision of child development to a curriculum policy which stresses greater diversity and learner-centred approaches.

During the consultations, early childhood practitioners expressed a 'local, situated and often personal view of the early childhood curriculum'

(Carr & May, 2000, p. 53). This view did not necessarily fit with the government objective of establishing a National Curriculum framework and many early childhood practitioners had difficulties with applying the word 'curriculum' to practice in early childhood settings. Despite this pressure, a curriculum framework was developed which integrated other visions of the curriculum. Smith (1999) argues that 'The introduction of holistic, open ended inclusive curriculum guidelines in New Zealand has been a huge success' (p. 15).

Carr and May describe the collaborative process that enabled this outcome as resulting from consultation and compromise where childhood organisations and practitioners were aware that they needed to offer an alternative 'defined' curriculum to prevent the New Zealand National Curriculum, which had been developed for primary and other educational sectors, 'trickling downward' into early childhood settings:

> During consultation it became clear that early childhood organizations and practitioners were wary that a national early childhood curriculum might constrain their current freedom of philosophy and practice. Nevertheless they saw that there was a danger in not defining an early childhood curriculum: the new national curriculum for schools might trickle downward into early childhood curriculum, particularly as the Government was introducing more systematic assessment guidelines during the early school years. Practitioners saw the value of an early childhood curriculum statement that would make clear links with school and would reflect the integrity of distinctive early childhood aims and practice.
>
> (Carr & May, 1993, p. 10)

There are, however, tensions that arise from this compromise between catering for children's individual needs and diversity while adhering to a national framework designed for a country with mass education and large groupings of pupils. McNaughton notes that in New Zealand early childhood settings the learner's actions are 'mediated through specific activities and it is through these activities that development takes place' (McNaughton, 1996, p. 191). Although a learner's needs are seen as central, the broader curriculum prescribes a developmental sequence, even if that sequence is seen as relatively flexible. In this situation the individual learner cannot be the sole source of curriculum development, as stated in the *Te Whāriki* document. There is, therefore, an inherent tension within the compromise struck by adapting a curriculum framework to learner-centred experiences. Opting to define a curriculum, even in a flexible manner, could restrict the child's active role in co-constructing and reconstructing personal meanings and limit the ability of teachers to co-collaborate with children through shared meanings and understandings where children take an active and inventive role. This tension is heightened by the acknowledgement of the sociocultural, Vygotskian framework as being central to the sociocultural emphasis of *Te Whāriki* (Smith, 1999, pp. 6–8).

Reggio Emilia

The final example examined in this paper represents another vision of a child-centred practice within an educational context. Reggio Emilia, like *Te Whāriki*, is based upon sociocultural principles and emphasises a learner-centred approach to teaching and learning. However, unlike *Te Whāriki*, Reggio Emilia is not a compromise between the demands of a National Curriculum framework and a learner-centred curriculum framework. In this example the tension between a learner-centred curriculum and having to implement prescribed, pre-selected guidelines and learning activities does not arise, because Reggio Emilia educators do not follow any predetermined national framework and is often referred to as an 'approach' or 'educational system' (see, for example, Mercilliott Hewett, 2001).

The Reggio Emilia approach can be firmly located at the progressive, learner-centred end of the continuum of beliefs that shape early childhood curricula. It is a community-supported, localised and activity-based schooling system which is a realisation of progressive education. It stems from the inspiration of one particular educator, Loris Malaguzzi, rather than from centralised policy making and national guidelines. The political contexts which Malaguzzi encountered during the Second World War and post-war Italy inspired him to engage in the struggle to implement his vision of a child-centred curriculum which would not be part of national guidelines.

Malaguzzi's work stems from his experiences of the war and a fascist regime, which had taught him that people who blindly conformed and obeyed were dangerous. He believed that a new society should nurture a vision of children who could act and think for themselves. This led him to give priority to children's views of the world and to design an early childhood education system founded on the perspective of the child. Children were seen as unique individuals with rights rather than just needs.

In order to achieve this vision, Malaguzzi left his state school teaching post to become involved in community initiatives to build and run schools created by parents near the town of Reggio Emilia in the Emilia Romagno region of Northern Italy. This move facilitated the implementation of his belief in a pluralistic approach which involved the commitment of children, parents, teachers, administrators and politicians. By 1967, all the parent-run schools were under the administration of the municipality of Reggio Emilia, which demonstrated its support by allocating 12% of the Town Council budget to funding the early childhood programme (Malaguzzi, 1995; Dahlberg, 2000). The inspiration for Malaguzzi's vision for working with young children can be seen to include the work of Dewey, Bronfenbrenner and Vygotsky.

One influence that can be seen in Malaguzzi's thinking is Dewey's notion of a learner-focused view of learning, which recognises and emphasises the experiences and understandings that the child brings to his or her experience of schooling. Malaguzzi, like Dewey, stressed interaction and participation in the learning process and the value of working through a project. Central to achieving this was a view of the development of knowledge through a collaborative partnership between children and adults (Mercilliott Hewett, 2001, p. 95). Malaguzzi also drew on Vygotsky, hence the nature of the relationship between child and adult is central to the work in Reggio Emilia. Patricia Ghedini, head of Early Years services in the Emilia Romagna region, highlights Reggio Emilia practitioners' belief in Malaguzzi's progressive philosophy with its emphasis upon individual difference, pluralistic approaches and processes, and their opposition to a focus on standardisation, outcomes and economic productivity. She states, 'If a society based on the myth of productivity (and therefore profit) needs only half human beings – steadfast doers, industrious reproducers – then it must be wrong and it must be changed. In order to change it, we need people who are capable of using their imagination' (cited in Whalley, 1995, p. 6).

Also central to the development of Malaguzzi's vision has been an ongoing dialogue within Reggio Emilia schools, which questions and challenges existing scientific, philosophical and educational viewpoints and accepted teaching practices and approaches. This dialogue is shared with the children, parents, teachers, administrators, politicians and educators from other countries. Through this ongoing dialogue, the teachers of Reggio Emilia have challenged the dominating discourse and accepted practices of early childhood pedagogy by 'deconstructing' the dominant ideas and theories that have shaped our conceptions and images of children and childhood (Dahlberg, 2000). This contrasts sharply with the development of other approaches to curricula discussed in this paper. Malaguzzi has articulated a distinctive vision of the child as a starting point for the curriculum. His ideas are grounded in his personal philosophy, which has been influenced by progressive educational theorists and from working with and listening to the views of parents, teachers, children and the wider community of other educators and stakeholders.

A criticism of the Reggio Emilia curriculum has been that in the absence of a written curriculum there is a lack of accountability to the wider society. Advocates of the Reggio Emilia approach argue that there is a detailed recording of the curriculum process, which opens their practice to criticism and scrutiny. This is achieved through documenting the children's work through photographs, slides and film, and in the form of publications and travelling exhibitions (Dahlberg, 2000). This is a very different form of accountability to the external inspection process, which often accompanies other curriculum frameworks and approaches. Malaguzzi's philosophy is to make the teaching of Reggio Emilia visible to others in order to share, extend and enrich his curriculum vision.

Summary

The curricula and debates examined in this paper have tended to be polarised around progressive, learner-centred views about formal versus informal learning and the role of play in learning and the acknowledgement of cultural difference in early childhood curricula. The examples we have looked at have also reached differing arrangements in the way in which they conform to or reject a National Curriculum and the pressures for centralised curricula in early childhood.

At the centre of the English Foundation Stage Curriculum Guidance is a view of the child as a future pupil. This has led to curriculum content which emphasises 'subject'-related learning goals and has resulted in practitioners feeling the need to prepare children for entry to school through more formal teaching approaches. Play is seen to be marginalised. In contrast, in Reggio Emilia the child is viewed as a powerful partner who 'actively co-constructs' the content of the curriculum with a more able 'other'. Within the *Te Whāriki* curriculum framework, although content is broadly mapped, the bicultural nature of early childhood is celebrated through a curriculum which allows for the individual mapping of 'strands and threads' to reflect the needs and interests of local groups, including members of the indigenous culture, parents and early childhood practitioners.

The Foundation Stage Curriculum in England is an example of a centralised, competency-oriented curriculum, as it establishes and specifies national educational goals and content in advance. An alternative viewpoint argues for more localised and individualised models, generated to meet local needs in order to support collaborative community visions for young children. The Reggio Emilia emergent curriculum offers this alternative view, as it regards a centralised, prescriptive approach as stunting the potential of children by formulating their learning in advance. Reggio Emilia educators advocate an approach in which adults outline flexible, general educational objectives, but do not formulate pre-specified goals. These two examples could be said to be at opposite ends of a continuum. Somewhere in between these two approaches is a 'framework consultative' approach to curricula, such as *Te Whāriki*, which provides the main values, orientations and goals for the curriculum but does not define how these goals should be achieved. Interpretation and implementation is left to local decisions (Bennett, 2001). These three examples could be said to fit along a continuum ranging from localised, individualised models through to centralised goal-oriented frameworks.

References

Anning, A. (2001) Interview transcript in Open University U212 *Childhood Audio Course Materials 2003* (Milton Keynes, Open University).

Anning, A. & Edwards, A. (1999) *Promoting Children's Learning from Birth to Five: Developing the new early years professional* (Buckingham, Open University Press).

Bennett, J. (2001) Goals and curricula in early childhood, in: S. Kamerman (Ed.) *Early Childhood Education and Care: International perspectives*, pp. 220–256 (New York, Institute for Child and Family Policy, Columbia University).

Carr, M. (2001) Interview transcript in Open University U212 *Childhood Audio Course Materials 2003* (Milton Keynes, Open University).

Carr, M. & May, H. (1993) Choosing a model. Reflecting on the development process of *Te Whāriki*: national early childhood curriculum guidelines in New Zealand, *International Journal of Early Years Education*, 9(2), pp. 7–21.

Carr, M. & May, H. (1996) *Te Whāriki*, making a difference for the under-fives? The New National Early Childhood Curriculum, *Delta*, 48(1), pp. 101–112.

Carr, M. & May, H. (2000) *Te Whāriki*: curriculum voices, in: H. Penn (Ed.) *Early Childhood Services: Theory, policy and practice*, pp. 53–73 (Buckingham, Open University Press).

Dahlberg, G. (2000) Everything is a beginning and everything is dangerous: some reflections of the Reggio Emilia experience, in: H. Penn (Ed.) *Early Childhood Services: Theory, policy and practice*, pp. 175–183 (Buckingham, Open University Press).

David, T. & Nurse, A. (1999) Inspection of under fives and constructions of early childhood, in: T. David (Ed.) *Teaching Young Children*, pp. 165–184 (London, Paul Chapman).

Department for Education and Employment (DfEE) (1999) *The National Curriculum: Handbook for primary teachers in England. Key Stages 1 and 2* (London, HMSO).

Dewey, J. (1900) *The Child and the Curriculum: The school and society* (Chicago, University of Chicago Press).

Dewey, J. (1916) *Democracy and Education* (London, The Free Press, Macmillan).

Dewey, J. (1938) *Experience and Education* (New York, Collier Books).

Dewey, J. (1939) *Freedom and Culture* (New York, Putman).

Dewey, J. (1963 [1938]) *Experience and Education* (London, Collier Books, Chicago Press).

Early years curriculum group (1989) *Early Childhood Education: The early years curriculum and the National Curriculum* (Stoke on Trent, Trentham Books).

Edwards, A. & Knight, P. (1994) *Effective Early Years Education: Teaching young children* (Buckingham, Open University Press).

Froebel, F. (1887) *The Education of Man* (New York, Appleton).

Hall, G.S. (1883) The contents of children's minds, *Princeton Review*, 11, pp. 249–272.

Hall, G.S. (1895) Child study, *Journal of Proceedings and Addresses of the National Educational Association, Session of the Year 1894*, pp. 173–179.

Hall, G.S. (1901) Ideal school based on child study, *Journal of Proceedings and Addresses of the Forty-First Annual Meeting of the National Educational Association*, pp. 260–268.

Kelly, A.V. (1994) A high quality curriculum for the early years, *Early Years*, 15(1), pp. 6–12.

Kliebard, H.M. (1987) *The Struggle for the American Curriculum 1893–1958* (New York, Routledge & Kegan Paul).

Malaguzzi, L. (1995) History, ideas and basic philosophy: an interview with Lella Gandini, in: C. Edwards, L. Gandini & G. Forman (Eds) *The Hundred Languages of Children: The Reggio Emilia approach to early childhood education*, pp. 41–89 (Greenwich, CT, Ablex).

May, H. (1997) *The Discovery of Early Childhood: The development of services for the care and education of very young children, mid eighteenth century Europe to mid twentieth century New Zealand* (Auckland, Auckland University Press, Bridget Williams Books).

May, H. & Carr, M. (1997) Making a difference for the under fives? The early implementation of *Te Whāriki*, the New Zealand national early childhood curriculum, *International Journal of Early Years Education*, 5(3), pp. 225–236.

McNaughton, S. (1996) Co constructing curricula: a comment on two curricula (*Te Whāriki* and the English curriculum) and their developmental bases, *New Zealand Journal of Educational Studies*, 31(2), pp. 189–196.

Mercilliott Hewett, V. (2001) Examining the Reggio Emilia approach to early childhood education, *Early Childhood Education Journal*, 29(2), pp. 95–100.

Miller, L. (2001) Shaping early childhood through the literacy curriculum, *Early Years, International Journal of Research and Development*, 21(2), pp. 107–116.

Miller, L., Soler, J. & Woodhead, M. (2003) Shaping early childhood education, in: J. Maybin & M. Woodhead (Eds) *Childhoods in Context* (Chichester, Wiley).

Ministry of Education (1993) *Te Whāriki: Draft guidelines for developmentally appropriate programmes in early childhood services* (Wellington, Learning Media).

Ministry of Education (1996) *Te Whāriki. He Whāriki Mātauranga mö ngä Mokopuna o Aotearoa: Early childhood curriculum* (Wellington, Learning Media).

Qualifications and Curriculum Authority (QCA) (1998) *The Baseline Assessment Information Pack: Preparation for statutory baseline assessment* (London, Qualifications and Curriculum Authority).

Qualifications and Curriculum Authority (QCA) (1999) *Early Learning Goals* (London, Qualifications and Curriculum Authority).

Qualifications and Curriculum Authority (QCA) (2000) *Curriculum Guidance for the Foundation Stage* (London, Qualifications and Curriculum Authority).

School Curriculum and Assessment Authority (SCAA) (1996) *Desirable Outcomes for Children's Learning on Entering Compulsory Education* (London, Department for Education and Employment/School Curriculum and Assessment Authority).

School Curriculum and Assessment Authority (SCAA) (1997) *Looking at Children's Learning* (Middlesex, SCAA).

Silcock, P. (1999) *New Progressivism* (London, Falmer Press).

Smith, A.B. (1999) The role of an early childhood curriculum: promoting diversity versus uniformity, paper presented at Enhancing Quality in the Early Years Conference, Dublin, 19–20 November 1999.

Staggs, L. (2000) Curriculum guidance for the early years, *Early Years Educator*, 2(6), pp. 21–23.

Vygotsky, L.S. (1978) *Mind in Society* (Cambridge, MA, Harvard University Press).

Whalley, M. (1995) Passion, power and pedagogy, in: W. Scott & P. Gura (Eds) *Reflections on Early Education and Care: Inspired by visits to Reggio Emilia*, pp. 5–7 (London, British Association for Early Childhood Education).

Chapter 4

Learning how to learn

Parental ethnotheories and young children's preparation for school

Liz Brooker

Source: *L. Brooker, International Journal of Early Years Education, 11(2), 117–128, 2003.*

Abstract

This paper discusses one aspect of the findings from an ethnographic study of the ways in which four-year-old children learn, and are taught, at home and in their Reception class. The children were from two distinctive cultural backgrounds within the same urban neighbourhood: one-half belonged to UK ('Anglo') families, and one-half to families from Bangladesh. They were observed and assessed throughout their first school year, and additional data were collected from interviews with parents, practitioners and the children themselves. Analysis of the data suggested that one way of understanding the variation in the children's experiences was through the ethnotheories, or cultural belief systems, of their home communities – such as their parents' concepts of childhood, and their theories of intelligence and instruction.

The paper argues that such differences in children's home preparation have consequences for their school experience, and carry implications for their school providers. The study of parental ethnotheories, therefore, may help to explain, and alleviate, the differences in school achievement of children from diverse backgrounds. However, accessing respondents' personal theories presents both ethical and methodological problems, particularly when the researcher is working with socially disadvantaged groups.

Introduction

This paper focuses on one aspect of the analysis of an ethnographic study of the home and school learning of 16 English four-year-olds. The study explored the processes and experiences presumed to influence children's attainment on entry to school, and their subsequent school progress. Since both the theories and practices of the children's families, and the theories and practices of the school staff, were regarded as contributory factors, the study attempted to describe both. But while school staff have some experience of articulating their beliefs and methods, and school practices were open to observation, the contribution of families was much more difficult to gauge. As the paper suggests, the process of uncovering parents' views, and evaluating the effects of their practices, was far from simple, and required a persistent effort to see past the taken-for-granted assumptions of both the respondents and the researcher.

The paper begins by outlining the relation of parental ethnotheories, or 'cultural belief systems' to children's early learning, and then offers a brief description of the context of the study, and some of the methodological and ethical concerns that it provoked. One set of themes arising from the 'home' data is indicated, and illustrated through a case study of one child and his family. Finally, the paper describes how the data was used to develop a theoretical explanation, which uses Bernstein's (1971, 1975) models of pedagogy, both to interpret the case study children's adaptation to school, and to reflect on the implications for practitioners.

Parental ethnotheories and children's learning

The relationship between parental ethnotheories and children's outcomes has only been fully theorised in recent years (Sigel *et al.*, 1992; Harkness & Super, 1996). Many aspects of this work, however (such as the origins of parents' beliefs in their class and community position, the relation of their beliefs to specific child-rearing patterns, and the consequences of such patterns for children's school behaviour) were prefigured by the work of the Newsons. Their longitudinal study of Nottingham families uncovered parental attitudes, and their effects, through the detailed probing of day-to-day parenting decisions – on bedtimes, chores, discipline, punishment and praise (Newson & Newson, 1968).

Harkness and Super (1992) term the beliefs that underlie such practices *parental ethnotheories,* and describe them as 'embedded in the experiences of daily life that parents have with their own children at particular ages, as well as being derived from the accumulated cultural experience of the community or reference group' (p. 374). Although inherited, in other words, these theories are continually evolving in response to ongoing experience, including the 'socialising' effect of the child on its caregivers.

But Harkness and Super argue too that, however we may theorise the relations between parental beliefs, parental behaviours, and child outcomes, in practice those qualities that are prized within a culture are those that most children acquire. As a result, 'Children's competence in the culturally marked areas is accelerated, whereas development in other domains lags if indeed it is even recognised' (Harkness & Super, 1992, p. 389). These authors define

a *developmental niche*, composed of the physical and social environment, culturally regulated child-rearing practices, and the psychology of the individual
caregivers, which offers a comprehensive description of the developing child's
unique environment (Super & Harkness, 1986). They identify similarities in
the underlying structures of this environment that constitute regulative principles similar to Bernstein's (1971) *codes*, or Bourdieu's ([1980] 1990) *habitus*.
As they put it:

> Regularities in the subsystems ... provide material from which the child
> abstracts the social, affective and cognitive rules of the culture, much as
> the rules of grammar are abstracted from the regularities of the speech
> environment
>
> (Super & Harkness, 1986, p. 552)

The disadvantaging effects of these 'rules' when the child from a working-
class or minority cultural background enters a middle-class or mainstream
educational setting have been shown in numerous contexts (Heath, 1983;
Dombey & Spencer, 1994; Vernon-Feagans, 1996).

   In the present study, which included children from families of English and
Bangladeshi origin, *individual* differences in parenting practices were sometimes subsumed within *group* differences in culturally regulated beliefs about
childhood and parenting. The developmental niche of the children, in other
words, was shaped by aspects of the collective practices of the Anglo and
Bangladeshi groups, respectively. The interview responses and observed practices of all the parents revealed strong but sometimes unconscious cultural
assumptions about good parenting. The case study of one family, which is presented later, illustrates how such assumptions were identified in the research
data, and how they were interpreted.

The context and conduct of the study

The study centred on a school in a poor neighbourhood in an English provin-
cial town. The 16 case study children were all entering the school's Reception
class (the first year of schooling for most English children, but a year prior
to the start of compulsory schooling). All could be predicted, on the basis
of large-scale studies (Davie *et al.*, 1972; Melhuish *et al.*, 2001), to have relatively poor school attainments. A recent government census had described
the neighbourhood they grew up in as characterised by overcrowded housing, unemployment, and a range of related social problems. Eight of the
sample children were from Bangladeshi families – still the lowest-achieving
minority ethnic group in the UK (Gillborn & Mirza, 2000) – and many of
these were younger children of large families (frequently defined as a 'risk
factor'). Both communities in the neighbourhood were poor, and most families were constantly vulnerable to financial and social crises. Within this shared

environment, the study attempted to uncover the fine-grained variations in children's daily experiences at home that contributed to the differences in their school achievement.

Access to the case study school, and to the families, was gained over the half year prior to the fieldwork, in which I volunteered in classrooms and accompanied outreach workers on home visits in the neighbourhood. My regular presence in the school meant that I was already familiar to many children and families before they were asked to participate in the study. All the Bangladeshi participants were visited at least twice in the months before their child started school, while the 'Anglo' families were approached informally in the school playground, or introduced to me by older siblings or by school staff. A sample of eight boys and eight girls from the new Reception intake, roughly matched by ethnicity, age in the year group and family position/birth order, had been constructed by the time the new school year commenced.

Evidence of the children's school experience throughout their Reception year was gained from participant observation, systematic observation, and a range of assessment measures, as well as interviews with staff. A picture of their home experience was constructed by means of two sequences of semi-structured interviews (with mothers plus any other family members who chose to contribute – fathers, grandfathers, aunts and teenage siblings), a questionnaire administered to all parents in the class, and field notes of conversations at school, in the street or on additional home visits. The children themselves, as well as offering their views in the process of daily informal chats, were also 'interviewed', semi-formally. They were happy to offer their opinions, and pleased to see their words written down, but their responses, like their parents', were frequently difficult to interpret.

The last piece in assembling the mosaic of children's home experience was supplied by observations of their classroom behaviour. Field notes described not only their learning of the school's 'official' curriculum, but also their more 'home-like' behaviours (such as tidying, cleaning up and putting dolls to bed) and the learning dispositions each of them displayed in the classroom. These observations triangulated with the accounts given by the children themselves and their parents, to build a picture of the ways each child had been prepared for school, and of the consequences of such preparation.

Analysis of the data was conducted both horizontally and vertically. A profile of each child and family was constructed, and explanations for the child's experiences and outcomes were sought within each individual case. Simultaneously, analyses were undertaken across the cases of the 16 children – of aspects of their experiences in the years from birth to four years old, of the home and school environments of their Reception year, and of their parents' perspective on their development. Some of the 'explanations' for individual and group differences that emerged from the data were found in the belief systems displayed by parents, which are discussed in the following pages.

Methodological issues: ethics and validity in research relationships

The complex and uncertain business of accessing and representing the beliefs and attitudes of research participants is fundamental to all interpretative research, and was a particular concern of this study. The long-standing 'insider-outsider' debate (Merton, 1972) has alerted us to questions of the validity, and propriety, of dominant-group researchers representing the views of dominated groups: whites researching blacks, males researching females, the middle classes researching the poor (Troyna & Carrington, 1993; Siraj-Blatchford, 1994a; Griffiths, 1998). This was clearly an issue for me: although not currently employed, in the eyes of my respondents I was a former teacher, highly educated and highly employable. We all knew that, however friendly and informal our relationships might be, I belonged to a more powerful and privileged group than any of them.

This unequal relationship raised two concerns. One was ethical: that in asking families to participate I was actually using my dominant position to make demands on their privacy. The other was epistemological: that information offered in a relationship of such inequality might not be reliable. Both these anxieties were gradually allayed, as the initially formal relationship with families evolved, in the course of daily encounters over many months, into a more informal acquaintance.

Seller (1994) has argued that the power relations between researchers and respondents can be dismantled through uncovering the 'commonalities' and common concerns that lie beneath their differences. In this study, a shared concern for the children's welfare, and shared observations of their progress and development, seemed to over-ride initial differences. Although I initiated the research interviews conducted with the families, it was the parents themselves who chose to come and find me at school to report bits of news, to ask how their child had coped with the day, or to request that I speak to the class teacher on their behalf. On the whole, therefore, I felt confident that the data I obtained from families were reliable, to the extent that it was freely given within a familiar relationship. Factual evidence at least – on mealtimes, bedtimes, literacy practices, religious observance – was trustworthy, and was borne out by my own observations. It was more difficult, however, to discern and describe the effects of parents' culturally regulated beliefs, in particular those they held unconsciously.

Identifying ethnotheories

Early analyses of the home data, which focused on conventional variables such as maternal education, paternal occupation, and family reading habits, showed no links with the children's relative success in the classroom. The two children whose mothers had the highest level of schooling – Cameron (Anglo boy) and

Tuhura (Bangladeshi girl) – were among the children who adapted least well to school, and achieved the lowest entry scores. The child with the highest score on a phonological awareness measure (regarded as a good predictor for literacy learning) was the youngest girl in the sample, Khiernssa, whose father was unemployed and whose mother had only five years of village schooling. These findings gave no hints about the patterns in children's everyday lives in their families that might be contributing to their early achievement. These patterns began to emerge as the first sequence of parent interviews was re-examined for evidence of the family beliefs and practices that were shaping the children's home experiences. A second sequence of interviews probed these issues more directly; for instance, by asking parents to describe how their children learned, and what made different children more or less 'clever' or successful as pupils. It was at this point that both researcher and respondents began to struggle to make meaning, as this extract shows:

Researcher: What is it, do you think, that makes some children better at learning than others, makes them find it easier?
[Rahena sighs before attempting to answer. Mrs Khan translates every phrase for me as she pauses.]

Rahena: It's a difference with the children, whether they want to learn, and some children don't bother. I can't tell everything about that ... but listen, I got a hand [she holds out her hand and points to each finger-tip in turn; I think she is referring to her nail polish] I got five fingers. Are they the same? Are they the same size? No, it doesn't happen: I know my five fingers are not the same, but they are all my fingers, my hand.
(21 March, record of home visit to interview Rahena, mother of Abu Bokkar)

Most parents were conscious of some of their beliefs, and could discuss the ways they attempted to implement them with their children. Other beliefs by contrast were aspects of 'taken-for-granted' knowledge that had been acquired unconsciously, and were more difficult for the respondents to articulate. These emergent theories were coded and ordered into a number of strands, each of which was gradually reinforced by evidence from other data sources until it made consistent sense. All of these 'home' theories were subsequently used in interpreting the children's school experiences:

- Beliefs about *childhood*, and about adult–child roles and relationships.
- Beliefs and practices about *the home*, including the use of time and space.
- Beliefs about the uses and purposes of *literacy* and the value of oracy.
- Beliefs about *children's learning*.

The study, inevitably, generated huge amounts of data, most of which cannot be reported here (but see Brooker, 2000, 2002). Instead, some aspects of these themes, selected from the data on all 16 children, are illustrated through a case study of one child and his family.

Family beliefs and practices: Abu Bokkar's family

Abu Bokkar is the youngest of seven children, all of whom have attended the local primary school. His mother Rahena can recite the names of all the teachers each of her children has had, and is full of praise for them all, but his father is more sceptical about the children's schooling. He shows me all his children's school reports, and points out that all were viewed as successful pupils at primary school, but were classified as low achievers, and put into low streams, when they started secondary school. He wonders what went wrong.

Abu Bokkar's family share many beliefs and practices with other Bangladeshi families in this neighbourhood. They hold high expectations for their children, and devote many hours to supporting their education at home – both the English literacy and numeracy that they see as vital to their children's school success, and the Bengali and Arabic instruction that will enable them to maintain their religious and cultural heritage. The children are brought up to show respect for adults, including teachers, and are expected to be obedient and co-operative in all aspects of their lives. The aspirations and expectations their parents hold are rather 'middle class', and there seems no obvious reason why the children should not succeed at school. A comparison of some of the strands of belief that shaped Bokkar's early home environment, with the beliefs underpinning the environment of his Reception class, offers some clues.

Conceptualising childhood

Discussions with all the mothers about their child's early years illustrated the culturally regulated nature of their views of childhood (James & Prout, 1997). Rahena, and the other Bangladeshi mothers, held an implicit but very specific view of what it meant to be a child, which differed significantly from the views of the Anglo community.

Anglo families in the neighbourhood, despite their marginal social status, shared the broadly 'child-centred' perspectives of their children's teachers. In general, mothers believed that their own role in their child's preschool years was to be involved in their children's play, and attentive to their enthusiasms and preferences. Those mothers who were not very involved assumed, apologetically, that they ought to be: quite literally they felt an obligation to get down to the child's level, and to acknowledge the child's point of view. (As Maisie, mother of Joshua reported: 'he *can* play on his own, but most of the time I'm there on the floor with him anyway'.) All of the Anglo respondents offered detailed accounts of the games and activities their children enjoyed as infants.

While their children are awake, most Anglo mothers try to make time for them in this way. But equally important is their practice of putting them to bed early enough in the evening for their parents to enjoy a separate, adult existence. Most four year olds, as their mothers emphasise, are expected to be out of sight from around 7.30 until it is time to get up in the morning.

Rahena's expectations were wholly different. She was bemused that I should expect her to know what her children played with, and indicated to the interpreter that playing is children's affair, and no business of adults. She could recall that Bokkar sometimes played with his brothers' computer games, or with small cars, but believed that in general 'he watches television, most of the day'. Like the other Bangladeshi children, Bokkar was expected to entertain himself with the children of neighbours, or simply to occupy himself around the house. He certainly would not expect his mother to abandon her own tasks and come and play, but had spent much of his time pottering at home alongside her, while she was fully occupied with her own chores.

Bangladeshi mothers' uninvolved stance towards 'childish' interests, however, does not exclude children from participating in all the family's daily routines, or from sharing in the sociable activities of older family members. Rather than inhabiting a separate childhood world, which is put away at bedtime, as the Anglo children do, the Bangladeshi children co-habit the family world of relatives of all ages. Instead of being seen as a separate social group, they are the newest recruits to a family life that spans the generations. The low priority Bangladeshi parents give to specifically *children*'s interests allows them to welcome children into their own lives as full family members. This view of childhood, and of generational relationships, shapes children's expectations of school, of teachers, and of the value attached by adults to 'playing'. It is also clearly manifest in the families' domestic routines.

Living in households

Abu Bokkar's family, in common with five of the other Bangladeshi households, have based their domestic routines on their former life in a Sylheti village. One aspect of this life is an 'integrated' day, in which children of all ages co-sleep with siblings or with their mother, and are permitted to fall asleep as and when (and where) they feel the need, rather than at set times or in specified places. The notion of 'bedtime', let alone 'story-time', is meaningless in families like these, where children nap and wake at will, and are consequently awake late into the night, when the restaurant workers return home. (On a day when Rahena completed a detailed diary for him, Bokkar slept on the sofa from 3.30 to 6.00, and then stayed up until the entire household went to bed around midnight.) Mealtimes are also flexible. Most mothers prepared large family meals freshly each morning, but many children also have rice or chips cooked for them at odd hours of the day. In consequence, young children and their mothers frequently sleep late into the morning, with disastrous effects on their punctuality on starting school. The school timetable is highly incompatible with restaurant workers' hours (11:00 a.m. to 3:00 p.m. and 5:00 p.m. to 2:00 a.m.) and with the 'village-like' daily rhythms that persist in many families. For these children, too, the school day with its rigid temporal requirements was a mystery.

Spatial routines in Bokkar's home were similarly distinctive, from a mainstream perspective. Like other former village families, his parents used their domestic space entirely flexibly. Rahena's 'front room', like many where I conducted taped interviews, contained children's bikes and a baby's cot, divans with sleeping nightworkers oblivious under duvets, and the paraphernalia of cooking and eating randomly distributed. Children brought up in such settings can make little sense of the orderly arrangements that underlie the apparent informality of Early Years settings. They could not detect, as some of the Anglo children could (particularly Joshua, son of a playgroup worker) the hidden rule that there is a time and a place for everything: a time to make a mess, and a time to clear it up; a place for the sand toys, and a place for the water toys; and rules that say the two shall not be mixed up.

The aspect of domestic routines that proved most difficult to investigate was parents' views of children's domestic responsibilities. Responses to direct questions (Does your child help at home? What kinds of things do they help with?) frequently contradicted the observational evidence. Rahena evidently found this question inappropriate: 'he says, "I will help you when I am big" – we don't expect our children to work'. Other Bangladeshi parents concurred: 'she's too young – she'll have to do that when she's married' (Rufia's father), and 'he doesn't work – his mother does the work' (Amadur's father). The majority of Anglo parents, however, reported that their children 'helped' in numerous ways, such as washing up, tidying, and cleaning. Many of these responses contradicted my impressions both of the somewhat indulgent childhood of many of the Anglo children, and of the rather grown-up responsibilities assumed by some of the Bangladeshi children.

Further probing revealed the differences in the way my question was understood by families. Anglo mothers, it seemed, interpreted 'helping' as another form of play, which was indulged more for the sake of the child's satisfaction than for any support it provided for the household. Thus, mothers whose children 'washed up' admitted that they 'had to do it all again' afterwards, or felt obliged to hide all the knives – 'she could cut herself' (Jemma's mother) – or hovered to protect their plates – 'they're not plastic, you know!'(Kelly's mother).

None of the Bangladeshi children was described as 'helping', or 'having any jobs to do in the house'. Yet many were observed at home in adult-like tasks, with no element of 'play' in sight (although the children were content and absorbed in their activities). Their contribution – chopping vegetables, serving food, soothing babies – was not remarked, but seen as the normal way to act within the family, where apprenticeship into household roles follows naturally from the integration of adults and children of all ages in activities. What Amadur's mother, when probed, described as 'putting his hand with mummy's hand' meant that children were introduced to sharp knives, and hot cooking-pots, at an age when some of their Anglo classmates were being kept out of the kitchen altogether, for fear of burning themselves.

Although each child's experience of home was unique, it seemed true in general to describe the Anglo group as *role-playing* adult responsibilities, whereas the Bangladeshi children were already beginning to assume responsible roles (Rogoff, 1990). Yet all were entering an explicitly 'child-centred' classroom environment.

Children's intelligence and learning

Rahena, as we saw, struggled to express her understanding of the reasons why some children do well at school. But, with further probing, her ideas about the ways children learn and succeed became clear:

> ... when Abu Bokkar knows 10 words, why are there children who will not know one word? Because when teacher is teaching them, they are listening in this ear and taking it out of the other ear: Bokkar doesn't do that, he is listening properly and putting it in his head ... intelligent, that means you remember something – with Bokkar, whatever you say, he never forgets!

Rahena's explanation was accompanied by a visual demonstration: head on one side, she indicated by pointing how information enters the head through the ear, and stays there. Like other Bangladeshi parents, she emphasised that parents must instruct their children to 'listen', 'learn' and, above all, 'remember' in order to do well at school. Her response to questions about children's early speech, and the importance of learning to communicate before starting school, was to down-play speaking, which was something children picked up naturally, without undue effort from adults, and emphasise the importance of listening.

A questionnaire administered to all parents in the class revealed that Anglo parents placed much more emphasis on their children's ability to talk than Bangladeshi mothers. Many mentioned their child's first words (a developmental milestone not referred to by Bangladeshi families), and described their children as 'always talking', 'she never stops'. Troy's mother informed me that she 'talked constantly' to her own sons, and was curious about the 'Indian' mothers: 'They never talk to anyone, so I wonder, do they talk to their children?'. The same mother was adamant that 'children aren't born thick or intelligent, it's how you bring them up: every child has the ability to be very intelligent, but the parents don't always exercise that'.

In practice, almost all respondents affirmed the importance of parental input, although not all input was the same. Some Anglo mothers describe the need for parents to 'give children a push', while there is a view among Bangladeshi mothers that parents can 'make children strong', and enhance their school success, through praise and encouragement. Jamila (Tuhura's mother) explains this process: 'we told a child that you are clever or intelligent because we give them some encouragement, and they will be thinking, "oh yes, I'm clever", or "I'm intelligent, I can do that", we give them this feeling'.

In describing an intelligent child, who would do well at school, Anglo mothers frequently resorted to phrases such as 'the way they come up to you and talk to you', 'you can tell by what they say', or simply 'how they communicate'. A more passive model of intelligence, however, was cited by the Bangladeshi parents, and shaped their children's preparation for school. Khiernssa's mother explained that parents must 'tell the child "you must listen, you must learn, you must do what the teacher says and don't play all the time"', oblivious of the fact that this school's explicit message to Reception children is that they *should* 'play all the time'.

The beliefs displayed by parents made sense, retrospectively, of field notes made in the children's first days and weeks of school. In this period, some children's failure to display the favoured learning dispositions of the Early Years environment – curiosity, independence, motivation, communicative competence – seemed to reflect the explicit and implicit messages of their school preparation. Amadur, for instance, had been told by his parents to 'be good at school, sit down and study', while Tuhura was instructed to 'behave well, listen to the teacher and do everything she says'. All the Anglo parents, on the other hand, were encouraging the type of behaviour – outgoing, active and chatty – which was fundamental to the pedagogy of the Reception class, and hence a prerequisite of school learning.

Systematic observations of the case study children during the first term (presented in full in Brooker, 2000) confirmed that Bokkar, in common with other Bangladeshi boys, spent a high proportion of his time in the classroom wandering from activity to activity without settling. The school's invitation to 'choose' and 'play', and the apparent freedom to use the time and space in the Reception area as they chose, left them at a loss, and they seldom became fully involved in the kinds of activities through which children were expected to access the curriculum.

Moving to theory

In common with all small-scale, ethnographic and interpretative studies, this study makes no claims to generality. Instead, its claims for relevance depend on the ways it explores or challenges theoretical propositions, and in so doing suggests implications for practice. In this instance the theoretical concepts explored and developed through the empirical work were taken from the projects of Bernstein and Bourdieu. Bourdieu's propositions about the forms of symbolic capital (Bourdieu, [1986] 1997) and the evolution of the *habitus* (Bourdieu, [1980] 1990) were used to describe both the kinds of capital individual children brought with them to school, and their dispositions to 'invest' such capital profitably. Bernstein's precise descriptions of the forms of pedagogic discourse and the ways they are manifest through the classification and framing practices of homes and schools (Bernstein, 1990) provided an analytic framework for the pedagogic practices experienced by the case study children in both settings (Brooker, 2002).

Bernstein's (1971, 1975) earlier discussions of school classrooms adopted the couplet of visible and invisible pedagogy to describe pedagogic practices that are more or less explicit and visible to the learner. His analysis extends also to the classification of 'official' and 'local' knowledge and to the ways such knowledge is *naturalised* in the everyday experiences of individuals, and *recontextualised* within the education system at every level (Bernstein, 1990). These terms help to explain the effects of group and individual beliefs and practices such as those already described.

Each child's experience of a unique 'home' pedagogy and curriculum influences that child's adaptation to the pedagogy and curriculum of the Reception class in which he/she is enrolled. Both the content of the curriculum (the 'natural curriculum' of the home and the official curriculum of the school), and the means used to impart it, contribute to this effect. Figure 4.1 offers one model for comparing different home experiences with each other, and with school practices.

In very general terms, the classroom the children were entering practised a pedagogy like that in the lower-left segment of this model. A quite strictly conceived curriculum was presented to the children largely through exploratory play or 'fun activities'. Rather than being 'taught to read', for instance, children

	Official knowledge taught by family members	Local knowledge taught by family/community
Visible pedagogy	Explicit instruction of a 'school' curriculum [e.g. ABC books taught, numbers learned and written, name copied].	Explicit instruction of a family or community curriculum [e.g. mosque school, Bengali classes, Sunday school].
Invisible pedagogy	Implicit instruction of a 'school' curriculum [e.g. educational toys, tapes and videos].	Implicit instruction of a family or community [e.g. home responsibilities, help in the household].

Figure 4.1 The curriculum and pedagogy of the home.

were invited to 'share books', an activity that defined the adult and child as partners in co-constructing a narrative from the illustrations. 'Teaching' and 'learning' were not terms used in the classroom, where children were encouraged to 'play, 'have fun', 'try things out' and so on. Most of the Anglo families had prepared their children for this pedagogic practice. They had tried not to 'teach' their child overtly, believing in the child's natural right to play, but most of their children had encountered educational toys at home (Lego-like blocks, magnetic letters and jigsaw puzzles) and had a good idea of what to do with them in the classroom.

Bangladeshi families, on the other hand, if they had attempted any preschool preparation, had taught their children (English, Arabic and Bengali alphabets in several cases) by sitting them down for an hour or more each evening, to copy, repeat and memorise. Their children's official knowledge was acquired through the pedagogy of the upper-left segment, and they would have found the suggestion that children 'learn' without being 'taught' somewhat naive. Their view of learning as transmission, although contrary to Western Early Years pedagogy, is the norm both in the majority world and in minority communities in the Western world (cf. Tizard *et al.*, 1988; Delpit, 1990).

A model like this does not imply a hierarchy of appropriate, or inappropriate, pedagogic practices. There is no easy solution to providing culturally relevant teaching and learning experiences (Ladson-Billings, 1992; Siraj-Blatchford, 1994b) to a cohort of children from diverse cultural traditions. What is suggested, however, is that both schools and families need to develop a greater awareness of the implications of their practices; and that it is the responsibility of schools, as the professional providers for all children, to make their own practices very explicit, both in communicating with parents *and* in interacting with children. Enabling children to access the pedagogy of their schools may remove some of the educational disadvantage experienced by children outside the cultural mainstream – children whose parents' dedicated instructional efforts in the preschool years may endow them with a cultural capital that does not transpose into the official education system.

Conclusion

This paper, in describing research findings constructed by eliciting and interpreting the views of culturally diverse respondents, has tried to suggest both the methodological difficulties of such a project and the implications that may be drawn from such findings. While the principal case study cited has been that of a Bangladeshi family, in practice the study found a continuum of beliefs and practices in which white working-class families were also frequently at odds with the school in their understanding of teaching and learning, and the roles of adults and children. The theoretical model introduced here for moving from data to theory can be applied equally well to the practices of families who are closer in ideology and background to their children's teachers. It is not a substitute for the detailed analysis of life in an individual family, but it enables us to discuss home–school relations at a more general level.

One last suggestion remains. In Bernstein's own earlier writings, and in subsequent discussion of them, the characteristics of *visible* pedagogy have been presented as those of the *formal* school, in which strong classification and framing create a pedagogy presumed to advantage children from certain backgrounds. The *invisible* pedagogy, by contrast, has been seen as that of the weakly framed and classified 'liberal-progressive' tradition. In other words, it seems, only *formal* methods can be made explicit, and available to children and their parents, while *informal* practices are necessarily implicit, and hidden from view. There seems no reason why this should be so (despite its 'naturalness'). If the link between formality, visibility and explicitness were broken – if it were possible to be explicit and visible in offering an informal pedagogy and curriculum – perhaps families from outside the cultural mainstream, in terms of both social class and ethnicity, might have easier access to the cultural goods that most teachers are striving to offer them.

References

Bernstein, B. (1971) *Class, Codes and Control, Volume 1: Theoretical Studies Towards a Sociology of Language* (London, Routledge & Kegan Paul).

Bernstein, B. (1975) *Class, Codes and Control, Volume 3: Towards a Theory of Educational Transmission* (London, Routledge & Kegan Paul).

Bernstein, B. (1990) *Class, Codes and Control, Volume 4: The Structuring of Pedagogic Discourse* (London, Routledge).

Bourdieu, P. ([1980] 1990) *The Logic Of Practice* (Cambridge, Polity).

Bourdieu, P. ([1986] 1997) The forms of capital, reprinted in: A. Halsey, H. Lauder, P. Brown & A. Wells (Eds) *Education, Culture, Economy, and Society* (Oxford, Oxford University Press).

Brooker, L. (2000) Pedagogy, class and culture. Unpublished Ph.D., University of London.

Brooker, L. (2002) *Starting School: Young Children Learning Cultures* (Buckingham, Open University Press).

Davie, R., Butler, N. & Goldstein, H. (1972) *From Birth to Seven. A Report of the National Child Development Study* (London, Longman).

Delpit, L. (1990) The silenced dialogue: power and pedagogy in educating other people's children, in: N. Hidalgo, C. Mcdowell & E. Siddle (Eds) *Facing Racism in Education* (Cambridge, MA, Harvard University Press).

Dombey, H. & Spencer, M. (Eds) (1994) *First Steps Together* (Stoke on Trent, Trentham).

Gillborn, D. & Mirza, H. (2000) *Educational Inequality: Mapping Race, Class and Gender. A Synthesis of Research Evidence* (London, OfSTED).

Griffiths, M. (1998) *Educational Research for Social Justice: Getting Off the Fence* (Buckingham, Open University Press).

Harkness, S. & Super, C. (1992) Parental ethnotheories in action, in: I. Sigel, A. Mcgillicuddy-Delisi & J. Goodnow (Eds) *Parental Belief Systems: The Psychological Consequences for Children* (Hillsdale, NJ, Lawrence Erlbaum).

Harkness, S. & Super, C. (Eds) (1996) *Parents' Cultural Belief Systems* (New York, Guilford).

Heath, S.B. (1983) *Ways With Words* (Cambridge, MA, Harvard University Press).

James, A. & Prout, A. (Eds) (1997) *Constructing and Reconstructing Childhood: Contemporary Issues in the Sociological Study of Childhood* (London, Falmer).

Ladson-Billings, G. (1992) Culturally relevant teaching: the key to making multi-cultural education work, in: C. Grant (Ed.) *Research and Multicultural Education* (London, Falmer).

Melhuish, E., Sylva, K., Sammons, P., Siraj-Blatchford, I. & Taggart, B. (2001) *The Effective Provision of Pre-School Education (EPPE) Project, Technical Paper 7: Social/Behavioural and Cognitive Development at 3–4 Years in Relation to Family Background* (London, University of London Institute of Education).

Merton, R. (1972) Insiders and outsiders, a chapter in the sociology of knowledge, in: W. Sollors (Ed.) *Theories of Ethnicity: A Classical Reader* (Basingstoke, Macmillan).

Newson, J. & Newson, E. (1968) *Four Years Old in an Urban Community* (London, Allen and Unwin).

Rogoff, B. (1990) *Apprenticeship in Thinking: Cognitive Development in Social Context* (New York, Oxford University Press).

Seller, A. (1994) Should the feminist philosopher stay at home?, in: J. Lennon & C. Whitford (Eds) *Knowing the Difference: Feminist Perspectives in Epistemology* (London, Routledge).

Sigel, I., Mcgillicuddy-Delisi, A. & Goodnow, J. (Eds) (1992) *Parental Belief Systems: The Psychological Consequences for Children* (Hillsdale, NJ, Lawrence Erlbaum).

Siraj-Blatchford, I. (1994a) *Praxis Makes Perfect* (Nottingham, Education Now).

Siraj-Blatchford, I. (1994b) *The Early Years: Laying the Foundations for Racial Equality* (Stoke on Trent, Trentham).

Super, C. & Harkness, S. (1986) The developmental niche: a conceptualization at the interface of child and culture, *International Journal of Child Development*, 9, pp. 1–25.

Tizard, B., Blatchford, P., Burke, J., Farquhar, C. & Plewis, I. (1988) *Young Children at School in the Inner City* (London, Lawrence Erlbaum).

Troyna, B. & Carrington, B. (1993) Whose side are we on? Ethical dilemmas in research on race and education, in: B. Troyna (Ed.) *Racism and Education: Research Perspective* (Buckingham, Open University Press).

Vernon-Feagans, L. (1996) *Children's Talk in Communities and Classrooms* (Cambridge, MA, Blackwell).

Play: Advances in theory and practice

Chapter 5

Playing in/with the ZPD

Lois Holzman and Fred Newman

Source: *L. Holzman and F. Newman, Playing in/with the ZPD, Lev Vygotsky: Revolutionary Scientist,
London: Routledge, 1993.*

> ...play is not the predominant feature of childhood but it is a leading factor
> in development.
>
> (Vygotsky, 1978, p. 101)

So begins the concluding section of Vygotsky's brief (twelve-page) discussion
of the role of play in development in *Mind in Society*. Read it again, for its
provocativeness might not be apparent from a quick reading. No doubt readers
are aware that many psychologists take play to be important for development
(often, however, because—in tautological fashion—they believe it to be the
predominant feature of childhood). In common belief and common practice in
most industrial societies play is taken to be the main feature of childhood, but
little consideration is given to its relevance for development or for learning. If
this weren't so, there would surely be much more play taking place in primary
(not to mention secondary) schools.[1]

Vygotsky, as the above quote makes clear, accorded play a critically important place in his overall theory of development. To our Vygotsky, therefore,
play is of concern as revolutionary activity. In this chapter we will investigate
play in its specific relationship to the dialectical unity, i.e. as an instantiation
of learning leading development in the ZPD. A critical question for revolutionary scientists is how and under what conditions play is or can be organized
as product and process of producing activity settings (creating ZPDs).

There has been very little Vygotskian-inspired research on play. Several
factors contribute to the paucity of work: Vygotsky himself wrote so little
on the topic; developmental psychologists (in our opinion overly focused on
cognitive development and pragmatic methodology) have adopted an information processing definition of creativity (as generatively transformative); and
Vygotskian developmental and educational psychologists and linguists, influenced by the issues which dominate their disciplines, have tended to focus on
the discourse and semiotic aspects of Vygotsky's findings.

Those (non-Vygotskian) contemporary researchers on play and specialists in early childhood who believe that play is important for development typically identify the following characteristics as contributing to cognitive and social development in particular: (1) in play children suspend the constraints of reality; (2) through play children learn social norms; and (3) play is rule—governed.[2] As Vygotskians examining play, we wish to ask what is meant by reality and rules in particular. Further, we seek to examine the concept of play itself in order to understand Vygotsky's contribution and its various uses by contemporary Vygotskians and others.

Play is associated with a host of other concepts and activities: games, imagination, fantasy, symbolic representation, pretending, performing, pleasure and fun, to name but a few. There are also different conceptual frameworks in which the concept play 'lives.' At least three meanings of play are important for our discussion of play's role in development: play as 'free' play, the pretend and fantasy activities of early childhood; play as games, the more structured, explicitly rule-governed activities that become pervasive in the school years and which are the dominant form of how adults play; and play as theater acting or performance, also common in early childhood but becoming more exclusive and formalized in adulthood. Only the first two kinds of play—free play and game play—have been examined to any degree by psychologists, especially developmental psychologists and psychoanalysts; theatrical play (acting) or performance has rarely been researched by psychologists of any kind, although theatrical concepts have been employed in analyses of children's symbolic and dramatic play (Erikson, 1977; Sutton-Smith, 1976). In addition, some sociologists and anthropologists have studied theater and/or used theatrical concepts in the study of other institutions (e.g., Goffman, 1971; McDermott, 1976; Sacks, 1974).[3] For reasons we will elaborate on here, we believe all three types of play are of critical importance in development and, further, that Vygotsky's life-as-lived (the performance of his life) suggests that he recognized this.

Vygotsky at play

Vygotsky's analysis of play is most interesting. More evocative than definitive, this discussion is less unified than others, e.g. those on concepts or language and thinking. He makes note of how play both 'liberates' and constrains the child, yet he does not fully discuss the contradiction between these nor complete the dialectical unity.

In his discussion of play and its role in development, Vygotsky (1978) examines several relationships and characteristics which in his day had been assumed to be defining features of play—for example, that it is associated with pleasure, that it satisfies ungratified desires, that it is symbolic, that it is rule-governed—and finds them all lacking, except for the fact that play is rule-based. With respect to pleasure, for example, Vygotsky points out that activities other than play give pleasure (e.g. sucking on a pacifier) and that, conversely, play is not always pleasurable (e.g. playing a game or sport and losing). Ignoring needs, desires and subjectivity, however, and considering play only from the perspective of how it contributes to the development of intellectual functions can result in 'a pedantic intellectualization of play' (1978, p. 92). Again Vygotsky is emphasizing the social production of needs, motives, desires and wants; in the dualistic framework of traditional psychology, these are usually referred to as characteristics of emotional, as opposed to intellectual, development. Here he is also stressing the monistic character of human development. He goes on to specify the needs and desires that develop in relation to play, what he refers to as immmediately unrealizable desires, which, he argues, begin to develop only in the preschool years and thus are critical to but do not explain play from the perspective of its own developmental course or its role in development more generally. Finally, defining play as symbolic does not differentiate it from the many other sign- and symbol-using activities in which human beings engage.

Vygotsky also makes claims about play which, at first reading, are counterintuitive—because, we would urge, our 'intuitions' are shaped by the dominant understanding of play. One is that, far from being 'free' in play, it is in play that the child exhibits the most self-control. Another is that in play what can be or stand for something else is not limitless, i.e. the child does not pretend or fantasize anything and everything. Vygotsky concludes that what is unique to play is the creation of an imaginary situation:

> Thus, in establishing criteria for distinguishing a child's play from other forms of activity, we conclude that in play a child creates an imaginary situation. This is not a new idea, in the sense that imaginary situations in play have always been recognized; but they were previously regarded as only one example of play activities. The imaginary situation was not considered the defining characteristic of play in general but was treated as an attribute of specific subcategories of play.
>
> (1978, pp. 93–4)

This defining characteristic of play—creating an imaginary situation—is linked theoretically with the presence of rules. Vygotsky claims that even the earliest forms of play contain rules and, further, that their importance grows with development. Any imaginary situation contains rules within its creation: 'Whenever there is an imaginary situation in play, there are rules—not rules that are formulated in advance and change during the course of the game but ones that stem from an imaginary situation' (p. 95). Thus even free play, where the creation of the imaginary situation dominates the child's activity, contains (hidden) rules. At the other end of the play continuum, every game with rules contains an imaginary situation.

> For example, playing chess creates an imaginary situation. Why? Because the knight, king, queen, and so forth can only move in specified ways; because covering and taking pieces are purely chess concepts. Although in the chess game there is no direct substitute for real-life relationships, it is a kind of imaginary situation nevertheless.
>
> (p. 95)

Vygotsky thus identifies the creation of the imaginary situation with the limitations placed on possible actions that occur in game play. It is in this way that rules and imagination are linked.

The developmental course of play is characterized by the changing positions of imaginary situations and rules in play activity: 'The development from games with an overt imaginary situation and covert rules to games with overt rules and a covert imaginary situation outlines the evolution of children's play' (p. 96). Play, then, begins with an emphasis on the imaginary situation and develops into the dominance of rules. What is the impact of this course of play development on development?

To answer, we must pursue the elements of this analysis further. Early play, according to Vygotsky, is very closely tied to reality; the imaginary situation is a reproduction or re-creation of a real situation. For example, when a child plays Mommy with another person or with a doll, she/he is re-creating what she/he has seen Mommy do. Similarly, when the child pretends that a stick is a horse and has it do 'horselike' actions, she/he is re-creating what she/he has seen horses do (or what people do with horses). Yet for the child to accomplish this re-creation entails operating with meanings separated from their usual, real life objects and actions (e.g. the meaning of stick and the object stick, the meaning of horse and the object horse, similarly of mother and child). The process of separating meanings from object and action in this way creates a contradictory situation which is of importance in understanding the role of play in development. On the one hand, the child detaches meanings from objects and, on the other hand, she/he fuses real actions and real objects. According to Vygotsky, the stick becomes a pivot for detaching the meaning of 'horse' from a real horse, which is then attached to the stick. This transfer of meaning, Vygotsky claims, is facilitated by the fact that for the young child the word is a property of the thing. At the same time, according to Vygotsky, it is through play activities like these that words become part of the thing.

> In play a child spontaneously makes use of his ability to separate meaning from an object without knowing he is doing it, just as he does not know he is speaking in prose but talks without paying attention to the words.

Thus, through play the child achieves a functional definition of concepts or objects, and words become parts of a thing.

(p. 99)

Paradoxes of play in reality/history

In one sense a child at play is free to determine his own actions. But in another sense this is an illusory freedom, for his actions are in fact subordinated to the meanings of things, and he acts accordingly.

(Vygotsky, 1978, p. 103)

In play—the creation of an imaginary situation—the child emancipates her/himself from situational constraints, such as the immediate perceptual field. Vygotsky describes this as the primary paradox of play—'the child operates with alienated meaning in a real situation' (p. 99). But being freed from situational constraints, the child, paradoxically, also faces constraints imposed by play: the rules of imagination. One such constraint, as Vygotsky understands it, is to act against immediate impulse. 'At every step the child is faced with a conflict between the rules of the game and what he would do if he could suddenly act spontaneously' (p. 99). The example he gives is refraining from eating a piece of candy in a game where the candy represents something inedible. Subordination to rules and restraining spontaneous action—again, paradoxically—is the means to pleasure. Here, Vygotsky seems to be talking less about free or pretend play and more about game play. It is when game play comes to dominate over performance play, when, as Vygotsky says, rules become overt and the imaginary situation covert, that these paradoxes of play emerge. This paradoxical 'moment' is highly significant for the child's development because

> play gives a child a new form of desires [rules]. It teaches her to desire by relating her desires to a fictitious 'I,' to her role in the game and its rules. In this way a child's greatest achievements are possible in play, achievements that tomorrow will become her basic level of real action and morality.
>
> (p. 100)

If this sounds strikingly similar to Vygotsky's description of the relationship between instruction and development, it is not accidental. Does play create a ZPD? Yes, but not in the same way as the ZPD is created in everyday nonplay situations. According to Vygotsky, the critical difference is that in everyday situations of real life, action dominates meaning, while in play, meaning dominates action. In play a child behaves differently from how she/he behaves in nonplay. Action in the imaginative sphere, as we have seen above, frees the child from situational constraints and, at the same time, imposes constraints of its own. Strict subordination to rules is not possible in real life, Vygotsky claims, but only in play. In this way,

> play creates a zone of proximal development of the child. In play a child always behaves beyond his average age, above his daily behavior; in play it is as though he were a head taller than himself.
>
> (p. 102)

Vygotsky continues,

> Though the play-development relationship can be compared to the instruction-development relationship, play provides a much wider background for changes in needs and consciousness. Action in the imaginative sphere, in an imaginary situation, the creation of voluntary intentions, and the formation of real-life plans and volitional motives—all appear in play and make it the highest level of preschool development. The child moves forward essentially through play activity. Only in this sense can play be considered a leading activity that determines the child's development.
>
> (pp. 102–3)

Davydov and his followers (e.g. Davydov and Markova, 1983) in the Soviet Union and elsewhere have taken Vygotsky's claim that play is a leading activity and conducted investigations with children to show that learning activity is based on play activity (see also Engestrom, Hakkarainen and Hedegaard, 1984).

Lest we be tempted to see play as a 'social catalyst' or 'context,' or even as 'the basis' for learning-leading-development, that is, not a ZPD at all, recall that psychology's proper object of study is history and that its particular tool-and-result is revolutionary activity. Again, what we mean by history is human beings creating and producing activity/activity settings 'in' and 'out of' the materials present in the dialectical environment of human existence that is revolutionary activity/societal behavior. Play makes, and shows, history most clearly through the paradoxes of play Vygotsky describes. For both real life and play are at once societal and historical. When organized as a ZPD, play is thus simultaneously more real (coherent with the dialectical environment of history/society) and less like real life.

The centrality of rules in Vygotsky's analysis needs examination. The question is: what kind of rules? We cannot accept the concept unexamined. For just as there are different kinds of tools—tool for result and tool-and-result—so too there are different kinds of rules. This 'for'—'and' distinction, critical to our understanding of the entire Vygotskian enterprise and to his specific discoveries regarding learning and development and thinking and speech, is useful, by analogy, in understanding play. We propose that rules are to the imagination what tools are to reality; there are *rules for results* and there are *rules-and-results*.

To our understanding, early play is characterized by rules-and results—the imaginary result informs the mode of performance (playing) as much as the performance informs the imaginary result. It is only later (when, as Vygotsky says, rules dominate) that the transformation from rules-and-result to rules for result occurs—in game play where rules are the how-tos, the instrumentation to an end result separate from, yet determined by, the mode of performance of the game. In this way, game play, like language-making, is a means of adaptation to reality, for it is nothing less than the repression of revolutionary activity—meaning-making, creating rules-and-results (imagination)—even as its development is made possible by revolutionary activity.

Armed with our new conceptual tool (-and-result) of the distinction rule for result and rule-and-result, we can view Vygotsky's analysis of the developmental course of play—from the primacy of creating an imaginary situation to the primacy of subordinating oneself to rules—and its significance for human development as an instantiation of the unity. Imagining, playing, performing, playing games—these are some of the uniquely human tool-and-result activities made possible by meaning-making and the unity. Creating an imaginary situation, regardless of its content, is revolutionary activity—although not all revolutionary activity is imaginary. Unlike beavers, who don't pretend (although they might play), our toolmaking, rule-making species creates in imagination rule-and-result; we use the predetermining elements of the life space in other than a predetermined way to create something other than what is predetermined. Recall Vygotsky's description of the rules of early, free play: 'Not rules that are formulated in advance and change during the course of the game but ones that stem from an imaginary situation' (1978, p. 95). The rules (-and-results) of play create the imaginary situation even as they stem from the creation of the imaginary situation. These rules (-and-results) are incomprehensible apart from the process of their development. The child playing at being Mommy is a rule (-and-result)-maker—the rules of playing at being Mommy are inseparable from playing at being Mommy. We propose that what Vygotsky identifies as action dominating meaning in real life is the revolutionary activity of creating tools-and-results; what he identifies as meaning dominating action in the imaginative sphere, we propose, is the revolutionary activity of creating rules-and-results. Free play (rule-and-result play, revolutionary activity, meaning-making) is necessary for the further development of play, i.e. game play (rule for result play, subordination to rules, societal behavior), because, and as, learning leads development in the ZPD.

Playing at Mommy and Daddy, even if following rules and imitating social roles, disrupts the organization of the life space. After all, the child is not Mommy. And Mommy doesn't play Mommy, she is Mommy. The strict subordination to rules (-and-results) of early play is the means by which the child is able to be more actively a producer of her/his own activity than in nonplay situations where action dominates. Vygotsky describes the situation where the child plays at what she/he is doing and gives the example of pretending 'it's night-time and we have to go to bed' to 'facilitate the execution of an unpleasant action' (1978, p. 102). He says that in play the child liberates her/himself from reality. Such liberation could mean an escape from reality or a means of getting closer to reality. We believe that in play the child gets closer to reality, because it is an attempt to make things more historical and less societal. By this we mean that it is more coherent with the dialectical environment history/society and less overdetermined by societal arrangements.

Play is at once an adaptation and an opposition to the adaptation. It is thus a conflicted response to alienation, for adapting to society is adapting to alienation—the separation of the process of production from the product. In everyday life one is guided—indeed, overdetermined—by perceptual, cognitive and emotional behaviors and is therefore less directly the producer of one's own activity. In play, as the producer, one has more control in organizing the perceptual, cognitive and emotional elements. In this sense, play is much more a performance than an acting. When children, for example, play Mommy and Daddy they are least like Mommy and Daddy because Mommy and Daddy are not playing or performing; they are acting out their societally predetermined roles. We are all cast by society into very sharply determined roles; what one does in a role is act it. Performance differs from acting in that it is the socialized activity of people self-consciously creating new roles out of what exists for a social performance. Children playing Mommy and Daddy are not acting but performing—creating new roles for themselves, reorganizing environmental scenes. In this sense, 'ZPD play' is a history game—the putting together of elements of the social environment in ways which help to see and show meaning-making as creative, productive activity—which produces learning-leading-development.

In an essay on the development of imagination written in 1932, based on a lecture delivered in that year, Vygotsky exposes the flaws both of the 'old' psychology and what he saw as the idealistic psychology of his contemporaries, including Freud and Piaget. Here he links imagination and thinking to the development of consciousness. In a concluding section, he describes the increasing complexity of forms of imagination in a way that is suggestive of our discussion:

> Alongside the images that are constructed in the immediate cognition of reality, man constructs images that he recognizes as part of the domain of imagination. At advanced levels in the development of thinking, we find the construction of images that are not found in completed form in reality. By recognizing this, we can begin to understand the complex relationship between the activity of realistic thinking and the activity of advanced forms

of imagination. Each step in the child's achievement of a more profound penetration of reality is linked with his continued liberation from earlier, more primitive forms of cognition. A more profound penetration of reality demands that consciousness attain a freer relationship to the elements of that reality, that consciousness depart from the external and apparent aspect of reality that is given directly in perception. The result is that the processes through which the cognition of reality is achieved become more complex and richer.

(1987, p. 349)

The writing game

... drawing and play should be preparatory stages in the development of children's written language.

(Vygotsky, 1978, p. 118)

We have departed somewhat from Vygotsky's own analysis of play and imagination. Recall that he claimed only that instruction (learning) leads development and that play leads development. Our discovery of the unity 'leads' us (in Vygotskian fashion) to posit a more specific relation between the two developmental processes—that play is an instantiation of learning-leading-development. Our argument is strengthened, we believe, by Vygotsky's (again brief) discussion of 'pre-written language' (1978). It not only is fascinating in its own right, but it provides further insight into his understanding of play and its role in development.

Vygotsky claims that becoming proficient in written language, however complex, disjointed or confusing it may appear on the surface, is not discontinuous but a unified process of development: 'In the same way as children learn to speak, they should be able to learn to read and write' (1978, p. 118). He presents experimental evidence of his own and others for the continuity from gestures to drawing to writing and for the preschoolers' capacity for 'primitive' written language (they can 'write' before they know how to write 'properly'), and urges that 'children be taught written language, not just the writing of letters' (1978, p. 119).

Central to Vygotsky's understanding is the difference between first-and second-order symbolism. He explains this distinction simply. First-order symbols directly denote actions or objects: a stick for a horse, pencil dots on a paper for running; second-order symbols denote symbols: written signs representing spoken words, a scribbled spiral for smoke. Both drawing and writing in the earliest stages are first-order symbolism. They are not representational, but indicatory; arising out of gestures, they are 'graphic speech.' Vygotsky describes the process of learning written language as one where first-order symbols become second-order symbols (the child comes to discover that one can represent spoken language by written abstract symbolic signs), only later to become first-order symbols again at a higher level of psychological process:

> [The] higher form ... involves the reversion of written language from second-order symbolism to first-order symbolism. As second-order symbolism, written symbols function as designations for verbal ones. Understanding of written language is first effected through spoken language, but gradually this path is curtailed and spoken language disappears as the intermediate link. To judge from all available evidence, written language becomes direct symbolism that is perceived in the same way as spoken language. We need only try to imagine the enormous changes in the cultural development of children that occur as a result of mastery of written language and the ability to read—and of thus becoming aware of everything that human genius has created in the realm of the written word.
>
> (1978, p. 116)

He cites experimental findings as well as anecdotal evidence from studies in which very young children were challenged to use written symbols to remember and/or represent objects. For example, Vygotsky's colleague Luria conducted experiments which created the moment of discovery that 'one can draw not only things but words' (p. 115). Children not yet able to write were given tasks in which they had to remember a certain number of phrases that exceeded their memory capacity. When the point was reached where the child was convinced she/he could not remember them all, she/he was given a piece of paper and told to record the words in some way. Although many of them were bewildered by the request, when aided by concrete suggestions from the experimenter, they complied. For the most part, the youngest children (3- to 4-year-olds) did not utilize the marks they made; they didn't even look at them when trying to remember. Nevertheless, as Vygotsky notes in summarizing Luria's results, there were occasionally 'some astonishing cases' where the child makes meaningless (to adults) lines and squiggles 'but when he reproduces phrases it seems as though he is reading them; he refers to certain specific marks and can repeatedly indicate, without error, which marks denote which phrase' (p. 114). To Vygotsky, this memory technique is the first precursor of written language. Children gradually replace these kinds of marks with pictures and figures, and then signs (letters and numbers).

Vygotsky also believed that play—specifically the pretend games children play—was another link between gesture and written language. He viewed children's play as a complex system of 'speech' through gestures that indicate the meaning of things—as, for example, when a pile of clothes becomes a baby through the child's own motions and gestures, e.g. of holding or feeding a baby. 'It is only on the basis of these indicatory gestures that playthings themselves gradually acquire their meaning—just as drawing, while initially supported by gesture, becomes an independent sign' (p. 108).

In another section of his discussion, Vygotsky offers more support for his view that make-believe, gestures, drawing and written language comprise a continuum of development. He describes the oft-observed developmental sequence of children's drawing aligned with speech—from initially communicating the basics in both marks on the paper and speech (Vygotsky likens the earliest children's drawing to telling a story), to drawing or scribbling something and suddenly discovering its meaning, to announcing beforehand what one is about to draw. Vygotsky also notes that children sometimes write separate phrases or words on separate sheets of paper, paralleling speech patterns, as further evidence that speech provides the model for writing.

Two observations concerning the relationship between speech, written language and play led Vygotsky to make strong recommendations as to how written language should be taught. First, speech initially dominates writing in children's earliest drawing and 'writing'; second, children are able to learn to write through discovering that they can draw speech. In that case, writing dominates speech. This is, we think, an interesting dialectical relationship. Vygotsky does not highlight it yet we believe it informs his contention that written language should be taught by 'exploiting' the continuity of the unity through creating environments in which reading and writing are necessary for play.

Vygotsky makes one other point about the importance of play in the development of written language. He cautions that without an 'inner understanding' of written language, it will be mere learning: 'Of course, it is necessary to bring the child to an inner understanding of writing and to arrange that writing will be organized development rather than learning' (p. 118). To do so, he argues, requires that drawing and play be organized so as to be preparatory stages in the development of written language. The concept of 'writing as organized development' is, to us, profound (and profoundly Vygotskian). To explain why, we summarize a contemporary Vygotskian study of written language and present our analysis of its use and misuse of Vygotsky.

McLane (1990) describes one of several recent research projects that explore writing as a social process.[4] Working with sixteen children (most aged 6 to 8) and two group workers in an afterschool program in a poor, inner-city community of Chicago, McLane observed and intervened in supportive and creative ways in the organization of the after-school program so as to enhance the children's writing experiences. The study is rich in useful ideas for teachers and child-care workers. We will concentrate on how McLane understands/uses Vygotsky's discovery regarding play and how it creates a ZPD.

According to McLane, the various writing activities in which the children and adults were involved suggest that 'adults in nonschool settings can support children's writing by helping them discover connections between more familiar symbol-using activities such as drawing, play and talking, and the less familiar one of writing' (p. 317). Moreover, McLane found it was necessary to support the adults to develop new ways of seeing the writing process, including their own relationship to it. She makes the important point that one must consider 'how to negotiate zones of proximal development with the children *and* the adults who work with them' (p. 317).

In discussing the significance of 'playful uses of writing,' McLane makes the following observation:

> Finally, play encourages the player to act as if he or she were already competent in the activity under consideration, to act, in Vygotsky's words, 'as though he were a head taller than himself' (1978, p. 102). Playing with the processes and forms of writing seems likely to give children a sense of 'ownership' of—or 'entitlement' to—this complex cultural activity. Through playful uses and approaches to writing, children may come to feel that they are writers long before they have the necessary skills and knowledge to produce mature, fully conventional writing. Such positive and proprietary feelings are likely to nourish assumptions and expectations about learning to write, as well as the motivation to work at developing increasing competence in writing.
>
> (p. 312)

Here we have a description of play that comes very close to identifying its meaning-making character, yet it misses the mark. The difference between McLane's extension of Vygotsky and ours turns on the seemingly slight distinction between 'as' and 'as if.' What McLane considers important in playful uses of writing is that children act *as if* they were writers. 'As if' establishes a separation between what is—they are not writers—and what might be—they could be writers; it accepts the duality of reality and fantasy; it locates the developmental aspect of play in the child's mind. We, on the other hand, take the significance of playful uses of language to be that children perform *as* writers, not 'as if' they were writers. Unlike 'as if,' 'as' embodies the dialectical relationship between being and becoming, between what is and what can be, between reality and pretense; it locates the developmental aspect of play in the child's activity. Following Vygotsky, we view play as an environment in which children perform beyond themselves. In play children learn/play that they are learners/players; they are performing as writers. Play is a ZPD for the unity (meaning-making/language-making).

But McLane persists in identifying play with changes in mental states, not in activity. For example, she emphasizes the 'sense of "ownership" of the cultural activity' that can come from acting *as if*; we emphasize the expression of revolutionary activity that comes from performing *as*. Ownership of an activity is effectively an expression of alienation. In order to own an activity which one produces, the activity must be reified and made into a product (commodified), separated from the process of its production (and thereby its producer). Furthermore, ownership of an activity implies a separation of oneself from the historical process of human productive/creative activities; it separates the one who owns from others. The situation is even more complex than this, because under capitalism one of the things human beings do is own; things, ideas, feelings and people have become commodities—why not activity? This means that the very process of production (including the process of the production of understanding production) which distances one from the human species— ownership of an activity—also brings one close to it, because human beings are, societally speaking, owners as much as we are writers.

McLane's assertion that 'children may come to feel that they are writers' in such play situations as she is describing (as when children play with language and writing) is not attentive to the meaning(-making)fulness of play that Vygotsky identified. Children may come to feel that they are writers 'through playful uses and approaches to writing,' but why is how children feel what is of critical importance? The word 'feel' in this context implies that there is a mismatch between feelings and the actual state of affairs. It does not merely emphasize feelings; it implies that the children, in fact, are not writers—they only feel that they are. But this denies the critical factor that makes learning lead development in the ZPD.

Children's writing activities of the sort McLane describes are evidence of children performing as historical writers (meaning makers). Not to see them as such is to take 'mature, fully conventional writing' (societal writing) as what writing is. It is to deny the unity (meaning-making/learning-leading-development) as the critical force behind language-making/thinking (which includes but is not reducible to 'mature, fully conventional writing'). It is children's play with written language that makes it possible for them to learn, eventually, the 'workings' of written language.

Another study employing Vygotsky's discovery that play creates a ZPD was conducted over a five-year period by McNamee (1990). Working with staff, parents and children at Chicago community centers that had Head Start and day care programs, McNamee set out to discover 'how story dictation and dramatization activities carried out in a literacy-rich preschool classroom environment that emphasized play as the main context and approach to learning might help children considered at risk for school failure and illiteracy' (p. 292). The report is replete with examples of classroom activities, teachers' stories and reports, and McNamee's own observations. It is valuable in its emphasis on the collaboration that developed among the teachers and researcher in the creation of ZPDs: 'ZPDs took shape between us as we acted together, spoke together, and wrote with and for each other' (p. 293).

However, when McNamee attempts to explicate Vygotsky's discovery, like McLane (1990) she 'elevates' activity to the realm of thought and thereby obscures the very point Vygotsky was making. Here is McNamee's interpretation of Vygotsky on play and the ZPD: 'Vygotsky says that play creates a ZPD; he meant that in order to grow and develop people need to be able to think of themselves in a way that is different from the way they are now'

(1990, p. 288). To corroborate her faulty thesis—there is no evidence Vygotsky meant this—she draws on the work of Paley, who explained why she told a child to ' "pretend" you are a boy who knows how to share' in the following way: ' "Pretend" disarms and enchants; it suggests heroic possibilities for making change, just as in the fairy tales' (Paley, 1984, p. 87). McNamee comments, 'Like Mrs Paley, Ms Stevens had discovered a way of speaking that helped her and the children establish a footing from which to change and grow in their classroom ZPD' (1990, p. 301).

In ascribing primary significance to what goes on in the child's mind, and attributing the power of pretending to the story the child acts out, McNamee misses what is in fact the extraordinary developmental occurrence that takes place 'in' play (and every other ZPD): meaning-making activity.[5]

Notes

1 Ethnographic and observational studies of preschool and primary school classrooms have found that play is an infrequently occurring phenomenon (Adelman, 1976; Eynard and Walkerdine, 1981; Wood, McMahon and Cranstoun, 1980). Adelman, quoting an unpublished PhD thesis by King (1977), makes the further point that when teachers do use play activities they do so to make school work more relevant and interesting; the children redefine such activities as work. Teachers thus turn play into work instead of turning work into play (Adelman, 1987, p. 27).

2 While a thorough examination of theories of play is well beyond the scope of this book, we would be remiss if we did not mention the influence of Piaget (1962), for whom play is essentially an assimilation of reality to the self, and Erikson (1977), for whom play is a critical means of 'working through' emotional conflicts. The work of even the most social of social constructionists shows the influence of Piaget's and Freud's dualistic and instrumentalist understanding of play. For example, Sutton-Smith, one of the leading play researchers in the United States, emphasizes that children's play provides evidence that they can take the role of the other (1976); Bruner, Jolly and Sylva (1976) introduce their impressive collection of numerous authors' work on the role of play in development and evolution by noting that one of the important things about play is that it is 'the first carrier of rule systems through which a world of cultural restraint is substituted for the operation of impulse' (p. 20). See Adelman (1987) for a review of nineteenth-century views of play among those now identified as important philosophers of education (e.g. Froebel and Rousseau).

3 For example, Goffman treats human beings and their interactions with social structures, institutions and relationships as dramas. As one example, consider the 'burdens sustained by normal appearances' when people need to keep an individual from suspecting something out of the ordinary is taking place. According to Goffman, they have 'two dramaturgical tasks': 'to play out roles that are alien to them, as when a policeman acts like a graduate student in order to penetrate a radical organization,' and to 'act natural' so as to conceal their concern about giving themselves away' (1971, p. 268). See Gouldner (1970) for a critique of Goffman's dramaturgical metaphor.

4 See the series of studies by McNamee and her colleagues (Harris-Schmidt and McNamee, 1986; McNamee, 1987; McNamee, McLane, Cooper and Kerwin, 1985; McLane and McNamee, 1990).

5 It is interesting but not surprising that much Vygotskian and neo-Vygotskian research outside of school settings sets up play situations (e.g. Wertsch's puzzle copying) but does not utilize Vygotsky's analysis of play. The everyday life settings set up by the researchers involved in the Vygotskian-inspired Rockefeller University ecological validity project discussed in Chapter 2 [of Holtzman, L. and Newman, F. (1993) *Lev Vygosky: Revolutionary Scientist*. London: Routledge] (such as cooking clubs and 'IQ bees') were in fact play situations, yet they were approached as cognitive problem-solving situations. The researchers approached play not historically (as revolutionary activity) but experimentally (as an experimental setting). In this, they strayed from Vygotsky's goal (a psychology of human, i.e. historical, beings) and his revolutionary practice.

References

Addelson, K.P. (1983). The man of professional wisdom. In S. Harding and M.B. Hintikka (Eds), *Discovering reality: feminist perspectives on epistemology, metaphysics, methodology, and philosophy of science*. Dordrecht: D. Reidel Publishing Company, pp. 165–86.

Adelman, C. (1976). *The use of objects in the education of 3 to 5 year old children*. London: Final Report to the Social Science Research Council.

Adelman, C. (1987). Self-activity and research into theories of play. *Evaluation and research in education, 1(3)*, 113–29.

Adorno, T.W. (1951). Freudian theory and the pattern of fascist propoganda. In G. Roheim (Ed.), *Psychoanalysis and culture*. New York: International University Press.

American Educator (1989).

Apfelbaum, E. (1986). Prolegomena for a history of social psychology: some hypotheses concerning its emergence in the 20th century and its raison d'être. In K.S. Larsen (Ed.), *Dialectics and ideology in psychology*. Norwood, NJ: Ablex Publishing Corporation, pp. 3–13.

Austin, J. (1962). *How to do things with words*. Oxford: Oxford University Press.

Bacon, F. (1960). *New organon*. New York: The Liberal Arts Press.

Bakhurst, D.J. (1986). Thought, speech and the genesis of meaning: on the 50th anniversary of Vygotsky's '*Myshlenie i rech*'. *Studies in Soviet thought, 31*, 103–29.

Bakhurst, D.J. (1988). E.V. Ilyenkov and contemporary Soviet philosophy. Unpublished D. Phil, dissertation, Exeter College, Oxford.

Barker, R.G. (1968). *Ecological psychology*. Stanford, CA: Stanford University Press.

Bateson, G. (1942). Social planning and the concept of deutero-learning. In Conference of Science, Philosophy and Religion (Ed.), *Science, philosophy and religion: second symposium*. New York, pp. 81–97. Reprinted in G. Bateson (1972), *Steps to an ecology of mind*. New York: Ballantine Books, pp. 159–76.

Bernstein, R.J. (1978). *The restructuring of social and political theory*. Philadelphia, PA: University of Pennsylvania Press.

Bickerton, D. (1981). *Roots of language*. Ann Arbor, MI: Karoma Publishers.

Biesta, G. and Miedema, S. (1989). Vygotskij in Harlem: de Barbara Taylor School. *Jeugd en samenleving, 9*, 547–62.

Blanck, G. (1990). Vygotsky: the man and his cause. In L. Moll (Ed.), *Vygotsky and education*. Cambridge: Cambridge University Press, pp. 31–58.

Bloom, L. (1970). *Language development: form and function in emerging grammars*. Cambridge, MA: MIT Press.

Bloom, L. (1973). *One word at a time: the use of single-word utterances before syntax.* The Hague: Mouton.

Bloom, L. *et al.* (1991). *Language development from two to three.* Cambridge: Cambridge University Press.

Bloom, L., Hood, L. and Lightbown, P. (1974). Imitation in language development: if, when and why. *Cognitive psychology,* 6, 380–420. Reprinted in L. Bloom *et al.* (1991), *Language development from two to three.* Cambridge: Cambridge University Press, pp. 399–433.

Brenner, E. (1992). Theater of the unorganized: the radical independence of the Castillo Cultural Center. *The drama review, 36(3),* 28–60.

Bronfenbrenner, U. (1977). Toward an experimental ecology of human development. *American psychologist, 32,* 513–31.

Broughton, J.M. (1987). An introduction to critical developmental psychology. In J.M. Broughton (Ed.), *Critical theories of psychological development.* New York: Plenum, pp. 1–30.

Brown, A.L. and Ferrara, R.A. (1985). Diagnosing zones of proximal development. In J.V. Wertsch (Ed.), *Culture, communication and cognition: Vygotskian perspectives.* Cambridge: Cambridge University Press, pp. 273–305.

Brown, A.L. and French, L.A. (1979). The zone of potential development: implications for intelligence testing in the year 2000. *Intelligence, 3,* 255–77.

Brown, P. (Ed.), (1973). *Radical psychology.* New York: Harper Colophon Books.

Bruner, J.S. (1975). The ontogenesis of speech acts. *Journal of child language, 2(1),* 1–19.

Bruner, J.S. (1983). *Child's talk: learning to use language.* New York: W.W. Norton & Co.

Bruner, J.S. (1985). Vygotsky: a historical and conceptual perspective. In J.V. Wertsch (Ed.), *Culture, communication and cognition: Vygotskian perspectives.* Cambridge: Cambridge University Press, pp. 21–34.

Bruner, J.S. (1987). Prologue to the English edition. In L.S. Vygotsky, *The collected works of L.S. Vygotsky. Vol. 1.* New York: Plenum, pp. 1–16.

Bruner, J.S., Jolly, A. and Sylva, K. (Eds) (1976). *Play: its role in development and evolution.* New York: Basic Books.

Brunswik, E. (1943). Organismic achievement and environmental probability. *Psychological review, 50,* 255–72.

Buck-Morss, S. (1975). Socio-economic bias in Piaget's theory and its implications for cross-cultural studies. *Human development, 18,* 35–49.

Bulhan, H.A. (1985). *Frantz Fanon and the psychology of oppression.* New York: Plenum.

Butterfield, H. (1962). *Origins of modern science.* New York: Collier Books.

Campione, J.C., Brown, A.L., Ferrara, R.A. and Bryant, N.R. (1984). The zone of proximal development: implications for individual differences and learning. In B. Rogoff and J.V. Wertsch (Eds), Children's learning in the 'zone of proximal development.' *New directions for child development,* no. 23. San Francisco: Jossey-Bass.

Chomsky, N. (1957). *Syntactic structures.* The Hague: Mouton.

Chomsky, N. (1965). *Aspects of the theory of syntax.* Cambridge, MA: MIT Press.

Clay, M.M. and Cazdan, C.B. (1990). A Vygotskian interpretation of Reading Recovery. In L. Moll (Ed.), *Vygotsky and education.* Cambridge: Cambridge University Press, pp. 206–22.

Cole, M. (1979). Epilogue: a portrait of Luria. In A.R. Luria, *The making of mind: a personal account of Soviet psychology*. Cambridge, MA: Harvard University Press, pp. 189–225.

Cole, M. (1990a). Cultural psychology: a once and future discipline? In J.J. Berman (Ed.), *Nebraska symposium on motivation: cross-cultural perspectives*. Lincoln, NE: University of Nebraska Press.

Cole, M. (1990b). Cultural psychology: some general principles and a concrete example. Paper presented at the Second International Congress of Activity Theory. Lahti, Finland.

Cole, M. and Cole, S. (1989). *The development of children*. New York: Scientific American Books.

Cole, M., Hood, L. and McDermott, R.P. (1978). *Ecological niche-picking: ecological invalidity as an axiom of experimental, cognitive psychology*. Working paper of the Laboratory of Comparative Human Cognition. New York: Rockefeller University.

Cole, M., Hood, L. and McDermott, R.P. (1979). *Ecological niche-picking: ecological invalidity as an axiom of experimental, cognitive psychology*. Working paper of the Laboratory of Comparative Human Cognition. New York, Rockefeller University, unpublished manuscript.

Corson, S.A. (1976). *Psychiatry and psychology in the Soviet Union*. New York: Plenum.

Davydov, V.V. and Markova, A. (1983). A concept of educational activity for children. *Soviet psychology, 21*, 50–76.

Davydov, V.V. and Radzikhovskii, L.A. (1985). Vygotsky's theory and the activity-oriented approach in psychology. In J.V. Wertsch (Ed.), *Culture, communication and cognition: Vygotskian perspectives*. Cambridge: Cambridge University Press, pp. 35–65.

Deleuze, G. and Guattari, F. (1977). *Anti-Oedipus: capitalism and schizophrenia*. New York: Viking Press.

Donaldson, M. (1978). *Children's minds*. New York: W.W. Norton & Co.

Engestrom, Y., Hakkarainen, P. and Hedegaard, M. (1984). On the methodological basis of research in teaching and learning. In M. Hedegaard, P. Hakkarainen and Y. Engestrom (Eds), *Learning and teaching on a scientific basis*. Aarhus, Denmark: Aarhus University, pp. 119–89.

Erikson, E. (1977). *Toys and reasons: stages in the ritualization of experience*. New York: W.W. Norton & Co.

Eynard, R. and Walkerdine, V. (1981). *The practice of reason: investigations into the teaching and learning of mathematics in the early years of schooling. Vol. 2: Girls and mathematics*. London: Thomas Coram Research Unit and the Leverhulme Trust.

Fanon, F. (1963). *The wretched of the earth*. New York: Grove Press.

Fanon, F. (1967). *Black skin, white masks*. New York: Grove Press.

Feyerabend, P. (1978). *Against method: outline of an anarchistic theory of knowledge*. London: Verso.

Forman, E. and McPhail, J. (1989). Positive benefits of peer interaction—a Vygotskian critique. Paper presented at American Educational Research Association Conference, San Francisco.

Foucault, M. (1978). *The history of sexuality. Vol. 1: an introduction*. New York: Pantheon.

Freire, P. (1972). *Pedagogy of the oppressed*. New York: Herder and Herder.

Fromm, E. (1973). *The crisis of psychoanalysis*. Harmondsworth: Penguin.

Fukuyama, F. (1989, Summer). The end of history? *The national interest, 16*, 3–18.

Fulani, L. (1988). Poor women of color do great therapy. In L. Fulani (Ed.), *The psychopathology of everyday racism and sexism*. New York: Harrington Park Press, pp. 111–20.

Gilligan, C. (1982). *In a different voice: psychological theory and women's development*. Cambridge, MA: Harvard University Press.

Gödel, K. (1962). *On formally undecidable propositions of Principia Mathematica and related systems*. London: Oliver and Boyd.

Goffman, E. (1962). *Asylums*. Chicago, IL: Adline Publishing Co.

Goffman, E. (1971). *Relations in public*. New York: Harper Colophon Books.

Goodman, Y.M. and Goodman, K.S. (1990). Vygotsky in a whole-language perspective. In L. Moll (Ed.), *Vygotsky and education*. Cambridge: Cambridge University Press, pp. 223–50.

Gornick, V. and Moran, B.K. (1972). *Woman in sexist society*. New York: NAL-Dutton.

Gouldner, A.W. (1970). *The coming crisis in Western sociology*. New York: Basic Books.

Green, D. and Newman, F. (1986). The divine right of white Americans: Eurocentric ideology in the United States. *Practice: The journal of politics, economics, psychology, sociology and culture*, 4(2), 8–26. Reprinted in L. Holzman and H. Polk (Eds) (1988), *History is the cure: a social therapy reader*. New York: Practice Press, pp. 103–25.

Greenfield, P.M. (1978). Structural parallels between language and action in development. In A. Lock (Ed.), *Action, gesture and symbol: the emergence of language*. New York: Academic Press.

Greenfield, P.M. (1984). A theory of the teacher in the learning activities of everyday life. In B. Rogoff and J. Lave (Eds), *Everyday cognition: its development in social context*. Cambridge, MA: Harvard University Press, pp. 117–38.

Gruber, H.E. and Voneche, J.J. (1977). *The essential Piaget*. New York: Basic Books.

Habermas, J. (1971). *Knowledge and human interests*. Boston, MA: Beacon Press.

Haley, J. (1984). *Ordeal therapy: unusual ways to change behavior*. San Francisco: Jossey-Bass.

Harding, S. and Hintikka, M.B. (Eds), (1983). *Discovering reality: feminist perspectives on epistemology, metaphysics, methodology, and philosophy of science*. Dordrecht: D. Reidel Publishing Company.

Harris-Schmidt, G. and McNamee, G.D. (1986). Children as authors and actors: literacy development through basic activity. *Child language, teaching and therapy, 2(1)*, 63–73.

Hedegaard, M. (1990). The zone of proximal development as basis for instruction. In L. Moll (Ed.), *Vygotsky and education*. Cambridge: Cambridge University Press, pp. 349–71.

Holzman, L. (1985). Pragmatism and dialectical materialism in language development. In K.E. Nelson (Ed.), *Children's language, Vol. 5*, pp. 345–67.

Holzman, L. (1986). Ecological validity revisited. *Practice: the journal of politics, economics, psychology, sociology and culture*, 4(1), 95–135.

Holzman, L. (1987). Humanism and Soviet psychology: friends or foes? *Practice: the journal of politics, economics, psychology, sociology and culture*, 5(2), 6–28. Reprinted in L. Holzman and H. Polk (Eds) (1988), *History is the cure: a social therapy reader*. New York: Practice Press, pp. 103–25.

Holzman, L. (1989). Vygotsky in Harlem, Somerset and on Capitol Hill. *Newsletter of the association of progressive helping professionals*, 1, 1–3.

Holzman, L. (1990). Lev and let Lev: a dialogue on the life and work of renowned psychologist/methodologist Lev Vygotsky. *Practice: the magazine of psychology and political economy*, 7, 11–23.

Holzman, L. (1992). When learning leads development: building a humane learning environment. *The community psychologist*, *25(3)*, 9–11.

Holzman, L. and Newman, F. (1979). *The practice of method: an introduction to the foundations of social therapy*. New York: Practice Press.

Holzman, L. and Newman, F. (1985). History as an anti-paradigm: work in progress toward a developmental and clinical psychology. *Practice: the journal of politics, economics, psychology, sociology and culture*, *3(3)*, 60–72. Reprinted in L. Holzman and H. Polk (Eds) (1988), *History is the cure: a social therapy reader*. New York: Practice Press, pp. 55–67.

Holzman, L. and Newman, F. (1987). Language and thought about history. In M. Hickmann (Ed.), *Social and functional approaches to language and thought*. London: Academic Press, pp. 109–21.

Holzman, L. and Polk, H. (Eds) (1988). *History is the cure: a social therapy reader*. New York: Practice Press.

Hood, L. (1977). A longitudinal study of the development of the expression of causal relations in complex sentences. Unpublished PhD dissertation, Columbia University.

Hood, L. and Bloom, L. (1979). What, when and how about why: a longitudinal study of early expressions of causality. *Monographs of the society for research in child development*, *44*. Reprinted in L. Bloom et al. (1991), *Language development from two to three*. Cambridge: Cambridge University Press, pp. 335–73.

Hood, L., Fiess, K. and Aron, J. (1982). Growing up explained: Vygotskians look at the language of causality. In C. Brainerd and M. Pressley (Eds), *Verbal processes in children*. New York: Springer-Verlag, pp. 265–85.Reprinted in *Practice: the journal of politics, economics, psychology, sociology and culture* (1983), *1(2–3)*, 231–52.

Hood, L., McDermott, R.P. and Cole, M. (1980). 'Let's try to make it a nice day'—Some not so simple ways. *Discourse processes*, *3*, 155–68. Reprinted in *Practice: the journal of politics, economics, psychology, sociology and culture* (1986), *4(1)*, 103–16.

Ingleby, D. (1974). The psychology of child psychology. In M.P.M. Richards (Ed.), *The integration of a child into a social world*. Cambridge: Cambridge University Press, pp. 295–308.

Ingleby, D. (1987). Psychoanalysis arid ideology. In J.M. Broughton (Ed.), *Critical theories of psychological development*. New York: Plenum, pp. 177–210.

Jacoby, R. (1975). *Social amnesia*. Boston, MA: Beacon Press.

James, W. (1916). *Pragmatism: a new name for some old ways of thinking*. New York: Longsmans, Green.

Joravsky, D. (1987). L.S. Vygotskii: The muffled deity of Soviet psychology. In M.G. Ash and W.R. Woodward (Eds). *Psychology in twentieth-century thought and society*. Cambridge: Cambridge University Press, pp. 189–211.

Joravsky, D. (1989). *Russian psychology: a critical history*. Oxford: Basil Blackwell.

Kant, I. (1929). *Critique of pure reason*. New York: St Martin's Press.

Kaye, K. (1982). *The mental and social life of babies*. Chicago, IL: University of Chicago Press.

Keller, E.F. and Grontkowski, C.R. (1983). The mind's eye. In S. Harding and M.B. Hintikka (Eds), *Discovering reality: feminist perspectives on epistemology, metaphysics, methodology, and philosophy of science.* Dordrecht: D. Reidel Publishing Company, pp. 207–24.

King, N. (1977). The hidden curriculum and the socialization of the kindergarten school. Unpublished PhD dissertation. University of Wisconsin.

Kozulin, A. (1984). *Psychology in utopia: toward a social history of Soviet psychology.* Cambridge, MA: MIT Press.

Kozulin, A. (1986a). The concept of activity in Soviet psychology. *American psychologist, 41(3),* 264–74.

Kozulin, A. (1986b). Vygotsky in context. In L.S. Vygotsky, *Thought and language.* Cambridge, MA: MIT Press, pp. xi–lvi.

Kozulin, A. (1990). *Vygotsky's psychology: a biography of ideas.* Cambridge, MA: Harvard University Press.

Kuhn, T. (1962). *The structure of scientific revolutions.* Chicago, IL: University of Chicago Press.

Labov, W. (1972). *Language in the inner city.* Philadelphia, PA: University of Pennsylvania Press.

LaCerva, C. (1992). Talking about talking about sex: the organization of possibilities. In J.T. Sears (Ed.), *Sexuality and the curriculum: the politics and practices of sexuality education.* New York: Teachers College Press, pp. 124–38.

Laing, R.D. (1983). *The politics of experience.* New York: Pantheon.

Lasch, C. (1976). The family as a haven in a heartless world. *Salmagundi, 35.*

Leont'ev, A.N. (1978). *Activity, consciousness, and personality,* Englewood Cliffs, NJ: Prentice Hall.

Levitan, K. (1982). *One is not born a personality: profiles of Soviet education psychologists.* Moscow: Progress Publishers.

Lewin, K. (1943). Defining the 'field at a given time.' *Psychological review, 50,* 292–310.

Lewis, C.I. (1990) *Mind and the world order: outline of a theory of knowledge.* New York: Dover.

Lichtman, R. (1977). Marx and Freud, part three: Marx's theory of human nature. *Socialist revolution, 7(6),* 37–78.

Lock, A. (Ed.) (1978). *Action, gesture and symbol: the emergence of language.* New York: Academic Press.

Lovejoy, A.O. (1960). *The revolt against dualism: an inquiry concerning the existence of ideas.* Second edition. LaSalle, IL: The Open Court Publishing Co.

Luria, A.R. (1978). Psychoanalysis as a system of monistic psychology. *Soviet psychology, 16,* 7–45. Reprinted in M. Cole (Ed.) (1978), *The selected writings of A.R. Luria.* White Plains, NY: Sharpe.

Luria, A.R. (1979). *The making of mind: a personal account of Soviet psychology.* Cambridge, MA: Harvard University Press.

Luxemburg, R. (1968). *The accumulation of capital.* New York: Monthly Review Press.

Luxemburg, R. (1972). *The accumulation of capital – an anti-critique.* New York: Monthly Review Press.

Lyons, J. (1981). *Language and linguistics: an introduction.* Cambridge: Cambridge University Press.

McDermott, R.P. (1976). Kids make sense: an ethnographic account of the interactional management of success and failure in one first-grade classroom. Unpublished PhD dissertation, Department of Anthropology, Stanford University.

McDermott, R.P. (1987). The acquisition of a child by a learning disability. Unpublished manuscript, Stanford University.

McLane, J.B. (1990). Writing as a social process. In L. Moll (Ed.), *Vygotsky and education*. Cambridge: Cambridge University Press, pp. 304–18.

McLane, J.B. and McNamee, G.D. (1990). *Early literacy*. Cambridge, MA: Harvard University Press.

McNamee, G.D. (1987). The social origins of narrative skills. In M. Hickmann (Ed.), *Social and functional approaches to language and thought*. New York: Academic Press, pp. 287–304.

McNamee, G.D. (1990). Learning to read and write in an inner-city setting: a longitudinal study of community change. In L. Moll (Ed.), *Vygotsky and education*. Cambridge: Cambridge University Press, pp. 287–303.

McNamee, G.D., McLane, J.B., Cooper, P.M. and Kerwin, S.M. (1985). Cognition and affect in early literacy development. *Early childhood development and cure*, 20, 229–44.

Marcuse, H. (1962). *Eros and civilization*. Boston, MA: Beacon Press.

Marx, K. (1964). *Economic and philosophical manuscripts of 1844*. New York: International Publishers.

Marx, K. (1967). *Capital. Vol. 1*. New York: International Publishers.

Marx, K. (1971). *Grundrisse: foundations of the critique of political economy*. New York: Harper & Row.

Marx, K. (1973). Theses on Feuerbach. In K. Marx and F. Engels, *The German ideology*. New York: International Publishers, pp. 121–3.

Marx K. and Engels, F. (1973). *The German ideology*. New York: International Publishers.

Merleau-Ponty, M. (1964). *Sense and non-sense*. Evanston, IL: Northwestern University Press.

Messer, D. (1991). Review of *The many faces of imitation in language learning. Journal of child language*, 18, 227–9.

Minick, N. (1987). The development of Vygotsk's thought: an introduction. In L.S. Vygotsky, *The collected works of L.S. Vygotsky. Vol. 1*. New York: Plenum, pp. 17–36.

Moerk, E.L. (1977). Processes and products of imitation: Additional evidence that imitation is progressive. *Journal of psycholinguistic research*, 6, 187–202.

Moll, L. (Ed.) (1990). *Vygotsky and education: instructional implications and applications of socio-cultural psychology*. Cambridge: Cambridge University Press.

Moll, L. and Greenberg, J. (1990). Creating zones of possibilities: combining social contexts for instruction. In L. Moll (Ed.), *Vygotsky and education*. Cambridge: Cambridge University Press, pp. 319–48.

Moshman, D., Glover, J.A. and Bruning, R.H. (1987). *Developmental psychology: a topical approach*. Boston, MA: Little, Brown & Co.

Moulton, J. (1983). A paradigm of philosophy: the adversary method. In S. Harding and M.B. Hintikka (Eds), *Discovering reality: feminist perspectives on epistemology, metaphysics, methodology, and philosophy of science*. Dordrecht: D. Reidel Publishing Company, pp. 149–64.

Neff, P. (1984). *Tough love: how parents can deal with drug abuse*. Nashville, TN: Abingdon.

Newman, D., Griffin, P. and Cole, M. (1984). Social constraints in laboratory and classroooom tasks. In B. Rogoff and J. Lave (Eds), *Everyday cognition: its development in social context*. Cambridge, MA: Harvard University Press, pp. 171–93.

Newman, D., Griffin, P. and Cole, M. (1989). *The construction zone: working for cognitive change in school*. Cambridge: Cambridge University Press.

Newman, F. (1978). *Practical-critical activities*. New York: Institute for Social Therapy and Research. Reprinted in *Practice: the journal of politics, economics, psychology, sociology and culture* (1983), *1(2–3)*, 52–101.

Newman, F. (1983). Talkin transference. *Practice: the journal of politics, economics, psychology, sociology and culture, 1(1)*, 10–31. Reprinted in F. Newman (1991), *The myth of psychology*. New York: Castillo International, pp. 16–44.

Newman, F. (1987). Crisis normalization and depression: a new approach to a growing epidemic. *Practice: the journal of politics, economics, psychology, sociology and culture, 5(3)*, 14–32. Reprinted in F. Newman (1991), *The myth of psychology*. New York: Castillo International, pp. 79–96.

Newman, F. (1989a). Seven theses on revolutionary art. *Stono, 1(1)*, 7.

Newman, F. (1989b). Panic in America. *Practice: the journal of politics, economics, psychology, sociology and culture, 6(3)*, 43–67. Reprinted in F. Newman (1991), *The myth of psychology*. New York: Castillo International, pp. 97–110.

Newman, F. (1991a). The patient as revolutionary. In F. Newman, *The myth of psychology*. New York: Castillo International, pp. 3–15.

Newman, F. (1991b). Community as a heart in a havenless world. In F. Newman, *The myth of psychology*. New York: Castillo International, pp. 140–57.

Newman, F. (1992). Surely Castillo is left—but is it right or wrong? Nobdy knows. *The drama review, 36(3)*, 24–7.

Newson, J. (1978). Dialogue and development. In A. Lock (Ed.), *Action, gesture and symbol: the emergence of language*. New York: Academic Press, pp. 31–12.

Paley, V. (1984). *Wally's stories*. Cambridge, MA: Harvard University Press.

Papert, S. (1980). *Mindstorms: children, computers and powerful ideas*. New York: Basic Books.

Peirce, C.S. (1957). *Essays in the philosophy of science*. New York: The Liberal Arts Press.

Petrovsky, A. (1990). *Psychology in the Soviet Union: a historical outline*. Moscow: Progress Publishers.

Piaget, J. (1929). *The child's conception of the world*. London: Kegan Paul.

Piaget, J. (1955). *The language and thought of the child*. London: Kegan Paul.

Piaget, J. (1962). *Play, dreams and imitation in childhood*. New York: W. W. Norton & Co.

Piaget, J. (1968). *Judgement and reasoning in the child*. Totowa, NJ: Littlefield, Adams.

Polkinghome, D. (1983). *Methodology for the human sciences*. Albany, NY: State University of New York Press.

Prigogine, I. (1984). *Order out of chaos: man's new dialogue with nature*. Toronto: Bantam. [First published in French under the title *La nouvelle alliance*.]

Quine, W.V.O. (1961). Two dogmas of empiricism. In W.V.O. Quine, *From a logical point of view*. Second edition. New York: Harper & Row, pp. 20–46.

Ratner, C. (1991). *Vygotsky's sociohistorical psychology and its contemporary applications*. New York: Plenum.

Ratner, N. and Bruner, J.S. (1978). Games, social exchange and the acquisition of language. *Journal of child language*, 5, 391–401.

Reich, W. (1970). *The mass psychology of fascism*. New York: Farrar, Straus & Giroux.

Riegel, K.F. (1979). *Foundations of dialectical psychology*. New York: Academic Press.

Rodney, W. (1974). *How Europe underdeveloped Africa*. Washington, DC: Howard University Press.

Rogoff, B. (1990). *Apprenticeship in thinking: cognitive development in social context*. New York: Oxford University Press.

Rogoff, B. and Gardner, W. (1984). Guidance in cognitive development: an examination of mother–child instruction. In B. Rogoff and J. Lave (Eds), *Everyday cognition: its development in social context*. Cambridge, MA: Harvard University Press, pp. 95–116.

Rogoff, B. and Lave, J. (Eds), (1984). *Everyday cognition: its development in social context*. Cambridge, MA: Harvard University Press.

Rosa, A. and Montero, I. (1990). The historical context of Vygotsky's work: a sociohistorical approach. In L. Moll (Ed.), *Vygotsky and education*. Cambridge: Cambridge University Press, pp. 59–88.

Russell, B. (1912). *The problems of philosophy*. London: Oxford University Press.

Sacks, H. (1974). An analysis of the course of a joke's telling in conversation. In R. Bauman and J. Sherzer (Eds), *Explorations in the ethnography of speaking*. New York: Cambridge University Press, pp. 337–53.

Schreiber, L.L. (1987). Vygotsky and Montessori: the process of learning in the preschooler. *American Montessori society*, 5–11.

Seve, L. (1978). *Man in Marxist theory and the psychology of personality*. Brighton: Harvester Press.

Slavin, R.E. (1983). *Cooperative learning*. New York: Longman.

Slobin, D. (1973). Cognitive prerequisites for the development of grammar. In C. Ferguson and D. Slobin (Eds), *Studies of child language development*. New York: Holt, Rinehart & Winston, pp. 175–208.

Speidel, G.E. and Nelson, K.E. (1989). The *many faces of imitation in language learning*. New York: Springer-Verlag.

Strickland, G. and Holzman, L. (1988). Developing poor and minority children as learners with the Barbara Taylor School Educational Model. *Journal of negro education*, *58(3)*, 383–98.

Sutton-Smith, B.(1976).*The psychology of play*. Salem, NH: Ayer Co. Publishers.

Szasz, T. (1961). *The myth of mental illness: foundations of a theory of personal conduct*. New York: Harper & Row.

Tharp, R.G. and Gallimore, R. (1988). *Rousing minds to life: teaching, learning and schooling in social context*. Cambridge: Cambridge University Press.

Thomas, R.M. (1992). *Comparing theories of child development*. Third edition. Belmont, CA: Wadsworth Publishing Co.

Travarthan, C. and Hubley, P. (1978). Secondary intersubjectivity: confidence, confiding and acts of meaning in the first year. In A. Lock (Ed.), *Action, gesture and symbol: the emergence of language*. New York: Academic Press, pp. 183–229.

Tudge, J. (1990). Vygotsky, the zone of proximal development, and peer collaboration: implications for classroom practice. In L. Moll (Ed.), *Vygotsky and education*. Cambridge: Cambridge University Press, pp. 155–72.

Valsiner, J. (1988). *Developmental psychology in the Soviet Union*. Bloomington, IN: Indiana University Press.

Van der Veer, R. and Valsiner, J. (1991). *Understanding Vygotsky: a quest for synthesis*. Oxford: Basil Blackwell.

Van der Veer, R. and Van Ijzendoorn, M.H. (1985). Vygotsky's theory of the higher psychological processes: some criticisms. *Human development, 28,* 1–9.

Vasta, R., Haith, M.M and Miller, S.A. (1992). *Child psychology: the modern science.* New York: John Wiley & Sons.

Vickers, J.M. (1991). Objectivity and ideology in the human sciences. *Topoi, 10(2),* 175–86.

Volosinov, V.N. (1987). *Freudianism: a critical sketch.* Bloomington, IN: Indiana University Press.

Vygotsky, L.S. (1962). *Thought and language.* Cambridge, MA: MIT Press.

Vygotsky, L.S. (1978). *Mind in society.* Cambridge, MA: Harvard University Press.

Vygotsky, L.S. (1982). The historical meaning of the crisis in psychology. In A.R. Luria and M.G. Iaroshevski (Eds), *L.S. Vygotsky: collected works. Vol 1,* Moscow: Pedagogika, [In Russian].

Vygotsky, L.S. (1986). *Thought and language.* Newly revised. Cambridge, MA: MIT Press.

Vygotsky, L.S. (1987). *The collected works of L.S. Vygotsky. Vol. 1.* New York: Plenum.

Vygotsky, L.S. (in press). *Problems of abnormal psychology and learning disabilities: the fundamentals of defectology.* New York: Plenum.

Walkerdine, V. (1984). Developmental psychology and the child-centered pedagogy: the insertion of Piaget into early education. In J. Henriques, W. Hollway, C. Urwin, C. Venn and V. Walkerdine (Eds), *Changing the subject: psychology, social regulation and subjectivity.* London: Methuen, pp. 153–202.

Walkerdine, V. (1988). *The mastery of reason: cognitive development and the production of rationality.* London: Routledge.

Watzlawick, P., Beavin, J. and Jackson, D. (1967). *Pragmatics of human communication: a study of interactional patterns, pathologies and paradoxes.* New York: W. W. Norton & Co.

Watzlawick, P., Weakland, J. and Fisch, R. (1974). *Change: principles of problem formation and problem resolution.* New York: W. W. Norton & Co.

Wertsch, J.V. (Ed.), (1981). *The concept of activity in Soviet psychology.* Armonk, NY: M.E. Sharpe.

Wertsch, J.V. (1985). *Vygotsky and the social formation of mind.* Cambridge, MA: Harvard University Press.

Wertsch, J.V, (1991). *Voices of the mind: a sociocultural approach to mediated action.* Cambridge, MA: Harvard University Press.

Whitehead, A.N. and Russell, B. (1962). *Principia mathematica.* Cambridge: Cambridge University Press.

Wittgenstein, L. (1953). *Philosophical investigations.* Oxford: Basil Blackwell.

Wittgenstein, L. (1961). *Tractatus logico-philosophicus.* London: Routledge.

Wittgenstein, L. (1965). *The blue and brown books.* New York: Harper Torchbooks.

Wood, D., Bruner, J. and Ross, G. (1976). The role of tutoring in problem-solving. *Journal of child psychology and psychiatry, 17,* 89–100.

Wood, D., McMahon, L. and Cranstoun, Y. (1980). *Working with under fives.* London: Grant McIntyre.

Yaroshevsky, M. (1989). *Lev Vygotsky.* Moscow: Progress Publishers.

Yaroshevsky, M. (1990). *A history of psychology.* Moscow: Progress Publishers.

Chapter 6

Togetherness and diversity in pre-school play

Ulf Janson

Source: U. Janson, *International Journal of Early Years Education*, 9(2), 135–143, 2001.

Abstract

Togetherness is seen as a function of shared activity, not just proximity in physical space. In the case of make-believe play, this activity is assumed to take place in three interrelated contexts: the physical, social and symbolical. Togetherness implies that each player has access to these contexts in order to participate in the process of co-construction and collective symbolisation characteristic of play. Through the study of blind and sighted pre-school children in play interaction the differences in the way players have access to physical space, experience social interaction and create meaningful symbols are demonstrated. Transcribed episodes of play negotiations illustrate how differences in visual ability may impede togetherness. As a conclusion it is posited that to understand such impediments differences in apprehension of the situation, as opposed to disabilities defined as individual characteristics, should be highlighted and made the focus of educational practice and intervention.

Togetherness and play

Broadly speaking, 'togetherness' stands for affliation, a sense of belonging together, forming one group. However, the phenomenon must also be related to activity. We do not merely 'belong together'. We belong together by jointly doing, thinking and expressing something. To specify the meaning of togetherness in *play* those specifc activities which constitute play must be identifed. Accordingly, I will concentrate here on make-believe play, where players, through the act of pretending, symbolically transform acts, objects and the self. The focus of this study will be collective forms of such play, where at least two players are involved (cf. Smilansky's concept of socio-dramatic play; in Wood & Attfield, 1996).

This activity characteristically takes place in a *play area* (cf. intermediate area; Winnicott, 1971), which is established as an imagined reality projected onto physical space. In group play it is co-constructed by participants gathered in physical proximity, handling the same set of objects and transforming the meaning of these objects in a process of collective symbolisation. Another person, for instance a pre-school teacher crossing the room, enters the same physical space, but not the actual play area.

Playing can also be conceived of as a two-level activity: *negotiation* and *enactment* (Doyle & Connolly, 1989). On the first level, symbols are collectively established in a play script. On the second, the script is enacted. Negotiation takes the form of metacommunication (Bateson, 1955), conceptualised by Giffin (1984) as varying along a continuum from within-frame to out-of-frame communication. The former means negotiation as part of enactment, without questioning the illusory world of pretence, whilst the latter negotiation is a more distant commentary on enactment itself. Therefore, negotiations out-of-frame can be said to question, or even threaten to dissolve, the play area into its everyday physical properties. Metacommunication is an important way not only of negotiating rules and transformations necessary for the play activity itself, but also of dealing with those underlying social experiences on which the script is based.

Enactment and negotiation situate play in three distinguished but inter-related contexts: the physical context of space, people and objects; the social context of communicative exchange; the symbolic context of pretence trans-forming persons, objects and action schemes (Janson, 1999). A shared play area is created by coordinated and parallel activity in these contexts. Togetherness will thus be taken to mean joint action in these three contexts.

Togetherness may be incomplete, limited to physical proximity, without communication or symbolic co-creation. People may share a room, but not a play area. Instead, they develop individual play areas without trying to enter the areas of others and without inviting others into their own area. To coordi-nate individual play areas the symbolic schemes making up these areas must be presented and negotiated. Children may differ in motivation for such coor-dination. Instead, the combination of physical togetherness and motivational differences may result in conflict. The metacommunicated play signal 'let us play' (Bateson, 1955) can, though not so intended, be interpreted as a power signal, a forceful intrusion resulting in the metacommunicated answer 'don't upset my circles'. These metacommunicative options will henceforth be termed 'power signal' and 'play defence', respectively.

Togetherness and horizontality

An additional aspect of togetherness concerns the nature of social relations, contended in the opposites 'horizontality/verticality'. The former represents the relation between partners of equal status and influence, whilst the latter stands for dominance/dependency relations. Horizontal peer relations promote solidarity and trust, the coordination of play themes, the management of emotions and socialised responses to aggression (Hartup, 1983, 1992; Odom *et al.*, 1992). They allow for mutual experimentation with social conventions by which a specific peer culture as part of, but also as a commentary on, social order is built (Corsaro, 1997). Such experimentation is particularly obvious in socio-dramatic play where experiences of everyday life are staged and acted out.

Nevertheless, play interactions are not always horizontal: they oscillates between horizontality and verticality, between instances of 'deep play' and 'power play', the latter occurring in attempts at controlling, rather than inspiring, others (Åm, 1993). While generally characterised by care and responsibility in the parent–child relation, verticality in peer relations may develop into a status order, a social system of dominance and dependency for its own sake. In such cases togetherness signifies a hierarchy where submissiveness is the less influential member's acceptance price.

Togetherness and diversity in play

Diversity, in terms of social, cultural and ethnic background or cognitive, physical and psychological prerequisites, is a characteristic of today's pre-school. Diversity in connection with terms like 'equality and full participation' expresses the strive for togetherness *in* diversity. In the pre-school context a specified meaning of 'equal and full participation' may be derived from the discussion of play and togetherness. *Full* participation necessitates access to all contexts of play. Players must have information about, and access to, the physical properties of the situation (other players, objects and spatial relations). To participate in the social context they must share a communication system, as well as norms for appropriate social interaction (cf. Guralnick, 1992). On the symbolic level, players must have some social experience in common if they are to contribute to the script. What happens during a train ride, in a hospital, in a kitchen?

Diversity, however, often means differences in access to these contexts. For instance, differences in visual ability mean different information about the physical context, resulting in different representations of the play area. This may influence social strategies in communication. Moreover, different ideas about what constitutes meaningful symbolisation may also be formed. Consider the following example.

Sara, a blind girl, and Julia, sighted, are playing 'hospital'. Julia brings her injured baby (a doll) to Sara, the nurse. Sara starts to bandage the doll's hand and wrist.

Julia: No Sara her forehead is hurt.
Sara: (ignores, continues with the doll's hand.)
...

Julia: No Sara put it on the forehead otherwise I'll tear it off.

...

Sara: But no she must have a bandage on the hand because then the forehead will heal, that's what happens here at my place.

Julia: But I decide where you should put it ... on the forehead.

Sara: But you can't have a bandage on the forehead.

Julia: Yes you can because I've seen it on television.

This is a conflict in the symbolical context. Different social constructions of injury and treatment are negotiated. Sara claims her authority with reference to medical treatment ('that's what happens ...'). Julia claims her right to know what's best for her baby ('but I decide ...'). These claims result in unsuccessful negotiations; togetherness in play is at risk. Upon closer inspection, however, it seems as if the conflict is representational, caused by differences in sensory input. The doll is big. In Sara's exploring hand, its forehead presents itself as a flat surface, without the affordance (Gibson, 1979) of being bandageable ('you can't have a bandage on the forehead'). The doll's hand, however, affords this. For Julia, a quick glance is enough to realise that bandaging the doll's head poses no problem. To her, Sara's solution ('she must have a bandage on the hand because then the forehead will heal') is absurd. On the other hand, Julia's reference to an outside authority (television) is meaningless to Sara. These differences in perceptual schemes result in the construction of different meanings and, consequently, different script proposals. Visual diversity thus seems to prevent togetherness.

Horizontality/verticality in play interaction between the blind and sighted

Equal participation in play may be understood as horizontal. Being vertically subordinated means not being treated as an equal contributor to the script. Proposals from such a player are ignored as he or she is only accepted as a submissive follower of the directives of others. Differences in perceptual, communicative or cognitive respects may reinforce tendencies towards such verticality. This is illustrated in a longitudinal study of social play between blind and sighted children. The study is reported elsewhere (Janson, 1993, 1999), but is briefly summarised here before some episodes are discussed in detail.

Twenty groups of age-matched pre-school children, two sighted and one blind, were video-recorded together with their teachers on six occasions over a period of 1 year. Social interaction was assessed with the ISB, Individual Social Behavior (White & Watts, 1973; modified by Guralnick & Groom, 1988). This instrument reflects the distribution of initiatives and responses and the form pro-social and competitive behaviour takes. Certain behaviour patterns (e.g. attention and assistance seeking, conflict and attempts at leading peers) are coded for 'success'. Furthermore, behaviour is coded for social direction, i.e. 'target person' (blind child, sighted child or teacher). If a target person is not discernible, behaviour is coded as 'zero directed', socially non-specified. Horizontality is defined in terms of symmetry (dominant versus dependent behaviour), success and social direction.

The relation between blind and sighted children is notably lacking in horizontality. Blind children tend to take a dependent and responsive position, whilst the sighted assume a dominant and initiating one. Blind children are vague in directing communication and, when explicitly addressing others, more adult-directed than sighted children. While dominant in relation to blind peers, the average sighted child demonstrates almost perfect symmetry in interaction with other sighted children. Consequently, interaction between sighted peers is horizontal, but *not* that between the sighted and blind. This is confirmed when success is studied. Sighted children are considerably more successful in influencing play, in getting attention and in conflicts with the blind. However, when seeking assistance or information, blind children are more successful, obtaining help in almost three attempts out of four. Thus, when trying to influence play blind children are relatively ignored, but when asking for help, i.e. acting from a subordinate position, attempts are successful. A circle of control and dependency, verticality rather than horizontality, seems to be established. It should be noted, however, that this verticality has a certain 'pseudo-adult' character. The average sighted child is not a dominant tyrant, but mostly caring and helpful. Whether this is 'good' or not is a matter of discussion. Nevertheless, it does not produce horizontality. Diversity seems to be assimilated into a vertical order of influence and status. The alternative is withdrawal and occupation with solitary play.

Play maintenance: Negotiation patterns between blind and sighted participants

'Play maintenance' is secured through a flow of contributions to play enactment and negotiation. The study indicates that blind children are less successful as contributors than sighted ones. One reason for this may be differences in the available information, as demonstrated by the 'hospital episode'. Another possibility may be differences in the social context. The average blind child is less peer-directed and more vague in interaction than the average sighted child. In the following episode a 'journey by train' script is negotiated. Until now the script has consisted of three roles: train driver, conductor and passenger. The blind child, Karin, is a passenger, while Jenny and Peter, both sighted, have alternated as driver and conductor. Karin, tired of her role, starts a discussion.

Karin: U. (recorder's name) the children never allow me to be the conductor, the children only allow me to be the passenger.

Jenny:	Karin.
Adult:	You have to address Jenny, Karin.
Karin:	Yes the children only allow me to be the passenger
Jenny:	Karin (puts conductor's cap on Karin) do you want to be the Conductor.
Karin:	No I want to be what do I want I want.
Jenny:	But you may if you want.

Karin addresses the adult recorder, not the peers she eventually has to influence. These are only referred to indirectly in an impersonal, collective way ('children'). Albeit ineffective in principle as an entry strategy into Jenny and Peter's common play area, Karin's opening seems to work. Jenny notes what is going on and addresses Karin. In spite of this Karin does not respond. She repeats her complaint to the adult, still referring to the other participants very impersonally. Jenny persists, generously offering Karin the role she is asking for. Karin hesitates: obviously she has something else in mind.

Karin:	How do you act if you are the passenger eh conductor … no conductor-driver. I will ask U (addressing U)… I want to be the conductor-driver.
U:	You can ask Jenny and Peter.
Karin:	But I think you cut tickets and drive cut tickets and drive cut tickets and drive hahaha. That's a conductor-driver.
Jenny:	But what are we going to do. Will you be the conductor or not?
Karin:	No, conductor-driver cut tickets and drive cut tickets and drive.
Jenny:	No, but Karin what are you going to do. Karin will you be the conductor or not.
Karin:	Cut tickets and drive cut tickets and drive. No I'll be the conductor-driver.
…	
Jenny:	Karin there is no such thing.
Karin:	Oh yes. On my pretend train there is a conductor-driver … shall we do conductor-driver?
Jenny:	Well you can do that yourself.

This negotiation is unsuccessful in maintaining play. Little by little play motivation fades away and finally the activity dissolves. One reason is the difference in social technique between the girls. Jenny directly addresses Karin and invites her into the play area. Karin's main target person is the adult. Her communication with Jenny consists of repetitiously proposing a role transformation not acceptable to the latter. Jenny finally gets tired of the whole thing and withdraws.

As well as different social techniques, different apprehensions of the script and of underlying social experience seem to be at hand. For Karin the role combination conductor-driver is quite possible; to Jenny, it is absurd. She and Peter have previously exchanged their roles as driver and conductor, thereby establishing the principle 'either driver or conductor' as part of their co-constructed meaning of a journey by train. This is also a norm for role distribution: there are three players and three roles. One person cannot occupy two parts. Karin's idea of a conductor-driver violates this social norm for ongoing interaction. It may also be that she is perceived as a power player, refusing to adapt her scheme to the others' play area. However, what is at stake might not so much be power *per se*, but differences in social strategies, different representations of the situation and different use of previous social experience. It seems apparent that the blind girl primarily bases her script on experiences outside the play area, unlike the sighted, who bases her script on co-constructed meaning within that area.

Representational diversity as a reason for conflict

Difficulties in togetherness may arise even when information about the physical situation is at hand and participants are highly motivated for coordination of play areas. As hinted at in the previous discussion, the reason may be differences in cognition, in the way social experience is stored and represented. Such representational differences may result in differences in symbol formation, preventing coordinated play. In the following episode Pia, blind, is the driver of a train; the train consists of chairs in a row. She stands beside the first chair, supposed to be the railway engine. Anna, a sighted passenger, is sitting on another chair. Pia makes 'train noises'.

Pia: Now the train is running.
Anna: No it isn't. First you must sit on your chair in the engine.
Pia: Not me.
Anna: Yes, you must.
... (Yes-and-no quarrelling for some time.)
T: Let's say the train has an autopilot, you just press a button and then the train runs by itself.
Pia: (Pretends to press a button.) Now the train is running.
Anna: It isn't. I can see it isn't.
Pia: (Moves herself in small circles beside the engine chair.) Now it's running.
Anna: I know it isn't. I know that.
Pia: Now I press again, now it stops (repeats circling movements), now it runs.
Anna: It isn't.

This episode depicts two conflicting ideas about what constitutes train movement and how it is to be enacted symbolically. Anna is governed by a predominantly visual scheme. Driving a train means being placed on the driver's seat. What must be preserved in the symbolic act is the correct position; this is a *sine qua non* in acting as a train driver. If not, Anna *cannot see* the train running ahead. To Pia, however, the symbol must preserve the moving sensation. Otherwise she *cannot feel* the train is running. Symbolic expression in play may be endlessly imaginative but still it must preserve some degree of realism. What constitutes necessary realism in this case differs to such a degree that coordination of play areas becomes impossible. Not even teacher authority is strong enough to construct a symbol of shared meaningfulness. Thus, togetherness is hampered by differences in the players' cognitive representations.

Role and script conflicts between blind and sighted players

As reported above, blind play participants tend to be losers in conflicts. Furthermore, conflicts between sighted players are more often solved by compromise than conflicts between the sighted and blind. One possible reason for this may be relative differences in the nature of conflicts: more object-centred between the blind and the sighted, more often about role distributions or script proposals between the sighted (Isheden *et al.*, 1995). In 'win-or-lose' conflicts about objects blind children predominantly argue in terms of personal motives ('I want to'), while the sighted also argue in terms of principles ('you have had it for so long') or by play proposals ('you can use this instead').

The following conflict is taken from yet another 'journey-by-train' session. The blind boy, Kalle, has been the conductor for quite a while, the sighted boy, Lars, the train driver and the sighted girl, Eva, the passenger travelling with her baby. Now she wants to change to the conductor's role.

Eva:	I want to be the one Kalle is.
Kalle:	No.
Lars:	Well let her.
Kalle:	No.
Eva:	Kalle has been for so long.
Susanne:	(teacher's name) has promised me I can be.
Kalle:	(calls to teacher) Susanne.
T:	I think you should change so you can all be conductor.
Kalle:	But what shall I be.
Eva:	You can be the baby's mother.
Kalle:	No.
...	
T:	Kalle, now it's Eva's turn to be conductor.
Kalle:	No.

T: But you have such a nice baby on your arm he wants to be cared for. Maybe you should have coffee in the dining car, you and the doll.

BB: OK (leaves the equipment to Eva).

This episode contains an extended period of yes/no quarrelling between Kalle and Eva about an attractive object (the conductor's bag). They are unable to find a solution to the conflict. Eva argues with reference to adult authority, but also in terms of principles ('Kalle has been [conductor] for so long'). Furthermore, she tries to find a solution by a play proposal ('you can be the baby's mother'), hinting at some kind of compromise by exchanging roles. Kalle, however, does not perceive any attractive alternatives. He only has access to those script possibilities connected with his present role. With limited access to the physical situation, his arguments are tied to this experience. They may seem egocentric, but he has little other choice. Only the teacher, pointing to script possibilities not immediately recognised by Kalle ('you have such a nice baby ... maybe you should have coffee in the dining car'), succeeds in solving the conflict. She expands the horizon of script meaning in a way that is attractive to all concerned. Play continues for a substantial period of time.

Conclusion

Togetherness in play is defined as joint presence and coordinated activity in the physical, social and symbolical contexts of play, resulting in a process of meaning co-construction. This interactionistic and contextual perspective has certain implications when trying to comprehend the difficulties in creating togetherness between players with functional differences, in this case specifically in terms of visual ability.

Firstly, *difference* rather than *disability* seems to create problems. Functional differences imply differences in information and affordance selection (Reed, 1993) and consequently in what is conceived of as potentially meaningful. What is at stake here are differences; not in individual characteristics, but in apprehension of the situation. All participants, blind as well as sighted, demonstrate limited ability, i.e. disability, in embracing the meaning of the others' proposals. Chosen examples illustrate how such differences restrict symbol co-construction. The reason for this is not the presence of some 'deviant individual', but diversity in information, social perception and representation of everyday reality.

Secondly, togetherness develops in coordinated meaning creation, but coordination and meaning may be in conflict. Where coordination demands that individual players refrain from what is genuinely meaningful for them, togetherness has to be implemented through other means. Such means may be power play, i.e. one participant's attempt to force someone else into compliance. As a result, verticality, as opposed to horizontality, is induced into the pattern of interaction. Verticality is indicated by persistent and rigid attitudes in negotiations or the use of threats, or even actual violence, though instances of the latter are very rare in the material referred to in this article. Irrespective of their outward character, such attempts must be regarded as symptoms. Beneath persistency is the inevitable need for meaning; behind power signals lies the defence of this meaning.

A further strategy in preserving meaningfulness is to withdraw from interaction, to establish a solitary play area. For the blind child, experiencing how attempts at influencing the common play project are frequently ignored, this seems to be a rational solution. Having established this, other's attempts at togetherness, be it invitations or entries, may easily be perceived as threats to sovereignty in this secluded realm. In line with this reasoning, solitude and a certain tendency to prefer adult interaction in many blind children's play is interpreted not as a disinterest in togetherness, but as the best compromise between the wish for social participation and the need for meaning.

Vertical togethernes s and sovereign solitude represent two contrasting solutions to the potential conflict between togetherness and meaningfulness in a pre-school group characterised by functional diversity. Neither solution satisfies the striving for equal and full participation. It is as if *attempts at* togetherness are paradoxically counteracted by the *conditions for* togetherness. Educational research as well as practice has to learn more about this. How are different forms of diversity affected by demands in the different contexts of play? How can educational planning and teacher intervention counteract situational demands which otherwise cause impediments to togetherness, turn diversity into conflict, create vertical status orders and promote withdrawal? Inclusive pre-school is in need of some answers.

References

Åm, E. (1993) *Leken-ur Barnets Perspektiv* (Stockholm, Natur och Kultur).

Bateson, G. (1955) A theory of play and fantasy, in: G. Bateson (Ed.) *Steps to an Ecology of Mind. Collected essays in anthropology, psychiatry, evolution and epistemology*, pp. 150–166 (Frogmore, St Albans, Paladin).

Corsaro, W.A. (1997) *The Sociology of Childhood* (Thousand Oaks, CA, Pine Forge Press).

Doyle, A.B. & Connolly, J. (1989) Negotiation and enactment in social pretend play: relations to social acceptance and social cognition. *Early Childhood Research Quarterly*, 4, pp. 289–302.

Gibson, J.J. (1979) *The Ecological Approach to Visual Perception* (Boston, MA, Houghton Mifflin).

Giffin, H. (1984) The coordination of meaning in the creation of a shared make-believe reality, in: I. Bretherton (Ed.) *Symbolic Play. The development of social understanding*, pp. 73–100 (London, Academic Press).

Guralnick, M. (1992) A hierarchical model for understanding children's peer-related social competence, in: S. Odom, S. McConnell & M. McEvoy (Eds) *Social Competence of Young Children with Disabilities*, pp. 37–64 (Baltimore, MD, Paul H. Brookes).

Guralnick, M.J. & Groom, J.M. (1988) Peer interactions in mainstreamed and specialized classrooms: a comparative analysis. *Exceptional Children*, 54, pp. 415–425.

Hartup, W.W. (1983) Peer relations, in: P.H. Mussen & E.M. Hetherington (Eds) *Handbook of Child Psychology*, Vol. 4, *Socialization, personality and social development*, pp. 103–196 (New York, NY, John Wiley & Sons).

Hartup, W.W. (1992) Peer relations in early and middle childhood, in: V. Van Hasselt & M. Hersen (Eds) *Handbook of Social Development: a lifespan perspective*, pp. 257–281 (New York, NY, Plenum Press).

Isheden, G., Abdollazadeh, A. & Farestveit, O.A. (1995) *Konflikt i Blinda och Seende Föreskolebarns Samspel*, Gruppen för Handikappforskning Report no. 6, Stockholm Universitet Pedagogiska Institutionen.

Janson, U. (1993) Preschool integration of handicapped children in Sweden, in: J.T. Sandvin & A. Frostad Fasting (Eds) *Intellectual Disability Research, Nordic Contributions*, Report no. 16/93, pp. 122–141 (Bodö, Nordlands-forskning).

Janson, U. (1999) Interaction and quality in inclusive preschool. Social play between blind and sighted children, in: *Interaction and Quality. Report of the CIDREE Collaborative Project on Early Childhood Education*, pp. 30–41 (Dundee, Scottish CCC).

Odom, S., McConnell, S. & McEvoy, M. (1992) Peer-related social competence and its significance for young children with disabilities, in: S. Odom, S. McConnell & M. McEvoy (Eds) *Social Competence of Young Children with Disabilities*, pp. 3–35 (Baltimore, MD, Paul H. Brookes).

Reed, E. (1993) The intention to use a specific affordance: a conceptual framework for psychology, in: R. Wozniak & K. Fischer (Eds) *Development in Context. Acting and thinking in specific environments* (Hillsdale, NJ, Erlbaum).

White, B.L. & Watts, J.C. (1973) *Experience and Environment. Major influences on the development of the young child* (Englewood Cliffs, NJ, Prentice Hall).

Winnicott, D.W. (1971) *Playing and Reality* (London, Tavistock).

Wood, E. & Attfield, J. (1996) *Play, Learning and the Early Childhood Curriculum* (London, Paul Chapman).

Chapter 7

'But I want to fly too!'

Girls and superhero play in the infant classroom

Jackie Marsh

Source: *J. Marsh, Gender and Education, 12(2), 209–220, 2000.*

Abstract

This article describes a study which was conducted in an inner-city school in the north of England, in a base which contained 57 children aged 6 and 7 years old. The purpose of the study was to explore the potential role of popular culture in the literacy curriculum. During the project, a socio-dramatic role-play area which was related to a popular superhero icon was set up in the classroom. Children's play in the area was recorded using a variety of methods, including field notes, video recording and photographs. Some of the previous research on superhero play has focused on the attraction the discourse has for boys or suggested that girls take on a non-female persona in such a play. The findings from this study suggest that superhero play is strongly attractive to girls, who explore agency and autonomy through such play and actively position themselves as females within a heroic discourse.

Introduction

Young children's fascination with superheroes and the incorporation of superhero narratives in play and writing have been explored in recent years (Paley, 1984; Kostelnik *et al.*, 1986; Sousa & Schneiderman, 1986; French, 1987; Dyson, 1994). Often, it is young boys' appropriation of the superhero discourse that has received critical attention (Paley, 1984; Davies, 1989; Clark, 1995; Jordan, 1995). However, this can mask the real interest some girls show in superhero narratives. This article outlines the findings of a research project which aimed to explore the potential role of popular culture in the literacy curriculum. The project was a successful venture for both children and staff in the school concerned (Marsh *et al.*, 1997) and provided some interesting insights into the lure of the superhero cult for children. For the girls, however, the project appeared to provide opportunities to challenge the usual boundaries constraining socio-dramatic role-play. This article outlines some of the responses made by the girls to the superhero discourse and discusses the implications of the introduction of such play into the classroom.

The case study took place in an inner-city school in the north of England, in a base which contained 57 children aged 6 and 7 years old. Twenty-eight of the children were girls and 29 were boys, and 38 of the children spoke English as an additional language. The children came from a variety of socio-economic backgrounds but the majority were from working-class families.

The study consisted of 10 days' observation of a role-play area which was constructed as the 'Batman[1] and Batwoman HQ'. The naming of 'Batwoman' was a deliberate attempt to construct the character as having equal status with Batman. Some of the children understood this:

Me: Why do you think I said the cave belonged to Batwoman as well as Batman?
Marcus: So that girls would have a turn.
Me: Why would that help them to have a turn?
Sajad: 'Cos if it's just Batman, they'd think, 'I can't do it'.
Edward: They'd think it's not for girls.

Data were gathered using field notes, video and the collection of children's writing within the cave. The number of literacy events children initiated was counted as well as the number of imaginative play activities the children engaged in. Semi-structured interviews were conducted with the teachers and a number of parents over the 10 days.

The cult of the superhero

Popular culture is a key feature of the leisure interests of many children, interests that are somewhat manipulated by the media and toy manufacturing industry. Children are attracted to the latest television series, video game or Disney video and are tempted by the commercial lure of related toys, books and comics. This 'commercialized supersystem' (Clark, 1995, p. 8) provides a rich source of imaginative play and narrative satisfaction for children (Hilton, 1996). Central to this consumerist universe is the superhero figure and we have seen a range of these characters enter the realm of popular culture over the years: Superman, Batman, Teenage Mutant Ninja Turtles, X-Men and Power Rangers amongst them.

A number of factors contribute to the dramatic appeal of the superhero figure to young children. Children can feel relatively powerless in their daily lives, regularly confronting the rules and regulations placed on them by parents, schools and society. Sousa & Schneiderman (1986), Kostelnik *et al.* (1986) and Kline (1993) suggest that children see superheroes as avenging this sense of powerlessness and serve as models for the kind of control they themselves want over a hostile environment. This is no new attraction for the human race. Myths and legends are full of powerful, omnipresent characters (French, 1987; Jordan, 1995). The figures in Greek myths are recognised as archetypes of the modern superhero (Coffin & Cohen, 1978; Kline, 1993) and some teachers have exploited this resonance in imaginative ways (Dyson, 1996). However, it is clear that there are equally pervasive symbols of benign, powerful individuals in cultures the world over, some of these with religious significance and others not. It would appear that superheroes fulfil a primeval function for the human race. Indeed, French (1987) asserts that:

> Jungian theory proposes a hero whose origins are rooted in the 'collective unconscious' which consists of a universal, inexhaustible collection of archetypes from which dreams, myths, fairy tales, epics and dramas are drawn.
>
> (French, 1987, p. 20)

Superheroes, then, may fulfil a deep-rooted need in the human psyche for the hope that humans can have some control over the chaotic forces of nature and evil. Children readily appropriate the struggles of superheroes as their own, using them as a cathartic force in the exploration of control in their own environment.

Children also appear to have a need to explore the world in terms of its opposed extremes: good/evil, male/female, right/wrong. Derrida (1967) suggests that these 'binary oppositions' govern our thinking and have pervaded the worlds of Western philosophy, the arts and sciences. It seems inevitable, then, that children explore these binaries in order to make sense of their world (Davies, 1997). As they grow older, they begin to deconstruct these oppositional discourses and reveal a world in which layers of meaning are woven into and around each other and nothing is as concrete or absolute as it first appears. This is the post-structuralist world. Children, however, live within the dualistic discourses of absolute right and wrong, good and evil and life and death. There are few opportunities as golden as superhero play for the enactment of these oppositions, both in terms of good/evil and male/female binaries. So it would appear that:

> In making use of popular and traditional cultural symbols (like Superman or Cinderella), children may position themselves within stories that reveal dominant ideological assumptions about categories of individuals and the relations between them.
>
> (Dyson, 1996, p. 472)

It is clear that the version of masculinity offered by superhero figures is particularly appealing to boys (Paley, 1984; Clark, 1995; Jordan, 1995). It is also clear that the cult of male superhero is repressive for boys, reducing the versions of masculinities on offer to them. It allows only one version of masculinity—strong, powerful, aggressive and usually anti-social. Achieving male personhood thus becomes a dichotomous process which, as Golden notes, 'seems to require a reduction in possible ways of being for boys ... at the same time as it promises the rewards of properly achieved maleness' (1994, p. 46).

If they provide this reductionist discourse for boys, what is on offer for girls? The male superhero figures live in a world where women are either wholly evil or wholly good. If they are wholly evil, they are to be resisted, hunted, captured and defeated. The good girls simper and whimper and if they are pretty enough, receive romantic attention from the heroes. The evil women at least manage some autonomous action in their characterisation but are usually portrayed as desexualised, physically unattractive characters. Female heroes, on the other hand, manage to be active and brave at the same time as looking like a Barbie doll. She-Ra, Wonder Woman and the like race around with silicon-like curves. Of course, they are not as brave and strong as the boys and when in direct competition with a man they are relegated to the category of 'girl' (Supergirl, Bat Girl). These female icons have not stirred the same passion in girls as the figures related to, for instance, My Little Pony and Polly Pocket narratives. Many have interpreted this as a lack of interest by girls in the superhero narrative. However, this lack of interest may be related to the fact that the female superheroes are generally located in patriarchal sites of power struggles and violence. Female superhero figures have been contextualised in a stereotypically masculine environment, an environment in which few girls have any meaningful interest. This is not surprising, given that the superhero discourse is primarily produced by men, for men and boys. As Luke (1998) points out:

> Cultural industries have a long history of male cultural productions of feminine stereotypes and misrepresentations which conceptualize women primarily either as objects of male adornment, pursuit and domination, or as mindless domestic drudges, brain-dead bimbos or saintly supermoms.
> (Luke, 1998, p. 19)

Dawkins (1991) suggests that if the male domination of the superhero discourse is challenged, girls would more than respond to the invitation to join in:

> Like many aspects of our daily existence, superhero play leaves girls on the fringe. If we become involved in the play, redirecting and rewriting the scripts, as suggested by the most recent early childhood writers on

the subject, we can seize the opportunity to both reduce the aggressive element and provide significant roles for the girls.

(Dawkins, 1991, p. 7)

One only has to consider the lure of icons such as the Spice Girls to understand that girls too have a need to identify with gendered symbols. Unfortunately, as we have seen, most of the time these symbols serve only to reinforce harmful stereotypes. Thus, what has the potential for female empowerment could become another tool of repression unless children are encouraged to question these images as well as enjoy aspects of them. This study found that, once the masculinist nature of the superhero discourse was dislocated and when presented with positive images of females as active agents, girls demonstrated a high level of interest in the superhero narrative.

Batwomen in action

The 'Bat cave' shared a space between two classes in an open-plan base. It was a small area, constructed from drapes and screens in order to produce a cavern-like effect. The main aim of the research project was to encourage literacy practices in the role-play area and therefore relevant resources were placed within it. The cave contained two desks, a computer, writing materials (notepads, pens, pencils, lined and unlined paper, two blank books labelled 'Batman's Diary' and 'Batwoman's Diary') and reading materials (maps, comics, messages, instructions). There was a dressing-up rack which contained home-made tabards, commercially produced Batman outfits, a cloak and a hat. Part of the way through the project a cardboard 'Batmobile' (the car used by Batman), which was made by the children, was placed in the cave. The children had contributed to the setting up of the cave, suggesting a range of resources for it and throughout the project they continued to produce new items to place in it (e.g. maps, radios).

When the cave was finally ready for its first superheroes, the children spent some time discussing the possibilities it offered. All the resources in the cave were introduced to them and suggestions were made by children, researcher and teachers as to their possible uses. Research by Morrow & Rand (1991) has indicated that when young children are given adult guidance about how to use literacy-related resources in role-play areas, there is an increase in the number of literacy-related events taking place there. Before taking part in the role-play, the children spent some time discussing the Batman character and the types of activity engaged in by the characters in the television programmes and films they had seen. Extracts from a Batman film were watched and discussed. This was important in order to ensure that all children could engage with the discourse when playing in the cave. The 'Bat cave' was firmly introduced to the children as a place where both girls and boys could take on superhero identities and the sexist nature of some of the video extracts seen was discussed by the children. The children were clear that girls could be Batwomen. Throughout the project, the children were introduced to selected images and texts which portrayed women in an active role, e.g. extracts in comics which featured characters such as Batgirl and She-Ra. Apart from this prior groundwork, the children were given no specific instructions about what to do in the cave as it was a place for child-directed play.

It was clear from the start that the girls were strongly attracted to the cave. On the first morning that it was set up, one teacher asked the children who would like to go into the cave. Almost all of the children in the class put their hand up. During the 10 days, the class teachers kept a high level of control over who entered the cave during the timetabled sessions as almost everyone wanted a turn. This may account for the fact that the girls visited the cave almost as often as the boys (see Fig. 7.1).

However, this level of interest by the girls was demonstrated even when entrance to the cave was not controlled, such as during playtimes:

> 10.25 and the cave is packed! I've decided to let the children decide when it is too full during playtimes and presumably they will not enter if there is no space. I thought that may mean that girls get pushed out but Ayesha, Saira and Rosewana are well ensconced in there! Josie and Natasha have also entered and are looking through the contents of the desk. That's five girls and four boys in so far.
>
> (Field notes, 9 January 1997)

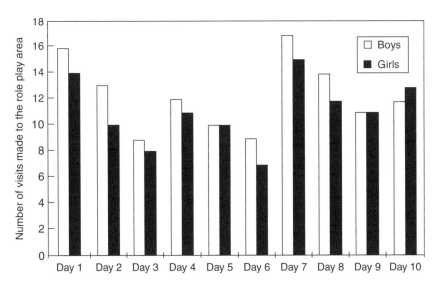

Figure 7.1 Comparison of the number of visits made to the role-play area by boys and girls.

> Girls were desperate to get in today at playtime. At one point, at least 6 girls were in there, jostling to grab whatever costumes and writing materials they could find!
>
> (Field notes, 15 January 1997)

There have been other studies which have identified girls' interest in superhero play. Singer & Singer (1981), in a study of young children's play, found that girls and boys both took part in dramatic play which focused on superheroes. Boys' level of superhero play was only marginally higher than that of the girls in the study. They state:

> Girls are moving closer to boys than ever before in their identification with heroic figures, adventurous achievement, and feigned aggression ... Even more specifically we can identify a special effect of television: the introduction of female superheroines, 'Wonder Woman', 'Bionic Woman', and 'Charlie's Angels'. Girls do seem to be identifying with such figures in make-believe although they play at male superhero roles as well.
>
> (Singer & Singer, 1981, p. 81)

Golden (1994) examined the narrative writing of children aged 6–9 years old and suggested that some of the girls found the position of male hero very desirable:

> As 'technologies of the self', the stories seemed to enable these girls imaginatively to construct and take pleasure in heroic selves, and through these selves explore themes such as love, adventure, courage, power and activity in the world.
>
> (Golden, 1994, p. 46)

In a study which involved the close observation of a class of children negotiating roles for their 'story-dramas', Dyson (1994, 1997) documented the desperate attempts of some girls to be included in the boys' superhero narratives. The boys persistently refused them entry to the narratives on equal grounds, assigning them minor, stereotypically feminine roles. The girls eventually responded by writing their own superhero narratives in which they themselves took key roles.

The fact that the cave contained so many literacy-related items may have been an enticing factor for the girls and legitimated their entry into it. There has been work which suggests that girls are more attracted to literacy activities than boys (Millard, 1997; Qualifications and Curriculum Authority, 1998), and in this study, girls did spend much of their time in the cave writing and reading. However, the difference in the number of acts of reading and writing engaged in by boys and girls was not significant. Over a period of 10 days, girls were engaged in 371 literacy events, in contrast to the 357 literacy events undertaken by boys. Nevertheless, there were differences in the nature of the reading and writing practices of boys and girls. Overall, boys tended to write short messages to the police and the Joker. If they did write longer narratives in 'Batman's diary', they focused on Batman as the heroic, solo character, saving the world from evil forces. Girls, however, tended to write longer letters to Batman, the police and the Joker. On these occasions, the writing the girls produced in the cave usually placed Batwoman in a supportive role to Batman:

> Batwoman and Batman they went looking for the Joker so the Joker she shouted Batman so he came running she told him that I know where the Joker is behind that wall she said. So he jumped over the wall and he had a fight with him at last he died.
>
> (Shakiel's writing, 17 January 1997)

When Batwoman was working autonomously in the stories and diary extracts, she was primarily rescuing children or old women. This supports evidence from other research, which has found that both girls and boys usually make males more active in their stories than females (Romatowski & Trepanier-Street, 1987; Marsh, 1998). That is, indeed, if boys include female characters at all. Without exception, girls wrote in *Batwoman's Diary* and boys wrote in *Batman's Diary*. At the end of the study, *Batwoman's Diary* contained 10 pieces of text. Batman featured in three of the narratives. *Batman's Diary* contained six pieces of text. None of them mentioned Batwoman.

The boys engaged in twice as much imaginative play as the girls (see Fig. 7.2).

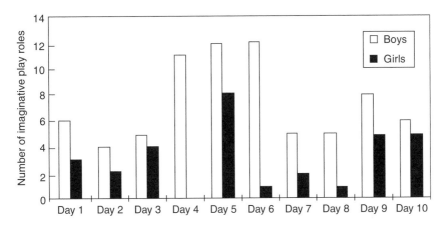

Figure 7.2 Comparison of involvement in imaginative play events by boys and girls.

In this case, 'imaginative play' was defined as those instances in which one or more children engaged in active, physical play that involved the creation of imaginative scenarios. However, it could be argued that all of the children who entered the cave were engaged in imaginative play all of the time. Without exception, every child who entered the cave dressed as a character in the discourse. Once dressed in Batman, Batwoman or Joker regalia, they either engaged in active imaginative play or sat to write and read in role. Only one girl in the two classes did not want to enter the cave in the 6 weeks it was *in situ*. The other 56 children all enthusiastically entered into the scenario at various times, taking on the role of Batman, Batwoman or the Joker each time they entered the cave. As Fig. 7.2 indicates, there were 74 instances of active imaginative play engaged in by boys. Girls took part in 31 instances. Comparing the total numbers of girls and boys engaged in this type of play, it was found that 24 boys (83% of the boys in the two classes) were responsible for these 74 instances, and 16 girls were involved in the 31 imaginative play events involving females (57% of the girls in the classes).

There were times when girls were keen to take on an active role as a superhero, as this extract from the video demonstrates:

Saira: I found the Joker! I found the Joker!
             [*Saira grabs Ayesha. Ayesha gets herself free, grabs the 'Batfile' and rushes off. She does not want to be the Joker. Saira jumps about, obviously being a superhero who is flying about. She grabs a chair and pulls it over to Adil who is writing, oblivious to the adventures of the superhero next to him.*]
Saira: Whoooooooosh!
             [*Saira stands on the chair and jumps off, arms flapping. Adil writes on, unperturbed. His friend Moshin comes over.*]
Moshin: The Joker is dead man, look behind you!
             [*Moshin leans on Adil's shoulder and shouts in his ear. Adil continues writing. Saira appears next to him.*]
Saira: Look behind you!
             [*Adil gives up and looks round at what is happening in the dressing up rack.*]

Some time later in the same session:

             [*The boys—Adil, Moshin and Zoaib are on the computer. Saira is putting the long black pair of gloves on. Ansa is watching her.*]
Saira: I'm gonna get the Joker now. Come on, we have to go and get the Joker.
             [*Saira rushes off on another adventure whilst the boys write.*]

The appeal of the superhero figure was widespread amongst the girls and it attracted children that the teachers had not expected to be interested in the theme. Ayesha was one such child. When asked before the start of the study if Ayesha was likely to enter a cave constructed as a Batman and Batwoman HQ, the teacher had said:

> I think that Ayesha would go in the area if it was a kind of more feminine theme. I think she didn't go in much when it was a space station and those sorts of things.

The average number of visits to the cave was four. Ayesha visited it seven times over the timetabled sessions and was often there during playtimes. She actively took up the role of Batwoman each time she entered the cave, sometimes engaging in imaginative play and sometimes involved solely in literacy activities.

The girls always dressed up as Batwoman when they entered the cave. There were four tabards with the Batman logo and one long green velvet cloak and hat. Many girls wore the tabards, but the main attraction for some girls became the cloak and hat, which they rushed to put on, even if it meant that the boys would try to confine them to the role of the Joker (the villain):

> Natasha is now resplendent in her favourite garb of green cloak and 'fur' collar. Wilf and James attempt to force her to be the Joker, but she refuses. This happened to her with Marcus earlier today. They persist and she eventually comes over to me and asks me to intervene.
>
> (Field notes, 8 January 1997)

The girls insisted that the cloak and hat belonged exclusively to them:

> Neil enters. 'Can I be Robin?' he asks eagerly. No one replies. He goes over to the dressing-up rack and puts on the green cloak. The girls have been watching his every move and at this Natasha rushes over. 'That's Batwoman's cloak!' she shouts and grabs it. Neil's loss is Saira's gain, and she puts the cloak on and rushes about a bit.
>
> (Field notes, 9 January 1997)

As a result, the boys eventually avoided the cloak as if it were contaminated:

> Josh and Sajad are putting on clothes. 'You have this', Josh tells Sajad, giving him the green cloak. 'No, that's girls!' Sajad replies, in horror.
>
> (Field notes, 15 January 1997)

This was a clear example of 'borderwork' (Thorne, 1993) or 'category maintenance work' (Davies, 1989).

Occasionally, the girls assumed identities of female superheroes other than Batwoman:

> Natasha is rushing about, green cloak behind her and arms open. 'I'm Supergirl!' she shouts.
>
> (Field notes, 15 January 1997)

Unlike in the Singer & Singer (1981) study, the girls did not emulate male superheroes. They were always female heroes but not necessarily always Batwoman. Golden (1994) asserts that assuming the position of hero involves agency and a necessity for girls to take up a position of becoming 'not females'. This is, she suggests, a result of the dualistic discourse which positions the male hero as active agent in opposition to females. In this study, some girls took on the persona of Batwoman and emphasised the nature of the active, powerful female discourse:

> Safeena and Naida are in full gear. Safeena has appropriated the green cloak again. Safeena runs over to the Batmobile and jumps in. 'Quick, get in! We've got to catch him!' Naida jumps in behind her. Marcus comes over and tries to get in the Batmobile. 'No! Get out! You can't be a Batwoman! You be the man Joker kills and we help you. Lie down over there!' Marcus moves away, refusing to be part of a narrative in which a boy plays second fiddle.
>
> (Field notes, 17 January 1997)

In these instances, the role of Batwoman did not appear to be constrained within the usual hegemonic discourses which result in highly gendered role-play. At these times, the girls were free to carry out their fantasies of power and control without any hindrance from the boys and the HQ appeared to provide them with an unusual opportunity to explore powerful adventures in which they were agents of their own destinies:

> Safeena, Nisha and Mena are all dressed up and ready to go. They write a note to the Joker. 'Say, "We're gonna get you"', Safeena suggests. Nisha runs about, cape spread out, on some private mission. Note completed, they all rush over to the Batmobile. 'You drive, I'll get the map', Safeena tells the others. Marcus enters 'Who's the Joker?' 'Nobody. Go away', Safeena tells him.
>
> (Field notes, 9 January 1997)

The desire by girls to take part in non-stereotypical superhero play was generally resisted by the boys:

> Neil and Shazaib are driving after some imaginary villain. They get out of the car and jump about, making 'whooshing' noises. Nisha has entered and put on the green cloak and hat. Neil tries to push her out of the way

and says, 'Get in the back. You wait and tell us when he's coming!' 'But I want to fly too!' insists Nisha. She moves away from them and jumps onto the chair. She jumps off into their path. Neil looks at her with a mixture of disgust and frustration. 'Come on, let's get out of here', he tells Shazaib and they get back into the 'Batmobile'.

(Field notes, 15 January 1997)

In this example, Nisha asserted her right to engage in the superhero play. There were other instances in which girls did not feel able to resist the reductive gendered positionings introduced by boys:

Natasha is 'climbing' up the wall using her 'Bat rope and anchor', her cape swinging behind her. She is humming the theme tune 'Na, na, na, na; Na, na, na, na, Batman!' Abdul rushes up. 'You the Joker! You the Joker!' The boys are always wanting to assign that position to the person they feel has the least power in the group. Natasha resists, 'No, I'm not! I'm Batwoman!' Nashid joins in, 'We're Batman. You be Joker! You be Joker and we get you!' Natasha gives up. 'All right, but no hitting'.

(Field notes, 17 January 1997)

At times, the girls actively took up the position of Batwoman but placed the discourse themselves within a constricting narrative that conformed to the usual binary pattern of male/female, strong/weak, active/passive. As in the example of the writing in the diaries, the girls who were acting out superhero roles sometimes placed Batwoman in a subordinate role to Batman:

Shezana and Naida enter the cave.

Shezana: Where's the computer?
Naida: That Joker took it.
Shezana: Joker can't come in here.
Naida: Yes he can, because we don't lock the door. But outside, outside, the gate is locked.
[*Shezana picks up the telephone.*]
Shezana: Hello Batman? Be quick! The Joker's took our computer. Be quick! Bye!
[*She starts flying about, then sits down to write.*]
Shezana: [*writing in notebook*] I'm telling Batman. He's resting. How do you spell 'resting'?
[*Naida spells it out for her. Shezana gets back onto the telephone.*]
Shezana: Batman! The Joker's taken our chair!' [*Reading from notebook*] Children at school and Batwoman. Yeah! Come quick 'cos he's taken the children's computer! Be quick then!
[*She puts the phone down and resumes writing in the notebook.*]

(Field notes, 10 January 1997)

The Batmen never relied on Batwomen in this way and, as we have seen, were generally resistant to girls getting involved in imaginative play at all as active agents. They preferred to direct the girls into passive roles, which did not allow them to have any control over the direction and nature of the play. Most of the girls actively resisted this. When the girls did insist on being autonomous Batwomen, the boys appeared to be resigned to letting them get on with it but made it clear that the play was to be kept separate:

> *Khaliq and Marcus have been sitting in the Batmobile for some time, reading comics. They get out to get their milk. The girls get into the Batmobile quickly as the boys go out. Shameem gets in at the end.*

Ruby: You drive!

Shameem: I need to look at the map. He is heading to the cave. We've got to catch him before he gets them. We'll catch him too.

Ruby: You'll look for the Riddler.

            [*Khaliq and Marcus re-enter the cave.*]

Khaliq: This is Batman's cave!

Ruby: We're looking for the Riddler.

Khaliq: Marcus, make them a car over there.

            [*Marcus makes a car consisting of two chairs. The girls move over and the boys get into the Batmobile, completely ignoring the girls' ensuing play.*]

(Field notes, 10 January 1997)

Like the boys, when engaged in active imaginative play the girls spent some of their time chasing after a villain, usually the Joker. In most of the boys' imaginative play, there was a need for a villain who could be physically handled and chased. However, the girls usually raced after an imaginary villain, the mainstay of their play focusing on the needs of the people who had to be rescued. The concept of a flesh and blood villain who could be wrestled to the ground did not appear to offer them the same emotional satisfaction that it gave to the boys. The girls got involved only occasionally in the physical handling of enemies, whereas the boys spent much of their time capturing the hapless children they had forced into the role of the Joker. If the girls did capture a child as the Joker and put her or him into prison, then they usually ensured that their prisoner had food and drink. The Batmen never did this. It was therefore clear throughout the 6 weeks of the project that there were differences within the gendered superhero discourses. Overall, Batwomen were generally focused on the active rescue of victims (often children) and maintaining good relationships with their co-heroes whilst Batmen were more concerned with the thrill of the chase and capture of villains.

Some question the extent to which girls should develop any of the characteristics associated with the powerful and adventurous superhero narratives (Hayes, 1994). The violence and aggression which appear to be an integral part of these warrior-hero discourses is something that we should be concerned to move boys away from, not girls towards. Moreover, apart from the vio-lence and sexism inherent in such discourses, there are issues relating to the endemic racism and xenophobia in children's popular culture, which are often ignored. 'Baddies' are frequently dark-skinned; only a few superhero narratives contain positive images of black characters. In addition, some villains speak with non-American accents, accentuating their 'foreignness'. Should not we be concerned to move all children away from these negative stereotypes? Such a move would also challenge the market forces that control and to some extent create these gendered narratives. However, the powerful attraction of these discourses for children suggests that such a course is not that simple. We need to involve children in challenging the inherent ideologies whilst acknowledg-ing the attraction that popular culture holds for them. In encouraging girls actively to position themselves within a heroic discourse, we can allow them to explore issues relating to autonomy and independence.

Conclusion

It is clear that the Bat cave provided girls with opportunities to move beyond the stereotypical framework operating in the highly gendered world of the primary classroom. Although the nature of the female superhero was very different from that of the male, many girls did engage in active play in which they were agents of action rather than passive onlookers. As suggested earlier, the major appeal of the cave for the girls could have been the opportunity to become involved in reading and writing activities. The superhero iconography was attractively framed for the girls, which enabled them to enter the discourse. However, once in it, there where times when they moved away from literacy practices and became involved in superhero narratives and imaginative play. Thus, the data contain images of girls flying about, jumping off chairs, driving Batmobiles and capturing villains. This is very different from the vision of girls involved in superhero play presented in some research:

> Thus it was not surprising to find that roles requiring someone to be strong and aggressive usually were played by boys ... As Superman they stop bullets with their bare hands ... Very seldom do girls accept such powerful roles ... They prefer weak, subordinate roles in which they can flutter about the room as sweet little angels, without anyone seeing them.
> (Wegener-Spohring, 1989, p. 45)

In order for girls to take more active roles in heroic discourses, teachers need to ensure that they create the conditions in which this can happen. Girls need to feel safe and be given the permission and space in which to explore these roles. Intervention in such play is also needed if boys are to be challenged into experimenting with alternative versions of masculinity (Jordan, 1995). Unless we try to shape the discourse in this way, girls and boys will continue to use superhero play to carve out gendered identities which cast in stone the stereotypes that are an integral part of children's popular culture.

Note

1 Batman is a character who originated in an American comic strip in the 1930s. The character has achieved iconic status over the years and has been the feature of television cartoons, television series, films, computer games, web sites, videos, books, comics and related merchandise. Batman is a superhero who outwits a variety of criminals and evil crooks, including one named the Joker. There is no Batwoman character in the discourse but there is a minor character named Batgirl. The Batmobile, mentioned later in the article, is a car specially designed for Batman.

References

Clark, E. (1995) Popular culture: images of gender as reflected through young children's story, paper presented at the *Annual Joint Meeting of the Popular Culture Association/American Culture Association*, Philadelphia. ERIC document no: ED 388966.

Coffin, T.P. & Cohen, H. (1978) *The Parade of Heroes* (New York, Anchor Press/Doubleday).

Davies, B. (1989) *Frogs and Snails and Feminist Tales: preschool children and gender* (Sydney, Allen & Unwin).

Davies, B. (1997) Constructing and deconstructing masculinities through critical literacy, *Gender and Education*, 9, pp. 9–30.

Dawkins, M. (1991) Hey dudes, what's the rap? A plea for leniency towards superhero play, *Australian Journal of Early Childhood*, 16, pp. 3–8.

Derrida, J. (1967) *Speech and Phenomena* (Chicago, Illinois, Northwestern University Press).

Dyson, A.H. (1994) The Ninjas, the X-Men, and the Ladies: playing with power and identity in an urban primary school, *Teachers College Record*, 96, pp. 219–239.

Dyson, A.H. (1996) Cultural constellations and childhood identities: on Greek gods, cartoon heroes, and the social lives of schoolchildren, *Harvard Educational Review*, 66, pp. 471–495.

Dyson, A.H. (1997) *Writing Superheroes: contemporary childhood, popular culture and classroom literacy* (New York, Teachers College Press).

French, J. (1987) *A Historical Study of Children's Heroes and Fantasy Play* (Research Report) (Boise, Idaho, Boise State University, School of Education. ERIC Document No: ED 310885).

Golden, J. (1994) Heroes and gender: children reading and writing, *English in Australia*, Part 110, pp. 42–52.

Hayes, S. (1994) Strong girls, brutal boys: contradictions in reading heroic action, *English in Australia*, 107, pp. 5–11.

Hilton, M. (Ed.)(1996) *Potent Fictions: children's literacy and the challenge of popular culture* (London, Routledge).

Jordan, E. (1995) Fighting boys and fantasy play: the construction of masculinity in the early years of school, *Gender and Education*, 7, pp. 69–86.

Kline, S. (1993) *Out of the Garden: toys and children's culture in the age of TV marketing* (London, Verso).

Kostelnick, M.J., Whiren, A.P. & Stein, L.C. (1986) Living with He-Man: managing superhero fantasy play, *Young Children*, 41, pp. 3–9.

Luke, C. (1998) Pedagogy and Authority: lessons from feminist and cultural studies, postmodernism and feminist pedagogy, in: D. Buckingham (1998) *Teaching Popular Culture: beyond radical pedagogy* (London, UCL Press).

Marsh, J. (1998) Gender and writing in the infant school: writing for a gender specific audience, *English in Education*, 32, pp. 10–18.

Marsh, J., Payne, L. & Atkinson, S. (1997) Batman and Batwoman in the classroom, *Primary English*, 3, 2, pp. 8–11.

Millard, E. (1997) *Differently Literate: boys, girls and the schooling of literacy* (London, Falmer Press).

Morrow, L.M. & Rand, M. (1991) Preparing the classroom to promote literacy during play, in: J.F. Christie (Ed.) *Play and Early Literacy Development* (Albany, NY, State University of New York Press).

Paley, V.G. (1984) *Boys and Girls: superheroes in the doll corner* (Chicago, IL, University of Chicago Press).

Qualifications and curriculum authority (QCA) (1998) *Can Do Better: raising boys' achievement in English* (London, Qualifications and Curriculum Authority).

Romatowski, J. & Trepanier-Street, M.L. (1987) Gender perceptions: an analysis of children's creative writing, *Contemporary Education*, 59, pp. 17–19.

Singer, J.L. & Singer, D.G. (1981) *Television, Imagination and Aggression: a study of preschoolers* (Hillsdale, NJ, Lawrence Erlbaum Associates).

Sousa, C. & Schneiderman, J. (1986) Preschoolers and superheroes—a dangerous duo, *Early Years*, November/December, pp. 75–77.

Thorne, B. (1993) *Gender Play: girls and boys in school* (Buckingham, Open University Press).

Wegener-Spohring, G. (1989) War toys and aggressive games, *Play and Culture*, 2, 1, pp. 35–47.

Chapter 8

Symbolic play through the eyes and words of children

Janet K. Sawyers and Nathalie Carrick

Source: *J. K. Sawyers and N. Carrick, Symbolic play through the eyes and words of children, in D. E. Lytle (ed.), Play and Educational Theory and Practice, US: Ablex Publishing Corporation.*

Introduction

Previous research on children's symbolic play has relied almost exclusively on adults' (parents, teachers, reseachers) interpretations of children's play. The purpose of this study was to expand our understanding of symbolic play through the eyes and words of children.

In their comprehensive review of research on play, Rubin, Fein, and Vandenberg (1983) noted the lack of knowledge about children's interpretations of symbolic play. In identifying questions concerning both content and methodolgy needed to advance our understanding of play, they suggested providing children with videotaped samples of children engaged in "make-believe" play to determine their "conceptions" of pretense. This methodology provided a different and insightful way to examine children's play.

Fantuzzo, Coolahan, Mendez, McDermott, & Sutton-Smith (1998) recently developed the Penn Interactive Peer Play-Scale. It was created in response to the need to "identify quality practices that are informed by valid assessment of the developmental needs and capabilities of young children" (p. 411) noted by the National Association for the Education of Young Children. They join a growing number of researchers concerned with the development of a contextually relevant understanding of children's behaviors (Pelligrini, 1992, cited in Fantuzzo et al., 1998). Thus, the concept of a contextually relevant understanding of play was another focus of this study.

Following the lead of Rubin *et al.* (1983) and Fantuzzo *et al.* (1998), children were directly asked questions regarding their symbolic play. Children were interviewed while watching previously videotaped segments of their symbolic play from their classroom. The parents and teachers were subsequently interviewed to gain further insight into the children's symbolic play. The interview questions were based on developmental aspects of symbolic play found in the literature.

Literature review: Elements of play

The elements of pretend play include themes, roles, object substitutions, and differentiation between fantasy and reality. An awareness of previous studies on these elements is necessary to set the stage for interpreting data in the present study.

Themes

The theme of a play scenario is defined by the events of the play, including children's actions and what they announce the play to be. Within the theme of the play is a script. A script is the action plan for the theme (Garvey, 1977).

Two theories explain scripts, script theory and emotive theory. In script theory (Shank & Abelson, 1977) it is thought that children's intentions during group pretend play are to imitate events that they have experienced. To do this successfully, children must share a common knowledge base about the script for dialogue with the play partner (Corasaro, 1983; Nelson & Gruendel, 1979; Nelson & Seidman, 1984; Short-Meyerson & Abbeduto, 1997; Snow, Shonkoff, Lee, & Levin, 1986). Emotive theory claims that during pretend play, children focus more on enacting events that allow them to express emotions (Fein, 1986, 1987, 1989, 1991). Fein's emotive theory suggests that children know that pretend play is not real; therefore, they are allowed to enact events that either have occurred but become distorted or are simply imagined. Children enact these events because there is a strong affective power to them. Consequently, in play they are able to play with the emotion of the event without actually feeling the emotion directly. Children can adjust the intensity of the emotion by either playing the event longer and in more detail or ending the play.

Roles

During the enactment of a theme, children engage in role-play. "Role" has been defined as a "behavior in which the child simulates the identity or characteristics of another person" (Fein, 1981, p. 101). Garvey (1977) identified four types of role-play: functional, relational, stereotype, and fictional. Functional, the first type, is determined by the script. The player performs the given function like serving food or driving a car. The second type is the relational role representing a family member, a friend, or a pet. Garvey labeled the third type stereotype because it is highly predictable and based on an occupation (cowboy or policeman). Roles taken from a story or television are labeled fictional. The third and fourth roles are both character roles. Garvey also noted an additional role that the children did not enact but rather talked about. She called this the "absent" role (imaginary person on the phone). With development in perspective-taking skills (Creasey, Jarvis, & Berk, 1998; Rubin & Pepler,

1980) and decentration (Fein, 1981), children are able to negotiate changes in the type of roles enacted from familiar and domestic to more fictional ones (Fein, 1981).

Object substitution

Object substitution follows a developmental sequence (Copple, Cocking, & Matthews, 1984; Lillard, 1993a; Trawick-Smith, 1990; Ungerer, Zelazo, Kearsely, & O'Leary, 1981; Vygotsky, 1978). By 12 months of age, children can symbolically transform a common object from its original purpose to a pretend purpose. At this age, children need an object that highly resembles the object of pretense. For example, they can pretend to drink from a real cup. The complexity of their substitution skills matures, and after the age of 3, children begin to decrease their reliance on the realism of the object for pretense. By school age, children are able to represent an object through gestures (Fein, 1975, 1981; Lillard, 1993a).

Fein (1975) and Matthews (1977) researched different levels of object substitution. By combining Fein's (1975) and Matthews' (1977) results, it appears that there are four levels of substitution: functional, high-level prototypical, low-level prototypical, and insubstantial. Functional substitution occurs when the child uses the object in the way that it is intended (a stick as a stick). High prototypical-level substitution occurs when the pretend object closely resembles the real object (a stick as a spoon). A low prototypical-level substitution occurs when the pretend object does not resemble the real object at all (a stick as a baby). Insubstantial substitutions occur when there is no object present, but the child pretends that there is something there (announces that there is a stick or moves hand to represent a stick). The use of these levels increases with age. However, once a new level has been attained, the lower-level substitutions may still be present in the child's play.

Fantasy and reality

The literature on children's understanding of fantasy and reality is extensive. Since the concept of children's understanding of fantasy and reality is extremely complex, blanket statements regarding children's ability to distinguish between the two can be misleading (Taylor, 1997). One reason is that the tasks utilized in the studies reveal only a fraction of the complete picture. For example, children are able to distinguish between mental images and real objects (Flavell, Flavell, & Green, 1987; Harris, Brown, Marriot, Whittal, & Harmer, 1991; Wellman & Estes, 1986); however, in Taylor and Howell's (1973) study, children had difficulty saying that a cartoon image in a picture was part of fantasy. Johnson and Harris (1994) asked children to imagine an item in a box and nothing in a control box. Children opened the box with the imagined item more often than the control box. On the other hand, Wooley and Phellps (as cited in Wooley, 1997) used a similar technique but added a consequential behavioral test at the end. After children were asked to imagine a pencil in a box, a stranger entered the test room and asked if there was a pencil that she could use. In this situation only a few children actually looked inside the box to give her the imagined pencil.

It appears that any emotions related to the items being used must also be considered in the children's performance on such tasks. In Samuels and Taylor's (1994) study, older children could differentiate between pictures depicting neutral, real, and fantasy situations as possibly occurring in real life, but younger children could not. However, when the photographs elicited frightening emotions, children were not able to make correct distinctions. Samuels and Taylor interpreted the children's statement that the frightening photographs representing real events could not happen in real life as a strategy for coping with their fear. The children in Harris, *et al.*'s (1991) study who had just imagined a scary object in a box did not want to be left alone in the room with that box. See Wooley (1997) for an extensive review of the literature on children's understanding of fantasy and reality.

Although children may have performed differently during experiments, their typical behavior during pretend play indicates that they do not confuse fantasy with reality (Lillard, 1993a). During pretend play, children can layer the pretend world onto the real world without losing the properties of the real world (Lillard, 1993a). For example, a child pretending that a block is a cookie will not attempt to eat the block. They are able to act among the layers of pretense and reality.

Children's understanding of pretense

Lillard (1993b, 1994, 1996) has researched an interesting side to children's understanding of pretense. She suggests that children see pretense as more of an action than a mental representation. During pretense, one creates an image of an object (a telephone) and places it on a real object (a block). The real object is then treated like the image of the desired object (telephone); a child puts the block to ear and speaks into it. Lillard makes the distinction that the major requirement for pretense to exist is the mental image of the telephone, not the action of putting it to the child's ear and speaking (Lillard, 1993b).

Lillard (1996) had children categorize different concepts as either mental (thinking, imaging, pretending, etc.) or physical (falling over, etc.) as requiring the mind, body, or both. Children between the ages of 3 and 6 said that mental acts required the mind more often than the body. However, there was a difference among the mental acts. Pretense received the lowest number of responses for needing a mind. This shows that some of the children had not yet made the link between needing mental representations during pretense. In follow-up questions, a few young children explained that pretense required "one's own body, an outfit, or a friend" (p. 1720), all of which are physical items.

In another study by Lillard (1993a), 4- and 5-year-olds were presented with a troll doll and were told that the troll did not know what a rabbit is and had never seen a rabbit. The experimenter made the troll move up and down, said the troll was hopping like a rabbit, and then asked the children if the troll was pretending to be a rabbit. Only 37% of 4-year-olds and 68% of 5-year-olds correctly answered that the troll was not pretending. The other children, who incorrectly answered the question, ignored the need for the troll to make a mental representation of a rabbit hopping in order to be actually pretending to be a rabbit.

In a later experiment in the study, the children were shown a picture of a child either thinking or not thinking about an action followed by another picture of the child enacting or not enacting the same action. Most children said that the child was pretending in the second picture, even when they were presented with the first picture of a child not thinking about the action and a second picture of the child enacting the same action. Both experiments show how children do not view pretending as primarily requiring mental representation.

Methodology

This study was conducted in a university laboratory preschool in Virginia. The selected children were in a morning program that operates for three and a half hours, five days a week. The school was equipped with video cameras in each classroom. The cameras, mounted on the walls, were operated from a location outside the classrooms. This placement of the cameras allowed the first author to see, record, and follow the selected children as they moved about the classroom in a non-intrusive manner.

Selection of participants

Teachers of a classroom with 4- and 5-year-olds were asked to nominate children who were frequently observed engaging in symbolic play and who had the verbal skills and propensity to respond to questions about their play. After conducting informal observations of the four children nominated, the first author chose two children for inclusion.

Participants

Hannah, a loquacious 5 year, 1 month old girl, frequently engaged in symbolic play with her friends or by herself with stuffed animals that she brought from home. She was a dominant figure in her group of friends, but not overly directive. She was able to initiate and follow different symbolic play episodes. Her play revolved around nurturing themes of play, including taking care of dolls, building homes for stuffed animals, and pretending to be mother or baby with her friends.

Skeeter was an active 5 year, 6 month old boy who appeared to prefer symbolic play to all other activities in the classroom. Skeeter had a large vocabulary and is very articulate. He rarely engaged in the art-based activities. He used the contructive play activities such as making an airport out of blocks to support his symbolic play. He was observed playing different themes with a diverse group of children. The two most frequent themes in Skeeter's play were emergency/recovery play and play involving "chemicals" in a "laboratory".

Procedures

Videotaping

The first author spent one week in the classroom of the target children interacting with all the children. This allowed time for her to build rapport with Hannah and Skeeter before videotaping their play. This rapport was believed necessary for the children to feel comfortable during the interview sessions.

The naturally occurring symbolic play of both Hannah and Skeeter was videotaped daily for four weeks. Excerpts of each child's symbolic play during a week were edited onto another videotape and given to the parents of each child at the end of the week. Edited segments ranged from one to three different episodes of symbolic play. The segments were representative of the important structural properties of symbolic play identified in the research literature on play: enacting a theme, taking on a role, or making an object substitution (Rubin *et al.*, 1983). Segments were edited to last no longer than 10 minutes. Immediately following each child's interview session, the next series of videotaping commenced, repeating the above procedure. Due to scheduling conflicts, only three child interviews were conducted. The entire four weeks of unedited video were analyzed.

Child interview sessions

The edited videotapes were given to the parents the day before the child interview session. They were asked to have the children watch the videotape at least once before the interview session in an effort to make the children feel comfortable and to familiarize them with the content of the video. The interview sessions took place in the child's home. Each child participated in one interview at the end of the week for three consecutive weeks.

INTERVIEW QUESTIONS

The interview questions used in the semi-structured interviews were drawn from the research literature and theories on symbolic play and were designed to uncover children's thoughts on themes' roles, object substitutions, and reality/fantasy.

A semi-structured interview was chosen because it allowed the interviewer the possibility of having set questions to begin a dialogue with the child and also the opportunity of following up on individual comments made by the child. This format allowed the researcher to distribute the questions systematically and strategically across the interviews rather than overwhelming the child with too many questions in any one interview or posing questions out of context. The first author audiotaped and transcribed each interview. The transcriptions were read and questions were noted to follow up on in subsequent interview/reflection sessions.

The questions related to themes were grounded in the prior research on the use of themes in symbolic play (Corasaro, 1983; Fein, 1986, 1987, 1989, 1991; Nelson & Gruendel, 1979; Nelson & Seidman, 1984; Shank & Abelson, 1977; Short-Meyerson & Abbeduto, 1997; Snow *et al.*, 1986). The questions were designed to elicit children's responses to preference in themes of emotions related to themes of negotiation and repetition of themes.

1   "Tell me about what you are playing here." (in relation to the video)
2   "Why did you choose that?"
3   "You were [smiling, frowning] in that play. Tell me what you were feeling while you were playing that."
4   "What kind of things do you like to pretend to do or play? Why? Which is you favorite? Why?"
5   "Are there things you don't like to pretend? Why?"
6   "If you could play [name of favorite theme of play] however you wanted, would you play it over and over again the same way or change it? Why?"
7   "If you could choose anybody to play [name of favorite theme of play] with you, who would it be? Mom, Dad, sister/brother, friend? Why?"
8   "Tell me about how you and your friends decided to play something."
9   "Are there things you like to pretend just by yourself? Why?"
10 "Tell me what it means to you to 'pretend' something."

The literature (Bretherton, 1989; Garvey, 1977, 1982; Miller & Garvey, 1984; Stockinger Forys & McCune-Nicolich, 1984) provided the basis for questions related to roles. The questions were designed to elicit responses regarding preference and choice of roles and restrictions of roles according to gender and age.

1   "Tell me about who you are pretending to be here." (in relation to the video)
2   "How did you choose that?"
3   "Tell me about your favorite thing to pretend to be."
4   "How does it make you feel to be that?"
5   "If you were playing house, would you ever be the mom (for a boy)/dad (for a girl)? Why?"

The questions about object substitution were drawn from previous research (Fein, 1975; Matthews, 1977; Vygotsky, 1978). The questions were intended to elicit information about choice of objects for substitutions and any limitations of specific objects for substitution.

1   "I see you are using a [name of object] here to [action]. What else could you use to do that? Could you use a [name of object with higher level of realism]? How about a [name of object with lower level of realism]?"
2   "Another child told me I could not use a block to pretend to brush my hair. What do you think? What else could I use?"
3   "If you could play this over again, what would you like to see the teacher put out for you to play with? Why?" (in relation to the video)

Teacher and parent interviews

The teachers and mothers were interviewed at the completion of videotaping and interviews with the children. This allowed the researcher the opportunity to discuss emerging findings (e.g., "Hannah [Skeeter] said that she [he] was not pretending in [a specific scene]. How do you see that?" Other questions were designed to gather background information on each child's symbolic play (e.g., "Tell me about Hannah's [Skeeter's] pretend play"), exposure to watching videotapes of themselves, and any reaction that their child had to watching the edited videotapes of their play. These interviews were also audiotaped and transcribed.

Results and discussion

"Cup or a cone": how themes are explained

The children elaborated more in answering questions about the theme of their play through the script theory (Shank & Abelson, 1977) perspective than emotive theory (Fein, 1986, 1987, 1989, 1991) perspective. Script theorists claim that children imitate the world around them in their play, while emotive theory sees play as more of an emotional expression.

Script theory

During one of the sessions, Hannah watched an episode of herself playing "ice cream." This play consisted of Hannah and her friends at the media table filled with sand. During the play she would ask a friend or teacher if the person wanted some ice cream by saying, "Do you want some ice cream, in a cup or a cone?" During the session, Hannah was asked what she was doing in the play episode. She described her play as an imitation of what actual people do who work in ice cream stores.

N *(interviewer):*   What are you doing here?

H *(Hannah):*   Well, we were saying "cups and cones" because we had these little things for the cups. And we were pretending like we said for real stuff, we said "in a cup or a cone" and like real people say, and all the people say cup and cone and that stuff.

N: You mean when you go to an ice cream shop that's what they say?

H: Yeah, they usually say "Do you want a cup or a cone?" and I say "Cup, or cone?"

N: So you were pretending to say just what the people say in the store.

H: Yeah.

To demonstrate, she then enacted this same script while watching the videotape. To better explain her "ice cream" play, she walked to the cabinet next to the television and pulled out different puzzle boxes. Each puzzle box represented the different flavors of ice cream.

Skeeter watched an episode of his play at the media table filled with shaving cream where he pretended to play "ice cream." While watching the videotape, he got out a book about an ice cream factory. The book showed cartoon illustrations of the progression of manufacturing ice cream with cartoon people at each stage of the manufacturing process.

While watching this episode of his play, Skeeter indicated which parts that the children playing with him were enacting (Skeeter points to each cartoon person in the book and labels each one as someone from his classroom play scenario: teacher, Hannah, himself).

N: So you in your play are pretending to be someone in a test lab [what the book calls where a person examines the ice cream].

S *(Skeeter):*   Yeah.

N: And Rachel [teachers] is [are] pretending to be someone at the taste lab [what the book calls where a person tastes the ice cream].

S: And, Hannah is, works right here [points at book] because she puts the chunks in to make sure they are stinky chunks.

Since Skeeter was imitating a book from home that he did not bring to school, the other children in the classroom were not playing with the same knowledge base as Skeeter. A shared knowledge base is reportedly needed for playing out a script (Corasaro, 1983). However, the children did not act in a way that violated Skeeter's interpretation of the script, so the play continued. One reason may be that the script of "every child makes a different part of the ice cream" was general enough to allow for variations. For example, Hannah making the ice cream "stinky" was not in the ice cream book but was an acceptable procedure to the children for making ice cream in their play. This appears to support Fein's (1991) idea that children are not as concerned with the details of play as the script theory literature claims. This slot filler (Nelson & Gruendel, 1979) of making ice cream "stinky" was appealing to the children because they liked the idea of people eating stinky ice cream.

Both children referred to having "parts" to their play as if following a script, without the interviewer's previously using that word. Hannah described how she negotiated a play scenario of making ice cream with a friend.

H: Me and Suzy we each have different parts and Suzy gives out the cakes because we have agreed which part is what. And Suzy agrees, see I say she makes cakes and she jumps up and down and says "I want to make cakes" and I jump up and down and say "I'll make the ice cream" and so we both agree on it and then we do it.

Skeeter explained what each child's part is in his "laboratory" play at the sink area.

N: What about Hannah and Emily [in the tape they are playing on the other side of the classroom sink from Skeeter and are not pretending the same thing as Skeeter]?

S: Well, they are down there because the part is when they are down there they aren't making something bad like us so usually the fire starts over on the sand table.

Skeeter spoke of what "usually" is done in a play episode of laboratory, even though he had played it only once.

S: Well, what we usually do if we don't is we don't come down, we watch there in the lab to know when.

(Said in another part of the interview)

S: Well, he usually does, what I usually do is I tap on him [Kenny] like this and if I can, hear his heart beating.

Hannah and Skeeter's use of the word "part" and Skeeter's use of the word "usually" made their play appear to follow a set flow of events similar to a script (Shank & Abelson, 1977). By following a script, the children were able to predict events and know how to act (Nelson & Gruendel, 1979). For example, Hannah knew that by imitating the people at the ice cream store, she could convey the intent of her play (serving ice cream), her role (employee), and her friend's role (customers). Since the other players knew what to do, this resulted in one of her longest episodes of sociodramatic play.

Emotive theory

During the interviews, the first author asked the children questions to explore their understanding of the emotional side of their play. Generally, their responses were short, and occasionally they did not respond at all. Hannah was able to express her favorite and least favorite roles (mermaid, tree), what a sad theme would be (the prince that she marries drowns), and why she liked to enact the role of mother (changing diapers) and baby (can ask to have diapers changed and take a nap). However, when asked to name a scary theme to play, she stared and was silent for the only time in all the sessions. When the first author told her that a scary theme that she played was going to the doctor to get a shot, Hannah seemed curious at first but then switched the subject.

Even though Hannah answered all but one question describing the emotional side of her play, she did not elaborate on the answers the way she did with other questions.

Skeeter's responses to what would be a happy or scary play were concrete. He said that a happy type of play would be when a fellow classmate who tends to hit other children apologizes for hitting them. A scary type of play would be playing hide-and-seek because some must say, "Boo." When asked why he does not like to play a father role, he said, "I don't know." After further probing to find an answer, he was silent. He was able to tell the first author that his favorite pretend play is being an inventor.

While watching the scene of Skeeter pretending to be a baby and play-fighting with David, the first author asked him what he was doing in the scene. He quickly replied, "Fighting," but then later when she asked if he was fighting, he lowered his voice and said, "No." He kept looking to the other room where his parents were present. He appeared to have been embarrassed that he was "fighting" even though he knew that he was only pretending. He then tried to justify his fighting by saying that the children playing with him knew that he was pretending.

N: What are you two doing there?

S: We're fighting there. (giggling)

N: You're fighting? (giggling)

N: So Suzy is the mom. So when you were playing with David, what were you doing?

S: Uh huh.

N: Were you fighting?

S: No. (He lowered his voice and appeared embarrassed. He looked into the kitchen.)

N: Were you just playing pretend fighting? (Said to show interviewer understood that he was only pretending so that he would not upset his parents.)

S: Uh huh. They [other children] know because of what we were doing.

N: Yeah, it looked like you were smiling (in the play scenario). Like you were just pretending.

During another time in a session, Skeeter looked to the room where his parents were when asked a question about emotions. During his play in the class room, he pretended to be a baby a few times. When the first author asked, "And you like to play the baby?" he responded, "Sorta, yeah" while looking in the other room. This may have been due to the arrival of a baby sister two months prior. He may have been working through emotions regarding his new sibling that he does not yet understand, so he was uncomfortable with the question.

The children's inability to elaborate or even answer the questions regarding emotions supports Fein's (1989) explanation that there is a subconscious aspect to symbolic play. Fein explained that as children develop their ability to create symbols, the tie between that which is signified and that which signifies becomes looser and even unclear. Children may not always understand why the emotional arousal is present in pretense, but it still exists and can be very strong for children. Skeeter associated emotions to enacting the role of baby, but he did not have the emotional or cognitive developmental ability to retrace the steps of why he associated good feelings to playing baby. Hannah was able to say that she liked playing baby because she can have her diapers changed, but this response was still very concrete. Changing diapers had associations with emotions that she did not or could not describe (being taking care of).

"To tell the truth, I'm a real chemist": distinctions in pretense of role play

While watching the videotapes, the children were repeatedly asked the question, "Who are you pretending to be here?" or "Are you pretending to be someone?" Surprisingly, the children most often replied that they were not pretending to be someone. For example, when Skeeter and the first author watched the segment of videotape in which he was pretending to make ice cream in the media table filled with shaving cream he was asked to tell when he was pretending to be someone. His very quick response was that he was not pretending to be somebody. The quickness in his reply and the directive tone in his voice indicated that he was shocked that the first author would ask him such a question.

N: Let me know when you are pretending to be somebody.
S: Well, I'm not pretending to be somebody at all.
N: The whole time you are not?
S: Uh huh.
N: So then who are you here?
S: Skeeter. (said very quickly)

After listing the instances when the children said that they were pretending and not pretending to be someone, a distinction between the types of roles being enacted became apparent.

Scenes in which the children said that they were not pretending to be someone included Hannah making cookies, Hannah caring for a doll, Skeeter making experiments in the laboratory, and both Hannah and Skeeter playing "ice cream." These roles were defined by Garvey (1977) as functional roles.

A functional role is used to enact the script, like a server of food. Interestingly, the children did not think that they had to pretend to be someone to enact these roles. One the other hand, Skeeter and Hannah said that they were pretending when they were taking the role of babies in their play. This role is, according to Garvey (1977), relational. Also, when asked "What are some roles you could pretend to be?" they responded, an airplane pilot, spy, chef, firefighter, nurse, mermaid, and inventor. These are what Garvey (1977) defines as character roles, either stereotypic or fictional.

Unlike adults who see all role-playing as pretense, Skeeter and Hannah appear to be making a distinction depending on the type of role. Also, as seen in a latter example, the same rules for when it is pretending for them do not apply to their playmates. During the first session, the first author asked Hannah if she ever pretended to be someone, and she immediately referred to the dress-up clothes in her closet.

N: Do you ever pretend to be somebody else?
H: Well, I have dressing stuff in my room and I pretend to be somebody.
       (Later in conversation)
H: And sometimes we pretend to be other things too.
N: Like what?
H: Like, all sorts of things, I can't explain every single thing cause my dresser is filled to the top.

In the last session, after Hannah said that she was not pretending to be the mother of her doll when she played with it, the first author asked her if she could give an example of when she was pretending to be someone with her doll. She first described going to the hospital with a big belly and giving birth and then being a nurse to the baby.

N: So let's say you took Shelline [doll] to the, at the hospital still, let's say she was sick. Could you pretend something then, could you pretend to be someone then?
H: I could well I could pretend she had an invisible mom, there was someone else her mom and I was the hospital girl, and the baby would lay down and I would (does pretend motion like fixing the doll).
N: So that's pretending?
H: Yeah, that's pretending.

Although Hannah said she did not have to pretend to be the mother of her doll, she did describe similar play with the doll by her friend Suzy.

N: I have a question, Shelline is your baby, so when Suzy holds it and takes care of it, she has to pretend to be somebody?
H: She pretends.

Skeeter explained that if the first author wanted to be a detective, she had to acquire certain props (credit card, license plate, and jet fuel). It appears that for the children to see a role as pretend, there must be a change in the appearance or capability of the person, including costumes, props, or doing something that is not possible (giving birth or being a nurse). When the children were making cookies or an experiment, they did not have to change themselves to engage in the play. They were not playing as if they were someone else (Bretherton, 1989). They saw themselves as Hannah and Skeeter playing, not Hannah and Skeeter, a baker or chemist, playing. When they were babies, there was a change in their behavior. They cried and sucked their thumbs. They were acting as if they were babies. They also referred to themselves as other people. Here are their descriptions while watching themselves playing "babies."

H: I was so mad at her [other friend playing with her].
N: You were mad at her? Why?
H: Cause she hit Hannah the baby.
N: She hit Hannah the baby?
H: Yes.
N: Emily the baby hit Hannah the baby?
H: Yes.
N: So here you are still playing babies. Oh did you see who came by? Who is that? [referring to a child dressed as a tiger going by to where Skeeter, Randy, Suzy and David were on the couch]
S: That's the tiger. Randy had to go after that because we pretend that that scares the babies so the dad has to go fight it off.
N: Oh the dad went to go fight off the tiger. So to protect the babies.
S: Uh huh, while the mom stays with us the babies.

The idea that the children must change themselves to pretend may be the reason that Hannah said that she was not pretending to be the mother to her doll. When asked if she was pretending to be a mom to her doll, she responded, "No, no, no way!" Garvey (1977) stated that some functional roles, like mother, can also be relational roles. Hannah treated being a "mother" as if it was a functional role. Hannah may not think that she is pretending to be the mother because she does not have to change herself to be a mother. She only needs to carry out the function of caring for a baby. Perhaps the type of doll that Hannah was caring for was responsible for this. This doll was highly realistic; it cried, ate, and even urinated. Hannah may not have felt the need to pretend with this doll because it was so realistic. Hannah may have said that Suzy was pretending when she played with Hannah's doll because the doll did not belong to Suzy. Suzy has to somehow change herself to have ownership of the doll.

Along this line, Skeeter was also engaged in a functional role during his "experiment" play. Since Skeeter is actually using materials during his experimenting, he may not think that he needs to pretend. His mother and teacher also agreed that since the materials are similar to what real experimenters use (baking soda, vinegar), he was actually a 5-year-old experimenter.

In both instances, they are performing actions with props and do not need to make a mental representations of the character (mother, experimenter). They are not changing anything about themselves to play. Hannah is pretending that the doll is real and that the food is real, but she herself is still the same. Skeeter is pretending that baking soda makes an explosion, but he himself is an actual experimenter.

Requiring a change to consider themselves, pretending shows pretense as a physical act. This supports Lillard's (1993b) suggestion that children understand their pretense as an action before they understand it as a mental representation. When asked about pretense, Skeeter and Hannah did not emphasize the importance of a mental image but focused more on the action made during pretense. For example, they made references to needing props and changing their behaviors in order to pretend.

The children's mothers offered interesting interpretations of why the children did not think that they were pretending. Greta reported that while trying to encourage Hannah's self-esteem, she tells Hannah to "just be yourself" and "you don't have to look at other people and wish that you could be who they are." Greta proposed that this might have an effect on Hannah's role-play. Greta also stated that Hannah does most of her play in her room with her brother, so Greta did not exactly know what kind of play she engaged in. Greta did report that she had never heard Hannah say that she was someone else.

Alice confirmed the finding that Skeeter did not say that he pretends to be someone when playing. When in his laboratory at home (behind a chair and under a table), Skeeter pretends that there are people there with him (Charles Lindbergh), but Skeeter never pretended to be someone else. She said that when Skeeter is alone, he does not engage in the type of symbolic play where he takes on a role, like an animal or other person. Occasionally, when playing with a younger female neighbor, Skeeter will be the father in the play at the neighbor's request.

"Only boys can be pilots and only girls can be flight attendants": how gender affects role-play

Both Hannah and Skeeter agreed that females could not pretend to take on male roles, and vice versa. However, children could take on adult and baby roles. Their ability to cross the generation line but not the gender line follows Garvey's (1977) and Miller and Garvey's (1984) findings. Skeeter explained that a girl could take on a male role if she was not imitating reality. Skeeter's response that girls could not be pilots is interesting because his mother said that Skeeter says Amelia Earhart lives in their house. Although he has extensive knowledge of a female pilot, he still said that girls could not be pilots.

Here, the interviewer asks Skeeter if she could pretend to play pilot with him:

S: Yeah, but only boys can be pilots only girls can be flight attendants.
N: Oh, ok. So if I wanted to pretend to play airplane with you …
S: You would be a flight attendant.
N: And you would be …
S: A pilot.
N: A pilot I see.
S: Or the co-pilot. Of course, I think co-pilots can be a girl.
N: Oh, co-pilots can be a girl. I wonder why we [girls] can be a co-pilot and not pilot, hmm. That's interesting, so even if it's just for pretend they can't be it.
S: Well you know what, you can but if you want to play like real life, that's how it goes.

During the second session, Hannah was asked if Skeeter could be the mother in their play, and she quickly laughed in disapproval. At the end of the third session, without prompting, Hannah stated that Skeeter had asked to be the mother in their play in the classroom and that she now thought that he could be the mother.

H: Do you remember that question one time you said "Can Skeeter be a mom?" And Skeeter said "Can I be a mom?" in class one time. [Laughs as if she's amazed]
N: Oh, and what happened?
H: And one time he wanted to be a sister and one time he wanted to be the baby girl baby.
N: And what did you do?
H: Well, we didn't do anything [said as if I should know that].
N: Was he the mom, did he pretend to be the mom?
H: Yes, and the baby and the sister.
N: That's so interesting.
H: Baby girl, a girl baby, a girl sister, and the mom.
N: So he could be all those things [said like a realization].
H: Yeah, if he wanted to, and Suzy could be the brother or the dad or the baby boy.

Ants, scorpions, and dolls: descriptions of objects substitutions

During the sessions, the first author asked questions that would evoke what the children thought about each level of object substitution (Fein, 1975; Matthews, 1977). Most questions were, "Could you use a [blank] for a [blank]?" or "If you did not have that [blank] object, what else could you use?" However, the most intriguing remarks came spontaneously. The children demonstrated many levels of object substitution in their symbolic play on the videotapes; however, these questions were designed to understand what they thought about object substitution.

One result was that Hannah did not consider objects that had a functional level of substitution (a plastic cup as a cup) (Matthews, 1977) to require pretense. Hannah does not have to pretend with her baby doll because it is so highly realistic (eats and cries) and has accessories that are really lifelike.

H: I don't pretend she's real, cause she's like a real baby because she goes, does all the stuff that real babies do.

This quote is not interpreted as Hannah's thinking the baby is actually real, but more as her stressing the point that the baby doll is like a real baby. This observation provides interesting support for Olszewki and Fuson's (1982) findings that highly prototypical objects can limit 5-year-old children's play. If Hannah does not think that she has to pretend with functional objects, then she may not extend her play in pretense. Actually, during the time that Hannah played with this doll in the classroom, she did not extend her play past caring for the baby. When it was suggested that she could make Play-doh food for the doll, she replied that she did not need to because the doll already had real packaged food. When asked what other objects the children could use in substitution for the objects that they had used in the play, they both suggested highly prototypical object substitutions. Hannah said a rolled-up piece of paper could become an ice cream cone, and Skeeter said the loft area could be used for a house. Hannah did not think that a pencil could be used to represent an ice cream cone because it would not be able to hold the ice cream, in this case, sand. Her inability to accept a low prototypical substitution is not typical of her age, since 5-year-old children are known to use low prototypical substitutions (Cole & LaVoie, 1985; Fein 1981).

The children were given an opportunity in the interviews to describe an insubstantial substitution (Matthews, 1977). In play, an insubstantial substitution occurs when the child either gestures or says that something is there when it is not. Hannah was asked, If she was in an empty room playing "ice cream shop," what could she do if she wanted to pretend a cone was there? Hannah was not able to say that she could just pretend the cone was there. Instead, she gave the following examples of what she could use.

H: If we were bored, and we had extra shirts on, just take our shirts off and use it as games [motions rolling up the shirts] [laughs]
N: What happens if you didn't even have that on?
H: We would be naked.
N: And what happens then if you wanted to play ice cream?

H: Take our nose off to pretend they were cups and we would take, actually our ears off to pretend they were cups and we would take our hands off to pretend they were cones.

Even though Hannah could not describe an insubstantial substitution for a cone, she continually made such substitutions while talking. She moved her hands to suggest rolling up a shirt and even holding an ice cream cone. She appeared to need what Vygotsky (1978) called a pivot in object substitution. She had to describe an actual object for the substitution, almost as a reference point of her understanding of the substitution. Vygotsky claimed that with age, children lessen this reliance on pivots during object substitution and eventually can make substitutions where the object used in pretense does not at all resemble the represented object. Hannah demonstrated this again when discussing here ice cream play in the classroom. On the videotape, her teacher asked for Chunky Monkey flavor ice cream, and Hannah scooped up sand and gave it to her. Another child later asked for bug and scorpion ice cream, and Hannah scooped the same sand and gave it to him. When asked to explain how she knew where which flavor was in a table with such a large amount of sand, her response was a description of what the flavor looked like.

H: For the bugs [bug ice cream] it's chocolate chips cause it's called bug ice cream because there are ants in it and it's really crazy cause there's ants, like ice cream they eat, and we call it bug ice cream cause ants are black and chocolate chips are black so we call it.

There really are no chocolate chips in the sand. However, instead of saying that she just pretends there are ants in the ice cream, she had to describe an in-between object (chocolate chips) that looked like ants. Interestingly, by saying that there were chocolate chips, she made an insubstantial substitution. However, it may have been too foreign for her to make a substitution for "ant ice cream," so she needed the chocolate chips as a reference point or pivot.

In the next description, she explained how Skeeter, who was also playing "ice cream shop" with her, knew that the sand represented scorpion ice cream. Again she used a pivot to describe the scorpions.

H: And like the chocolate ants are chocolate chips, well scorpion, do you know why we call it scorpion ice cream they have these red kind of bubble gum in it and you chew it all up and it looks like scorpion. They are shaped like scorpion and the chocolate chips are shaped like ants.

N: Oh, so that's why he [Skeeter], he's pretending that those little red things are scorpions. [On the videotape, Skeeter said there were scorpions in the sandbox.]

H: Yeah.

N: But are there little red things in the sand box?

H: Well, no, we are just pretending.

N: So, Hannah you are pretending that there are red things in the ice cream and Skeeter is pretending that the red things are scorpions. I get it.

When Skeeter was asked how he could play ice cream if there was nothing there, he simply said he would get a bucket and pretend there was ice cream inside it.

N: If you are playing in a room and you wanted to play ice cream like you were at school that day, and you didn't have those toys to play with, what else do you think you could pretend to be ice cream? What kinds of things could you use to be ice cream?

S: Well, I'd just imagine there was ice cream.

N: Just imagine, like what?

S: Take a box full of nothing and then just pretend fill it with stuff and stir it (gestures with hands).

N: So you can just take a bucket and pretend there's ice cream in it?

S: Uh huh.

N: And what could you use for the cone?

S: Pretend you go [gestures holding a cone and eating from it].

Since children's ability to make object substitutions develops with age (Fein, 1981), it is not surprising that Hannah was unable to describe an insubstantial substitution. It may also stem from Hannah's interpretation of the question. She may have thought that she was being asked for another object that she could use.

For real–real? Fantasy versus reality

The children were asked questions to elicit their thoughts on the distinction between fantasy and reality in their play. Since the interviews were conversational in their structure, the children did not have force-choice answers as in more structured experiments like Samuel and Taylor (1994) or Flavell *et al.* (1987).

Therefore, the children's responses did not reveal as much of their actual understanding of the difference between fantasy and reality as expected, but the responses did demonstrate an interesting side to the children's view on fantasy and reality. During the four weeks of videotaping and during the interview sessions, the children did not appear to confuse fantasy with reality in their behavior. For example, the children did not eat plastic food or run out of the room while pretending that there was a fire.

It appeared that the children were able to understand the different layers of pretense and act within those layers (Lillard, 1993a). However, when questioned if something was "real or not real," they reacted in a way that suggests they wanted to keep the illusion of pretense present (Griffin, 1984). This conclusion comes from not only their verbal responses but also their non-verbal cues, such as whispering or smiling as in jest.

Both Hannah and Skeeter's responses below indicated more of a desire to believe and act imaginatively than confusion in distinguishing between fantasy and reality.

N: Now can I ask you something, is it really going to burn you those experiments?
S: Particularly, at least if you put a lot a lot of mixture, yes.
N: But when you are playing here, is that a real experiment or just a pretend experiment?
S: Actually they can be real if you put enough bad stuff in.
N: Then you really have to put your gloves on.
S: And then the more and more you experiment with the same experiment it will turn into a real explosion.

While watching a videotape segment of Skeeter and Kenny playing in the laboratory, Skeeter told me that Kenny died because the chemicals (sand, water, and soap) that he was mixing together killed him. He was then asked if his chemical was real.

N: Is it a real chemical?
S: I try not to breathe mine [chemical] because I try to make mine real. I try not to breathe it.

It appeared that Skeeter wanted to believe that his pretend scenarios of chemicals and death of his friend were real. This desire to believe in fantasy was also present in Hannah's answers. In the following example she spoke in a quiet voice when proclaiming that the oven that she had made to cook Play-doh cookies was real.

N: Hannah can I ask you something? Is it a real oven?
H: [in a quiet, soft voice] It's a pretend oven.

When Hannah wanted to demonstrate the "ice cream" episode that she had played in the classroom during our interview at her home, she took out puzzle boxes to represent the ice cream flavors. When the first author said the word "box" in reference to the pretend ice cream flavors, she was upset that the illusion of fantasy was broken.

The interviewer asked what Hannah was doing in a play episode:

H: I'll show what we are doing [goes to cabinet]. Say this is the ice cream [takes out puzzle box].

N: The box is the ice cream.

H: Well, don't say the box.

During the conversations about pretense and reality, the difficulty in questioning children about their understanding became apparent. As Taylor (1997) explained, when children are asked questions about play, they must step outside the play scenario to answer them. The child may then still continue to act "playful" in the response. Hannah and Skeeter demonstrated a "playfulness" with their desire to act imaginatively. Another obstacle was found in the use of the word "real." Whereas fantasy and reality are usually thought of as two opposing concepts, the children showed that during the act of pretense, an item may be and people may act "for real." In this example the first author asked Hannah if the oven that she drew on a piece of paper was real.

H: Well, no, it's a real oven.

N: It's a real oven.

H: Yeah, for us, we're just pretending.

N: So, it's real when you pretend.

H: Yes, well, the cookies are not pretend either.

N: The cookies are not pretend?

H: No.

N: Can you eat those cookies?

H: [Nods yes]

N: You can eat those cookies right there that we are looking at right now.

H: [strange voice with a smile] Yes.

N: All the time?

H: [Nods no with an embarrassed look]

N: Just for pretend you can eat them. I get it.

People may also act "for real" during pretend. Hannah described her teacher pretending to eat ice cream made out of sand as being real within the terms of pretend.

N: So here she [teacher] is eating it [ice cream].

H: Yes.

N: Is she really eating it?

H: No, just for pretend.

N: She's pretend eating it.

H: But for pretend she's really eating it.

N: For pretend she really eats it, there's a difference.

Implications

This methodology opens avenues for both learning more about children's understanding of play and using videotapes as a methodology to study play.

Through their responses and behaviors, the children shared their ideas about a number of important aspects of play. They were better able to discuss the script of their play than any emotions that they attached to their play. This observation supports Fein's research that children do not always understand their emotions during play (Fein, 1989). In keeping with Lillard's (1993b, 1994, 1996) work on pretense, it appeared that the children did not yet understand that pretense requires mental representation. Gender affected their choice of role-play, as seen in Garvey's work (1977). Finally they demonstrated that while they understood the difference between fantasy and reality, they preferred to sustain the playfulness of fantasy in their responses (Taylor, 1997).

The edited videotaped segments or the children's play served as a wonderful catalyst to spark conversation between the children and researcher. Having a tangible illustration of abstract concepts such as object substitution or roles depicted in the videotaped play segments, the interviewer was able to ask specific questions about complex concepts that otherwise may not have been possible. For example, the interviewer and children were able to pause the video and refer to actual images of the children's play. This was a common occurrence during all the interviews. The videotapes also provided a distance between the children and their actual play. This distance allowed the children to look at their play and answer questions about it without being disrupted in their play. The use of clips of their own play appeared to maintain a meaningful context for the children to reflect. Further, the multiple interview sessions allowed the researcher to spread out the questioning about themes, roles, object substitution, and the distinction between fantasy and reality.

Due to the small number of participants, the findings of this study are better cast in the form of possible avenues for future research rather than as specific conclusions. The children were excited to view the tapes and discuss their play with an interested adult. Seeing play from the eyes of children and in their words may help researchers reclaim their sense of wonder about symbolic play.

References

Bretherton, I. (1989). Pretense: Acting "as if." In J. J. Lockman & N. L. Hazen (Eds.), *Action in social context* (pp. 239–274). New York: Plenum Press.

Cole, D., & La Voie, J. (1985).Fantasy play and related cognitive development in 2-to 6-year olds. *Developmental Psychology. 21*, 233–240.

Copple, C., Cocking, R., & Matthews, W. (1984). Objects, symbols, and substitutes: The nature of the cognitive activity during symbolic play. In T. D. Yawkey & A. D. Pelligrini (Eds.), *Child's play: Developmental and applied* (pp. 105–124). Hillsdale, NJ: Erlbaum.

Corasaro, W. (1983). Script recognition, articulation and expansion in children's role-play. *Discourse Processes, 6*, 1–19.

Creasey, G., Jarvis, P., & Berk, L. (1998). Play and social competence. In O. N. Saracho & B. Spodek (Eds.), *Multiple perspectives on play in early childhood education* (pp. 116–143). Albany: State University of New York Press.

Fantuzzo, J., Coolahan, K., Mendez, J., McDermott, P., & Sutton-Smith, B. (1998). Contextually-relevant validation of peer play constructs with African American Head Start children: Penn interactive peer play scale. *Early Childhood Research Quarterly, 13*, 411–431.

Fein, G. (1975). A transformational analysis of pretending. *Developmental Psychology, 11*, 291–296.

Fein, G. (1981). Pretend play in childhood: An integrated review. *Child Development, 52*, 1095–1118.

Fein, G. (1986). The affective psychology of play. In A.W. Gottfried & C. C. Brown (Eds.), *Play interactions* (pp. 31–50). Lexington, MA: Lexington Books.

Fein, G. (1987). Pretend play: Creativity and consciousness. In D. Gorlitz & J. Wohlwill (Eds.), *Curiosity, imagination, and play* (pp. 283–305). Hillsdale, NJ: Erlbaum.

Fein, G. (1989). Mind, meaning and affect: Proposals for a theory of pretense. *Developmental Review, 9*, 345–363.

Fein, G. (1991). Bloodsuckers, blisters, cooked babies, and other curiosities: Affective themes in pretense. In F. S. Kessel M. H. Bornstein, & A. J. Sameroff (Eds.), *Contemporary constructions of the child* (pp. 143–158). Hillsdale, NJ: Erlbaum.

Flavell, J. H., Flavell, E. R., & Green, F. L. (1987). Young children's knowledge about the apparent-real and pretend-real distinctions. *Developmental Psychology, 23*, 16–22.

Garvey, C. (1977). *Play*. Cambridge, MA: Harvard University Press.

Garvey, C. (1982). Communication and the development of social role play. In D. L. Forbes & M. T. Greenberg (Eds.), *Children's planning strategies* (pp. 81–102). San Francisco: Jossey-Bass.

Griffin, H. (1984). The coordination of meaning in the creation of a shared make believe reality. In I. Bretherton (Ed.) *Symbolic play: The development of social understanding* (pp. 73–100). New York: Academic Press.

Harris, P. L., Brown, E., Marriot, C., Whittal, S., & Harmer, S. (1991). Monsters, ghosts, and witches: Testing the limits of the fantasy-reality distinction in young children. *British Journal of Developmental Psychology, 9*, 105–123.

Johnson, C., & Harris, P. L. (1994). Magic: Special but not excluded. *British Journal of Developmental Psychology, 12*, 35–51.

Lillard, A. (1993a). Pretend play skills and the child's theory of mind. *Child Development, 64*, 348–371.

Lillard, A. (1993b). Young children's conceptualization of pretense: Action or parental representation state? *Child Development. 64*, 372–386.

Lillard, A. (1994). Making sense of pretense. In C. Lewis & P. Mitchell (Eds.), *Children's early understanding of mind: Origins and development* (pp. 211–234). Hove, U.K.: Earlbaum.

Lillard, A. (1996). Body or mind: Children's categorizing of pretense. *Child Development, 67*, 1717–1734.

Matthews, W. (1977). Modes of transformation in the initiation of fantasy play. *Developmental Psychology, 13*, 212–216.

Miller, P., & Garvey, C. (1984). Mother–baby role play: Its origins in social support. In I. Bretherton (Ed.), *Symbolic play: The development of social understanding* (pp. 101–130). New York: Academic Press.

Nelson, K., & Gruendel, J. (1979). At morning it's lunchtime: A scriptal view of children's dialogues. *Discourse Processes, 2*, 73–94.

Nelson, K., & Seidman, S. (1984). Playing with scripts. In I. Bretherton (Ed.), *Symbolic play: The development of social understanding* (pp. 45–72). New York: Academic Press.

Olszewski, P., & Fuson, K. (1982). Verbally expressed fantasy play of preschoolers as a function of toy structure. *Developmental Psychology, 18*, 57–61.

Rubin, K., Fein, G., & Vandenberg, B. (1983). Play. In P. H. Mussen (Series Ed.) & E. M. Hetherington (Vol. Ed.), *Handbook of child psychology: Vol 4. Socialization, personality, and social development* (pp. 693–774). New York: Wiley.

Rubin, K., & Pepler, D. (1980). The relationship of child's play to social congnitive growth and development. In F. C. Foot, A. J. Chapman, & J. R. Smith (Eds.), *Friendship and social relationships in children* (pp. 209–234). New York: Wiley.

Samuels, A., & Taylor, M. (1994). Children's ability to distinguish fantasy events from real-life events. *British Journal of Developmental Psychology, 12*, 417–427.

Shank, R., & Abelson, R. (1977). *Scripts, plans, goals and understanding*. Hillsdale, NJ: Erlbaum.

Short-Meyerson, K., & Abbeduto, L. (1997). Preschoolers' communication during scripted interaction. *Journal of Child Language, 24*, 469–493.

Snow, C., Shonkoff, F., Lee, K., & Levin, H. (1986). Learning to play doctor: Effects of sex, age and experience in hospital, *Discourse Processes, 9*, 461–473.

Stockinger Forys, S., & McCunce-Nicolich, L. (1984). Shared pretend: Sociodramatic play at 3 years of age. In I. Bretherton (Ed.), *Symbolic play: The Development of social understanding* (pp. 159–194). New York: Academic Press.

Taylor, B. J., & Howell, R. J. (1973). The ability of three-, four-, and five-year-old children to distinguish fantasy from reality. *Journal of Genetic Psychology, 122*, 315–318.

Taylor, M. (1997). The role of creative control and culture in children's fantasy/reality judgements. *Child Development, 68*, 1015–1017.

Trawick-Smith, J. (1990). The effects of realistic versus non-realistic play materials on young children's symbolic transformation of objects. *Journal of Research in Childhood Education, 5*, 27–35.

Ungerer, J., Zelazo, P., Kearsely, R., & O'Leary, K. (1981). Developmental changes in the representation of objects in symbolic play from 18 to 34 months of age. *Child Development, 52*, 186–195.

Vygotsky, L. (1978). *Mind in society*. Cambridge, MA: Harvard University Press.

Wellman, H. M., & Estes, D. (1986). Early understanding of mental entities: A reexamination of childhood realism. *Child Development, 57*, 910–923.

Wooley, J. (1997). Thinking about fantasy: Are children fundamentally different thinkers and believers from adults? *Child Development, 68*, 991–1011.

Theme III

Policy generation and implementation

Chapter 9

Governance of early childhood education and care

Recent developments in OECD countries

Michelle J. Neuman

Source: *M. J. Neuman, Early Years, 25(2), 129–141, 2005.*

Abstract

Since the 1990s, many OECD countries have expanded their early childhood services and developed more coherent and coordinated policies. Through this process, countries have adopted very different approaches to governing their early childhood systems. Drawing from findings of a 12-country comparative study, this article explores cross-national approaches to the governance of early childhood systems, as well as some possible implications for future policy development. The article discusses the roles of the national government, the local authorities, the private sector and other stakeholders, such as teachers and parents, in making key decisions about how the system operates in different countries. The article calls for empirical research on the effects of governance on the nature of policies and programmes for young children and their families in different nations.

Introduction

Over the past decade, many OECD countries have expanded their early childhood services and developed more coherent and coordinated policies. Yet, countries have adopted very different approaches to *governing* their early childhood systems. This article seeks to answer the following questions: what is governance and why is it important for the early years? What are the key policy dimensions on which countries vary? What are the roles of national and subnational governments, the private sector and other stakeholders – particularly teachers and parents – in making key policy decisions? After exploring cross-national approaches to the governance of early childhood systems, the article proposes some implications of this analysis for policy development and raises issues for further scholarly attention.

This paper draws on data from the OECD Thematic Review of Early Childhood Education and Care Policy (see OECD, 2001). The author was the Project Leader for this study between 1997 and 2001. Recognising the importance of the early years as a foundation for lifelong learning (OECD, 1996), the OECD initiated a landmark study of early childhood education and care (ECEC) in 1998.[1] The study sought to analyse current policy issues and concerns, identify feasible policy options suited to different contexts, and highlight innovative policies and practices. As part of the review process, each participating country prepared a Background Report and hosted a review team for an intensive case-study visit. After each country visit, the OECD produced a Country Note, which draws together background materials and the review team's observations. These country-specific reports, as well as the synthesis comparative report, *Starting strong: early childhood education and care* (OECD, 2001), provide detailed cross-national information on policies and provision for young children in 20 of the 30 OECD member countries.[2]

Increasing policy attention to the early years

Early childhood education and care (ECEC) soared on to the policy agendas of OECD countries in the 1990s (OECD, 2001). Policy interest in the early years has been spurred by brain research, showing that the first few years of life are critical for a child's early development and learning (Shore, 1997; Shonkoff & Phillips, 2000). At the same time, the growing proportion of working mothers has created a pressing need for child care (OECD, 1999a). Policy-makers, business leaders and parents increasingly recognise the dual role of quality early childhood services in promoting children's cognitive skills, school readiness and social behaviour (Karoly *et al.*, 1998; OECD, 1999b), and in supporting their working parents (OECD, 2001; Committee for Economic Development, 2002).

With strong policy and public attention to the early years of education, many OECD countries focused on expanding access, improving quality, and developing more coherent ECEC policies and programmes in the 1990s. Indeed, children in most OECD countries now have access to at least two years of free ECEC before primary school (OECD, 2001). Several countries established legal entitlements to ECEC in the late 1980s and 1990s. In Belgium, France, Italy and The Netherlands, for example, national legislation entitles access to free pre-school from age 30 months, 36 months and four years, respectively. In Denmark, Finland and Sweden, access to early care and education for children under 7 is a legal right, with parents paying low, income-based fees (OECD, 2001). Other countries upgraded and reformed their pre-school teacher training (e.g. Sweden, Portugal, Italy) and developed mechanisms to coordinate policies and practices (e.g. Denmark, France, The Netherlands, the UK) during this period (OECD, 2001).

Despite similar goals, governments have adopted very different strategies for ECEC *governance*, that is how nations allocate responsibility for decision-making and delivery within and across administrative departments, levels of government, and public and private actors (EC Childcare Network, 1996; Oberhuemer & Ulich, 1997; Kamerman, 2000; OECD, 2001). Governance is a current policy issue that affects all levels of education (e.g. Cole, 2001; Conley, 2002), including the early childhood years. In the USA, for example, there have been heated debates about whether the Head Start pre-school programme should be transferred from the US Department of Health and Human Services to the US Department of Education, as well as whether the federal programme should be devolved to the states as a block grant (National Head Start Association, 2003; Wetzstein, 2003; Gilliam & Ripple, 2004). Sweden made a landmark governance change in 1996 by shifting responsibility for all ECEC services from the Ministry of Social Affairs to the Ministry of Education (Lenz Taguchi & Munkammar, 2003). Policy discussions in France have focused on whether 2-year-olds belong in universal pre-schools within the education system or in infant/toddler programmes within the less extensive child care system (Neuman & Peer, 2002). In light of such recent developments, it is timely to take stock of how countries are governing their ECEC systems.

What is governance?

According to Cole (2001), 'Theorists typically understand governance to be wider than "government", and to be a useful descriptor for the compound of diverse internal and external pressures that have reshaped traditional patterns of public administration in Western liberal democracies since the 1980s' (p. 708). *Exogenous* governance refers to the changing structure of government as a result of global economic pressures, the work of supranational institutions like the European Union, and increased transnational policy diffusion and exchange. In the policy domain of education, governance is primarily an *endogenous* process influenced by internal changes, such as more independent actors in the policy-making process, the rise of meso-level governments, decentralisation and fragmentation of the state, and greater involvement of private actors in policy-making (Rhodes, 1996; Stoker, 1998; Cole, 2001). Scholars have linked these changes to new types of networked/interdependent relationships, the blurring of the boundaries between public, private and voluntary sectors, and rushed policy-making (Rhodes, 1996).

In addition to its policy relevance, studies of governance can contribute to theoretical debates about the effects of institutions on public policy in the political science literature. The 'new institutionalism' argues that politics and policy outcomes do not depend only on individual preferences, but also on the process of individuals operating through institutions (March & Olsen, 1984).[3] Over the past two decades, scholars have explored the role of political institutions (e.g. who controls the legislature; the balance between central and local governments) in shaping rules and other aspects of the strategic environment to give priority to certain groups and ideas over others (Hall & Taylor, 1996). Some scholars in this tradition (e.g. Cohen, 2001) have argued that the fragmented governance can help explain why we find much more limited public support of ECEC in the USA, a federal system, than in Sweden and Denmark, nations with unitary systems of government. This article only begins to explore the extent to which governance institutions shape ECEC policy.

Why is governance important for early childhood education and care?

Comparative studies of education governance have accorded scant attention to the pre-school years (e.g. Karlsen, 2000; Cole, 2001; Cole & John, 2001; Menéndez Weidman, 2001; Astiz *et al.*, 2002). In part, this omission can be explained by the fact that many ECEC services are not part of the education system, but rather under social or health auspices; but it also reflects the reality that in many countries pre-school education has not been treated as a major force in debates about education reform. Yet, the organisational complexity of ECEC may make it more challenging than compulsory education to govern. Historically, 'child care' and 'pre-school' have evolved as separate systems (Kamerman, 2000). While a primary goal of 'child-care' policy has been to subsidise the cost of care for low-income working parents, 'pre-school' has focused on preparing children for school. Recently, these distinctions have become blurred as stakeholders recognise that quality early experiences provide both 'care' and 'education' (EC Childcare Network, 1996; Kagan & Cohen, 1997; OECD, 2001). Yet, multiple agencies, levels of government and providers are vestiges of this past and can lead to fragmentation, overlap and gaps or inconsistencies in policies and programmes (Hodgkin & Newell, 1996; Kagan & Rigby, 2003).

Governance is a critical component of an early childhood system, because it can determine whether or not services meet quality standards, are affordable, meet local demand, promote cost effectiveness and achieve equity goals (Kagan & Cohen, 1997). Governance can help ensure more coherent policy-making across government agencies, levels of government and programmes (Hodgkin & Newell, 1996), making the ECEC system easier for families to navigate (Kagan & Cohen, 1997). Governance helps match the supply of programmes with the needs of different types of families and different geographical areas (Gallagher & Clifford, 2000). In the absence of strong governance, some parents end up piecing together different ECEC arrangements with varying quality to meet their family's needs, while others fall through the cracks. Children may experience inappropriate discontinuities as they are jostled from setting to setting, and their parents may have difficulties finding reliable services to stay employed (Capizzano & Adams, 2000; Moore & Vandiviere, 2000; Kagan & Rigby, 2003).

In this paper, 'governance' of ECEC refers to efforts by different levels of government and public/private bodies to organise, administer and implement ECEC policy and services (Gormley, 1996; Kagan & Cohen, 1997). I focus on the governance of early childhood *systems*, rather than the governance of early childhood programmes or services, such as an individual pre-school or kindergarten. Governance of individual entities involves more day-to-day management needs and decisions and, though critically important, is beyond the scope of this review. To date, discussions in the ECEC field have focused more on governance as the management of discrete programmes (e.g. pre-school, child care) or policies (e.g. subsidies, curriculum) than on governance as the 'glue' that holds the pieces of the early childhood system together.

What are some cross-national approaches to governance?

Given the potential importance of governance to policies and programmes for young children, it is critical to explore how different countries are organising and operating their early childhood systems. The following review of the literature suggests that despite facing similar challenges, OECD countries have adopted diverse approaches to governance. Specifically, nations vary on three key institutional dimensions of governance: administrative integration, decentralisation and privatisation. (Kamerman, 2000; Kagan *et al.*, 2002). These diverse approaches are likely to have consequences for which actors are involved in ECEC policy-making.

Administrative integration

Most countries around the world (e.g. Australia, Belgium, Czech Republic, France, Italy, The Netherlands, Portugal, the USA) have developed *divided* administrative auspices for 'care' and 'education'. This administrative division at the national level generally follows the age of the child, with 'pre-school' arrangements for children from about the age of 3 years based in the Ministry of Education, together with primary schooling. 'Care' services for infants and toddlers generally fall under the responsibility of the Ministry of Social Welfare and/or Health (Kamerman, 2000; OECD, 2001). In some cases, there may be multiple agencies with overlapping or *parallel* responsibilities for programmes and target groups. In the USA, for example, 69 federal programmes provided or supported education and care for children under 5 years in 1999. Nine different federal agencies and departments administered these programmes, though most were operated by the US Department of Health and Human Services and the US Department of Education (US General Accounting Office, 2000).

These administrative divisions have led to parallel or even contradictory policies of funding, regulation, staff training and compensation, and curriculum content for young children, depending on their age or whether the programme they are attending is viewed as 'care' or 'education'. In general, in the social welfare or health systems, services tend to employ lower-paid and lower-trained staff, open a full day and charge a fee to parents, whereas services that fall under education auspices tend to have staff who are trained and compensated at levels comparable to primary teachers, open part-day, and are free to parents (EC Childcare Network, 1996; Oberhuemer & Ulich, 1997; OECD, 2001).

In contrast, a small, but increasing, number of countries (e.g. Denmark, England, Finland, New Zealand, Norway, Scotland, Spain and Sweden) have developed integrated systems under *unified* administrative auspices. For example, in Norway, the Ministry for Children and Family Affairs administers all ECEC services for children under age 6. In these countries, policies tend to be more consistent across the early years from birth to around 6 years; staff training, working conditions, opening hours, fee policies, and programme emphasis tend to be similar for services for infants/toddlers and pre-schoolers. Indeed, often children under 6 attend the same settings, work with the same staff and follow the same curriculum guidelines throughout their pre-school years (EC Childcare Network, 1996). Evidence suggests that this integrated approach may provide more coherent early childhood experiences for children with less fragmentation and fewer inequities than the divided auspices approach (EC Childcare Network, 1996; Oberhuemer & Ulich, 1997; OECD, 2001; Meade & Podmore, 2002).

Regardless of the administrative structure adopted, many countries have created a range of mechanisms to carry out governance functions for children and youth across different departments and sectors (e.g. education, social services, health) (Hodgkin & Newell, 1996; Lenz Taguchi & Munkammar, 2003). In Denmark, for example, an Inter-Ministerial Committee on Children was set up in 1987 as an interdisciplinary body of 15 ministries responsible for encouraging cross-sector initiatives to improve the living conditions for children and youth. In the USA, several state and local governance structures (e.g. governors' cabinets for children, public/private governance boards, inter-agency councils) have emerged to make ECEC policy and oversee implementation (Cauthen et al., 2000; Groginsky, 2002). Emphasis on young children within these inter-agency coordination structures may vary. Coherent policy across sectors and age groups may be difficult to implement in practice if policymakers, administrators, staff and parents do not share a holistic vision of an ECEC system (OECD, 2001).

An interesting trend that calls for further investigation is the increasing tendency to organise all ECEC settings for children from birth to compulsory school age under the auspices of education (Kamerman, 2000; OECD, 2001; Cohen et al., 2004). The decision to integrate all early childhood services into the national education system raises important political and philosophical issues. Some worry that bringing together some areas of responsibility for children could marginalise child welfare, health, and other services from ECEC, and exacerbate coordination barriers with non-education sectors (OECD, 2001). Another concern is that integration might lead to the loss of early childhood traditions and practices to a dominating schooling model that is focused on a more narrow set of academic concerns (Kherroubi & Plaisance, 2000). Indeed, in Belgium, France and the UK, as ECEC becomes more integrated with primary education, there are signs of 'schoolification'. The dominant culture of the school system has eroded some of the specific pedagogical methods of the pre-schools, particularly the traditional emphasis on children's creativity and self-initiative (Goutard, 1993; Oberhuemer & Ulich, 1997; Bertram & Pascal, 1999; Kherroubi & Plaisance, 2000).

The institutional positioning of ECEC within the education system may strengthen the political status of the field on the national policy agenda. In countries such as France, integrating pre-schools into the school system has secured an important status of the field in political and policy discussions, in large part due to the role of the powerful teachers' unions. For example, issues related to pre-school teacher recruitment and curriculum are addressed within more general debates about French education policy and thus receive more attention than in other countries (Kherroubi & Plaisance, 2000). There is a risk that pre-school will lose political attention, and possibly resources, to the more weighty system of compulsory education. In her comparison of France and North Carolina, Le Floch (2000) cautions that, 'While early childhood education may gain in viability as part of the public school system, it may lose some specificity and policy may lose some distinctiveness' (p. 31).

Despite these concerns, an integrated system under education auspices also provides opportunities for promoting ECEC as a public good, expanding access, and encouraging continuity in, children's learning (Neuman, 2001). Shifting the responsibility to the Ministry of Education and making early childhood an important part of the educational system suggests that these services are right for children (not just a service for working parents) and should be available free of charge to all children, as is the case in Belgium, Italy and France for children over age 3. It also may enlist the support of a powerful and established interest group of teachers.

Since transferring responsibility for pre-schools, family day care, open pre-schools and leisure-time activities from the Ministry of Social Welfare to the Ministry of Education in 1996, Sweden has created a new curriculum framework with common themes across the education system, upgraded teacher training for pre-school teachers, and introduced a free universal pre-school session for 4- and 5-year-olds. While Swedish reforms are still fairly recent, reviews suggest that the integration of early childhood services under education auspices has led to an increasing public understanding that early childhood services combine care and learning, and that quality provision for children in the first six years of life is a necessary part of the educational process (Gunnarsson *et al.*, 1999; Moss & Petrie, 1999; Moss, 2001; Cohen *et al.*, 2004). The early childhood period is not viewed solely as a preparation for primary school, but as a distinctive phase of education, with its own intrinsic value and unique characteristics (Gunnarsson *et al.*, 1999; Neuman, 2001; Lenz Taguchi & Munkammar, 2003). This suggests that it is important to consider both the institutions and the ideas that underpin them.

Decentralisation

Countries also vary in the extent to which the authority for governance and accountability in education and social services has been transferred to local (and to a lesser extent, regional) authorities. Cross-nationally, governments justify increasing decentralisation to achieve common goals such as promoting local democracy, bringing decision-making closer to those who are being served, reducing bureaucracy, and encouraging more client-oriented services (Oberhuemer & Ulich, 1997). Decentralisation is a strong emerging theme in many OECD nations (Weiler, 1990; De Vries, 2000; Karlsen, 2000) and has been a consistent trend in the USA for some time, where block grants (funding with fewer strings attached) have been used to devolve decision-making, regulations, and resource allocation for social, welfare, and education services from the federal government to the states (Conlan, 1998; Cohen, 2001; Kagan *et al.*, 2002).

In many countries, national framework documents and broad policy goals are replacing more centralised and prescriptive approaches to decision-making, regulation, steering, monitoring and evaluation. The goal is to reduce the role of the central government and to give sub-national authorities the flexibility to address local concerns about quality, access, etc. While some countries (e.g. Italy, Belgium and France) maintain national regulations and inspections for ECEC, others (e.g. Denmark, Sweden, The Netherlands and the USA) have accorded responsibility to state/local government for providing sufficient numbers of places, monitoring quality and ensuring sufficient resources. Municipalities across much of Europe now decide the appropriate balance of services (e.g. family day-care homes versus centres) and also are free to contract with private services as they see fit. A common challenge for central governments is how to balance local control with the need to address equity concerns, such as the limited access and quality in rural areas, inner cities and children in need of special support (low-income, minority and special education needs) (Kröger, 1997). Country experiences suggest that within a decentralised framework, localities need adequate funding and technical assistance to meet national goals and policy objectives (OECD, 2001).

A potential positive development resulting from loosening central control is that some local authorities have blended funding streams and experimented with integrating administration and policy development across age groups and sectors. In Denmark, Italy, Norway, Sweden and the UK, for example, an increasing number of local authorities have reorganised responsibility for ECEC and schools (and sometimes other children's services) under one administrative department and political committee – often education. Municipalities in parts of Norway have integrated kindergartens, leisure-time activities, schools and child welfare services into a Department for Growing Up, with responsibility for a child's total environment. Despite the challenges of bringing together staff from different professional backgrounds, these mechanisms can lead to more interdisciplinary ways of working and, possibly, a more efficient allocation of resources to children (OECD, 2001).

Decentralisation often means giving considerable latitude to individual ECEC settings, and to staff and parents. While central governments and/or local authorities are expected to provide the broad goals, frameworks and resources to foster quality, centralised enforcement instruments, such as detailed curricula and monitoring by government inspector, are giving way to devolution of control and management to individual programmes (Oberhuemer & Ulich, 1997). There is a trend towards engaging a wide range of stakeholders in quality assurance and evaluation (OECD, 2001). For example, in Denmark, Norway, Sweden and parts of Italy, municipal pedagogical advisers work alongside teachers and parents to define programme goals and document their progress towards achieving them. There is great variation in the extent to which parents are involved in decision-making. Denmark is an exemplar. Parents form the majority of the management councils for kindergartens and family day care and make key decisions about staffing, curriculum and programme organisation.

Privatisation

In some countries, decentralisation, sometimes accompanied by deregulation, has been used as a mechanism to introduce market-driven policies into the ECEC sector (Oberhuemer & Ulich, 1997). In other cases, privatisation has been imposed on locals by a conservative national government eager to reduce the roles of all levels of government (Feigenbaum *et al.*, 1999). Privatisation is commonly justified as a tool for parental choice and for raising the quality of the entire system through competition. Countries are more likely to involve non-profit and for-profit providers in delivering services for infants and toddlers than for pre-schoolers, who are often served within the public school system. The for-profit sector is quite small in most European countries. In all countries, privatisation is strongly linked to ideology about the roles of government and families.

Privatisation may also be a strategy to expand the supply of services. The Dutch government contracts with the non-profit and for-profit sectors to provide many ECEC services for children under 4, particularly to groups that are hard to reach through mainstream services. England has set up local Early Years and Childcare Development Partnerships (EYCDP) across the country as a governance tool for expanding and improving services in partnership with public, for-profit, and non-profit providers. Although public funding and policy-making authority is decentralised to the local level, national standards and regulations exist for all types of programmes (Bertram & Pascal, 1999).

Indeed, most countries require quality standards for private and public providers if they are to receive direct or indirect public subsidies and, in many cases, if they are to operate at all (e.g. Belgium, Denmark, The Netherlands and Sweden). This reflects a view that ECEC is a public responsibility, even if it is provided by private entities. The USA has adopted a more market-oriented approach than other OECD countries. About 90% of child-care services are privately operated centres or family child-care homes, and more than half of these operate for profit. There are no federal quality regulations, and the states are free to set their own standards (Cauthen et al., 2000). As a result, there are wide disparities in staff–child ratios, staff training requirements, and even health and safety requirements. Some US states, for example, exempt religious, school-based, part-day and family child-care providers from any government oversight (Kagan & Rigby, 2003). This suggests that while greater market involvement can lead to more diversity of providers and choice for parents, governance safeguards are necessary to minimise inequities across public and private provision (OECD, 2001).

Cross-national themes and future research directions

Several cross-national themes and topics for further study emerge from this brief review. First, countries have followed very different models for organising their early childhood systems, with potential implications for the quality regulations and staffing, access and funding, and coherence of services. One of the most important governance decisions concerns the number of ministries or departments involved in ECEC policy at the national level. More research is needed on the extent to which divisions between 'care' and 'education' foster turf competition and policy fragmentation. The trend towards integrating ECEC services within the education system presents both risks and opportunities. Preliminary evidence suggests that as ECEC becomes integrated with education, strong interest groups (e.g. teachers) and ideas embedded within the education system (e.g. learning, achievement) dominate policy development. We need more information on the consequences of integration for raising the political status of the field and also for the risk of 'schoolification'.

Second, there is a trend towards the decentralisation of responsibilities for ECEC to more efficiently meet local needs and circumstances. The national government often sets broad goals to be achieved without specifying the means or methods to follow. Decentralisation seems to have led to greater involvement of a wide range of local stakeholders – parents, practitioners, community members – in making policy decisions about quality, access, staffing and programme content. For equity reasons, more information is needed on the extent to which decentralisation indeed meets local needs but also may foster greater disparities in access and quality across different geographical areas.

Third, the size and involvement of the private sector in ECEC varies across OECD countries. In most countries, all ECEC settings, regardless of whether they are publicly or privately operated, are subject to public regulation. The private sector has expanded to meet the diverse needs of families, but also reflects ideology favouring a market approach to service delivery. There is limited information available on the size of the private sector, the types of children enrolled, the level of quality offered, and the relationship between public and private services. To what extent does the involvement of the private sector in ECEC provision contribute to a two-tiered system for children based on their family background or area of residence?

In conclusion, this article has elucidated the role of governance in the early years of education, positioned OECD countries on three main governance dimensions (administrative integration, decentralisation and privatisation), and highlighted recent cross-national trends and developments. It is hoped that this exploratory work will provide the foundation for further empirical study of the extent to which institutions privilege certain actors and ideas over others in the policy-making process. Moreover, there is a need for further research on the consequences of different governance arrangements for policy outcomes that affect children's early learning and development: quality, access and coherence. Such information will be critical to inform ongoing cross-national policy debates about the merits of integrating pre-school into the school system, decentralising responsibilities to lower levels of government and expanding the role of the private sector.

Notes

1 This article uses the definition for ECEC (early childhood education and care) that has been adopted by the countries involved in the OECD review and includes the full range of 'care' and 'education' services: organised home-based, centre-based and school-based arrangements for children below compulsory school age, regardless of administrative auspices, funding sources, staffing or programme emphasis.

2 The OECD reviewed 12 countries between 1998 and 2000: Australia, Belgium, the Czech Republic, Denmark, Finland, Italy, The Netherlands, Norway, Portugal, Sweden, the UK and USA. A new wave of country reviews is under way and includes: Canada, France, Germany, Hungary, Ireland, Korea, Mexico and Spain. Reports from the study are available at: http:// www.oecd.org.

3 Until the mid-twentieth century, what is now known as 'old institutionalism' focused on the legislature, the executive, the bureaucracy of the executive branch and organised interests as static. These scholars studied the major institutional aspects of political systems in order to provide normative analyses of what comprised good government (Thelen & Steinmo, 1992).

References

Astiz, M. F., Wiseman, A. W. & Baker, D. P. (2002) Slouching towards decentralization: consequences of globalization for curricular control in national education
systems, *Comparative Education Review*, 46(1), 66–88.

Bertram, A. D. & Pascal, C. (1999) *Early childhood education and care policy in the United
Kingdom* (Background Report prepared for the OECD Thematic Review of Early
Childhood Education and Care Policy) (Worcester, Centre for Research in Early
Childhood).

Capizzano, J. & Adams, G. (2000) *The number of child care arrangements used by children
under five: variation across states* (No. B-12) (Washington, DC, Urban Institute).

Cauthen, N. K., Knitzer, J. & Ripple, C. H. (2000) *Map and track: state initiatives for
young children and families* (New York, National Center for Children in Poverty).

Cohen, B., Moss, P., Petrie, P. & Wallace, J. (2004) *A new deal for children? Re-forming
education and care in England, Scotland and Sweden* (Bristol, The Policy Press).

Cohen, S. S. (2001) *Championing child care* (New York, Columbia University Press).

Cole, A. (2001) The new governance of French education? *Public Administration*, 79(3),
707–724.

Cole, A. & John, P. (2001) *Local governance in England and France* (London and New York,
Routledge).

Committee for Economic Development (2002) *Preschool for all: investing in a productive
and just society* (New York, CED).

Conlan, T. (1998) *From new federalism to devolution: twenty-five years of intergovernmental
reform* (Washington, DC, The Brookings Institution).

Conley, D. T. (2002) *The new patterns of American educational governance: from local control
to state and federal direction of education policy* (Policy Perspective series) (Eugene, OR,
ERIC Clearinghouse on Educational Management, University of Oregon).

De Vries, M. S. (2000) The rise and fall of decentralization: a comparative analysis of
arguments and practices in European countries, *European Journal of Political Research*,
38, 193–224.

European Commission Childcare Network (1996) *A review of services for young children in the European Union 1990–1995* (Brussels, European Commission Childcare
Network).

Feigenbaum, H., Henig, J. & Hammett, C. (Eds) (1999) *Shrinking the state: the political
underpinnings of privatization* (Cambridge and New York, Cambridge University
Press).

Gallagher, J. & Clifford, R. C. (2000) The missing support infrastructure in early
childhood, *Early Childhood Research and Practice*, 2(1), 1–24.

Gilliam, W. S. & Ripple, C. H. (2004) What can be learned from state-funded
pre-kindergarten initiatives? A data-based approach to the Head Start devolution
debate, in: E. Zigler & S. J. Styfco (Eds) *The Head Start debates (friendly and otherwise)*
(Baltimore, Brookes Publishing).

Gormley, W. T., Jr. (1996) Governance: child care, federalism, and public policy, in:
S. L. Kagan & N. E. Cohen (Eds) *Reinventing early care and education: a vision for a
quality system* (San Francisco, CA, Jossey-Bass), 168–174.

Goutard, M. (1993) Preschool education in France, in: T. David (Ed.) *Educational
provision for our youngest children: European perspectives* (London, Paul Chapman),
35–55.

Groginsky, S. (2002) *Child care and early education coordination in the states: a statutory overview* (Denver, CO, National Conference of State Legislatures).

Gunnarsson, L., Martin Korpi, B. & Nordenstam, U. (1999) *Early childhood education and care policy in Sweden* (Background Report prepared for the OECD Thematic Review of Early Childhood Education and Care Policy) (Stockholm, Ministry of Education and Science in Sweden).

Hall, P. A. & Taylor, R. C. R. (1996) Political science and the new institutionalisms, *Political Studies*, 44, 936–957.

Hodgkin, R. & Newell, P. (1996) *Effective government structures for children: report of a Gulbenkian Foundation inquiry* (London, Gulbenkian Foundation).

Kagan, S. L. & Cohen, N. E. (1997) *Not by chance: creating an early care and education system for America's children* (Report of the Quality 2000 Initiative) (New Haven, CT, Yale University Bush Center).

Kagan, S. L., Mitchell, A. & Neuman, M. J. (2002) *Governing American early care and education: retrospective and prospective perspectives.* Unpublished ms.

Kagan, S. L. & Rigby, E. (2003) *Improving the readiness of children for school: recommendations for state policy* (A discussion paper for the Policy Matters Project) (Washington, DC, Center for the Study of Social Policy).

Kamerman, S. B. (2000) Early childhood education and care: an overview of developments in the OECD countries, *International Journal of Educational Research*, 33(1), 7–30.

Karlsen, G. E. (2000) Decentralized centralism: framework for a better understanding of governance in the field of education, *Journal of Education Policy*, 15(5), 525–538.

Karoly, L. A., Greenwood, P. W., Everingham, S., Houbé, J., Kilburn, M. R. & Rydell, C. P. et al. (1998) *Investing in our children: what we know and don't know about the costs and benefits of early childhood interventions* (Santa Monica, CA, Rand).

Kherroubi, M. & Plaisance, E. (2000) Making a modernist pedagogy: changes in elementary and pre-elementary schooling, *Journal of Education Policy*, 15(1), 83–91.

Kröger, T. (1997) The dilemma of municipalities: Scandinavian approaches to child day-care provision, *Journal of Social Policy*, 26(4), 483–507.

Le Floch, K. C. (2000) From periphery to passage: the politics of early childhood legislation, paper presented at the *American Educational Research Association*, New Orleans, LA, April.

Lenz Taguchi, H. & Munkammar, I. (2003) *Consolidating governmental early childhood education and care services under the Ministry of Education and Sciences: a Swedish case study* (Working Paper) (Paris, Unesco).

March, J. G. & Olsen, J. P. (1984) The new institutionalism: organizational factors in political life, *American Political Science Review*, 78(3), 734–749.

Meade, A. & Podmore, V. N. (2002) *Early childhood education policy co-ordination under the auspices of the Department/Ministry of Education* (Early Childhood and Family Policy series No. 1) (Paris, Unesco).

Menéndez Weidman, L. K. (2001) Policy trends and structural divergence in educational governance: the case of the French national ministry and the US Department of Education, *Oxford Review of Education*, 27(1), 75–84.

Meyers, M. K. & Gornick, J. C. (2001) Cross-national variation in ECEC service organization and financing, in: S. B. Kamerman (Ed.) *Early childhood education and care: international perspectives* (New York, The Institute for Child and Family Policy, Columbia University), 143–176.

Moore, K. A. & Vandiviere, S. (2000) *Turbulence and child well-being* (No. B-16) (Washington, DC, Urban Institute).

Moss, P. (2001) Beyond early childhood education and care, paper presented at the *OECD Early Childhood Education and Care Conference*, Stockholm, Sweden, June.

Moss, P. & Petrie, P. (1999) *Rethinking school: some international perspectives* (London, Joseph Rowntree Foundation).

National Head Start Association (2003) *Dismantling Head Start: the case for saving America's most successful early childhood development program* (A National Head Start Association White Paper) (Washington, DC, National Head Start Association).

Neuman, M. J. (2001) Hand in hand: improving the links between ECEC and schools in OECD countries, in: S. B. Kamerman (Ed.) *Early childhood education and care: international perspectives* (New York, The Institute for Child and Family Policy, Columbia University), 177–217.

Neuman, M. J. & Peer, S. (2002) *Equal from the start: promoting educational opportunity for all preschool children – learning from the French experience* (New York, French-American Foundation).

Oberhuemer, P. & Ulich, M. (1997) *Working with young children in Europe: provision and staff training* (London, Paul Chapman).

OECD (1996) *Lifelong learning for all: meeting of the Education Committee at the ministerial level, 16–17 January 1996* (Paris, OECD).

OECD (1999a) *A caring world: the new social policy agenda* (Paris, OECD).

OECD (1999b) *Education policy analysis 1999* (Paris, OECD).

OECD (2001) *Starting strong: early childhood education and care* (Paris, OECD).

Rhodes, R. A.W. (1996) The new governance: governing without government, *Political Studies*, 44(4), 652–667.

Shonkoff, J. P. & Phillips, D. A. (Eds) (2000) *From neurons to neighborhoods: the science of early childhood development* (Washington, DC, National Academy of Sciences).

Shore, R. (1997) *Rethinking the brain* (New York, Families and Work Institute).

Stoker, G. (1998) Cinq propositions pour une théorie de la gouvernance, *Revue Internationale des Sciences Sociales*, 155, 19–30.

Thelen, K. & Steinmo, S. (1992) Historical institutionalism in comparative politics, in: S. Steinmo, K. Thelen & F. Longstreth (Eds) *Structuring politics: historical institutionalism in comparative analysis* (Cambridge, Cambridge University Press), 1–32.

US General Accounting Office (2000) *Early education and care: overlap indicates need to assess crosscutting programs* (No. GAO/HEHS-00-78) (Washington, DC, Government Printing Office).

Weiler, H. N. (1990) Comparative perspectives on educational decentralization, *Educational Evaluation and Policy Analysis*, 12(4), 433–448.

Wetzstein, C. (2003) Bush's Head Start plan gets cheers, jeers, *Washington Times*, 6 February.

Chapter 10

Transforming the early years in England

Kathy Sylva and Gillian Pugh

Source: *K. Sylva and G. Pugh, Oxford Review of Education, 31(1), 11–27, 2005.*

Abstract

The goal of this paper is to explore the design and implementation of early years educational policy in England in the period 1997–2004. First to be described are the innovations in policy (i.e. the promise), followed by the 'evidence base' for new policy (i.e. the research), the delivery of new services (i.e. the achievement), and finally the tensions and gaps which remain (i.e. the shortfall). The paper will focus on evidence concerning expansion of services and on the benefit of early years education on children's development. It is argued that early years education in England has been transformed through the following: *integration of education and care* at local and national level, the introduction of the *Foundation Stage Curriculum 3–6 years* and its birth–3 years supplement, and the firm *focus on families* as well as children in the delivery of services. There are, however, gaps and tensions to be resolved before the overall vision can be achieved.

Part 1: The promise

While the nineteenth century was distinguished by the introduction of primary education for all and the twentieth century by the introduction of secondary education for all, so the early part of the twenty first century should be marked by the introduction of pre-school provision for the under fives and childcare available to all.

(Rt Hon Gordon Brown, MP, Chancellor of the Exchequer, 2004
Comprehensive Spending Review)

With its resounding electoral victory in 1997, Labour set about increasing services and support for young children and their families. Not only did they plan to increase spending on early years provision, they intended to alter its nature and the way services were delivered. In 1998 the 'National Childcare Strategy' was unveiled and this went far beyond education. It called for: free nursery education places for all four year olds whose parents wished it, Ofsted (Office for Standards in Education) inspections to assure quality of provision of free nursery education places, and 25 Early Excellence Centres to be set up across the country which would serve as 'models' for high quality practice integrating early education with childcare. Labour's vision was to meet the educational needs of young children but also the needs of their families for childcare and parent support or education.

The new government put early years high on its agenda of reform. They were not working from a blank slate, for during their years in opposition there had been a series of influential reports recommending an expansion in early education and an integrated approach to services for young children and their parents (see DES, 1990; Ball, 1994; Audit Commission, 1996, for example). The model for early excellence centres had been articulated by Pugh (1994), drawing on developments which went back to the earliest days of nursery education, but more specifically on the small number of 'combined nursery centres' which had been established since the 1970s.

In 1998 the Green Paper *Meeting the Childcare Challenge* was published. It went far beyond extending a half-day free educational place to three year olds. Some 1.6 million places were promised by 2004, and child care and early education were to become one experience for children and a seamless service for families. Responsibility for all 'day care' services for children under eight was transferred from the Department of Health to the Department of Education and Employment, which was to take a lead in 'joining up' the provision and funding of services for young children and their families. With its concern for expanding child care to support parents' return to work, the Department of Work and Pensions also had a stake in these services. Within months of coming into office, the government also established a Treasury-led cross-departmental review of services for children under eight, which led to proposals for the establishment of the Sure Start initiative, whereby some 250 (and later 500) local Sure Start programmes were to be set up in disadvantaged neighbourhoods, providing community-based support for parents and children under four. Financial support was offered to families on low incomes through the Working Families Tax Credit. The Foundation Stage was established for children from three until the end of reception year (aged five/six), a curriculum framework entitled *Curricular Guidance for the Foundation Stage* (DFEE/QCA, 2000). This was followed by *Birth to Three Matters*, a complementary framework for practitioners working with the growing number of children under three in early years services (DfES/Sure Start, 2003). All were part of an explosion of initiatives, programmes and funding streams.

The goal of this paper is to explore this recent history in terms of innovation in policy (i.e. the promise), the grounds for change (i.e. the research), delivery of new services (i.e. the achievement), and the tensions and gaps which remain (i.e. the shortfall). The paper will focus heavily on research evidence in terms of the effects of early years provision on children. Will the new policies make a difference for children and their families?

Part II: The research

Why are the early years important?

From its very first days Labour promised policies which would be 'informed by evidence'. Their speeches and reports on the early years were infused with research findings, all providing the rationale for policy initiatives.

Two lines of research explain why early learning is important. First are the many studies on the development of the brain, suggesting that early learning contributes to the brain's developing architecture. Scientists made clear that early learning stimulates optimal brain development (Blakemore & Frith, in press). Although the brain research is beguiling (Bruer, 1997; House of Commons, 2000a), the more powerful research comes from developmental psychology (see Gopnik *et al.*, 1999) which shows how the earliest interactions between child and carers provide the cultural structure that underpins the development of intellectual schemas. In essence, the neurological research confirmed the importance of learning in the early years whereas the psychological studies suggested which kind of learning was best (Sylva, 1994a; Melhuish, 2004). Children learn from conversations with adults and older peers, and it is through these conversations that young children acquire the cultural 'tools' to aid them in setting and achieving goals and in becoming part of communities (Bruner, 1986). Sylva extended the argument by showing that early learning experiences shape children towards a 'mastery' orientation in learning or a 'performance' one. Well before entering school the young child has acquired learning dispositions as well as key cognitive skills (Sylva, 1994b).

Finally, there were scores of studies, especially from the USA, which demonstrated the powerful effects of early education on children's readiness for school and for their attainment throughout education and even employment. Melhuish (2004) reviewed the international literature on the effects of early education and care, concluding 'for provision for three years onwards the evidence is consistent that pre-school provision is beneficial to educational and social development for the whole population ... the evidence on childcare in the first three years for disadvantaged children indicates that high quality childcare can produce benefits for cognitive, language and social development. Low quality childcare produces either no benefit or negative effects'. Note that the word 'quality' has entered the debate.

Most striking in the international literature are the Perry Pre-school study (Schweinhart *et al.*, 1993) and the Abercedarian study (Ramey & Ramey, 1998). Both used randomised control designs and both demonstrated the lasting effects of early education and care, especially for children from disadvantaged backgrounds. The Perry studies were especially persuasive because they showed that early education (half day, ages three to five years) improved high school grades, decreased delinquency and adult crime, and improved employment status and earnings. Even more important, early education saved the taxpayer money because for each $1 of investment in the service, $7.16 was saved in social, health and justice systems later on (Barnett, 1996).

Research in the early years has been substantial in the UK. Throughout the Labour government a large-scale longitudinal research study on effective education in the early years has been carried out by the EPPE team (Sylva *et al.*, 1999), commissioned by the government in 1997. This has been influential in guiding the development of policy and has been used by ministers and the Treasury as the 'evidential base' for expanding universal services and targeting enhanced provision for the poor.

The Effective Provision of Pre-School Education (EPPE) project is the first major European longitudinal study of a national sample of young children's development between the ages of three and seven years. To investigate the effects of pre-school education, the EPPE team collected a wide range of information on 3,000 children. They also studied their parents, home environments and the pre-school settings children attended. Settings (141) were drawn from a range of providers (local authority day nursery, integrated centres, playgroups, private day nurseries, nursery schools and nursery classes). A sample of 'home' children (who had no or minimal pre-school experience) were recruited to the study at entry to school for comparison with the pre-school group. In addition to investigating the effects of pre-school provision, EPPE explored the characteristics of effective practice (and the pedagogy which underpins it) through twelve intensive case studies of settings with positive child outcomes. EPPE has demonstrated the beneficial effects of high quality provision on children's intellectual and social/behavioural developmental measured at school entry as well at the end of Years 1 and 2 (Sammons *et al.*, 2002, 2003; Sylva *et al.*, 2004).

Key findings on the effects of pre-school at age five and also at age seven

- *Impact of attending a pre-school – lasting effects* (Sammons *et al.*, in press)

  - Pre-school experience, compared to none, enhances all-round development in children.
  - The duration of attendance is important, with an earlier start being related to better intellectual development.
  - Full time attendance led to no better gains for children than part-time provision.
  - Disadvantaged children in particular can benefit significantly from quality pre-school experiences, especially where they are with a mixture of children from different social backgrounds.

- The beneficial effects of pre-school remained evident throughout Key Stage 1, although some outcomes were not as strong as they had been at school entry.

- *Does type of pre-school matter?*
  - There are significant differences between individual pre-school settings and their impact on children; some settings are more effective than others in promoting positive child outcomes.
  - Good quality can be found across all types of early years settings; however even after taking account of a child's background and prior intellectual skills, the type of pre-school a child attends has an important effect on developmental progress. EPPE found that integrated centres (these are centres that fully combine education with care and have a high proportion of trained teachers) and nursery schools tend to promote the strongest intellectual outcomes for children. Similarly, fully integrated settings and nursery classes tend to promote better social development even after taking account of children's backgrounds and prior social behaviour.

- *Effects of duration*
  - The number of months a child attended pre-school continued to have an effect on their progress throughout Key Stage 1, although this effect was stronger for academic skills than for social behavioural development.

- *Effects of quality*
  - Pre-school quality was significantly related to children's scores on standardised tests of reading and mathematics at age six. At age seven the relationship between quality and academic attainment was somewhat weaker and the effect of quality on social behavioural development was no longer significant.
  - Settings that have staff with higher qualifications have higher quality scores and their children make more progress.
  - Effective pedagogy includes interaction traditionally associated with the term 'teaching', the provision of instructive learning environments and 'sustained shared thinking' to extend children's learning (Siraj-Blatchford et al., 2002).

- *The importance of home learning*
  - For all children, the quality of the home learning environment promotes more intellectual and social development than parental occupation or qualification.

The EPPE study has demonstrated the positive effects of high quality pre-school provision on children's intellectual and social behavioural development up to the end of Key Stage 1 in primary school. The EPPE research indicates that pre-school can play an important part in combating social exclusion and promoting inclusion by offering disadvantaged children, in particular, a better start to primary school. Figure 10.1 shows clearly that disadvantaged children fail to meet the 'expected level' (level 2) in reading and writing if they do not attend pre-school education. The EPPE findings indicate that pre-school has a positive impact on children's progress over and above important family influences. The quality of the pre-school setting as well as the quantity (more terms but not necessarily more hours/day) are both influential.

EPPE has also shown that individual pre-school centres vary in their effectiveness in promoting intellectual progress over the pre-school period, and indicate that better outcomes are associated with some forms of provision. Likewise, the research points to the separate and significant influence of the home learning environment. These aspects (quality and quantity of pre-school and home learning environment) are more susceptible to change through policy initiatives than family characteristics such as SES. Early childhood services are a powerful lever in reducing inequalities and government used this message in 1999–2004 as a rationale for policy (House of Commons, 2000b, 2004; Inter-departmental Childcare Review, 2002).

EPPE results were replicated in a study in Northern Ireland (Melhuish, 2002, 2003) suggesting that the benefits of early education were to be found throughout the UK. Moreover EPPE findings were supplemented by small-scale studies, such as Bertram *et al.* (2002), suggesting that integrating services and focusing on families were the 'best' ways to promote child development and family capacity to support their children.

Part III: The achievement

In the period since 1997 there has been substantial investment in services for young children and their families, some of it universal and some targeted at the most disadvantaged communities (for further details of programmes and expenditure see http://www.nao.org.uk/publications/nao_reports/03-04/0304268.pdf, p. 22). The £2 billion annual government expenditure in 1997 had soared by 75% to £3.5 billion by 2003 (see Figure 10.2). Indeed, some £14 billion has been spent on early years services since 1998 (National Audit Office, 2004). However, as is evident in Figure 10.3, parents still make the major financial contribution to the cost of care – around 45% of the national childcare bill in 2002–2003, although part-time early education is free for three and four year olds.

With this level of investment, the sector has experienced some dramatic changes in the landscape, with a considerable number of centres both opening and closing, as nurseries in the private and voluntary sectors struggle to make

Reading at key stage 1,
SES and pre-school
experience

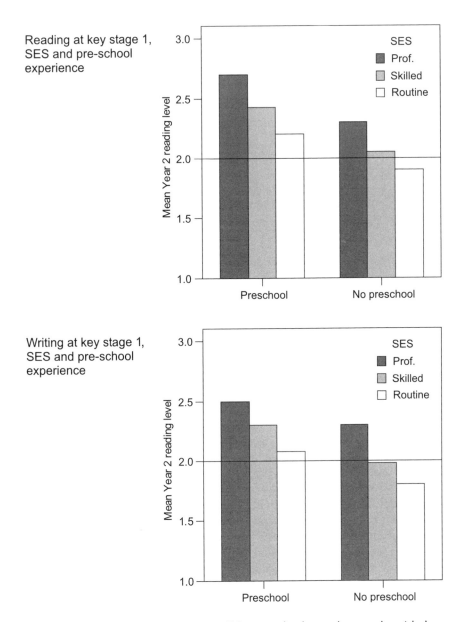

Writing at key stage 1,
SES and pre-school
experience

Figure 10.1 Children's attainment at age 7 by pre-school attendance and social class.
Source: Sammons *et al.* (2004).

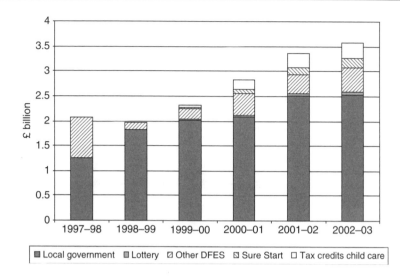

Figure 10.2 Government expenditure on early years since 1997.
Source: National Audit Office (2004).

ends meet. As can be seen from Figure 10.4, in the childcare sector each year there are nearly half as many closures as there are new places. The most rapid expansion has been in full day care places and in out-of-school clubs (some of which include places for children under five) (Table 10.1), along with expansion of part-time early education. Nursery education is the only universal service for all three and four year olds whose parents wish to take advantage of it. The numbers of children using these free places has risen by over 40% since 1998, from around 800,000 to 1,150,000 (Figure 10.5). The public funding to provide 12.5 hours a week in term time for children of three and four is available to nursery and primary schools in the statutory sector and to private and voluntary sector nurseries and pre-school groups, provided they meet nationally approved standards. For parents who wish to use more than this two and a half hours a day, and also to find provision during the holidays, there is a commitment to increase the amount of 'joined up' provision through children's centres and 'wrap around care' (see below) but parents will probably have to pay, unless they are eligible for working tax credit, or live in an area in which the local authority has subsidised the cost of the provision.

Working tax credit, introduced in 1998 as Childcare Tax Credit, was intended to assist low income families with up to 70% of their childcare costs. However, the take-up has been low. Only 15% of eligible couples and 24% of lone parent families receive the child care element and according to the National Audit Office 20% of low income parents still pay all costs themselves (National Audit Office, 2004).

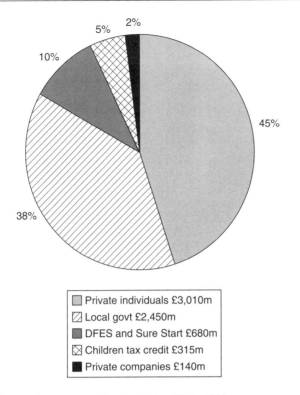

Figure 10.3 How early years provision is paid for, 2002–2003.
Source: National Audit Office (2004).

Much of the expansion in service provision has been targeted on those areas with the highest level of need. The initiative that has reached the greatest number of children is Sure Start, where some 520 local programmes have been set up with a catchment area of between 500 and 900 children under four and their families. With a focus on the emotional, social and intellectual development and health of young children, and support for their parents, the programmes are managed by a local partnership board involving parents and professionals from health, education and social services. There is an extensive evaluation underway, but there are as yet few published reports on outcomes; those that are available from the very early programmes show 'a positive but limited effect' (National Evaluation of Sure Start, 2004).

The flagship of integrated services, providing seamless care and education for children from a few months old until five, were 'Early Excellence Centres', some 107 'one stop shops' providing all day all year care and education for children, support for parents and often access to adult education as well. Few of these were new centres: most were built on existing centres or networks of

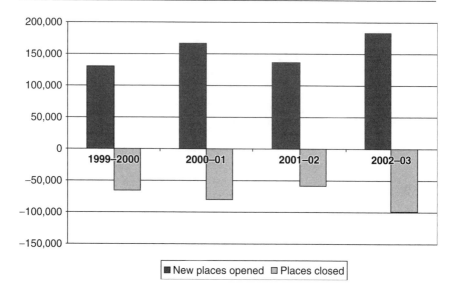

Figure 10.4 Annual changes in childcare places, 1999–2003.
Source: National Audit Office (2004).

Table 10.1 Number of childcare places in England (excluding nursery education or sessional pre-school places)

	Places for children (registered)	
	1997	2004
Childminders	365,200	322,100
Full daycare	193,800	483,600
Out of school clubs	78,700	332,400
Total	637,700	1,138,100

Source: Daycare Trust (2004).

services, with the provision of a little additional funding to extend the service and encourage the centre to take on a training and dissemination role. The initial evaluation of these centres (Bertram *et al.*, 2002) suggested substantial benefits for children, families and the wider community through the bringing together of a range of services that met families' needs without the stigma associated with specialist provision.

A further plank of the expansion of early years provision has been the Neighbourhood Nurseries Initiative, which has aimed to meet the needs of children and parents in disadvantaged areas with a 'mixed economy' approach within

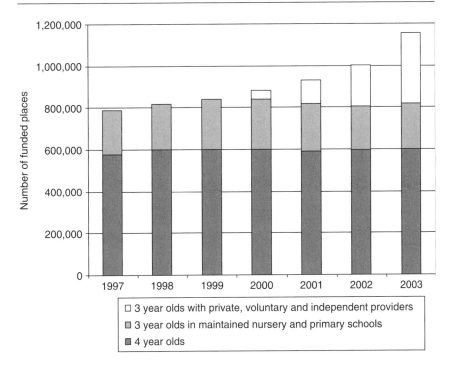

Figure 10.5 Number of children in early years (nursery) education, 1997–2003.
Source: National Audit Office (2004).

the private, voluntary and statutory sectors. Some 1400 neighbourhood nurseries are planned by March 2005 but some have closed already, and many are now becoming children's centres.

In 2003 the government launched its 'children's centre' programme, building on early excellence centres and neighbourhood nurseries through a promise of a centre in the 20% most disadvantaged communities. Children's centres are less generously funded than early excellence centres, but they do have an additional emphasis on health, being required to provide a base for midwives, health visitors and speech and language therapists, as well as information and support for parents, and training and support for childcare workers (see Pugh, 2003). From 2006 local Sure Start programmes will be integrated into children's centres, and the forthcoming Ten Year Strategy is likely to promise children's centres in every community by the end of the next parliament (Prime Minister's speech, November 2004).

The Foundation Stage curriculum has been well received and enthusiastically adopted by early years professionals (Aubrey, 2004). The *Foundation Stage Guidance* (DfEE QCA, 2000) and, more recently, *Birth to Three Matters* (DfES/Sure Start, 2003) provide a clear framework for all years practitioners working with children up to the age of six. Both are based on clear principles and on the central importance of learning through play, but within a structure in which there are opportunities for children to engage in activities planned by adults as well as those they plan or initiate themselves. Both the three to six and the birth to three frameworks also recognise the centrality of social, emotional and creative development, as well as literacy and numeracy. The government has made the radical step of specifying developmental objectives and pathways for its youngest children.

The EPPE research cited above found that a key to the quality of the provision and good outcomes for children was the level of qualification of the staff working in early years settings. Table 10.2 outlines the qualifications and age of the workforce, illustrating not only the discrepancy between teaching and non-teaching staff in qualifications and levels of pay, but also how little many staff are paid. It is not surprising that the Equal Opportunities Commission recommended to the Select Committee on Child-care (2004) that government should 'invest in the workforce. Staff should be better paid and receive good quality training ...'

The EPPE researchers (Taggart et al., 2000) showed a hierarchy in staff qualifications across the sectors: 'Nursery classes and nursery schools ... could be viewed as the most highly qualified, followed by combined centres, then private day nurseries and local authority centres together, and finally, playgroups that have the lowest proportion of qualified staff'. Qualifications in the workforce and equity of pay and conditions remains a major problem as will be discussed below.

Government has clearly seen both quality and integration of provision as a key to transforming early years provision, and in this it has been supported by findings from the EPPE study and by the evaluation of the early excellence centres. But how good is the quality of our early years provision? The 2003 Ofsted Early Years report concluded that 'on the whole, childcare providers have reached the level set out in the national standards'. But as the final section of this paper shows, whilst the promise was clear and the delivery swift, problems remain in realising the longer term vision.

Table 10.2 Characteristics of the childcare workforce

	Women	Under 25	NVQ3	Hourly pay
Childcare workers	98%	41%	52%	£5.50
Childminders	99%	6%*	15%	N/A
Nursery workers	99%	16%	76%	£7.10
Playgroup workers	99%	7%	44%	£5.40
Teachers (for comparison)	72%	5%	97%	£11.07

*20–29 years.
Adapted from Daycare Trust (2004) and Moss (2004).

Part IV: Tensions remaining – the shortfall

The authors of this paper are not alone in applauding the government's achievements. 'Tremendous progress has been made in children's services in England since the first OECD review took place in December 1999. Most noteworthy are the significant increase in investment, the expansion of (local) Sure Start schemes and new moves towards children's centres and extended schools' (private communication from John Bennett, author of the forthcoming OECD report on early years, 2004).

While the past seven years have seen considerable increases in the level of provision, and a commitment to ensuring high quality, even more is promised. The DfES ten year strategy for early years and childcare, to be published at the end of 2004 and heralded in a speech given by the Prime Minister in November 2004, promises 2,500 children's centres by 2008 and a universal offer by 2010, some to be developed out of existing provision, including primary schools. In addition every school is to offer extended opening hours in order to support parents' working patterns. Given the challenges in sustaining the quality and quantity of existing services these are extraordinarily ambitious targets. Let us examine briefly some of the issues that are raised – the integration of care and education, whether services are sustainable, and the quality of the services, including the calibre of the workforce.

The concept of children's centres assumes, from the child and family's perspective, an integrated service, offering high quality education and care, available all the year round and for a long working day, providing support for parents, access to training and employment, and with health care and outreach into local communities. This is the vision at the centre of the government's Change for Children agenda, as embodied in the Green Paper *Every Child Matters* and the Children Act 2004. Within this, children's centres are the key to joined-up service delivery, as are extended primary and secondary schools for children and young people aged 5–16. But it is a far cry from the current maze of different providers and services that parents must navigate. There are currently only 71 children's centres – a long way for one in every community. The universal vision is an excellent one – but can we travel this far so fast, given the reluctance of professionals to work in integrated teams and the challenges of bringing together different professional cultures, patterns of training, working practices and salaries, and conditions of service?

Whilst joining up services is a challenge, it is nothing to the size of the expansion required, nor the challenges of sustaining the growth already experienced, at a price that parents can afford. The government's 'offer' to parents for children before the age of five is for two and a half hours of free nursery education a day for three and four year olds in term time only. Anything beyond this (including provision for children under three) is paid for by parents, with some subsidy provided for some parents through working tax credit. As has been shown, working tax credit reaches only a relatively small number of parents (parents are either earning too much or not earning at all) and even for those who claim, the amount received is far from the actual cost of a place. In one London borough, for example, it costs on average £250 per week for a child care place. In order for parents to be able to afford this, the borough has to subsidise all places by £80 per week to help parents to bridge the gap (London Borough of Camden, 2004). In areas in which there is no subsidy, many parents cannot afford the fees.

Those providing early education – whether in the statutory, voluntary or independent sector – are equally unable to meet the costs without subsidy and, as has been shown, the level of turnover amongst providers is rising. Government figures show that between April 1997 and March 2004 over one million childcare places were created, but there was only a net gain of 540,000 places (Hansard column 1050W, 17 June 2004). Any further increase in the number of places will therefore require substantially increased subsidies for both parents and providers.

A government with elections to win is likely to put increased quantity higher on its agenda than improved quality, and yet the research evidence cited in this paper shows that it is only early education of high quality, provided by staff who are well qualified, that is effective in the longer term. There is currently a very wide variety in the quality of children's experiences in early years services. Government inspectors rate 54% of childcare as satisfactory rather than good, and much of the workforce is poorly trained and under qualified, particularly in the voluntary and independent sectors, with high staff turnover. Only 50% of staff in day nurseries are qualified to NVQ level 3 (some way below graduate level) and there are significant differences in pay and conditions between those with a teaching qualification and those without. The new Children's Workforce Council is charged with improving the qualifications and training of all who work with children but it remains to be seen how closely they are able to work with the Teaching Training Agency to bring some cohesion to the early years workforce. Additional funding is urgently required to improve training and qualifications, and to pay the increased salaries that these better-qualified staff will be able to demand.

Even within nursery classes situated in primary schools, many children are in classes where teachers are not qualified to work with three and four year olds. A recent study of children's experiences in reception classes concluded: 'If the purpose of the Foundation Stage was to extend to four and five year olds in primary/infant schools the best practice in the education of three and four year olds, then it has not succeeded. There is a demonstrable gap between the quality of children's experiences in the reception classes (the year preceding Year 1) and the quality of their experiences earlier in the Foundation Stage...' (Adams et al., 2004). There are huge implications here for the training and ongoing professional development of the early years workforce, all of which have considerable resource implications.

As this quotation illustrates, there is concern that the Foundation Stage curriculum, intended to guide the practice of those working with children aged three, four and five years up until the end of the reception year, is not being implemented as it was intended. The Foundation Stage guidance and *Birth to Three Matters* have been widely welcomed across the early years sector. But a high priority for government now must be to extend the Foundation Stage to incorporate the birth to three phase, and to ensure that the foundation phase is seen as the first stage of education, for all children from birth to five/six years.

Another tension concerns the government's commitment to a mixed market. EPPE (Sylva *et al.*, 1999) and other research has shown that there is higher quality in the state sector than the voluntary and private sectors. Will further expansion of the non statutory sectors compromise quality? Further, Moss (1999) questions the over-arching 'preparation for school' rationale of early years education, and calls for a re-investigation of the very nature of childhood (see also Montgomery *et al.*, 2003). This, he believes, would result in fundamental changes to the way early years education is conceived and approached. Early years practitioners have long argued that this first phase of education must be seen as of value in its own right, and not as training for academic skills needed in school (DES, 1990).

And finally – is this expansion primarily focused on the needs of children for high quality early education in the first years of their lives, or is it driven by the wish to enable as many parents as possible to return to work? Can 'early education' be reconciled with 'childcare for working parents'? Much of the drive for additional places has come from a commitment, led by the Chancellor of the Exchequer, to dramatically reduce the number of children living in poverty. The most effective way of doing this, it is argued, is by enabling parents in workless households to return to work, which they could do if there were adequate childcare. The expansion of 'childcare' places is long overdue and welcomed by parents and early years professionals alike, but expansion cannot be at the expense of quality, and parents must feel that they have some choice. As the EPPE research has shown, the educational environment of the home and the support that parents give their children is key to all aspects of their future development, but many parents feel torn by the dual messages of 'work' and 'be better parents' and under some pressure to return to work before they are ready.

Much has been achieved, and the ten year strategy promises yet more. Yet the vision is still hazy. Over the past year the integrated education and care of young children has been referred to by government as nursery education, day care, childcare, early years services, the foundation stage/phase and early education. Is it to be high quality early education led by well trained staff, or edu-care offered by a poorly qualified and low-paid workforce? As the expansion continues, there are nettles to be grasped and adequate resources to be found if the quality of early education is to be central to all early years services, and if care and education are to be truly integrated.

Acknowledgements

The authors are grateful to James Walker-Hall for bibliographic assistance and help with figures and tables.

References

Adams, S., Alexander, E., Drummond, M. J. & Moyles, J. (2004) *Inside the foundation stage: recreating the reception year* (London, Association of Teachers and Lecturers).

Aubrey, C. (2004) Implementing the foundation stage in reception classes, *British Educational Research Journal,* 30(5), 633–656.

Audit Commission (1996) *Counting to five* (London, Audit Commission).

Ball, C. (1994) *Start right: the importance of early learning* (London, Royal Society of Arts).

Barnett, W. S. (1996) Lives in the balance: Age-27 Benefit-cost analysis of the high/scope perry preschool program. *Monographs of the high/scope educational research foundation,* 11 (Ypsilanti, High/Scope Press).

Bertram, T., Pascel, C., Bokhari, S., Gasper, M. & Holtermann, S. (2002) Early Excellence Centre pilot programme, DfES *Research brief RB 361.*

Blakemore, S. & Frith, U. (2005) *The learning brain* (Oxford, Blackwell Publishing).

Bruer, J. T. (1997) Education and the brain: a bridge too far. *Educational Researcher,* 26(8), 4–16.

Bruner, J. (1986) *Actual minds, possible worlds* (London, Harvard University Press).

Daycare Trust (2004) *A new era for universal childcare?* www.daycare.trust.org.uk.

Department for Education and Employment (1998) *Meeting the childcare challenge.* http://www.dfes.gov.uk/childcare/chldcare.doc.

Department of Education and Skills (1990) *Starting with quality: report of the committee of enquiry into the educational experience offered to 3 and 4 year olds* (Rumbold Report) (London, HMSO).

DfEE/QCA (2000) *Curriculum guidance for the foundation stage* (London, Qualifications and Curriculum Authority).

DfES/Sure Start (2003) *Birth to three matters, an introduction to the framework* (London, HMSO).

Gopnik, A., Meltzoff, A. & Kuhl, P. K. (1999) *The Scientist in the crib: what early learning tells us about the mind* (New York, William Morrow).

Hansard written answers to questions (2004) *Attainment Gap.* Volume no 422, part no 103, column 1050W.

House of Commons (2000a) Early years learning. *Post,* 140 (London, Parliamentary Office of Science and Technology).

House of Commons (2000b) Education and employment committee. *Early years* (London, The Stationery Office).

House of Commons (2004) *Early years: progress in developing high quality childcare and early education accessible to all* (London, The Stationery Office).

Inter-Departmental Childcare Review (2002) *Delivering for children and families* (London, Department for Education and Skills/Department for Work and Pension/HM treasury/Women and Equality Unit).

London Borough of Camden (2004) *The shortage of under fives childcare in Camden.*

Melhuish, E. C. (2002). Prospects for research on the quality of the pre-school experience, in: W. W. Hartup & R. K. Silbereisen (Eds) *Growing points in Developmental Science* (Hove, Psychology Press).

Melhuish, E. C. (2003) Daycare, in: B. Hopkins *et al.* (Eds) *Cambridge encyclopaedia of child development* (Cambridge, Cambridge University Press).

Melhuish, E. (2004) *A literature review of the impact of early years provision on young children, with emphasis given to children from disadvantaged backgrounds* (London, National Audit Commission).

Montgomery, H., Burr, R. & Woodhead, M. (Eds) (2003) *Changing childhoods: local and global* (Wiley, The Open University).

Moss, P. (1999) Renewed hopes and lost opportunities: early childhood in the early years of the Labour Government, *Cambridge Journal of Education,* 29(2), 229–238.

Moss, P. (2004) *Why we need a well qualified early childhood workforce.* Powerpoint presentation.

National Audit Office (2004) *Early Years: progress in developing high quality childcare and early education accessible to all* (London, The Stationery Office) (http://www.nao.org.uk/publications/ nao_reports/03–04/0304268.pdf).

National Evaluation of Sure Start (2004) *Towards understanding Sure Start local programmes* (London, DfES).

Office for Standards in Education (2003) *Early years: The first national picture* (London, Ofsted Publications Centre). (http://www.ofsted.gov.uk/publications/ index.cfm?fuseaction=pubs.display-file&id=3372&type=pdf).

Prime Minister (2004) Speech to the Daycare Trust conference, November 11.

Pugh, G. (1994) Born to learn, *Times Education Supplement* (http://www.tes.co.uk/ search/story/?story_id=9504).

Pugh, G. (2003) Children's centres and social inclusion. *Education Review,* 17(1), 23–29.

Ramey, C. T. & Ramey, S. L. (1998) Early intervention and early experience. *American Psychologist,* 53, 109–120.

Sammons, P., Smees, R., Taggart, B., Sylva, K., Melhuish, E., Siraj-Blatchford, I. & Elliot, K. (2004) *The effective provision of pre-school education project (EPPE). Technical paper 2: special educational needs in the early primary years: primary school entry up to the end of year 1* (London, DfES/Institute of Education, University of London).

Sammons, P., Sylva, K., Melhuish, E., Siraj-Blatchford, I., Taggart, B. & Elliot, K. (2002) *The Effective Provision of Pre-School Education Project (EPPE). Technical paper 8a: measuring the impact of pre-school on children's cognitive progress over the pre-school period* (London, DfES/Institute of Education, University of London).

Sammons, P., Sylva, K., Melhuish, E., Siraj-Blatchford, I., Taggart, B. & Elliot, K. (2003) *The Effective Provision of Pre-School Education Project (EPPE). Technical paper 8b: Measuring the impact of pre-school on children's social/behavioural development over the pre-school period* (London, DfES/Institute of Education, University of London).

Sammons, P., Sylva, K., Melhuish, E., Siraj-Blatchford, I., Taggart, B., Elliot, K. & Marsh, A. (2004). *The effective provision of pre-school education project (EPPE). Technical paper 11: The continuing effects of pre-school education at age 7 years* (London, DfES/Institute of Education, University of London).

Schweinhart, L. J., Barnes, H. V. & Weikart, D. P. (1993) Significant benefits: the high/scope perry preschool study through age 27, *Monographs of the high/scope educational research foundation,* 10 (Ypsilanti, High/Scope Press).

Siraj-Blatchford, I., Sylva, K., Muttock, S., Gilden, R. & Bell, D. (2002) *Researching effective pedagogy in the early years* (Norwich, DfES/Queen's Printer).

Sylva, K. (1994a) The impact of early learning on children's later development, in: C. Ball *Start right: the importance of early learning* (London, RSA).

Sylva, K. (1994b) School influences on children's development, *Journal of Child Psychology and Psychiatry,* 35(1), 135–170.

Sylva, K., Melhuish, E., Sammons, P. & Siraj-Blatchford, I. (1999) *The effective provision of pre-school education project (EPPE). Technical paper 1: Introduction to the effective provision of pre-school education project (EPPE)* (London, Institute of Education, University of London).

Sylva, K., Melhuish, E., Sammons, P., Siraj-Blatchford, I. & Taggart, B. (2004) *The effective provision of pre-school education project (EPPE). Technical paper 12: Effective pre-school education* (London, DfES/Institute of Education, University of London).

Sylva, K., Siraj-Blatchford, I., Melhuish, E., Sammons, P., Taggart, B., Evans, E., Dobson, A., Jeavons, M., Lewis, K., Morahan, M. & Sadler, S. (1999). *The effective provision of pre-school education project (EPPE). Technical paper 6a: characteristics of the pre-school: an introduction to the EPPE project* (London, DfES/Institute of Education, University of London).

Taggart, B., Sylva, K., Siraj-Blatchford, I., Melhuish, E., Sammons, P. & Walker-Hall, J. (2000) *The effective provision of pre-school education project (EPPE). Technical paper 5: characteristics of the centres in the EPPE study: interviews* (London, DfES/Institute of Education, University of London).

The Treasury and Department of Education and Skills. (2003) *Every child matters* (London, The Stationery Office).

Chapter 11

The 'childcare champion'? New Labour, social justice and the childcare market

Stephen J. Ball and Carol Vincent

Source: *S. J. Ball and C. Vincent, British Educational Research Journal, 31(5), 557–570, 2005.*

Abstract

Childcare as a policy issue has received unprecedented attention under New Labour, through various aspects of the National Childcare Strategy introduced in 1998. This policy focus looks set to continue, with the government announcing the first ever 10-year plan for childcare in December 2004, and childcare playing a major role in the 2005 manifesto and general election. Early years care and education is a productive area for New Labour as initiatives here can address several agendas: increasing social inclusion, revitalising the labour market, and raising standards in education. The provision of childcare is seen as having the potential to bring women back into the workforce, modelling child-rearing skills to parents understood as being in need of such support, and giving children the skills and experience they need to succeed in compulsory education. This article offers an overview of recent policy on childcare, drawing in places on a two-year study of the choice and provision of childcare in London. The article examines the developments in childcare planned and set in motion by the government, identifying some points to be welcomed as well as areas of concern. The authors demonstrate that even for privileged middle-class consumers, such as those in their research, the current childcare market is a very 'peculiar' one, especially when compared to the markets of economic theory. In conclusion, the authors argue that social justice in childcare is more than a matter of access, and highlight the lack of parental voice shaping the future direction and development of the childcare market.

Introduction

> You can't put a price on the safety and happiness of your child.
>
> (Grace, Battersea mother)

This article offers an overview of recent policy on childcare. The childcare sector is an important one to research in relation to social justice as it is currently dynamic and developing, having experienced both massive expansion of private sector provision and high levels of government intervention. We consider New Labour's recent initiatives in childcare and argue that the focus has been on increasing provision, a necessary, but not sufficient approach to make meaningful choice in childcare available to all. The article goes on to demonstrate that even for privileged middle-class consumers, the childcare market is a very 'peculiar' one, especially when compared to the markets of economic theory. We conclude that social justice in childcare is currently understood to be primarily a matter of access, overlooking issues of form and content, and with a lack of parental voice shaping the future direction and development of the childcare market.

At various points in the article we draw on data collected during an Economic and Social Research Council funded project on choice of pre-school childcare (R000239232). Our project investigated choice and provision of pre-school child care, and the interactions of parents with the childcare market. We focused on professional middle-class users, sometimes referred to as members of the 'service class',[1] a sizeable group of users in the formal marketplace where the costs involved in accessing care are high, especially in London where our research was located. We focused on two inner London areas, Stoke Newington and Battersea (for a detailed explanation of this approach, see Vincent *et al.*, 2004). The two areas both have sizeable service class populations, although of different kinds. Our sample in Battersea was dominated by private sector employees, especially those that work in households where one adult at least is employed in the City, whilst the Stoke Newington respondents were more likely to be welfare or arts professionals. Our research cohort was a skilled and privileged group of consumers: mostly white, mostly heterosexual and all highly educated, the vast majority having a first degree.[2] Yet even these multiply-advantaged consumers sometimes struggled in their interactions with the market, their difficulties due to the particular characteristics of childcare services.

New Labour childcare policy

Until the advent of the 1997 Labour government childcare was indeed a neglected area of public policy. As Denise Riley (1983) has noted, 'the very term "childcare" has a dispiriting and dutiful heaviness hanging over it ... it is as short on colour and incisiveness as the business of negotiating the wet kerb with the pushchair' (cited in Brennan, 1998, p. 3). However, the rising number of mothers with small children who were returning to the labour market was a phenomenon that demanded a response.[3] In addition, and importantly, early years care and education is a productive area for New Labour as initiatives here can theoretically address several agendas: increasing social inclusion and in particular combating child poverty, revitalising the labour market, and raising standards in education. The provision of childcare is seen as having the potential to bring women back into the workforce, thereby increasing productivity as well as lifting families out of poverty, modelling child-rearing skills to parents understood as being in need of such support, and giving children the skills and experience they need to succeed in compulsory education. It is worth noting, however, that these different agendas are only partially complementary.

Until recently, and as is the case in the USA (Uttal, 2002), the private sector has been the major beneficiary of the increasing number of women returning to work. In the period between 1990 and 2000 the UK day nursery market quadrupled, and day nurseries account for about 30% of registered child care places. The day nursery market is worth £2.66 billion (Blackburn, 2004) and in 2003, grew by 13%. The sector is currently experiencing a period of mergers and acquisitions among the larger operators, with Nord Anglia buying two other major but struggling chains, Leapfrog and Jigsaw, in 2004, making it the market leader in terms of size. Asquith Court, the former market leader, and kidsunlimited also announced a merger over the summer of 2004 to form the Nursery Years Group. However, this was then called off as being 'commercially unviable' (statement from kidsunlimited, reported in *Nursery World*, 11 November 2004). Despite this, more mergers and acquisitions are likely to follow, resulting, eventually, in perhaps three or four major players dominating the market, paralleling the history of the residential care sector (although independent small businesses are unlikely to completely disappear). However, at the moment the private day nursery sector remains a competitive, fragmented market. Currently, private sector providers outside London are complaining that their viability, in a period of falling birth rates, is further at risk from government funded Sure Start initiatives scooping up the limited numbers of children and staff in particular localities (Vevers, 2004a). Blackburn's 2004 report also notes a rise in vacancy rates nationwide for the second year running (Blackburn, 2004).

Through the National Childcare Strategy (Department for Education and Skills [DfES], 1998) and the new Ten Year Strategy (Her Majesty's Treasury [HMT], 2004), New Labour is committed to 'a longer term vision of the childcare market in which every parent can access affordable, good quality childcare' (Baroness Ashton, DfES, 2002, cited in Mooney, 2003, p. 112; also HMT, 2004, p. 1). This is to be achieved through a plethora of initiatives, particularly directed at disadvantaged areas and lower income families. However, the rhetoric is increasingly of universal childcare (Vevers, 2004b; Labour Party,

2005), with services being provided through Children's Centres (integrated services on one site eventually planned to be in every local community, but initially in the most disadvantaged areas). The pace of expansion quickened markedly in 2004. As part of the Spending Review, the Chancellor announced in the summer of 2004 that 2500 Children's Centres will be open by 2008, and the 2005 manifesto promises 3500 Children's Centres by 2010 ('a universal local service' [Labour Party, 2005, p. 75]).[4] The DfES five-year plan published in 2004 (DfES, 2004) also talks of a vision of integrated 'educare', with services available to families from 8 a.m. to 6 p.m., 48 weeks of the year. The emphasis is clearly on one-stop provision, drawing together a range of health, education and welfare and care services available eventually to all families. (There is, of course, a considerable body of literature on the difficulties of inter-agency collaboration. For one recent review, see Campbell & Whitty [2002].) The umbrella for these many projects is Sure Start,[5] which now incorporates Children's Centres and the Neighbourhood Nurseries Initiative (designed to bring affordable care to disadvantaged areas). The future of Sure Start is contested (see Glass, 2005; Hodge, 2005) but local programmes will be wound up within the next two years as Children's Centres appear. Glass (2005) asserts that 'little [of the philosophy and ways of working] will remain but the brand name'.

The recently-published Ten Year Strategy (HMT, 2004) announced Labour's key proposals. The strategy takes account of earlier criticisms that Labour's plans were directed primarily at adult workers rather than children, by emphasising the benefits of pre-school education for children, and acknowledging 'a policy that gives too much emphasis to helping parents work could come at the expense of the needs of children' (HMT, 2004, para. 2.4). The strategy lays out plans for the extension of paid maternity leave to nine months from 2007 with a planned extension to 12 months by 2010. Some of that leave may be transferable to fathers. Children's Centres should number 3500 by 2010 (one in every 'community'), although they will be at their most numerous and most extensive in disadvantaged areas. Three-and four-year-olds will receive a phased extension of their free provision up to 15 hours per week (for 38 weeks a year) by 2010, with an ultimate goal of 20 hours per week. There is no mention of universal provision for one-and two-year-olds, however.

New Labour has also made tax credits available to lower income families, and from April 2005 an extension was announced of the childcare voucher scheme to offer working parents in participating companies income relief on the first £50 they earn each week. With regard to planning provision and ensuring well-trained staff, local authorities have been given the role of developing and supporting local provision. There will be a Transformation Fund from 2006 which will contain £125 million to 'help raise quality and sustainability'. A new training and qualifications structure is already being planned. An increase in Child Tax Credit will be introduced, and £5 million is to be invested in pilot schemes in London in recognition of the capital's particularly high childcare costs.

There are many praiseworthy government initiatives here. The Chancellor, Gordon Brown, was hailed as a 'childcare champion' in March 2004 by the pressure group and childcare charity the Daycare Trust. This was in response to the 2004 Budget, which directed increased spending of £669 million on early years education and childcare by 2008, and the July Spending Review, which saw an extra £100 million for the development of Children's Centres. Thus, the Sure Start budget will rise by 17% in real terms from 2004/05 to 2007/08.

Nonetheless, there has been concern expressed by those in the field that the expansion which seeks to improve access to care has not been entirely thought through, although, as we note above, the Ten Year Strategy clearly seeks to address some campaigners' concerns. Writing just after the publication of the strategy, it seems that the following concerns (expressed in summer 2004) are still pertinent. A special report in the practitioner journal, Nursery World, described the aims of the Spending Review and the five-year education plan as 'laudable' but also noted 'concerns over the level of funding, the absence of clear mechanisms for delivery, a perceived yawning gap in staff training and an unrealistic timescale' (Vevers, 2004c, p. 10).[6]

Affordability is likely to remain as a stumbling block to access. Childcare costs, even with the various subsidies and funding streams in place, are still high, especially in London, with parents bearing 75–85% of the costs.[7] The Daycare Trust's 2004 survey found that whilst a full-time nursery place for an under-two cost an average of £134 a week, or over £7000 per annum, the inner London equivalent is £168 a week, over £8730 per annum. Another recent survey by the Daycare Trust into the impact of the childcare element of the Working Tax Credit (now the integrated Children and Working Tax Credit) on parents and childcare providers in the capital found that the average cost of childcare in London is 'significantly' higher than the rest of the country, meaning that even with tax credits, childcare is unaffordable for many parents (research reported at www.daycaretrust.org.uk). The Ten Year Strategy (HMT, 2004) signalled a rise in Children's Tax Credit to a maximum of £175 for one child, which is clearly necessary. However, the CTC still excludes informal care and take-up is low. Duncan et al. (2004) quotes figures from 2002 revealing that only 13% of those eligible receive the benefit. Whilst there are signs of recent improvement, there are still complaints that CTC is complex to apply for and the administration is poor (Howard, 2004). Duncan et al. (2004) also cite Hilary Land's argument (2002) that childcare provision, unlike school education or healthcare, is not provided as a free universal service, and thus 'meaningful choice' (Alakeson, 2004; Collins & Alakeson, 2004) is unavailable to families with lower incomes.

Another common criticism (which the government's proposals will address when they reach fruition) is that childcare options currently depend on where you live. London, our research suggested, is a 'sellers' market'. There has also been some concern over Sure Start's targeting of the most disadvantaged areas, the criticism being the same as that for any area-based initiative: many families in poverty are also to be found outside the designated areas. One recent example was provided by a street in Newham in London, which was divided by a Sure Start boundary. As a result, services were available to families on one side and not the other, However, the council succeeded in integrating various funding streams and thereby expanding services to all parents within the borough (Curnow, 2004).

In our study, in contrast to some other areas of the country, both Battersea and Stoke Newington had an inadequate supply of childcare places. State funded provision was unavailable to these middle-class families in Battersea (B) and heavily oversubscribed in Stoke Newington (SN). The transcripts were littered with similar complaints and amazement: 'couldn't find a nursery place – waiting lists' (Grace, B); 'It's a sellers' market for childminders' (Madison, SN); 'they were fully booked' (Marie, SN); 'the nurseries were full' (Isabel, B); 'I had his name down before birth' (Lynn, B); 'There just aren't many childminders, they are difficult to find' (Mia, SN); 'private nurseries were full … simply not enough … waiting lists as long as your arm' (Elsa, SN); 'I was in the market too late at 6 mths pregnant' (Nicole, SN). The families in both localities were unanimous that it 'sounds like a lot of choice but there isn't' (Margaret, B). Indeed, when the mothers talked about 'competition' they did not mean among providers but between choosers – 'everything's so sort of competitive around here' (Grace, B); 'you always hope they will give you preferential treatment on the waiting list because you had a child there before, because it's so competitive' (Madison, SN); 'finding the right childcare is very competitive' (Rachel, SN); 'everything is so competitive around here' (Alice, B). The issue of variability in both supply and quality of provision presents a continuing challenge for policy makers (Duncan, 2004).

Particular difficulties are likely to be the perception held by some that the expansion focuses on access but avoids the much contested issue of 'quality' care. The BBC television programme *Nurseries Uncovered*, which screened in August 2004, dramatically illustrated that in three apparently reputable care settings, the quality of carer–child interaction and the levels of hygiene both left a lot to be desired. The undercover reporter found young children, toddlers in some cases, being shouted at and treated with little dignity by some staff. The issue of staffing in the sector is a crucial one, as acknowledged by the Ten Year Strategy (HMT, 2004; see, for instance, paras 3.34–3.35). There is already a problem with recruitment and retention, as the young women who traditionally make up the bulk of the caring workforce can find better paid employment elsewhere. Presumably in recognition of this, the Office for Standards in Education (Ofsted) now allows providers to count 17-year-old trainees in staffing ratios (Evans, 2004). Working with young children is exhausting and draining. Yet nursery assistants in the private sector in

2003 received an average starting salary of £4.50 an hour, going up to £4.80. Qualified nursery nurses earned £4.92 going up to £5.30 an hour. Even nursery managers' top rates of pay were little over £8 an hour.[8] Unsurprisingly, there are currently recruitment difficulties, especially at the more senior levels, with Sure Start research reporting 79% of settings having difficulties in recruiting supervisors.[9]

As the number of nurseries has nearly doubled in the last five years, the need for new staff is intense. Sure Start estimates that between 175,000 and 180,000 new staff are needed in the sector between 2003 and 2006. Concerns have also been raised about the levels to which staff are trained and the need to professionalise the childcare workforce. Lisa Harker of the Daycare Trust argues that the focus of initiatives needs to be the substance of the child's experiences: 'We have chosen to go down the route of "inspecting out" poor quality, rather than investing in a highly trained workforce that can be depended on to deliver optimal experiences for children'. She draws attention to New Zealand, whose government has recently embarked on its own 10-year plan to improve the quality of its childcare provision, by setting a target of 100% teacher-trained workforce by 2012 (Harker, 2004). Outcomes here are currently uncertain, as a consultation process on the childcare workforce is under way, but the Ten Year Strategy (HMT, 2004) recognises the need for improving the training of professionals, particularly in the private sector (para. 3.4), which will include increasing the graduate workforce (para. 6.8).

Peter Moss develops Harker's point further, arguing strongly for the importance of having a well-thought-out answer to 'two critical questions. What is our image or understanding of the child? What is our image or understanding of institutions for young children? (2004b, p. 20). Clearly, our different images and understandings of the child produce different ways of providing services for and working with children. Moss presents a strong case for understanding institutions for young children as 'children's spaces', spaces where children are understood holistically, 'the child with the mind, body, emotions, creativity, history and social identity' (2004b, p. 21), Such a vision goes 'beyond childcare', the latter term denoting as it does 'an image of "childcare" services as private producers selling a product "childcare" to individual consumers' (2004b, p. 21). It is not clear whether New Labour, focusing on encouraging adults back into the labour market and producing children geared up for the performative world of primary school, shares Moss's vision, nor indeed has any other clearly thought-out ideas about the substance of children's experience in the new Children's Centres, beyond the rhetorical mantras of 'quality' and 'educare'. Glass (2005) makes the same criticism in relation to Sure Start, identifying the growing thrust of the government's drive for childcare: to get parents back into the labour market. He notes that, in contrast,

> the early Sure Start documents make very little reference to 'childcare', in the sense of somewhere where children can be looked after to enable

their parents to work; it was all about child development … [However] Sure Start, originally a child centred programme, became embroiled in the childcare agenda and the need to roll out as many childcare places as possible to support maternal employment.

The Ten Year Strategy (HMT, 2004) confirms the recognition from the Labour Party that childcare is a public good, but for most families it is still treated as a private good, something individual parents find for themselves and purchase. As in other areas of education and welfare, New Labour's emphasis is on the individualisation of responsibility, based on a notion of individual families sifting possible childcare options (unhindered by concerns with affordability, availability or quality) in order to make an appropriate choice. Thus, choosing childcare is understood by New Labour as a precursor of the choice process that parents (again apparently unproblematically) conduct in order to find primary and secondary schools. Our own research demonstrates the private and gendered nature of these choice-making processes, understood solely as a problem of management for individual women (Grace, 1998). For childcare is still seen as 'allowing' women, rather than parents, to enter the labour market. It is mothers who return to paid work who have to find care, often pay for it, and then organise participation in two worlds – of home and paid work – which have contrasting rhythms and values. This remains a process fraught with ideological and practical difficulties (Vincent et al., 2004). As McMahon comments, 'the political, organisational and ideological contradiction between those spheres [caring at home and paid work] are reduced to the private problem of organising and scheduling, a private problem of balancing' (1995, p. 206).

Another fundamental issue related to the nature of childcare provision is that many families, particularly working-class and black and minority ethnic families, prefer informal care, seeing formal childcare arrangements as not offering the 'same degree of flexibility, trust, reciprocity that informal childcare arrangements can and do' (Land, 2002; Wheelock & Jones, 2002; Daycare Trust, 2003a, b; Lewis, 2003; Scottish Executive, 2004). There is a distrust amongst some social groups of leaving young children with 'strangers', a distrust unlikely to be diminished by programmes such as *Nurseries Uncovered* or screaming headlines such as those in summer 2004 that long hours in nursery care leads to emotionally damaged and behaviourally disrupted children. The preferences of many parents may be being overlooked by the rush to expand nursery provision at the expense of other alternatives. This seems to have been recognised at least partially by government plans to extend paid maternity leave. We do not wish to debate the merits of day nurseries here as against other forms of provision, but rather to note the remarkable absence of parental voice in the recent expansion of childcare, a point to which we return later.

Research on choice, such as our own (Vincent & Ball, 2006) and that of Simon Duncan and colleagues (e.g. Duncan et al., 2003; Edwards, 2002), shows that parental decisions concerning childcare are a complex mixture of practical and moral concerns; social relations are at least as important as economic relations. Duncan (2005) supports the point made by Glass cited earlier when he argues that childcare policy sees care in economic terms as a mechanism to allow the mother to work. Wendy Ball and Nickie Charles (2003) make a similar point. In their article analysing policy discourses around childcare in Wales, they identify the dominance of a 'role equity discourse' which couples childcare with paid work, thereby resonating with a liberal discourse of equal opportunities and economic efficiency, aiming to allow women to operate in the workplace on equal terms with men (Ball & Charles, 2003). Duncan and colleagues argue that most families do not, indeed cannot, share this view of themselves as purely actors in the labour market; what they call the 'adult worker model'. This is a highly limited model which would allow 'little consideration of the wider social, moral and emotional components of parenting or childcare' (Duncan et al., 2004, p. 255). Thus they suggest that Labour's childcare policy is in its genesis, a 'rationality mistake' (Duncan et al., 2004, p. 256):

> People do not act in an individualistic economically rational way. Rather they take such decisions with reference to moral and socially negotiated views about what behaviour is right and proper, and this varies between particular social groups, neighbourhoods and welfare states.

Recent research on childcare (e.g. Holloway, 1998; Mooney et al., 2001; Edwards et al., 2002; Uttal, 2002; Duncan et al., 2003) demonstrates that 'it is not just a question of the quantity of childcare but also of its quality and nature, and these judgements about quality and nature will vary socially and geographically. The mere provision of childcare is not adequate as a policy response to the problems of combining caring with children with employment' (Duncan et al., 2004, p. 263). Whilst we would argue that the government's planned expansion of childcare, 'the new frontier of the welfare state' as the Prime Minister has termed it, is too major an intervention to be described as 'mere provision', we agree with the general thrust of Duncan and colleagues' argument.

It is clear that the current composition of the market in childcare is likely to be altered if the government's proposals for 'universal' childcare reach fruition. A quasi-market in childcare, similar to those in education and health, may one day be the result, or, more optimistically, Children's Centres may provide 'a bridgehead for introducing a more social democratic orientation into early childhood policy, holding out the prospect of integrated and inclusive centres as basic provision for all young children' (Moss, 2004a, p. 633). Yet that all seems a long way ahead. At the moment, given the 'extraordinary diversity in existing patterns of provision' (Randall, 2004, p. 4), the operation of local markets is key in determining parents' choice of and use of childcare (Harris et al., 2004).

Thus, we aim in the remainder of this brief article to give some sense of the 'lived reality' of the childcare market as experienced in our two areas of London (for fuller development of these arguments, see Vincent & Ball, forthcoming).

A peculiar market

Let us continue by looking at how the formal childcare market works and explaining what we mean here by a peculiar market. The childcare market is peculiar, we suggest, in a number of different ways. First, it just does not work like markets are supposed to. It is a practical market that is very different from a theoretical market – and it is very inefficient. Second, it is peculiar inasmuch as the services which are required by consumers are complex and unusual, with social, moral and emotional components (Duncan *et al.*, 2004). As our respondents unanimously see it, they want 'safety, happiness and love'. They are willing to pay, in part for an emotional engagement: 'You want someone who will kiss and cuddle them' (Grace, Battersea) and in part for a sense of security, someone you can 'trust'. This is a market which, as the quotation at the start of the article indicates, involves putting a price on things beyond price. This is in that sense an impossible market. The financial exchange is inadequate as a way of representing the relationships involved. Trust is at a premium, and doubt, anxiety and guilt abound. It is a market that rests on multiple ambivalences.

Thirdly, and related, this is a market, as Lane (1991, p. 77) put it, 'saturated with emotions'. The processes involved here are far removed from the concept of market rationality, with its assumption of 'a kind of emotional neutrality' (Lane, 1991, p. 58) that is in this case 'totally unrealistic' (p. 58). Choice of childcare is both very rational and very emotional. Indeed, for many families difficult compromises are involved which trade off emotional and rational responses to the market around both sensitivity to price and questions of access and availability. As one mother put it, 'If you really need childcare you turn a blind eye'. Nonetheless, these compromises are unevenly distributed across families in relation to the ability to pay. Also, as Lane argues, against economic orthodoxy, but again appositely in this peculiar market, the 'final goods' here are 'satisfaction or happiness and human development' (p. 3), although as suggested already, parents are not, indeed cannot, be totally unconcerned about efficiency, utility and cost. Indeed, our respondents made repeated complaints about these aspects of the childcare market.

Fourthly, there is little evidence of 'consumer sovereignty' in these local London markets, partly because of shortages on the supply side, and partly because the consumer is often in a position of relative ignorance in relation to forms of expertise which are part of the purchase of services. As one of our pilot provider respondents saw it, 'Parents are, for want of a better term, a captive market' (Chain Director). He went on to describe the providers as 'price-makers' and was critical of what he saw as excessive profits being made by some nursery chains in London.

Fifthly, and again related, this is a highly gendered market. The main players in both supply and demand are women (97.5% of the childcare workforce is female; www.daycaretrust.org.uk). It is very much a woman's world (Vincent, Ball & Pietikaninen, 2005). As Kenway and Epstein (1996) point out, most literature on marketisation is silent on gender and also on the role of emotions. Again this challenges the traditional economic assumptions about the theoretical consumer. As Kenway and Epstein (1996, p. 307) suggest, 'the free standing and hyper-rational, unencumbered competitive individual who can operate freely in the morally superior market can only be an image of middle class maleness'. Several of these characteristics simply do not apply here. As we noted earlier, 'the reality for many families is that childcare is organised by women in order to facilitate their own entry and that of their family members into paid work' (McKie et al., 2001, p. 239).

Sixthly, as mentioned above, this is currently a highly segmented and diverse market, with many very different types of providers, both public and private. The segmented nature of the market is also related to social class and class fractions in terms of different lifestyles, working arrangements and childcare practices and beliefs and, of course, price. The providers are clearly very aware of themselves operating in a hierarchical, classed market, and within this market relations are niched, and nuanced. In effect the providers are finely tuned to the family structures, lifestyles and childcare practices of their family types. Furthermore, the childcare market also has a very highly developed 'grey market' sector – with many informal, unregistered, 'cash-in-hand' providers. Some of these are avoiding tax, others are non-UK citizens, some without work permits. And alongside this there is in the population at large, although not in our sample, the extensive use of friends and family members to do childcare work. In some respects, then, there is exploitation in this market. However, this social care market, like many others, is regulated by the state. There were, by early 2005, 48 different quality assurance schemes with more to come. These are accredited by Sure Start as Investors in Children and intended to provide reassurance to consumers. Providers are supposed to be registered, inspected, trained and subject to health and safety regulations. But, clearly, as the previous point indicates, only parts of the market are actually regulated (and the efficacy of Ofsted visits as a form of regulation has been questioned, with Ofsted itself encouraging parents to inform it of any less than desirable practice which they witness,[10] and some parts of the formal market are still only lightly regulated, e.g. nannies. Finally, parts of the childcare market position parents as employers of individual service providers – nannies specifically – to work in their own homes. Again the relations of exchange here are very complex, involving both personal/ emotional and formal/financial aspects (see Vincent & Ball, forthcoming). As Gregson and Lowe (1994, p. 190) put it, 'the social relations of nanny employment are characterised by an elision as fundamental as that between the nanny as child care professional and as mother substitute ... [and] are constructed by and shaped through wage and false kinship relations'.[11] A very peculiar market indeed!

Conclusion

This is a market which does not work as markets are meant to do; it does not guarantee quality or efficiency and it dispenses services in a highly inequitable fashion. As an instrument of childcare policy it is at present deeply flawed. In part we want to conclude by suggesting that these problems within the market are irresolvable in so far as there are important paradigmatic differences between the nature of market relations and the nature of the social relations embedded in childcare and brought to the market by parents seeking to 'buy' childcare. So while, as Anderson (1991, p. 182) suggests, 'perhaps the most characteristic feature of markets is their impersonality', intimacy and commitment are key elements parents are searching for in childcare. This may be not only a peculiar market, it may ultimately be an impossible market inasmuch as it can only function either as not a proper market or to the extent that it does operate as a proper market, it removes from childcare essential aspects of its social relations (Anderson, 1991, p. 202).

New Labour's emphasis on access, on bringing childcare to those families who did not have such options, is highly laudable. Given the neglected state of childcare as an issue on the policy agenda, and the lack of provision available, the government's initiatives have transformed the landscape of care. However, New Labour's emphasis on the politics of distribution and redistribution – the concern with access to care – are not sufficient, we suggest, to render this market less peculiar, less impossible. A focus on distributive justice, of access to a particular social good, is incomplete without an accompanying focus on content. Whilst those who work in early years may be able to substantiate the rhetorical assertion of the need for 'quality care', the evidence in our research leads us to suggest that parents find it harder to do so (see Vincent & Ball, forthcoming). Lacking meaningful information about daily life in care settings, they find themselves having to trust the provider. Indeed, parents' voices in general have been muted in the expansion of childcare to date, and in our research we were struck by the absences and silences characterising the relationships between parents and carers in the sample. On a national scale, Glass (2005) argues that the demise of local Sure Start programmes, planned in collaboration with parents, will simply return many parents living in disadvantaged communities to the margins of decision-making with regard to local children's services. The Daycare Trust (2004) has recently published a booklet on parents' forums, with suggestions for including parents in childcare services. However, a number of the case studies quoted in the booklet focus on involving parents in intervention projects (for example, healthy eating, supporting young fathers and so on), rather than involving parents in decision-making aboout service provision. A similar criticism is often made of parents' relationships with schools, that parents are co-opted as supporters and learners, rather than participants (Vincent 1996, 2000). We have argued elsewhere (Vincent & Ball, forthcoming) that there is a lack of appropriate vocabulary open to parents and carers with which to conduct full and meaningful conversations about the children's development and well-being, and also a lack of tradition to support those conversations (see also Uttal, 2002). This is true not just of relationships between individuals but at the level of public policy. Moss and Penn (2003) suggest this as a reason for the sharp distinction between acute parental concern over their children's well-being and their lack of awareness about the nature of the care and education they receive from providers, noting 'the lack of vision at a public and political level and the consequent low level of public discussion. When it comes to early childhood services, Britain suffers a poverty of expectation and a low level of awareness of issues arising from years of [policy makers'] neglect and indifference' (Moss & Penn, 2003, p. 24).[12]

Alongside the welcome expansion of and public investment in childcare, we surely require a public debate about the care of our very young children, asking, at the very least, three sets of questions: whether the market is an appropriate form through which and in which to organise the provision of childcare, what types of care we wish as a society to see available, and what are and what should be the goals of caring for young children in home and group settings?

Notes

1 As Goldthorpe (1995, p. 314) makes very clear, 'the service class is a class of employees'. The main problem of demarcation is that of distinguishing them from other sorts of employees. There are two elements to this: first, benefits of employment over and above salary (pension rights and so on); and second, some degree of professional autonomy and managerial or administrative authority. Despite ongoing changes in the labour market these criteria do still provide a fairly robust basis for distinguishing service class employees from other middle-class groups, specifically the 'intermediate' middle class, that is, those employed in routine, low-autonomy, white-collar jobs.

2 The research as a whole involved a respondent group of 71 parents from 59 families, 21 care providers and 5 'others' (local council personnel, representatives of provider organisations).

3 The 2004 Ten Year Strategy for Childcare (HMT, 2004) cites figures of 64% maternal employment, with 40% of mothers working part time, paras 2.33–2.34.

4 In Gordon Brown's statement to the House introducing the Spending Review in July 2004, he said:

> But there is one additional reform that has the potential to transform opportunity for every child and be a force for renewal in every community, and on which the Government wishes to make further progress today. While the nineteenth century was distinguished by the introduction of primary

education for all and the twentieth century by the introduction of secondary education for all, so the early part of the twenty first century should be marked by the introduction of pre-school provision for the under fives and childcare available to all ... So that from the 269 Children's Centres this year and the 1700 proposed in the Budget, we can now move the number of Children's Centres we build and open between now and 2008 up to 2500 Children's Centres – as we advance further and faster towards our goal of a Children's Centre in every community and in every constituency in our country.

5 Sure Start is focused upon young children and their parents living in 20% of the most disadvantaged areas of the UK, there are 524 local programmes, and approximately 400,000 children involved. Expenditure will reach £1.5 billion by 2006. For a critique of the conception of Sure Start, see Moss (2004a).
6 See also National Day Nurseries Association (2004).
7 The London Development Agency has recently produced 'gap funding' to allow the launch of over 30 Neighbourhood Nurseries, whose appearance was in jeopardy due to the high cost of land and building works in London (*Nursery World*, 15 July 2004, p. 5).
8 The survey was conducted mostly amongst private day nurseries (90% private day nurseries, remainder not-for-profit community nurseries) and the maintained sector does pay a little better. It was conducted by IDS, the information and research service on employment issues in 2004 (*Nursery World*, 5 August 2004, p. 6).
9 Sure Start report (2002/2003) Childcare and Early Years Workforce Survey – Day nurseries and other full day care provision, published May, 2004.
10 Reported in the *Guardian*, 1 September 2004.
11 False kinship is a term Gregson and Lowe use to describe the positioning of nannies by many mothers as 'part of the family'. The risk to the nannies here was that such a relationship can be used to persuade them to do unpaid favours.
12 A recent example of this simplistic public debate can be seen from the press reaction to speeches from the Prime Minister and the Leader of the Conservative Party on childcare in November 2004. The issues were reduced to crude ideological formations, with the Daily Express talking of Labour's plans to 'corral children like battery hens in schools for most of their waking hours' and Melanie Phillips, a conservative commentator, damning the Tories' plans for increased maternity benefits as 'nationalising motherhood' (reported in the *Guardian*'s press review, 13 November 2004).

References

Alakeson, V. (2004) 2020 vision, *Nursery World*, 21 October, 10–11.
Anderson, E. (1991) The ethical limits of the market, *Economics and Philosophy*, 6(2), 179–205.
Ball, W. & Charles, N. (2003) Social movements and policy change: childcare and domestic violence policies in Wales, paper presented at '*Alternative futures and popular protest*' *conference* at Manchester Metropolitan University, April.
Blackburn, P. (2004) *Children's nurseries: UK market sector report 2004* (London, Laing & Buisson).
Brennan, D. (1998) *The politics of Australian child care* (Cambridge, Cambridge University Press).

Campbell, C. & Whitty, G. (2002) Inter-agency collaboration for inclusive schooling, in: C. Campbell (Ed.) *Developing inclusive schools* (London, Institute of Education).

Collins, P. & Alakeson, V. (2004, 3 December) Pennies for the parents, *Guardian*.

Curnow, N. (2004) Council pools funds to level services, *Nursery World*, 7 October, 8.

Daycare Trust (2003a) *Parents eye project* (London, Daycare Trust).

Daycare Trust (2003b) *Informal childcare: bridging the childcare gap* (London, Daycare Trust).

Daycare Trust (2004) *New guide to involving families in childcare services* (London, Daycare Trust).

Department for Education and Skills (DfES) (1998) *Meeting the childcare challenge* (London, DfES).

Department for Education and Skills (DfES) (2004) *Five year strategy for children and learners* (London, DfES).

Duncan, S. (2004) Speech delivered to the 'Choice and provision in local pre school childcare' seminar, Institute of Education, 21 October.

Duncan, S. (2005) Mothering, class and rationality, *Sociological Review*, 53(1), 50–76.

Duncan, S., Edwards, R., Reynolds, T. & Alldred, P. (2003) Motherhood, paid work and partnering: values and theories, *Work, Employment and Society*, 17(2), 309–330.

Duncan, S., Edwards, R., Reynolds, T. & Alldred, P. (2004) Mothers and childcare: policies, values and theories, *Children and Society*, 18, 254–265.

Edwards, R. (Ed.) (2002) *Children, Home & School: regulation, autonomy or connection* (London, Routledge Falmer).

Evans, M. (2004) Age and experience, *Nursery World*, 15 January, 14–15.

Glass, N. (2005, 5 January) Surely some mistake? *Guardian, Society Guardian*.

Goldthorpe, J. (1995) The service class revisited, in: T. Butler & M. Savage (Eds) *Social change and the middle classes* (London, University College London Press).

Grace, M. (1998) The work of caring for young children – Achieving integration, *Women's Studies International Forum*, 21(4), 401–413.

Gregson, N. & Lowe, M. (1994) *Servicing the middle classes: class, gender and waged domestic labour in contemporary Britain* (London, Routledge).

Harker, L. (2004, 11 November) Lessons from Reggio Emilia, *Guardian*.

Harris, T., La Valle, I. & Dickens, S. (2004) *Childcare: how local markets respond to national initiatives*. Research report no. RR526 (London, Department for Education and Skills).

Her Majesty's Treasury [HMT] (2004) *Choice for parents, the best start for children: a ten year strategy for childcare* (London, Her Majesty's Treasury).

Hodge, M. (2005, 8 January) Our baby is thriving, *Guardian*, comment.

Holloway, S. (1998) Local childcare cultures: moral geographies of mothering and the social organisation of pre-school children, *Gender, Place and Culture*, 5(1), 29–53.

Howard, M. (2004) *Tax credits: one year on* (London, Child Poverty Action Group).

Kenway, J. & Epstein, D. (1996) The marketisation of school education; feminist studies and perspectives, *Discourse*, 17(3), 301–314.

Labour Party (2005) *Britain, forward not back: the general election manifesto* (London, The Labour Party).

Land, H. (2002) Spheres of care in the UK: separate and unequal, *Critical Social Policy*, 22(1), 13–32.

Lane, R. (1991) *The market experience* (Cambridge, Cambridge University Press).

Lewis, J. (2003) Developing early years childcare in England, 1997–2002: the choice for (working) mothers, *Social Policy and Administration*, 37(3), 219–238.

McKie, L., Bowlby, S. & Gregory, S. (2001) Gender, caring and employment in Britain, *Journal of Social Policy*, 30(2), 233–258.

McMahon, M. (1995) *Engendering motherhood* (New York, Guilford Press).

Mooney, A. (2003) Mother, Teacher, Nurse, in: J. Brannen & P. Moss (Eds) *Rethinking childrens' care* (Buckingham, Open University Press).

Mooney, A., Knight, A., Moss, P. & Owen, C. (2001) *Who cares? Childminding in the 1990s* (London, Family Policy Studies Centre).

Moss, P. (2004a) Sure Start, *Journal of Education Policy*, 19(5), 631–634.

Moss, P. (2004b) Setting the scene: a vision of universal children's spaces, in: Daycare Trust, *A New Era for Universal Childcare?* (London, Daycare Trust).

Moss, P. & Penn, H. (2003) *Transforming nursery education* (London, Paul Chapman).

National Day Nurseries Association (NDNA) (2004) *Promoting quality in the early years* (Brighouse, NDNA).

Randall, V. (2004) The making of local child daycare regimes: past and future, *Policy and Politics,* 32(1), 3–20.

Scottish Executive (2004) *Parents' access to and demand for childcare in Scotland* (Edinburgh, Scottish Executive).

Vevers, S. (2004a) Feeling the squeeze, *Nursery World*, 29 July, 10–11.

Vevers, S. (2004b) Invest in staff first, providers tell MPs, *Nursery World*, 7 October, 4.

Vevers, S. (2004c) By numbers, *Nursery World*, 22 July, 10–11.

Vincent, C. (1996) *Parents and Teachers: power and participation* (London, Falmer).

Vincent, C. (2000) *Including parents? Education, citizenship and parental agency* (Buckingham, Open University Press).

Vincent, C. & Ball, S. (2006) *Childcare, choice and class practices* (London, Routledge).

Vincent, C., Ball, S. J. & Kemp, S. (2004) The social geography of childcare: making up a middle class child, *British Journal of Sociology of Education*, 25(2), 229–244.

Vincent, C., Ball, S. & Pietikaninen, S. (2005) Metropolitan mothers: mothers, mothering and paid work, *Women's Studies International Forum*, 27(5), 571–587.

Uttal, L. (2002) *Making care work: employed mothers in the new childcare market* (New Brunswick, NJ, Rutgers University Press).

Wheelock, J. & Jones, K. (2002) 'Grandparents are the next best thing': informal childcare for working parents in urban Britain, *Journal of Social Policy*, 31(3), 441–463.

Chapter 12

Childhood and social inequality in Brazil

*Fúlvia Rosemberg**

Source: *F. Rosemberg , Childhood and social inequality in Brazil, in H. Penn (ed.), Unequal Childhoods: Young Children's Lives in Poor Countries. London: Routledge, 2006, pp. 142–170.*

Summary

Brazil was a Portuguese colony from 1500 to 1822. When the Portuguese began their journeys of conquest to the Brazilian territories, they encountered between three and five million indigenous people organized into approximately one thousand different nations. Portuguese society was rigidly structured, 'centred in hierarchy, founded in religion; service to God and service to the king were the parameters of social activity' (Paiva 2000:44). The Portuguese Empire had the support of the Catholic religious orders in the colonization process, especially the Jesuits who used formal education of indigenous children as one of their strategies. The Portuguese began to enslave the indigenous people in 1536. The Jesuit priest Manuel de Nóbrega, who founded the Jesuit mission in Brazil, wrote the following to Dom João III, king of Portugal, in 1551:

> When the priests realized that the grown people were so rooted in their sins, so obstinate in their evil ways, gratifying themselves by eating human flesh, and that they called it the true ambrosia and seeing how little can be done with them because they are so full of women, so fiercely engaged in war and given over to their vices, and that is one of the things which most disturbs reason and takes away all meaning, the priests decided to teach the children the ways of salvation so that later, they can teach their parents. Thus going out to the villages, they gathered them together to teach them Christian doctrine.
>
> (Cited in Chambouleyron 2004:59)

Thus, in the sixteenth century, there began an uninterrupted narrative by the North about the inhabitants of the South, its children and adults, interpreting, as a rule, the specificity of the South as sin, vice, pathology, anomie, underdevelopment, incompetence; a specific which required instruction and counsel from the North so that the natives could acquire civilization. From then until the present day, pirates, colonizers, criminals, travellers, diplomats, queens and princes, governors, academics, scientists, artists, politicians, activists from international and humanitarian organizations, Brazilianists, and advisors to non-governmental and multilateral organizations have interpreted Brazil and its people based on their own parameters, interests, languages and sources. Often, like the Jesuits, they have proposed or imposed solutions. Such solutions, at times, are incorporated by the South itself, which describes itself according to the point of view of the North.

This chapter describes and discusses how social and economic inequality impacts on young Brazilian children (under 6 years of age). It emphasizes how social policies to address inequality have also been defined in the context of North–South relations.

A brief state of the art

This chapter is based on published and widely available macro data. Brazil has a public agency responsible for national statistics, the Brazilian Institute of Geography and Statistics (*Instituto Brasileiro de Geografia e Estatística/* IBGE) which has been undertaking demographic census since 1872, and annual national household surveys (PNADs) since 1976. Generally, statistical information is reliable and of good quality. Researchers, activists and technical personnel from public agencies who are users of this information, perform critical analyses of its quality and are regularly consulted by the IBGE in order to improve it.[1] On the whole the literature on early childhood is now wide-ranging, particularly with the publication of *Primeira Infância* (Young Childhood) (IBGE 2001a). There is a literature on early childhood care and education (ECCE), infant and child mortality and malnutrition.[2]

Academic production is dispersed throughout various publications, predominantly in journals of education, psychology, social service, history and public health.[3] Childhood and adolescence have had more attention from educators and social workers, while the fields of sociology and anthropology have shown less interest (Nunes 1999). In Brazil, there has not been the same emphasis towards childhood studies or the sociology of childhood reported in the northern hemisphere (James and Prout 1990; Montandon 2001; Sirota 2001; Rosemberg 2003b).

There has been a long progressive tradition of the human and social sciences in Brazil, heavily influenced by Marxism. In line with this tradition, early childhood activists and researchers have drawn on European psychology – Piaget, Wallon, Vygostsky – rather than on the Anglo-Saxon experimental psychology tradition. (Anglo-Saxon influence has been felt most intensely in the activities of the multilateral organizations such as UNICEF and the World Bank (Rosemberg 2003a)). This long progressive tradition also explains, in part, the priority focus of Brazilian studies: childhood which is forsaken, poor; adolescents considered to be in 'situations of risk' ('street children', prostitution, adolescent pregnancy, etc.); themes of high media visibility and great international appeal. However, as elsewhere, it is easier to research the poor, who, due to their very condition of subordination, are more welcoming to researchers than the Brazilian middle class, who are more resistant to researchers invading their intimacy.

Writing on childhood by academics, activists and Brazilian governmental agencies shows the same bias as writing from the northern hemisphere about the southern hemisphere: the focus is to treat social inequality from the point of view of the dominated rather than the dominant. Thus, what is problematic are the poor, the blacks, the indigenous, i.e. the 'others'. Rarely is the issue framed from the reverse point of view: what it means to be white, of European origin, to belong to the economic and political elites, to speak a dominant and hegemonic language. We do not examine the effective strategies we use to maintain their (our) dominant position.

At present, the Department for Children and Adolescents within the Ministry of Justice is the national agency responsible for promoting and defending the rights of children and adolescents. Public policies for young children are fragmented (Campos *et al*. 1992) and are interspersed among federal, state and municipal agencies for education, social welfare and health.[4] We have Councils for Children and Adolescents at all three levels of government. The specific legislation, the Statute on Children and Adolescents, is considered to be quite advanced, but suffers from the same tensions observed in the International Convention on the Rights of Children (Boyden 1990; Rosemberg and Freitas 2001). This tension resides between the right to protection and the right to autonomy, the guiding concept being individual, and not collective, rights. The most recent Constitution agreed in 1988 extends the rights of children and adolescents, of women, of the disabled, of the aged, of blacks and of the indigenous. For example, it criminalizes racism and recognizes the collective ownership of the ancestral territories of blacks and indigenous peoples. It also recognizes children's right to education in daycare and preschools, which should fulfill the double role of education and care.

During the 1970s and 1980s, the feminist movement mobilized to struggle for daycare for the young children of working women. At the moment its political agenda is centred on adult women (combating domestic violence, decriminalizing abortion, etc.). Brazilian feminist theory now, like international feminist theory, tends to assume children and childhood are unchanging and not particularly relevant (Rosemberg 1996b). The Brazilian black movement centres more attention on older children, adolescents and adults.

Two Brazilian organizations presently stand out as advocacy organizations for young children: the Interforum Movement for Early Childhood Care and Education of Brazil (MIEIB) and the Pastoral Commission for Children.

The MIEIB is a lay organization, created in 1999, with a national presence, whose goal is to monitor ECCE. The Pastoral Commission for Children is an agency connected to the Catholic Church, with national coverage, which acts through voluntary community agents (women) who give maternal-child assistance to the low income population (Pastoral da Criança 2002).

Brazilian public attention is directed more toward older children, adolescents and young people. The multilateral organizations (UNESCO, UNICEF, the World Bank) prioritize elementary education for children over the age of 7 in Brazil, as does the Brazilian government. This priority appears to derive from their greater visibility in the public arena. Adults, both Brazilian and foreign, see the behaviour of older children as potentially disruptive and dangerous. Young children, however, are more likely to be at home or confined within closed spaces, and have less public visibility. Unlike older children they are not yet labelled as victims, nor considered to be a threat – the sentiments which appear to mobilize adult public attention. The relative lack of public attention to young children is not a reflection of parental attitudes in Brazil – but to the very low negotiating power of young children and poor women (Rosemberg 2000a).[5]

If we get some distance from the stereotyping and stigmatizing eye trained to observe the spectacle – such as Sebastião Salgado's photographs, or the images used to illustrate the reports of the multinational organizations or fundraising advertisements in the North (such as 'adopt a child from the South for fifty dollars a year') – we encounter clear indications of the appreciation of Brazilian parents for their young children. There are strong signs of change. Recent urbanization, the penetration of the individualistic values of modernity, nearly universal access to television, the drop in infant mortality and fertility rates and the intense expansion of ECCE over the last three decades are social conditions that fuel this changing conceptualization (Rosemberg 1996b).

Early childhood is set off from the other stages of childhood: new spaces in the labour and consumer market are staked out. Parents recognize changes in understandings and patterns of child rearing. The young child is considered to be intelligent, making demands on, but dependent upon, adults. The impact of modernity (television, violence) is feared. The right tone in education is sought, and the role of fathers in caring for their children is being rethought (Moro and Gomide 2003).

Finally, in this section I would like to make two general points about my analysis. It is worth noting that Portuguese, the hegemonic language of Brazil, unlike English, uses two different terms for children: *filho/a* (*filius* in Latin) and *criança* (*puer*). Thus, the translation of this text, like all production of information and studies of childhood, leaves room for ambiguities deriving from differences in meanings associated with the terms 'child' and '*criança*' (Rosemberg 2003b).

Social inequality in Brazil

Brazil occupies a territory of 8.5 million km^2 in the east of Latin America, inhabited by one hundred and seventy million people who generate an annual per capita gross domestic product of US\$2,129 (data from 2000). On a world-wide comparison, its per capita income level places it in the upper third of world countries, which means that '77 per cent of the world population lives in countries with a lower per capita income than Brazil' (Barros *et al.* 2000:17). Given the intense concentration of world income, Brazil is in a good position among the developing countries. Therefore, Brazil is not a poor country, but a country with intense inequality in the distribution of income, which results in having a small number of rich people and a large percentage of poor. The percentage of poor in the country has revolved around 30 per cent to 50 per cent in the 1980s and 1990s, reaching 57.1 million people (34 per cent) in 2002[6] (see Table 12.1.)

The Gini index rating of inequality is one of the highest in the world – around 0.60. In Brazil, the wealthiest 20 per cent enjoy an average income thirty times higher than the poorest 20 per cent of the population (Barros *et al.* 2000:22–3).

The incidence of poverty over time shows an important decline in the 1970s; but beginning in 1980, there is stagnation, and then a higher rate of poverty (Medeiros 2003:10). This suggests inequality in Brazil is historical and structural. 'The levels of inequality in Brazil have not been significantly modified by urbanization, industrialization, democratization, secularization and growth in the aggregate product of Brazilian society' (Medeiros 2003:16).

Brazilian social inequalities exhibit two marked tendencies: the social sectors that receive less income are also those that have less access to the benefits of public policy and lesser political participation. These inequalities are persistent. Thus, indicators such as life expectancy at birth, access to schooling (along with the ability to remain in school and be successful) and basic sanitation, show clear improvements in recent years throughout

Table 12.1 The evolution of poverty

Year	Percentage of poor people	Number of poor (in millions)
1982	43	51.9
1985	44	56.9
1992	41	57.3
1995	34	50.2
2002	34	57.1

Sources: PNAD 1982 and 1995 (cited in Barros *et al.* 2000:15); PNAD 2002 (cited in *Folha de S. Paulo*).

the national territory, yet, at the same time, maintain the pattern of inequality.

Political participation in the political parties, unions or the organizations of civil society, shows a strong correlation with personal income and education (Schwartzman 2004). This situation indicates that the economic elite are also the political elite in Brazil. The professions declared by members of the fifty-second legislative session of the National Congress (2003) are mostly high-earning professions.

> The large majority of the individuals who occupy positions among the political elite, represented by the members of congress, belong to the economic elite. If the economic elite are also the political and social elite, their power is not limited to managing their own wealth in accord with individual and group interests, this power also extends to the management of the wealth of third parties, including public funds.
>
> (Medeiros 2003:9)

Social inequality in Brazil shows a strong association to color/race, geographical region of residence and age of the citizen: higher incomes and greater social benefits are appropriated by the white, adult, residents of the south and southeastern regions. The position of women is more ambiguous and will be explored further in this chapter.

Inequality and race

The enslavement of Africans lasted for more than three centuries and Brazil was the last country to abolish it. Domination of black Africans during the slave-holding regime extended beyond the slaves, also affecting free black people. Colonizers or travellers brought to Brazil the vision reigning in Europe about Africa, the Africans and miscegenation.

> With few exceptions, all the young black girls have no concern beyond that of being mothers. It is an idée fixe that takes hold of their spirits, from the time of puberty, and that they put into practice as soon as they have occasion. This fact, that the ardor of African blood is perhaps sufficient to explain, is above all then a calculated result. In truth, does maternity not lead them with all certainty to well being, to the satisfactions of self love, to the usufruct of sloth, to coquetry and to consume delicacies? A wet nurse is hired for more than a laundress, a cook or a maid ... At the time of farewell, some even shed tears ... but what all lament infinitely is [the loss of] the indolent life, the luxury of the clothes, the abundance of all that it is necessary to leave behind.
>
> (Charles Expilly, French traveller to Brazil 1862, pp. 202–20, cited in Leite 2001:31–2)

The abolition of slavery was gradual and regulated by specific legislation. In 1859 transatlantic traffic of African slaves was prohibited; in 1871 freedom was granted to those born of slave mothers and in 1885 to the aged slaves; finally in 1888 the law granting overall liberation of the slaves was promulgated.

Brazilian society at the end of the nineteenth century displayed the following configuration:

> a small white elite, the remainders of a slaveholding economy in decadence, and a multitude of freed slaves, bastard children, descendents of Indians, poor whites and poor immigrants brought from Europe and Japan. They lived mostly in the country, often on large plantations, but for the most part as sharecroppers, producing, at most, enough to survive; but also in the cities as vendors, artisans, clerks, oddjobbers, household servants, the unemployed and occasional beggars. Very similar to Marx's 'dangerous classes', but, far from being residuals from a social and economic order in transition, they were the majority of the population of a country in formation.
>
> (Schwartzman 2004:20)

After the abolition of slavery, social and political relations between blacks and whites were shaped by three main processes:

1   The country did not adopt legislation to ensure racial segregation (unlike the United States and South Africa), and therefore there was no legal definition of racial identity.
2   The country had no specific policies for integration of the recently freed blacks into the evolving society, which served to strengthen the historical social inequalities between blacks and whites, which have lasted into the present.
3   The country encouraged white European immigration during the transition from the nineteenth to the twentieth century: a state policy of whitening the population in consonance with the eugenic racist policies developed in Europe in the nineteenth century.[7]

To escape the fate of a mixed race country, so despised by Europe, Brazil encouraged European immigration by conceding advantages for Europeans to settle in Brazilian territory, especially in the South and Southeastern regions. This policy caused an increase in the percentage of whites (from 44.0 per cent in 1890 to 63.5 per cent in 1940), and the forcing of the black populations into the Northeast region, which was already showing economic decadence. Today, the Northeast constitutes the poorest region in Brazil and also has the greatest percentage of blacks (blacks and browns). By contrast, the South and Southeast are the wealthiest regions and have the largest percentage of whites (Table 12.2).

Table 12.2 Racial composition and income distribution by geographical region, Brazil, 2001

Regions	Composition		Income level (in MW*)					
	Whites	Blacks	Under ½ MW	½ to 1 times MW	1 to 2 times MW	2 to 3 times MW	3 to 5 times MW	5 times MW
North (N)	27.9	71.8	28.7	29.5	21.2	7.4	5.4	5.0
Northeast (NE)	29.5	70.2	37.0	28.1	17.2	5.5	4.3	4.5
Southeast (SE)	63.5	35.0	12.1	21.8	26.6	12.6	10.5	11.6
South (S)	84.0	15.0	11.9	22.1	29.2	13.1	10.4	10.8
Central-West (C-W)	43.8	55.4	18.1	27.6	24.4	9.5	8.0	9.8
Brazil	53.4	46.0	18.9	24.1	24.5	10.6	8.6	9.6

Source: PNAD 2001, cited in IBGE 2003.

Note
*MW = minimum wage.

This historical process, updated later by structural and symbolic racism, shaped the pattern of race relations in Brazil. Classification now takes the following forms:

- a system of racial classification based on appearance resulting from the simultaneous apprehension of physical traits (skin colour, facial features, hair), socio-economic status and region of residence;
- a large black and mixed-race population (which identifies as brown, not white) – 46 per cent of the population;[8]
- living with patterns of race relations which are simultaneously vertical, producing intense inequality of opportunity and horizontal, where overt hostility and racial hatred are not observed. (This can result in amicable relationships in certain social spaces under certain circumstances.)

This last particularity of race relations in Brazil, which also appears as intense miscegenation, allied to the process of racial classification based on appearance, resulted in the dissemination, at home and abroad, of the myth of Brazilian racial democracy. This myth presupposes not just amicable, cordial relations, but equality of opportunity as well. Further, the social and economic inequalities between whites and blacks in Brazil were attributed solely to the slaveholding past and class inequality.

The constitutive historical and contemporary racism in Brazil society is evident when the Human Development Index (HDI) is calculated separately for the white and black populations: for whites it is the equivalent of 0.791 (41st place) and for blacks, it is 0.671 (108th place).

The myth of racial democracy has been challenged since the 1950s by both black and white researchers, and especially by black activists at the end of the 1970s. They have pointed out the undeniable racial inequality in access to both symbolic and material goods, and have interpreted this as an expression of structural and ideological racism. They have proposed policies to overcome racism. In 1996, the Brazilian government recognized, for the first time, that the country is structurally racist and acknowledged its historical debt to blacks. Young black children who are residents of the Northeast are the poorest of all children.

Children under 6 years old

The 2000 Census counted 23 million children under 6 years old, making up almost 13.6 per cent of the population in Brazil. This percentage has been in steady decline as a result of the reduction in fertility and birth rates: from 1990 to 2000, the birth rate per 1,000 inhabitants fell from 23.05 to 20.04 and total fertility from 2.70 to 2.2.

Income distribution

Despite the reduction in the proportion of children under 6 years old in the population, this group shows the highest percentage of poor and chronically poor people and has the worst ratings on social indicators (Rosemberg and Pinto 1997; Hasenbalg 2001; Sabóia and Sabóia 2001).

The majority of Brazilian children under 6 years old live with the status of children *(filius)* in two-parent families (71.6 per cent). Less frequently children live in extended families (10.3 per cent) or only with the mother (13.5) (PPV, cited in Hasenbalg 2001:13). As in the overall population, the majority (52 per cent) of children are white, residing in urban areas (76.5 per cent), predominantly in the Northeast (32.4 per cent) and Southeast (38.7 per cent) (IBGE: PNAD 1999) (see Table 12.3).

Table 12.3 Percentage of people with an income of less than half the minimum wage, by age and year, in the Northern region of Brazil, 1992 to 1999

Age (years)	1992	1993	1995	1996	1997	1998	1999
under 6	58.03	54.31	41.27	41.28	41.91	44.37	45.54
7 to 14	53.58	50.03	35.47	36.93	36.63	38.42	40.08
15 to 17	44.71	41.49	26.84	28.25	28.48	29.78	32.06
18 to 24	39.13	36.97	23.28	24.74	25.03	25.87	27.64
60 to 66	22.98	20.40	8.45	10.28	9.87	9.26	9.32
over 67	20.51	19.80	7.23	9.29	8.78	7.64	7.80

Source: Various PNADs.

A comparison among different types of families that have children under 6 show that across social classes they always occupy an unfavourable position when compared to families which do not have young children (Sabóia and Sabóia 2001).[9] The persistence of such indicators about the unfavourable position of families and households with young children 'would justify a national policy of support for these families ... It indicates that programmes directed to children of school age should be preceded by programmes directed to young children' (Sabóia and Sabóia 2001:45). This suggestion, however, has not been taken up by the Brazilian government.

Hasenbalg (2001:10) highlights two aspects regarding the relation between poverty and early childhood: differences in fertility which may explain the disproportionate concentration of young children at the lower levels of income; and oscillations in the level of poverty in the Brazilian population according to the ups and downs of the economy over recent decades. In addition, families that have young children tend to be at the beginning of their working lives; and the present pattern of fertility means that couples are having children closer in age to each other. The school schedule makes working outside the home difficult for mothers with young children, so family income falls. The state accepts a redistributive role and offers some social support, e.g. social security, and some programmes to maintain poor children from the ages of 7 to 14 in school (called *Bolsa-Escola*). Barros and Carvalho argue that 'Although all these programmes lead to a reduction of poverty at all age levels however, the reduction is much more marked among old people than among children' (2003:8) since the amount of resources allocated by the social welfare net is greater for the elderly than for small children.

Living conditions

The low priority assigned to young children by economic and social policies is shown in their conditions in life and death. Inequality is not just a matter of income distribution, but also of the benefits of public policies.

An analysis of poverty indicators shows:

• Improvement over recent decades for the country overall and for each region.
• Marked and persistent differences among them according to region, rural or urban residence, racial segment, family income level, the schooling of the mother and head of the family. Generally, the worst indicators are observed among black and indigenous children,[10] residents of the Northeast region, the rural areas, those coming from families with lower incomes and whose mothers had little educational opportunity. A large number of the indicators also show worse conditions for children residing in households headed by women, but there are exceptions, as for example

in access to basic sanitation, where the indicators are better for households headed by women (Rosemberg and Pinto 1997).

- A general improvement in the indicators has not contributed to reducing inequalities. The gap that separates children with better indicators (coming from higher income levels and receiving greater benefits from social policies in housing, sanitation, education, etc.) from children who show worse indicators remains.
- The literature is contradictory in its use of indicators. UNICEF (2004), for instance, weights mother's education, or lack of it, as a causal factor in mortality and malnutrition whereas Simões (2002) considers it to be just a proxy; family income and sanitation conditions are more likely to cause mortality and malnutrition.

Information available about some of these indicators is summarized in the following sections on housing, nutrition and mortality.

Housing

Approximately one third of the population live in conditions of high density (favelas or shanty towns) and lack an adequate supply of water, sanitary sewers and trash collection (IBGE 2001a, Northeast and Southeast regions). Such living conditions tend to affect the daily lives of small children more than the other residents of these households, in so far as their circulation in other spaces is more restricted and they depend on older people.

In research on living conditions of young children according to racial background, Rosemberg and Pinto (1997) observed an important racial difference in the access of children from urban areas to adequate sanitation conditions, even when controlling for household income and area of residence. In Brazil, especially in urban Brazil, black populations tend to live in areas alongside poor whites. They do not have access to good services, but they are more likely to be able to deal with racism.

Intense regional inequality and the poverty and lack of opportunity in rural areas have led to continued internal migration and consequent growth of the metropolitan areas. Thus, the rate of urbanization for Brazilians is high (83.9 per cent) and three metropolitan areas house 33.7 million people, i.e. 20 per cent of the Brazilian population: the São Paulo metropolitan area with 18.2 million residents, Rio de Janeiro with 11.0 million and Belo Horizonte with 4.7 million inhabitants (IBGE: PNAD 2001). Mostly migrants congregate in peripheral areas of cities, in favelas or shanty towns, and are in effect environmentally segregated from the city.

The distribution of services and urban infrastructure is deficient in these peripheral areas of the large cities: transport is precarious, adding additional hours to long working days; sanitation is deficient, to which is added non-existent drainage, greater exposure to the occurrence of floods and landslides during the rainy season and cuts in water supply during the dry season. There are fewer opportunities for formal employment, for access to the professions, for access to information; for access to leisure facilities, or to the legal system, or to the administrative apparatus; difficulty in access to health services, school and daycare; greater exposure to violence both from the police and criminals (Maricato 2003:152). Inadequate basic sanitation and its unequal distribution have been considered one of the factors responsible for the persistently high rates of malnutrition and infant and child mortality.

Mortality

Two different expressions refer to the death of young children: infant mortality, which refers to the death of children before completing a year of age, and child mortality, which refers to children who die before completing their fifth year. Both rates refer to deaths within a group of one thousand people (see Table 12.4).

The same trends emerge again and again: young children coming from families with lower incomes, and black children who reside in the Northeast, whose mothers have had few educational opportunities, have the least chance of living beyond 5 years (Simões 2002). Their chances of surviving would be better if they lived in households with adequate basic sanitation.

As a reflection of the low investment in services throughout the 1990s, the drops in child mortality related to basic sanitation were not very significant among children residing in poor households, despite the evident progress in child vaccination and the implementation in 1998 of the Programme for the Comprehensive Care of Diseases Prevalent in Childhood (Atenção Integrada às Doenças Prevalentes na Infância (AIDPI)).

Nationally, on average, the drop was 14 per cent during the periods from 1988 to 1992 and 1995 to 1998, a value similar to that observed in the

Table 12.4 Rates of infant mortality (under 1 year old) and child mortality (under 5 years old) by year and region (%), Brazil, 2000

Regions	Infant (under 1 year, per 1,000 population) 2000	Child mortality (under 5, per 1,000 population) 2000	Family income, per capita	Child mortality (under 5 years, per 1,000 population)
North	33.01	41.3	1st quintile	81.6
Northeast	52.31	66.8	2nd quintile	54.0
Southeast	24.09	29.9	3rd quintile	48.2
South	20.34	23.9	4th quintile	34.1
Central-West	24.00	28.2	5th quintile	29.8
Brazil	33.55	41.8	Brazil	57.4

Source: Census and PNADs, cited in Simões 2002:55 and 62.

Northeast and Southeast regions of the country. In the South and Centre-west the drop in mortality was more accented (22 per cent and 28 per cent respectively) and was practically double that observed for the other regions of Brazil. From this we can infer that in the Northeast, more than in other regions of the country, the reduction in child mortality still depends essentially on measures directed to distribution of income and access to basic sanitation services (Simões 2002:74).

The most recent macro-economic reforms (of the 1990s and 2000s), valuing the minimal state and seeking to contain the public debt (internal debt and interest on debt incurred to the World Bank) have reduced infrastructure investment, including basic sanitation. Young children living in lower income households have a greater probability of dying because the government withdraws investments in sanitation to pay these debts, in order not to frighten off international investors.

Malnutrition

The present federal government – led by Luíz Inácio Lula da Silva – gained national and international notoriety in proposing the *Fome Zero* (Zero Hunger) project as its main social project. The project, presently being reformulated, has sparked controversy and criticisms even among progressives (Monteiro 2003:7). The economic and media manipulation of hunger has been under discussion in Brazil and the northern hemisphere for a long time (Brunel 1990; Monteiro 2003). Sylvie Brunel (1990) calls the international statistics on hunger 'an international hoax'. Like Brunel (1990), Monteiro (2003) emphasizes that the three concepts – poverty, malnutrition and hunger – are not identical. Information available about small children refers to their state of nutrition or malnutrition. Thus, rates of child malnutrition refer to the percentage of children (under 5 years old) with low height – low height is defined at that which diverges from the averages expected for age and sex, according to the international growth standards recommended by the World Health Organization (WHO 1995, cited in Monteiro 2003:11).

Brazil has a percentage of 10.4 children (under 5 years old) with low height, an indicator of malnutrition. As for other indicators, malnutrition rates show important local variations: higher in rural areas than urban, higher in the North and Northeastern regions than in the Central-West, Southeast and South (Table 12.5); higher for black than white children and those between 2 and 4 years old (Lustosa and Reichenheim 2001:104–7). The better indicator for children under 1 year old is possibly correlated with breast-feeding which takes place up to 9.9 months (on average) in urban Brazil in 1999.[11]

These figures show improvement over the last three decades, but this improvement is patchy. Based on figures from the period 1989–96, the goal of controlling malnutrition – i.e. reaching an index of 2.3 per cent – will be

Table 12.5 Prevalence (%) of malnutrition in childhood, Brazil, 1996

Region	Area		
	Urban	Rural	Total
North	16.6	–	–
Northeast	13.0	25.2	17.9
Centre-south*	4.6	9.9	5.6
Brazil	7.7	18.9	10.4

Source: PNDS, cited in Monteiro 2003:11.

Note
*Includes the Central-West, Southeast and South regions.

achieved at very different times according to the region under consideration: in 2003 for the urban southern regions; in 2013 for the urban Northeast; in 2031 for the urban North; for the rural Central-West in 2035 and only in 2065 for the rural Northeast (Monteiro 2003:13).

Regional differences persist when comparing levels of child malnutrition even when the children come from households with similar purchasing power. This suggests that the malnutrition of children is influenced by other factors, beyond income, such as availability of public health services, education and basic sanitation (Monteiro 2003:12).

Brazilian educational policy during the 1990s followed the prescription of the World Bank, prioritizing, almost exclusively, elementary education as a strategy to combat poverty and bring the country economic progress. This prioritization was based on the theory of human capital (Torres 1996). Thus, the federal government abandoned its initial commitment to ECCE (early childhood care and education for children under 6 years of age) and concentrated its resources on elementary education (Rosemberg 2003a).

Public schools were required to implement feeding programmes for children from 7 to 14 years of age. But children this age are likely to suffer less from the impact of malnutrition than younger children! Moreover, pressures from the International Labour Organization (ILO) in its campaign to eradicate child labour (and to avoid an international boycott of its exported products), led the the federal government to create, during the 1990s, the *Programa Bolsa Escola* (School Scholarship Programme) for children aged between 7 and 14 from families with low income to enable them to remain in school and not work. In 2001 the federal government finally created a parallel programme, the *Programa Bolsa Alimentação* for children under 6 years of age. But this was done without a linked strategy of expanding vacancies in daycare centres and preschools, so the poorest young children, who were less likely to be attending provision, did not benefit.

Further, the amount passed on by the federal government to purchase food for daycare centres and preschools under contract, was worth, up until July of 2004, only half the value of that passed on to feed children aged between 7 and 14. These policies could be read as discrimination against young children.

Early childhood care and education

ECCE reflects the intense social segregation in the urban areas of Brazil. Despite the poor living conditions in these segregated areas (poor sanitation, crowded households, contaminated outside spaces) UNICEF (in the 1980s) as well as the World Bank (in the 1990s) suggested that caring for young children in the household (family daycare) for Brazil meant lowcost care. It reduced public investment whilst it expanded coverage. This was justified in the name of 'cultural proximity', i.e. daycare homes would reflect the cultural conditions of the children being looked after!

In 2001, 10.6 per cent of children under 3 years of age and 65.6 per cent of those in the 4- to 6-year age range, attended some kind of ECCE. The offer of ECCE in Brazil is mostly public (63.5 per cent in daycare and 75.4 per cent of preschools in 2000) and among the private sector, for-profit education is responsible for 57.0 per cent of enrolments in daycare and 75.3 per cent in preschools (Rosemberg 2003a).

Despite showing high growth between 1970 and 1990 (Rosemberg 2003a), studies of the 1990s (Kappel *et al.* 2001; Rosemberg 2003a) have shown that ECCE was the level of education that grew least during the 1990s.

White children from the higher income levels have better access to ECCE. However, because of the low-cost schemes to provide ECCE in poor areas as a strategy to combat poverty, the distribution of the attendance rates can be misleading (Rosemberg 2003a). This policy of low-cost ECCE expansion for regions considered 'politically dangerous' (the 'poverty pockets' in the Northeast) during the last years of the military dictatorship subsequently influenced the pattern of attendance rates: it is the Northeast region which shows the better rates (see Table 12.6). Paradoxically higher rates of ECCE attendance in Brazil are associated with lower indicators of quality (Rosemberg 1999). The Northeast shows, at the same time, high coverage and the worst quality indicators: it has the highest rate of 'lay' teachers, who receive the lowest salaries and who work in establishments with the worst physical conditions (i.e. in schools without any basic sanitation) (see Table 12.7).

This model of low cost ECCE expansion seems to suggest that ECCE shows the greatest focus on the poor: it indicates that 'the poorest have greater access than the wealthiest' (Barros and Foguel 2001:119). This is the result, however, of a perverse and paradoxical process, deriving from the fact that these daycare centres and preschools were created precisely for the poor, and due to their poor quality, repelled families with higher income levels. The ECCE

Table 12.6 Rate of ECCE school attendance by age range, colour, quartiles and geographic regions, Brazil, 1999

Region	Age range (years)	White Income quartiles					Not white (black, brown and indigenous) Income quartiles					Total
		1st	2nd	3rd	4th	Subtotal	1st	2nd	3rd	4th	Subtotal	
North*	Under 3	1.3	3.8	8.5	12.8	6.1	2.6	6.5	6.4	12.5	5.8	5.9
	4–6	39.6	53.3	55.7	71.1	54.3	39.0	47.8	53.1	70.1	49.2	50.8
	Total (0–6)	15.5	25.7	28.9	36.9	26.1	18.2	24.5	28.5	39.6	25.2	25.5
Northeast	Under 3	6.6	10.4	16.7	24.4	11.1	6.3	9.0	11.7	26.2	8.4	9.3
	4–6	51.9	64.2	76.4	88.1	63.4	49.8	57.8	66.9	79.4	55.1	59.4
	Total (0–6)	24.5	33.3	41.6	52.2	32.6	9.5	31.6	37.0	52.1	29.9	30.7
South east	Under 3	7.0	7.4	7.8	19.6	10.8	5.7	8.5	7.0	13.2	7.7	9.7
	4–6	43.6	48.9	57.4	75.7	58.4	38.0	47.3	51.1	62.5	47.1	54.0
	Total (0–6)	22.9	24.3	28.8	44.9	31.2	20.4	26.4	27.5	36.3	25.9	29.2
South	Under 3	6.3	5.6	12.2	21.9	10.9	3.5	10.6	12.5	24.4	8.8	10.5
	4–6	31.4	35.0	45.7	62.3	43.0	28.5	32.2	35.8	43.8	32.4	41.1
	Total (0–6)	16.9	18.5	27.0	40.3	25.0	14.7	20.9	24.7	34.4	20.1	24.2
Central-West	Under 3	3.3	5.4	6.5	14.2	7.3	6.0	3.7	6.1	10.9	5.8	6.6
	4–6	31.8	38.2	46.0	69.1	46.3	31.2	35.7	45.9	56.5	38.7	42.5
	Total (0–6)	15.4	19.6	23.5	38.4	24.2	17.0	18.6	22.7	33.6	20.6	22.4
Brazil	Under 3	6.2	7.2	9.8	20.0	10.4	5.8	8.2	8.6	16.6	7.8	9.2
	4–6	42.7	47.2	55.4	73.4	54.5	44.5	49.7	54.4	66.4	49.5	52.1
	Total (0–6)	21.4	24.1	29.4	43.9	29.3	23.3	27.3	29.8	40.4	27.0	28.2

Source: IBGE 1999.

Note
*Exclusively rural population from the North region.

Table 12.7 Number of preschool establishments by physical characteristics of the school and geographic region, Brazil, 1997

Region	Total establishments	Establishments that do not have:						Adequate bathrooms	
		Water supply		Electricity		Playground			
		Total	%	Total	%	Total	%	Total	%
North	6,399	902	14.1	2,348	36.7	5,719	8.94	5,448	85.1
Northeast	39,154	4,880	12.5	12,730	32.5	34,661	88.5	33,729	86.1
Southeast	19,754	314	1.6	1,086	5.5	10,350	52.4	10,980	55.6
South	11,115	38	0.3	36	0.3	5,898	53.1	6,735	60.8
Central-West	4,539	40	0.9	251	5.5	2,738	6.03	2,959	65.2
Brazil	80,961	6,174	7.6	16,451	20.3	59,366	73.3	59,851	73.9

Source: 1997 School Census (accessed via the internet, 17 September 1998), cited in Rosemberg 1999.

reinforces the process of social segregation in providing 'poor programmes for poor people'. Oliveira (1994) observed strong racial segregation in the public daycare centres under contract to the city government of São Paulo; but these centres were *meant* to serve children from black families with low income levels.

Children under 3 years of age are those with lowest access to ECCE. Yet it is exactly within the 2- to 4-year age range that children show the highest and most persistent rates of malnutrition. The federal government acknowledges the problem but only supplies the daycare centres with nutritional supplements at *half the value* (which is already low) given to elementary schools.

Children under the age of 3 have the lowest chance of attending daycare; and children under 4 have the highest malnutrition rates. Rather than seeing better daycare as a solution, however, the latest UNICEF report on Brazilian childhood and adolescence stigmatizes daycare as a care and education option for children under the age of 3. In its latest report on *Diversity and Equity in Brazil*[12] one finds the following passage, a masterpiece of diplomacy (or cynicism):

> **Daycare:** UNICEF considers it important for children to have a good beginning in life, and thus takes the position that under 3 years of age they should benefit from family living and parental care.
>
> In this document an analysis of data on early childhood does not include educational indicators for children under 3 years old, given that, despite being recognized by UNICEF as a right, daycare is not the only education possibility for education at this stage of life. It is fundamental that attention offered by parents and adults responsible for caring for the development of children under 3 years of age be valued as well.
>
> (UNICEF 2004:52)

The statistics about, and analysis of, ECCE in the 2004 UNICEF report do not include children under the age of 3, who, for UNICEF, have ceased to exist except as embedded in their family.

The devaluation of ECCE has resulted in its having the lowest annual average cost (public and private) per student in the Brazilian educational system. According to the OECD (2000), the average Brazilian cost for ECCE was US$820 (28th place), while the cost for higher education was US$10,791 (10th place).

ECCE expansion has been paid for by family and by teachers (thanks to their low salaries). This has had negative consequences for its quality. In fact it is possible to argue that Brazilian ECCE has been paid for by young children themselves – receiving far less than a decent entitlement. The multilateral organizations (UNESCO, UNICEF and the World Bank) continue to disseminate the idea that the costs of Brazilian ECCE can and should be reduced even further.

The issue of quality in ECCE reached the agenda only in the mid 1990s. Until then, the model used by welfare agencies was of emergency programmes to combat poverty. The propagation via UNESCO, UNICEF and the World Bank of low cost models of public investment meant that the expansion was prioritized at any cost. This resulted in a low quality standard of functioning; educators without formal training, insufficient and inadequate toys, books and interior and exterior spaces.

In this political context, the models for evaluating quality produced in the United States (for example, Developmentally Appropriate Practice (DAP) produced by the NAEYC (National Association for the Education of Young Children)) have had little circulation in the country because of the absence of context or any discussion of values. The ECCE community in Brazil needed to discuss the concept of ECCE on the political plane, exploring the values and the social actors involved. Since the debate about ECCE quality began, a main conceptual tool in Brazil has been the discussion paper produced by the European Community, *Quality in Services for Young Children: A discussion paper* (Balaguer *et al*. 1992).

In this sense, diversity in Brazil meant inequality. The contemporary effort has been, therefore, to define an acceptable national minimum so that daycare centres and preschools respect children, rather than reinforce inequality in the name of cultural diversity. But this needs to be done in the wider frame of discussion about values.

Overcoming inequality

How do we overcome such inequality in income distribution and in access to public services when the neoliberal model reigns supreme and the utopia of world revolution has no more followers? The responses of the multilateral organizations and Brazilian economists and administrators (Barros *et al*. 2000; Faria 2000; Medeiros 2003) suggest three areas for reform: an increase in the amassed wealth of the country, population reduction and a change in the distribution of social benefits via public policy.

Economic growth

Economic growth is considered one of the routes to reducing inequality and combating poverty. 'A growth rate of 3 per cent per year in per capita income, for example, tends to reduce poverty in an amount approximately equal to a percentage point every two years' (Barros *et al*. 2000:27). That is, it would take 25 years to reduce the level of poverty to below 15 per cent, if other conditions remained constant (which is highly unlikely). However, the Brazilian economy has not been growing at this rate: between 1995 and 2004, the accumulated Brazilian average is 2.2 per cent, the world average is 3.7 per cent and that of the emerging countries is 4.9 per cent. The most recent macro-economic reforms reduced inflation but promoted inequalities. The option to contain the increase in the public debt limited investment in infrastructure. Paying the public debt (domestic and foreign) and the cost of servicing it, imposed an enormous increase in the tax burden, but redirected it. Between 1995 and 2001, collection of social tax contributions increased 33 per cent (as a percentage of GDP) and social spending by the government increased by just 13 per cent.

Considered by some as the 'indispensable morphine', the Brazilian foreign debt, its negotiation with creditors and the agreements with the IMF for loans destined to compensate for deficits, is a producer of inequality: 'From 1994 to 1998 the country remitted R$128 billion on debt service and debt payment and in 1999, more than R$67 billion. In the same years, the federal government destined R$12 billion to education and R$9 billion to health services' (Souza 2002:l).[13] Presently, Brazilian foreign debt has now reached an amount close to US$120 billion.

Despite the United States being Brazil's major creditor, Brazilian foreign debt began during the Empire period in the nineteenth century, when Brazil inherited Portugal's debt to England as a result of the Aberdeen Treaty. The last payment on this debt was made in 1957. Brazilian foreign debt increased greatly during the military dictatorship (from US$12.5 billion to US$46.9 billion in 1979) which opted for accelerated growth during the 1970s (a 6.8 per cent average rate increase between 1974 and 1979) thanks to the support of loans. The debt got beyond tolerable limits with the world recession of 1981 and the increase in North American interest rates.

Brazil's present Minister of Education, Tarso Genro, has supported the Argentine initiative of negotiating with international institutions to use debt relief for basic education (Dianni 2004:1). To reach the goals set for ECCE by the National Plan for Education (which contemplates an expansion and improvement in quality) in 2006, an expenditure totalling 37.4 per cent of the refinancing of the federal debt service would be needed (Gomes 2004:64). A miracle would be needed in the present economic and political situation for Brazil's creditors to soften their hearts on behalf of young children.[14]

Birth control

Birth control has been considered by the neo-Malthusians to be one of the most effective strategies to reduce poverty. After carrying out a simulation of the impact of reducing the number of children of the Brazilian poor, Medeiros concluded:

> Brazilian poverty cannot be associated with the high number of children in families. If no Brazilian family had more than four children under 5 years of age, the percentage of poverty would be the same – 33 per cent. If the control were more extreme and in Brazil there was not even one child

under 5 years of age, the number of the poor (and the population overall) would diminish, but the percentage would drop by only one percentage point.

(Medeiros 2003:11)

Despite this fact, the World Bank continues to attribute important weight to the reproductive patterns in producing poverty in Brazil: 'the three factors most associated to the probable causes of poverty are: being located in a poor area, having a low level of schooling and having a large family' (World Bank 2001:8).

Explaining poverty by causes attributable to poverty itself such as reproductive patterns, linked to 'cultural' explanations of people's poverty, suggests that the moral scorn of the colonizers has not changed very much. The poor and poverty are still stigmatized. The metaphor of the 'vicious circle' of the reproduction of poverty and the 'virtuous circle' for combating it can be interpreted as a form of ideological pressure.

To illustrate the 'vicious circle' of poverty in Brazil, the World Bank gives a 'real-life' of Pedro's mother and her children. This groups together stereotypes about children's poverty, education and work:

- Pedro's mother is illiterate and of rural origin, therefore, poverty is associated with rural–urban migration.
- Pedro's mother comes from a family with thirteen children; she has ten children (a large family is responsible for the cycle of poverty).
- His mother lives with Pedro's step-father who makes two minimum wages (poverty is reproduced through a 'disorganized' family).
- None of Pedro's mother's children go to school because they cannot afford school supplies.
- It is Pedro's mother who decides who should leave school: 'I told them: you have to get some kind of job to be able to buy all those supplies'.
- Pedro's mother's children work, the boys stay on the street.

(World Bank 1995:66)

This fable is presented as 'a recent study done by a Latin American institute with support from UNICEF' (cited in Rosemberg and Freitas 2001:101–2).

This process of stigmatization was acutely perceived by Sharon Stephens during the Global Forum of ECO-92 in Rio de Janeiro, when she referred to the images of children in the discourse of environmentalists:

The first is an image of innocent children in a beautiful environment, this is the image of quality of life that we outline for 'all of us' when we engage in environmental actions. These children are usually white. The second image is of a mass of starving children, who fill the photographic frame and who destroy the environment. As far as I could tell, these children are black, although many of the children of the Third World are Asian, and naturally many of the poor children of the world are white.

There is an undeniable racist component to illustrate 'over-population' – this excess population that needs to be reduced so that 'our children' have the quality of life illustrated by the first set of images.

(Stephens 1992:12)

In this paragraph, Sharon Stephens sums up the emphasis that guides discourses, analyses and proposals issued by the international, inter-governmental as well as the national agencies, about poor childhood and adolescence in the developing world generally, and in Brazil in particular. These emphases, which are ideological, revolve around two main axes:

* Underdevelopment is homogeneously identical throughout the continents and within the same continent: Latin America is homogenous and its poor are equal.
* In this context of poverty, poor families practice excesses that put their children at 'risk'. In poor families, women are seen, above all, as out-of-control reproducers, who cause and perpetuate poverty and put global ecology and economy at risk.

In these ways the processes of social domination are reinforced.

Public policies

During the 1940s, the Brazilian State created specific agencies for child protection for the first time, strongly inspired by European experiences. The National Department for Children (DNCR) was created in 1940, linked to the then Ministry of Education and Health. The Brazilian Legion for Assistance was created in 1942. DNCR gradually centralized the assistance policies for mothers and children in Brazil over a 30-year period, making changes of a normative, educational and moralizing nature. It was the DNCR which regulated the few philanthropic daycare centres created in Brazil at the end of the 1960s. Its moralizing nature was underscored by Vieira (1988:7): 'The predominant cause everywhere, in Europe as here, of high infant mortality is the incompetence of mothers in the matter of childrearing' (Oliveira 1940, cited in Vieira 1988:7) – a concept not far from that disseminated by UNICEF in 2004.

Iniquity and poverty form a vicious circle of self reproduction. Poor children are inserted into intergenerational cycles of poverty and exclusion. When this paradigm is not broken, they will be fathers and mothers of children who are also poor. Thus, malnourished children grow up and become malnourished mothers who give birth to low weight babies; parents who lack access to information crucial for becoming capable of feeding and caring for children in a healthful way; and illiterate parents have more difficulties in helping with the learning process of their children. To transform this negative circle into a positive one, a reduction of iniquity and poverty should be given more attention with regard to childhood, without forgetting other phases and situations of life.

(UNICEF 2004:47)

Barros and Carvalho, evaluating the challenges for Brazilian social policy to 'combat poverty', point out:

the lack of integration among existing social programmes, the absence of co-ordination among the three levels of government, a precarious focus on the neediest population, as well as the rare evaluations that have contributed to the transformations which Brazilian social policy has undergone, have not been sufficient to achieve significant reduction in the degree of inequalities of income in the country.

(2003:15)

Analysing social policies for young Brazilian children, I would argue that they are underwritten by the policy of spectacle – the very poor, the weak and hopelessly vulnerable, the violent. The intervention of international organizations (of the United Nations and the NGOs) build on the policy of spectacle in order to shape Brazilian public policy on childhood.

After the International Year of the Child (1979), multilateral organizations, especially UNICEF, began to develop campaigns in favour of children in situations of 'risk'. There began a process of fragmenting poverty into subgroups or themes such as 'street children', 'child prostitution', 'adolescent pregnancy', 'eradication of child labour'. These campaigns, no doubt humanitarian, focused on these subgroups as representative of underdeveloped poverty in general. Starting with 'guesstimates', they arrived at a catastrophic number which appealed for focused, urgent governmental action. In their oversimplified explicatory models, they stigmatized children and families.

In 1981, the then advisor to UNICEF in New York on issues related to abandoned children and those without a family, Peter Taçon, brought to public light what was perhaps the first estimate of 'street children' in the world:

Perhaps there exist no more intensely exploited and abused children in our present world than those who are forced to survive on city streets – descendents of economic miracles and human tragedies. Any reasonable estimate can evaluate their number at around one hundred million – and it is possible that half of them live in Latin America.

(Taçon 1981a:13)

Two components merit highlighting in this text: the exorbitance of the number of street children and the allegory of 'street children' being descendants of the economic miracle and of human misery.

The one hundred million estimated by Taçon fell to seventy million in the underdeveloped world' in the book written by Maggie Black (1986) on the history of UNICEF. The category of 'street children' gained sophistication and was attributed to 'an irregular family situation', accentuating the family of origin and its difficulties:

> Concerned individuals, voluntary organizations and governmental departments estimate that approximately seventy million children throughout the developing world fall under the broad definition of being in 'irregular family situation' meaning that they live totally or virtually without parental support ... Among these children forty million live in Latin America where industrialization has been more intense than in Asia and Africa. This means that one in every five Latin American and Caribbean children live in a very different way than the traditional dependence on a family and relatives.
>
> (Black 1986:360)[15]

Families that abandon their children, men and women who do not distinguish between good and evil are the dominant – and insulting – discourses:

> Many personalities have related what happens to abandoned minors in Brazil. Thirty million according to some, thirty-two to thirty-six according to others. The boys *naturally* become delinquents (robbery, holdups, attacks on the aged, etc.) and the girls are prostitutes at an early age.
>
> (International Federation of Democratic Jurists 1986:106, emphasis mine)

Such issues, due to their media appeal, mobilize national governments who channel resources to specific programmes for 'street children', to combat 'child prostitution', to the 'eradication of child labour', etc. This is the same defensive process as in the nineteenth century, when Gobineau cursed our miscegenation. That is, issues of greater media visibility come to receive resources proportional to that visibility, disconnected from an overall policy for childhood.

The examples have been numerous over recent decades. Taking the example of daycare, international agencies, like UNICEF in Brazil, have chosen to emphasize parental discourses, improving parenting as a means of combating poverty. Levison (1991) analysing data from Brazil, showed that the most important factor determining whether Brazilian children from the ages of 7 to 14 work rather than study is the existence of a preschool-age sibling. If the mother of a young child has no care alternative for her child, either she stops working and the family allocates the responsibility to earn to another family member or she keeps working and another family member cares for the younger child. Families are not separate individuals living together by chance, but are inextricably interconnected, as the abundant literature from the 1980s on survival strategies has shown.

Conclusion

So if there are no daycare centres for children under 3 years old, what do the mothers who work do? And what do the women heads of families do who have young children? Should they stop working and beg with a child on the lap? Should they abandon the child? Should they leave the baby with an older child or contract a neighbour to care for the baby? These are the options in Brazil. Who would this person be, capable of caring for a baby for reduced payment while the mother works? The main option is a young female adolescent who is as poor, or poorer. Thus inequality is reproduced: the international advisor from far away creates the problem, which in order to be solved, requires his/her competence, salary, travel, seminars, publications, etc. At the same time, the international advisors mount campaigns to eradicate the domestic work performed by poor and often black Brazilian girls. Whose is the vice?

I have reversed the usual way of interpreting inequality in early childhood – good agencies teaching us the best way to develop ECCE – by listing the twenty capital *sins* of the multilateral organizations on public policies ECCE issues.

Twenty cardinal sins

- Disregard the local prior history of ECCE.
- Disregard earlier interventions by international organizations.
- Disregard local trends and current conflicts.
- Disregard local ECCE experiences (propose models, programmes) without having visited local daycare centres and preschools.
- Commission studies to support project/programme models decided upon beforehand to guide the taking of decisions.
- Learn about local ECCE experiences just by references to the literature that circulates among international organizations, without returning to the original sources.
- Transpose experiences and diagnoses of underdeveloped countries in general to Latin America and the Caribbean in particular.
- Transpose experiences and diagnoses of Latin America and the Caribbean in general to a country in particular.
- Transpose conclusions from some experiences in the North to the South.
- Transpose specific local experiences from elsewhere to Brazil, and vice-versa.
- Be guided exclusively by economic analyses (cost/benefit models).

- Disregard the multiplicity of issues, including values about childhood, family, education and work in implementing programmes.
- Establish deadlines to respond to bureaucratic or institutional needs and not reasons intrinsic to the proposal.
- Lose sight of the fact that the first commitment of programmes for children, proposals and projects should be to improve present conditions in the lives of children and their families.
- Disregard the fact that there are often divergences among the interests of the child, the parents, the professionals, the technicians, the governments and the international organizations.
- Disregard the local and international political setting (the correlation of forces) in which the proposals are being discussed or implanted.
- Develop proposals for programmes where administrative costs (including those of headquarters) and the costs of implementation are disregarded or minimized.
- Propose low cost programmes as miraculous, capable or eradicating poverty.
- Use women's labour as voluntary.
- Do not independently evaluate their local interventions.

Notes

* Fúlvia Rosemberg is Brazilian, a senior researcher with the Carlos Chagas Foundation, and a full professor of social psychology at the PUC-SP, where she coordinates the Nucleus for Studies on gender, race and age relations (NEGRI). Her academic and political activities have dealt with issues related to the creation and overcoming of social inequalities. To access her publications in Portuguese or another language go to www.cnpq.br/platformalatts/indexnovo.htm. The translation from Portuguese to English was done by Ann Puntch.

1 I have not used statistics and indicators systematized and published by UNICEF and the World Bank, references which are almost obligatory in analyzing the poverty of the South. This was (and has been) a political option, since I and other researchers and activists consider that international agencies propose policies for Brazilian childhood that, as a rule, reinforce stigma and social inequalities, and the statistics they use reinforce these perceptions.

2 Two publications from the 1980s deserve to be highlighted: *Infância e Desenvolvimento* (Childhood and Development) (Magalhães and Garcia 1993) and *Criança pequena e raça* (Young children and Race) (Rosemberg and Pinto 1997).

3 The academic journal that comes closest (to gathering these materials) is entitled *Revista Brasileira de Crescimento e Desenvolvimento* (The Brazilian Journal of Growth and Development), created in 1992.

4 Since 1889 Brazil has been a federal republic comprised of 26 federal units and a federal district. The federated units (the states) are subdivided into municipalities (5,560 in the overall federation).

5 Infant mortality in a rural region of the state of Pernambuco was the subject of an award winning interpretation by a North American academic. Through this one can perceive that the anathema launched over Brazilian poverty can also have its origin in academic writing, even when motivated by 'good intentions'. I am

referring to *Death without Weeping*, a book by Nancy Scheper-Hughes, who began travelling to Brazil at the start of the dictatorship as a member of the Peace Corps (USAID-North American). Her book deals with the negligence of poor rural mothers in the region of Pernambuco known as the Zona da Mata, as one of the intermediaries of premature death of infants.

It is a Brazil observed by Americans and includes visions of primitivism and primevalism as well as the hardened emotiveness and distorted characterizations of the poor people who are shaken by misery and violence in a country that has still not experienced full development. 'American national anthropology reinforces its dominant pose, and Brazil, poor and primitive, aids in the construction of this anthropology' (Scott 2004:3–4). The author has not published a single text in Portuguese, which makes a debate with the national academic community difficult. The impact of this book extends beyond anthropology, escaping the walls of academia. The maternal negligence related by Scheper-Hughes in this circumscribed region came to be reported in the media as poor Brazilian mothers who kill their children. e.g. *Publishers Weekly*. 'In Brazil's shantytowns, poverty has transformed the meaning of mother love. The routineness with which young children die, argues University of California anthropologist Scheper-Hughes, causes many women to affect indifference to their offspring, even to neglect those infants presumed to be doomed or "wanting to die". Maternal love is delayed and attenuated, with dire consequences for infant survival, according to the author's two decades of fieldwork'.

6 Brazil does not have a legal definition of a poverty line. Here we use the criterion that the poor are people who do not have the minimum income level necessary to satisfy basic needs. There is a national debate about the validity of measuring inequality in Brazil, in so far as the rich tend to omit reporting part of their income (Hoffmann 2000).

7 A European of the nineteenth century, who was outstanding in the propagation of racist theories in Brazil, was Count Gobineau (1816–82), author of the *Essai sur l'inégalité des races humaines*, who served here as the head of the French diplomatic delegation. A monogeneticist, Gobineau introduced the notion of 'degeneration of the race', 'understood to be the final result of mixing different human species'. Following are two excerpts from his writing:

> The two varieties of our species, the black race and the yellow race are the gross background, the cotton and the wool, that the secondary families of the white race soften, mixing their silk into them, while the Aryan group, putting its finer fabric into circulation through the ennobled generations, apply their arabesques of silver and gold to the surface, in an amazing masterpiece.
>
> (Gobineau 1940, vol. II:539)

8 Brazil can be considered the second largest country, after Nigeria, with a majority black population in the world (composed of blacks and browns).

9 This conclusion is based on a study by Sabóia and Sabóia (2001) based on data from the PPV 96/97 which analysed eight types of families using ten variables by the grouping method of analysis. The sole exception found was for families headed by men residing in the Southeast region.

10 The indicators for indigenous children are not always available since, in addition to having received little attention from indigenists and anthropology (Nunes 1999), their low presence in the population generates difficulties in interpretation of the data collected in research by sampling.

11 In recent decades, Brazilian mothers have been nursing their babies longer. Between 1989 and 1999 the average age for weaning babies increased by 4.4 months (Ministry of Health, cited in Brazil 2003: note 39).

12 The report was developed under contract with the IBGE, the official Brazilian agency which has been collecting data on daycare since 1995, under pressure from the social movements.

13 One US dollar is approximately equal to R$3 (July 2003).

14 See Chapter 3 [of Penn, H. (Ed.) (2005) *Unequal Childhoods: Young People's Lives in Poor Countries*. London: Routledge.] and comments by the Inter-American Development Bank.

15 During the 1990s several studies were done that estimated the number of children and adolescents in a street situation in Brazil. All arrived at much lower numbers than the international media estimates. I co-ordinated a study that did the counting in the city of São Paulo (1993). We found fewer than 5,000 children and adolescents during the day (the large majority working) and fewer than 900 during the night (Rosemberg 2000b).

References

Abley, M. (2003) *Spoken Here: Travels amongst Threatened Languages*, New York, Random House.

Alderson, P. (2000) *Young Children's Rights*, London, Save the Children/Jessica Kingsley.

Alexander, T. (1996) *Unravelling Global Apartheid*, Cambridge, Polity Press.

Amin, S. (1990) *Maldevelopment: Anatomy of Global Failure*, London, Zed Books.

Balachander, J. (1999) 'World Bank Support for Early Childhood Development: Case studies from Kenya, India and the Philippines', *Food and Nutrition Bulletin*, 20(1) also at www.unu.edu.unupress/food/v201e

Balaguer, J., Mestres, J. and Penn, H. (1992) *Quality in Services for Young Children: A Discussion Paper*, European Commission on Childcare Network.

Barbarin, O. and Richter, L. (2001) *Mandela's Children*, London, Routledge.

Barnett, T. and Whiteside, A. (2002) *AIDS in the Twenty-First Century*, Basingstoke, Palgrave/Macmillan.

Barnett, W., (1995) 'Long Term Effects of Early Childhood Programs on Cognitive and School Outcomes', *The Future of Children*, 5(3), 25–50.

Barros, R.P. and Carvalho, M. (2003) *Desafios para a política social brasileira*, Discussion Paper 815, Rio de Janeiro, IPEA.

Barros, R.P. and Foguel, M.N.(2001) 'Focalização dos gastos públicos sociais em educação e erradicação da pobreza no Brasil', *Financiamento da educação no Brasil, Em Aberto*, 74 (18 July):106–20.

Barros, R.P., Henriques, R. and Mendonça, R. (2000) 'Evolução recente da pobreza e da desigualdade: marcos preliminares para a política social', *Cadernos Adenauer*, 1:11–22.

Bauman, Z. (1995) *Life in Fragments: Essays on Postmodern Morality*, Oxford, Blackwell.

Bergesen, H. and Lunde, L. (1999) *Dinosaurs or Dynamos? The. United Nations and the World Bank at the Turn of the Century*, London, Earthscan.

Berman, P. (ed.) (1995) *Health Sector Reform in Developing Countries*, Cambridge, MA Harvard University Press.

Bernard, D., Cantwell, N., Cherp, A., Falkingham, J. and Letarte, C. (2000) *Societies in Transition: A Situational Analysis of the Status of Children and Women in the Central Asian Republics and Kazakhstan*, Almaty, UNICEF.

Bickel, R. and Spatig, L. (1999) 'Early Achievement Gains and Poverty-Linked Social Distress: The Case of Post Head-Start Transition', *Journal of Social Distress and the Homeless*, 8(4): 241–54.

Biersteker, L. (1996) *Non-formal Education in the Early Childhood Development Sector and Women's Empowerment: Experiences of Some Women Trainers in the Western Cape*, Evaluation study submitted to the Centre of Adult and Continuing Education, Cape Town, University of the Western Cape.

Black, M. (1986) *Children First: The Story of UNICEF*, Oxford, Oxford University Press.

Boli, J. and Thomas, G. (eds) (1999) *Constructing World Culture*, Stanford, CA, Stanford University Press.

Bourgois, P. (1998) *Families and Children in Pain in the U.S. Inner City*, in N. Scheper-Hughes and C. Sargent (eds) *Small Wars: The Cultural Politics of Childhood*, Berkeley, CA, University of California Press, pp. 331–51.

Boyden, J. (1990) 'Childhood and the Policy Makers: A Comparative Perspective on the Globalization of Childhood', in A. James and A. Prout (eds) *Constructing and Reconstructing Childhood*, London, Falmer Press.

Brazil, Ministério da Saúde (2003) *Relatório sobre saúde infantil*, Brasília, Ministério da Saúde.

Bradbury, B. and Jantii, M. (1999) *Child Poverty Across Industrialized Nations*, Florence, UNICEF Innocenti Centre, EPS 71.

Bredekamp, S. and Copple, C. (eds) (1997) *Developmentally Appropriate Practice in Early Childhood Programs*, Washington, National Association for the Education of Young Children.

Briggs, J. (1970) *Never in Anger: Portrait of an Eskimo Family*, Cambridge, MA, Harvard University Press.

British Medical Journal (2002) 'Global Voices on the AIDS Catastrophe', *British Medical Journal*, 7331, 26 January.

Bronfenbrenner, U. (1974) *Two Worlds of Childhood: US and USSR*, London, Penguin.

Bruer, J. (1999) *The Myth of the First Three Years*, New York, The Free Press.

Brunel, S. (1990) *La faim dans le monde*, Paris, Hachette.

Burman, E. (1995) *Deconstructing Developmental Psychology*, London, Routledge.

Campbell, C. (2003) *Letting them Die: Why HIVAIDS Prevention Programmes Fail*, Oxford, James Currey.

Campbell, F., Pungello, E., Miller-Johnson, S., Burchinal, M. and Ramey, C. (2001) 'The Abecedarian Project: The Development of Cognitive and Academic Abilities: Growth curves from an early childhood educational experiment', *Developmental Psychology*, 37: 231–42.

Campbell, F., Ramey, C, Pungello, E., Sparling, J. and Miller-Johnson, S. (2002) 'Early Childhood Education: Young Outcomes from the Abecedarian Project' *Applied Developmental Science*, 6(1): 42–7.

Campos, M.M., Rosemburg, F. and Ferreira, I.M. (1992) *Creches e Pré-escolas ne Brasil*, São Paulo, Cortez.

Chambers, R. (1997) *Whose Reality Counts? Putting the First Last*, London, Intermediate Technology.

Chambers, R. (2002) *Power, Knowledge and Policy Influence: Reflections on an Experience*, in K. Brock and R. McGee (eds) *Knowing Poverty: Critical Reflections on Participatory Research and Policy*, London, Earthscan, pp. 135–65.

Chambouleyron, R. (2004) 'Jesuítas e as crianças no Brasil Quinhentista', in Mary Dez Priore (ed.) *Hist Prioree as crianças no Bra*, São Paulo, Editora Contexto, pp. 55–83.

Childcare Information Exchange Home Page: www.ccie.com

Chomsky, N. (2003) *Power and Terror*, New York, Seven Stories Press.

Chua, A. (2003) *World on Fire*, London, Heinemann.

Chugani, H.T., Phelps, M.E. and Mazziota, J.C. (1987) 'Positron Emission Tomography Study of Human Brain Function Development', *Annals of Neurology*, 22: 487–97.

Church of England/Christian Aid (2000) *New Start Worship*, London, Church of England.

Chussodovsky, M. (1997) *The Globalization of Poverty: The Impacts of IMF and World Bank Reforms*, London, Zed Books.

Cole, M. (1990) *Cultural Psychology: A Once and Future Discipline*, Cambridge, MA, Bellknap Press/Harvard University Press.

Cornia, G. and Sipos, S. (1991) *Children and the Transition to the Market Economy*, Aldershot, Avebury.

De Vylder, S. (1996) *Development Strategies, Macro-economic Policies and the Rights of the Child*, Stockholm Discussion Paper for Radda Barnen.

De Waal, A. (2002) *Famine Crimes: Politics and the Disaster Relief Industry in Africa*, Oxford, James Currey.

De Waal, A. (2003) 'Review of Aids in the 21st Century', *London Review of Books*, July.

DeLoache, J. and Gottlieb, A. (eds) (2001) *The World of Babies: Imagined Childcare in Seven Societies*, Cambridge, Cambridge University Press.

Demberel and Penn, H. (2005) *Education in Nomadic Society: An Autobiography*, Oxford, Bergahn Books.

Dianni, C. (2004) *Tarso Genro discutiu com ministro argentino acordo*, Folha de São Paulo online, www.bookfinder.us/review2/0520075374.html.

Diderichsen, F. (1995) 'Market Reforms in Health Care and Sustainability of the Welfare State', in P. Berman (ed.) *Health Sector Reform in Developing Countries*, Boston, Harvard University Press, pp. 183–98.

Epstein, A. and Weikart, D. (1979) *The Ypsilanti–Carnegie Infant Education Project: Longitudinal Follow- Up*, Monographs of the High/Scope Educational Research Foundation, No. 6, Ypsilanti, Michigan, High/Scope Press.

Evans, J., Myers, R. and Ilfeld, E. (2000) *Early Childhood Counts: A Programming Guide on Early Childhood Care for Development*, Washington, World Bank Institute.

Falkingham, J. (2000) *From Security to Uncertainty: The Impact of Economic Change on Child Welfare in Central Asia*, Innocenti Working Paper 76, Florence, UNICEF.

Faria, V.E. (2000) 'Estabilização e o resgate da dívida social', *Cadernos Adenauer*, 1: 23–33.

Folha de São Paulo, 27 June 2004.

The Future of Children (1995) 'Long-term Outcomes of Early Childhood Programs: Analysis and Recommendations', Washington, *The Future of Children*, 5(3, Winter).

Gasperini, L. (1999) *The Cuban Education System: Lessons and Dilemmas*, Human Development Department LCSHD Paper, Series no, 48, Washington, World Bank.

Geldof, B. (2004) 'Brand New Aid', *Guardian*, 27 February, p. 27.

George, S. and Sabelli, F. (1994) *Faith and Credit: The World Bank's Secular Empire*, London, Penguin.

Ghosh, A. (1998 edition) *In an Antique Land*, London, Granta, p. 200.

Giddens, A. and Hutton, W. (2001) 'Fighting Back', in W. Hutton and A. Giddens (eds) *On the Edge: Living with Global Capitalism*, London, Vintage, pp. 213–24.

Gilliam, W. and Zigler, E. (2001) 'A Critical Meta-Analysis of all Evaluations of State-Funded Pre-school from 1977–1998: Implications for Policy, Service Delivery and Programme Evaluation', *Early Childhood Research Quarterly*, 15: 441–73.

Glover, J. (2003) 'Can we Justify the Killing of Children in Iraq?', *Guardian*, G2, 5 February: p. 6.

Gobineau, Joseph Arthur, comte de (1940) *Essai sur l'inégalité des races humaines* (1st edition pub. 1854), Paris, Firmin-Didot & Cie.

Gomes, C.A. (2004) 'Financiamento e custos da educação infantile', in Coelho, R. de C and Barreto, Â.R. (eds) *Fundamento da Educação infantil*, Brasília, UNESCO, pp. 31–72.

Goodnow, J. and Collins, A. (1990) *Development According to Parents*, New Jersey, Lawrence Erlbaum.

Goody, J. (1990) *The Interface between the Written and the Oral*, Cambridge, Cambridge University Press.

Gottlieb, A. (2004) *The After-life is Where We Come From: The Culture of Infancy in West Africa*, Chicago, Chicago University Press.

Gupta, A. (2001) 'Governing Population: The Integrated Child Development Services Program in India', in T. Hanson and F. Stepputat (eds) *States of Imagination: Ethnographic Explorations of the Post-Colonial State*, Durham, Duke University Press.

Guardian (2002) 'The Life of a Tennis Ball', G2, 5 February, 24.

Hancock, G. (1991) *Lords of Poverty*, London, Mandarin (revised edn published 1996).

Harkness, S. and Super, C. (1996) *Parent's Cultural Belief Systems: Their Origin, Expressions and Consequences*, New York, Guilford Press.

Harper, C, Marcus, R. and Moore, K. (2003) 'Enduring Poverty and the Conditions of Childhood: Lifecourse and Intergenerational Poverty Transmissions', *World Development*, 31(3): 535–54.

Hasenbalg, C. (2001) 'Condições de socialização na primeira infâneia', in IBGE (ed.) *Primeira infância*, Rio de Janeiro, IBGE, pp. 9–24.

Head, B. (1993) *The Cardinals*, Cape Town, David Philip.

Heap, B. and Kent, J. (2000) *Towards Sustainable Consumption: A European Perspective*, London, The Royal Society.

Hensher, M. and Passingham, S. (1996) 'The Impact of Economic Transition on Kindergartens in Kazakhstan: Problems and Policy Issues', *Compare*, 26(3): 305–13.

Hertz, N. (2001) *The Silent Takeover: Global Capitalism and the Death of Democracy*, London, Arrow.

Hinton, W. (1970) *Fanshen: A Documentary of Revolution in a Chinese Village*, London, Penguin (reprinted 1997, University of California Press).

Hochschild, A. (2001) 'Global Care Chains and Emotional Surplus Value', in W. Hutton and A. Giddens (eds) *On the Edge*, London, Vintage.

Hoffman, R. (2000) 'Mensuração da desigualdade e da pobreza no Brasil', in R. Henriques (ed.) *Desigualdade e pobreza no Brasil*, Rio de Janeiro, IPEA, pp. 81–107.

Hrdy, S. (1999) *Mother Nature: A History of Mothers, Infants and Natural Selection*, New York, Random House.

Hubel, D.H. and Weisel, T.N. (1977) *Functional Architecture of the Macaque Monkey Visual Cortex*, Proceedings of the Royal Society of London, B, 198: 1–59.

Hulme, D. and Edwards, M. (eds) (1997) *NGOs, States and Donors: Too Close for Comfort?*, Basingstoke, Macmillan.

Hulme, D., Moore, K. and Sheperd, A. (2001) *Chronic Poverty: Meanings and Frameworks*, Working Paper 2, Manchester, Chronic Poverty Research Group.

Hutton, W. and Giddens, A. (eds) (2001) *On the Edge: Living with Global Capitalism*, London, Vintage.

IBGE, *Pesquisa Nacional por Amostra de Domicílios* (PNAD) 1982, 1985, 1995, 1996, 1997, 1998, 1999, 2001 and 2002.

IBGE (1999) *Microdados da PNAD 1999*, Rio de Janeiro, IBGE.

IBGE (2001b) *Censo Demográfico 2001*, Resultados Preliminares, www.IBGE. gov.br

IBGE (2001a) 'Pesquisa sobre padrões de vida, 1996, 1997' (PPV) in *Primeira infância*, Rio de Janeiro, IBGE.

IBGE (2003) *Síntese de indcadores sociais 2002*, Rio de Janeiro, IBGE.

Inter-American Development Bank (1999) *Breaking the Poverty Cycle: Investing in Early Childhood*, Washington, Inter-American Development Bank.

The Inter-American Development Bank (1999) *Breaking the Poverty Cycle: Investing in Early Childhood*, New York, Inter-American Bank.

International Federation of Democratic Jurists (AIJD: Association Internacionale des Jurisites Democrates) (1986) *Bulletin d'Informacion sur les Activités de l'AIJD en 1986*, Brussels, AIJD, pp. 29–30.

Jahoda, G. and Lewis, I. (1987) *Acquiring Culture: Cross-cultural Studies in Child Development*, London, Academic Press.

James, A. and Prout, A. (eds) (1990) *Constructing and Reconstructing Childhood: Contemporary Issues in the Sociological Study of Childhood*, London, Falmer Press.

Jaramillo, A. and Mingat, A. (2003) *Early Childhood Care and Education in Sub-Saharan Africa: What Would it Take to Meet the Millenium Development Goals?*, Mimeo, Washington, The World Bank: Africa Region.

Justice, J. (2000) 'The Politics of Child Survival', in L. Whiteford and L. Manderson (eds) *Global Health Policy, Local Realities: The Fallacy of the Level Playing Field*, London, Lynne Reinner Publishers.

Kagan, J. (1998) *Three Seductive Ideas*, Cambridge, MA, Harvard University Press.

Kaldor M. (1999) *New and Old Wars*, Cambridge, Polity.

Kappel, M., Dolores B., Kramer, S. and Carvalho, M. Cristina (2001) 'Perfil das crianças de 0 a 6 anos que frequentam creches, pré-escolas e escolas: uma análise dos resultados da pesquisa sobre padrões de vida', *Revista Brasileira de Educação*, 16 (January–April): 35–47.

Kessen, W. (1981) 'The Child and Other Cultural Inventions', in E. Kessel and S. Siegel (eds) *The Child and other Cultural Inventions*, New York, Praeger.

Khor, M. (2001) *Rethinking Globalization: Critical Issues and Policy Choices*, London, Zed Books.

Kirschenbaum, L. (2001) *Small Comrades: Revolutionizing Childhood in Soviet Russia 1917–1932*, London, Routledge.

Krugman, P. (2003) 'The Good News', article from *New York Times* reprinted in *This Day*, 2 December, p. 22, Johannesburg.

Kumar, A. (2003) *World Bank Literature*, Minnesota, University of Minnesota Press.

Kunbur, R. (2001) *Economic Policy, Distribution of Poverty and the Nature of Disagreement*, paper presented to the Swedish Parliamentary Commission on Global Development, 2000, Revised January 2001, www.people.cornell.edu

Kuper, H. (1978) *Sobhuza II: Ngwenyana and King of Swaziland*, London, Duckworth.

Kuper, H.(1980) *An African Aristocracy*, New York, Africana Publishing Co.

Lamb, M. (1999) *Parenting and Child Development in 'Non-Traditional' Families*, New Jersey, Lawrence Erlbaum.

Lamb, M. and Sternberg, K, (1992) 'Socio-cultural Perspectives on Non-Parental Care', in M. Lamb, K. Sternberg, P. Hwang and A. Goteborg (eds) *Child-care in Context: Cross-cultural Perspectives*, New Jersey, Lawrence Erlbaum, pp. 1–26.

Leite, M.M. (2001) 'A infância no século XIX', in M.C. de Freitas (ed) *História social da infância no Brasil*, São Paulo, pp. 25–38.

Levin, R. (1997) *When the Sleeping Grass Awakens*, Johannesburg, Witwatersrand University Press.

Le Vine, R. (2003) *Childhood Socialization: Comparative Studies of Parenting, Learning and Educational Change*, Hong Kong, Comparative Education Research Centre.

LeVine, R., Dixon, S., LeVine, S., Richman, A., Leiderman, P., Keefer, C, and Brazleton, T. (1994) *Childcare and Culture: Lessons from Africa*, Cambridge, Cambridge University Press.

Levison, D. (1991) *Children's Labour Force Activity and Schooling in Brazil* (tese de doutorado), Ann Arbor, Michigan.

Lloyd, E. *et al.* (2004) *How Effective are Measures Taken to Mitigate the Impact of Armed Conflict on the Psychosocial and Cognitive Development of Children aged 0–8?*, www.eppi.ioe.ac.uk, accessed March 2004.

Lustosa, T.Q.O. and Reichenheim, M.E. (2001) 'Perfil nutricional da primeira infância', in IBGE (ed.) *Pesquisa sobre padrão de vida, 1996–1997*, Rio de Janeiro, IBGE, pp. 89–127.

Magalhães, A.R. and Garcia, W. (1993) *Infância e desenvolvimento*, Brasília, IPEA.

Magagula, C.M. (1987) *An Inventory of Preschools in the Kingdom of Swaziland*, Mbabane Swaziland Institute of Educational Research, UNISWA with support of Bernard van Leer Foundation.

Mamdani, M. (1996) *Citizen and Subject: Contemporary Africa and the Legacy of Late Colonialism*, New Jersey, Princeton University Press.

Maricato, E. (2003) *Alternativas para a crise urbana*, Petrópolis, Vozes.

Masse, L. and Barnett, S. (2003) *A Benefit/Cost Analysis of the Abecedarian Early Childhood Intervention*, www.nieer.org at March 2004.

Mayall, B. (2002) *Towards a Sociology of Childhood: Thinking from Children's Lives*, Bucks, Open University Press.

Medeiros, M. (2003) *Os ricos e a formulação de políticas de combate à desigualdade e à pobreza no Brasil*, Discussion Paper 984, Brasília, IPEA.

Montandon, C. (2001) 'Sociologia da infância: balanço dos trabalhos cm língua inglesa', *Cademos de Pesquisa*, 112 (March); 33–61.

Monteiro, C.A. (2003) 'A dimensão da pobreza, da desnutrição e da fome no Brasil', *Revisla de Estudos Avançados*, 48 (May–August): 7–20.

Moore, K. (2001) *Frameworks for Understanding the Inter-generational Transmission of Poverty and Well-being in Developing Countries*, Working Paper 8, Manchester, Chronic Poverty Research Centre.

Moro, C. de S. and Gomide, P.I.C. (2003) 'O conceito de infância na perspectiva de mães usuárias e não usuárias de crèche', *Paidéia*, 13(26, July–December): 171–80.

Munyakho, D. (1992) *Child Newcomers in the Urban Jungle*, The Urban Child in Difficult Circumstances series, Kenya/Florence, UNICEF.

Myers, R. (2000) *Thematic Studies: Early Childhood Care and Development*, Paris, UNESCO.

Narayan, D., Patel, R., Schafft, K., Rademacher, A. and Koch-Schulte, S. (1999) *Can Anybody Hear Us?*, Washington, World Bank/Oxford, Oxford University Press.

Narayan, D., Chambers, R., Shah, M.K. and Petesch, P. (2000) *Crying Out for Change*, Washington, World Bank/Oxford, Oxford University Press.

National Association for the Education of Young Children (NAEYC) (1995) *Developmentally Appropriate Practice*, USA, NAEYC.

New Internationalist (2003) *The World Guide: An Alternative Reference to the Countries of Our Planet*, London, ITGD Publishing.

Nichter, M. and Lock, M. (2002) *New Horizons in Medical Anthropology*, London, Routledge.

Norberg-Hodge, H. (1992) *Ancient Futures: Learning from Ladakh*, London, Rider/Random Century.

Nunes, Â. (1999) *A sociedade das crianças a'uwê-xavante*, Lisboa, Institute de Inovaçâo Educacional.

Ochs, E. and Schieffelin, B. (1984) 'Language Acquisition and Socialization: Three Developmental Stories and their Implications', in R. Shweder and R. LeVine (eds) (1984) *Culture Theory; Essays on Mind, Self and Emotion*, Cambridge, Cambridge University Press, pp. 276–320.

OECD (2000) *United States: Early Childhood Education and Care Country Note*, 1 July, Paris, OECD. Also on web at www.oecd.org

OECD (2001) *Starting Strong: Thematic Review of Early Education and Care*, Paris, OECD.

Oliveira, E, de (1994) *Relações raciais nas creches paulistanas*, São Paulo, PUC-SP.

Paiva, J. M. (2000) 'Educaçâo jesuítica no Brasil colonial', in E.M. Tehal Lopes (ed.) *500 anos de Educaçâo no Brasil*, Belo Horizonte, Autêntica, pp. 43–60.

Pastoral Da Crianca (2002) 'Portal Pastoral da criança', www.pastoral dacrianca.org.br. Accessed 2 July 2004.

Penn, H. (1994) 'Working in Conflict: A Dynamic Model of Quality', in P. Moss and A. Pence (eds) *Valuing Quality*, London, Paul Chapman/Teachers College Press, pp. 10–28.

Penn, H. (1997) 'Diversity and Inclusivity in Early Childhood Studies in South Africa', *International Journal of Inclusive Education*, 1(1): 1204–114.

Penn, H. (1999) 'Researching Childhood in the Majority World', in B. Mayall and S. Oliver (eds) (1999) *Social Policy Research: Issues of Power and Prejudice*, Buckingham: Open University Press, pp. 25–39.

Penn, H. (2001) 'Research in the Majority World', in T. David (ed.) *Promoting Evidence Based Practice in Early Childhood Education: Research and its Implications*, London, JAI, pp. 289–308.

Penn, H. (2004a) *Childcare and Early Childhood Development Programmes and Policies: Their Relationship to Eradicating Child Poverty*, Child Poverty Research Centre, London, Save the Children Fund.

Penn, H. (2004b) *Understanding Early Childhood: Issues and Controversies*, Maidenhead, Open University Press/McGraw Hill.

Penn, H. (2005) 'Parenting and Substitute Parenting', in G. Bendey and R. Mace (eds) *Alloparenting in Human Societies*, Cambridge, Cambridge University Press, forthcoming

Penn, H. and Gough, D. (2002) 'The Price of a Loaf of Bread: Some Conceptions of Family Support', *Children and Society*, 16.

Phipps, S. (2001) 'Values, Policies and the Well-being of Young Children in Canada, Norway and the United States', in K. Vleminckx and T. Smeeding (eds) *Child Well-being, Child Poverty and Child Policy in Modern Nations: What Do we Know?*, Bristol, The Policy Press, pp. 79–98.

Pieterse, J.N. and Parekh, B. (eds) (1995) *The Decolonization of the Imagination: Culture, Knowledge and Power*, London, Zed Books.

Pollitt, E. and Triana, N. (1999) 'Stability, Predictive Validity, and Sensitivity of Mental and Motor Development Scales and Pre-school Cognitive Tests among. Low-income Children in Developing Countries', *Food and Nutrition Bulletin*, 20(1, March).

Prout, A. and James, A. (1990) *Constructing and Reconstructing Childhood*, London, Falmer Press.

Quarles van Ufford, P. and Giri, A. (2003) *A Moral Critique of Development: In Search of Global Responsibilities*, London, EIDOS/Routledge.

Rabain, J. (1979) *L'enfant du Lignage*, Paris, Payot.

Raffer, K. (1992) *What's Good for the United States Must be Good for the World*, Kreisky Forum Symposium, Vienna, reprinted by Jubilee (2000).

Rahnema, M., Bawtree, V. (eds) (1997) *The Post Development Reader*, London, Zed Books.

Rampal, S. (1999) *Debt Has a Child's Face*, Unicef Website, unicef.org/pon99/debtcom

Rawls, J. (2000) *A Theory of Social Justice*, Oxford, Oxford University Press.

Republic of Kazakhstan (2001) *Preschool Education and Training: Main Regulations*, Astana, Ministry of Education and Science.

Reynolds, P. (1989) *Children in Crossroads: Cognition and Society in South Africa*, Capetown, David Philips.

Reynolds, P. (1991) *Dance, Civet Cat: Child Labour in the Zambezi Valley*, London, Zed Books.

Reynolds, P. (1996) *Traditional Healers and Childhood in Zimbabwe*, Ohio, Ohio University Press.

Rorty, R. (1989) *Irony, Contingency and Solidarity*, Cambridge, Cambridge University Press.

Rosaldo, R. (1993) *Culture and Truth: The Remaking of Social Analysis*, London, Routledge.

Rose, S. (ed.) (1998) *From Brains to Consciousness? Essays on the New Science of the Mind*, London, Penguin.

Rosemberg, F. (1990) *Panorama da educação infantil brasileira nos anos 1990*, São Paulo, Fundação Carlos Chagas, mimeo (2003).

Rosemberg, F. (1996a) 'Contemporary Trends and Ambuiguties in the Upbringing of Small Children', in E. Barretto and D. Zibas (eds) *Brazilian Issues on Education Gender and Race*, São Paulo, FCC, pp. 87–110.

Rosemberg, F. (1996b) 'Teorias feministas e subordinação de idade', *Pro-posições*, 7(3): 17–23.

Rosemberg, F. (1999) 'Expansâo da educação *infantil* e processus de exclusão', *Cadernos de Pesquisa*, 107 (June): 7–40.

Rosemberg, F. (2000a.) 'Ambiguites in Compensatory Policies: A Case Study from Brazil', in R. Cortina and N. Stromquist (eds) *Distant Alliances: Promoting Education for Girls and Women in Latin America*, New York and London, Routledge Falmer, pp. 261–94.

Rosemberg, F. (2000b) 'From Discourse to Reality: A Profile of the Lives and an Estimate of the Number of Street Children and Adolescents in Brazil', in A.M. Rosely (ed.) *Children on the Streets of Americas*, London and New York, Routledge, pp. 118–35.

Rosemberg, F. (2003a) 'Multilateral Organizations and Early Child Care and Education Policies for Developing Countries', *Gender and Society*, 17(2): 250–66.

Rosemberg, F. (2003b) 'Quelques points d'un plan de recherche sur la sociologie de l'enfance', *Journées francophones de sociologie de l'enfance*, Lisbon, October.

Rosemberg, F. and Andrade, L.F. (1999) 'Ruthless Rhetoric: Child and Youth Prostitution in Brazil', *Childhood*, 6(1, February): 113–32.

Rosemberg, F. and Freitas, R. (2001) 'Will Greater Participation of Brazilian Children in Education Reduce their Participation in the Labor Force?', *International journal of Education Policy Research and Practice*, 2(3): 249–66.

Rosemberg, F. and Pinto, R.P. (1995) 'Saneamento básico e raça', *Revista Brasileira de Crescimento e desenvolvimento humano*, 112 (January–December): 23–38.

Rosemberg, F. and Pinto, R.P. (1997) *Criança pequena e raça*, São Paulo, Textos FCC, 13.

Roy, A. (1999) *The Greater Common Good*, Bombay, India Book Distributors.

Ruel, M., Levin, C, Armar-Klemesu, M., Maxwell, D. and Morris, S. (1999) *Good Childcare Practices can Mitigate the Negative Effects of Poverty and Low Maternal Schooling on Children's Nutritional Status: Evidence from Accra*, FCND Discussion Paper 62, Washington, International Food Policy Research Institute.

Sabóia,J. and Sabóia, A.L. (2001) 'Condições de vida das famílias com crianças até 6 anos', in IBGE (éd.) *Primeira infância*, Rio de Janeiro, IBGE, pp. 25–48.

Sange Agency (2001) *Listening to the Poor*, Almaty, UNDP.

Scheper-Hughes, N. (ed.) (1983) *Child Survival*, Dordrecht, Holland, D. Reidel Publishing Co., pp. 293–324.

Scheper-Hughes, N. (1993) *Death Without Weeping*, Berkeley, CA, University of California Press.

Scheper-Hughes, N. and Sargent, C. (eds) (1998) *Small Wars: The Cultural Politics of Childhood*, Berkeley, CA, University of California Press.

Schwarcz, L.M. (2004) *O espetáculo das raças*, São Paulo, Companhia das Letras.

Schwartzman, S. (2004) *As causas da pobreza*, Rio de Janeiro, FGV.

Schweinhart, L. (2003) *Benefits, Costs and Explanation of the High/Scope Perry Preschool Program*, Paper presented at the Meeting of the Society for Research in Child Development, Tampa, Florida.

Schweinhart, L. and Weikart, D. (1997) 'The High/Scope Preschool Curriculum Comparison Study Through Age 23', *Early Childhood Research Quarterly*, 12: 117–13.

Schweinhart, L., Barnes, H. and Weikart, D. (1993) *Significant Benefits: The High/Scope Perry Preschool Study Through age 27*, Monographs of the High/Scope Educational Research Foundation, 10.

Scott, J.C. (1989) *Weapons of the Weak: Everyday Forms of Peasant Resistance*, New Haven, Yale University Press.

Scott, J.C. (1998) *Seeing Like a State: How Certain Schemes to Improve the Human Condition Have Failed*, New Haven, Yale University Press.

Scott, K., Avchen, R. and Hollomon, H. (1999) 'Epidemiology of Child Development Problems: The Extent of the Problems of Poor Development in Children from Deprived Backgrounds', *Food and Nutrition Bulletin*, 20(1): 2, also on www.unu.edu/unupress/food

Scott, P. (2004) *Antropologias nacionais e articulações internacionais, Brasil e Estados Unidos*, Recife, UFPE.

Sen, A. (1999) *Development as Freedom*, Oxford, Oxford University Press.

Serpell, R. (1993) *The Significance of Schooling: Life Journeys in an African Society*, Cambridge, Cambridge University Press.

Serpell, R. (1999a) 'Local Accountability in Rural Communities: A Challenge for Educational Planning in Africa', in F. Leach and A. Little (eds) *Education, Cultures and Economics: Dilemmas for Development*, London, Falmer Press, pp. 111–39.

Serpell, R. (1999b) 'Theoretical Conceptions of Human Development', in L. Eldering and P. Leseman (eds) *Effective Early Education: Cross-cultural Perspectives*, London, Falmer, pp. 41–66.

Shweder, R. and Le Vine, R. (1984) *Culture Theory: Essays on Mind, Self and Emotion*, Cambridge, Cambridge University Press.

SIDH (1996) *Culture and Gender Beliefs*, Mussoorie, Society for Integrated Development of Himalayas.

SIDH (1999) *A Matter of Quality: A Study of People's Perceptions and Expectations from Schooling in Rural and Urban Areas of Uttarakhand*, Mussoorie, Society for Integrated Development of Himalayas.

SIDH (2001) *Primary Study on Incidence of Disablity in Jaunpur*, Sansodhan–Block Tchri District, Mussoorie, Society for Integrated Development of Himalayas.

SIDH (2002) *Child and the Family: A Study of the Impact of Family Structures upon Children in Rural Ullarakhand*, Mussoorie, Society for Integrated Development of Himalayas.

Simões, C.C. (2002) *Perfis de saúde e de mortalidade no Brasil*, Brasília, OPAS.

Sirota, R. (2001) 'Emergência de uma sociologia da infância: evolução do objeto e do olhar', *Cadernos de Pesquisa*, 112 (March): 7–32.

Soros, G. (2000) *Open Society: Reforming Global Capitalism*, New York, Public Affairs.

Souza, Silvio Araujo (2002) 'A impagável dévida externa', CMI Brazil, www.midiaindependente.org, Accessed 27 October 2003.

Spiro, M. (1990) 'On the Strange and the Familiar in Recent Anthropological Thought', in J. Stigler, R Shweder and G. Herdt (eds) *Essays on Comparative Human Development*, Chicago, Chicago University Press, pp. 47–61.

Stephens, S. (1992) *And a Little Child Shall Lead Them: Children and Images of Children at the Conference on Enviroment and Development*, Trondheim, Mimeo.

Stephens, S. (1995) *Children and the Politics of Culture*, New Jersey, Princeton University Press

Stigler, J., Shweder, R. and Herdt, G. (1990) *Cultural Psychology: Essays on Comparative Human Development*, Cambridge, Cambridge University Press.

Stiglitz, J. (2002) *Globalization and its Discontents*, London, Penguin.

Stirrat, R. (1999) 'Economics and Culture: Towards an Anthropology of Economics', in F.E. Leach and A. Little (eds) *Education, Cultures and Economics*, London, Falmer, pp. 33–47.

Super, C. and Harkness, S. (1986) 'The Developmental Niche: A Conceptualization at the Interface of Society and the Individual', *Journal of Behavioural Development*, 9: 545–70.

Sure Start (2003/4) www.ness.bbk.ac.uk.

Sutton-Smith, B. (1986) *Toys as Culture*, New York, Gardner Press.

Sutton-Smith, B. (1999) 'The Rhetorics of Adult and Child Play Theories', in S. Reifel (ed.) *Advances in Early Education and Day Care*, 10, London, JAI pp. 149–62.

Taçon, P. (1981 a) *El seminario sobre el menor en situación de abandono y/o atención al niño*, New York, UNICEF.

Taçon, P. (1981b) *My Child Minus One*, New York, UNICEF.

Theroux, P. (2003) *Dark Star Safari: Overland from Cairo to Cape Town*, New York, Houghton Mifflin.

Tobin, J. (1995) 'Post-structural Research in Early Childhood Education', in J. Hatch (ed.) *Qualitative Research in Early Childhood Settings*, Connecticut, Praeger, pp. 223–43.

Tobin, J. (1996) *Making a Place for Pleasure in Early Childhood Education*, New Haven, Yale University Press.

Toroyan, T., Roberts, I., Oakley, A., Laing, G., Mugford, M. and Frost, C. (2003) 'Effectiveness of out-of-home day care for disadvantaged families: randomized controlled trial', *British Medical Journal*, 327: 906–9.

Torres, R.M. (1996) 'Melhorar a qualidade da educação básica? As estratégias do Banco Mundial', in De Tommasi, L., Warde, M. and Haddad, S. (eds) *O Banco Mundial e as políticas educacionais*, São Paulo, Cortez, pp. 125–93.

UNGTAD (1999) *Trade and Development Report*, New York, United Nations.

UNDP (2003a) *Perceptions of Corruption in Kazakhstan: By Parliamentarians, Public Officials, Private Business and Civil Society*, Sange Research Centre, Almaty, UNDP.

UNDP (2003b) *Human Development Report 2003: A Compact Amongst Nations to End Human Poverty*, New York, United Nations.

UNESCO (2000a) *World Education Forum 2000: The Dakar Framework for Action*, Paris, UNESCO.

UNESCO (2000b) *World Education Forum 2000: Thematic Studies: Early Childhood Development and Care*, Paris, UNESCO.

UNESCO (2002) *Workshop on Young Children Affected by HIVAIDS*, Paris, UNESCO.

UNESCO/MoE (2000) *Case Study: Kazakhstan Preschool Education System at the Doorstep of the 21st Century*, Astana, MoE.

UNICEF (2000) *Societies in Transition: A Situational Analysis of the Status of Children and Women in the Central Asian Republics and Kazakhstan*, Almaty, UNICEF.

UNICEF (2001) *Annual Report for Swaziland*, Mbabane, UNICEF.

UNICEF (2002a) *The Right to Qualify Education: Creating Child-friendly Schools in Central Asia*, Florence, MONEE/Innocenti Centre.

UNICEF (2002b) *Early Childhood Development in the Central Asian Republics and Kazakhstan*, prepared by Konstantin Osipov and Cherie Etherington-Smith, Almaty, UNICEF.

UNICEF (2004) *Relatório sobre infância e adolescência no Brasil: equidade e diversidade*, Brasília, UNICEF.

van der Gaag, J. and Tan, J. (1998) *The Benefits of Early Child Development Programs: An Economic Analysis*, Washington, World Bank Education Section, 18992, V. 1.

Vieira, L.M. (1988) 'Mal necessário: creches no Departamento Nacional da criança', *(1940–1970) Cadernos de Pesquisa*, 67 (November): 3–16.

Viruru, R. (2001) *Early Childhood Education: Postcolonial Perspectives from India*, London, Sage.

Vleminckx, K. and Smeeding, T. (eds) (2001) *Child Well-being, Child Poverty and Child Policy in Modem Mations: What Do we Know?*, Bristol, The Policy Press.

Wade, R. (2001) 'Showdown at the World Bank', *New Left Review*, Second Series, 7: 124–37.

Walt, G. (1994) *Health Policy: An Introduction to Process and Power*, London, Zed Books.

Whiteford, L. and Manderson, L. (eds) (2000) *Global Health Policy, Local Realities: The Fallacy of the Level Playing Field*, London, Lynne Reinner Publishers.

Whitfield, S. (1999) *Life Along the Silk Road*, London, John Murray.

Whiteside, A., Hickey, A., Ngcobo, N. and Tomlinson, J. (2003) *What is Driving the HIV/AIDS Epidemic in Swaziland and What More Can we do About It?*, Mbabane, National Emergency Response Committee on HIV/AIDS (NERCHA) and United Nations Programme on HIV/AIDS (UNAIDS).

WHO (1999) *A Critical Link: Interventions for Physical Growth and Psychological Development: A Review*, Geneva, WHO, Department of Child and Adolescent Health and Development.

WHO (2004) *The Importance of Caregiver-child Interactions for the Survival and Healthy Development of Young Children: A Review*, Department of Child and Adolescent Health and Development, Geneva, WHO.

Woodhead, M. (1997) *In Search of the Rainbow: Pathways to Quality in Large Scale Programmes for Young Disadvantaged Children*, The Hague, Bernard van Leer Foundation.

Woodward, D. (1992) *Debt, Adjustment and Poverty in Developing Countries: The Impact of Debt and Adjustment at the Household Level in Developing Countries*, London, Pinter Publications / SCF.

World Bank (1998) Project information BRPA 6525, Washington, World Bank.

World Bank (2001) *O combate è pobreza no Brasil, Vol. 1, resumo do relatório*, Departamento do Brasil, Setor de Redução da Pobreza e Manejo Econômico, Região da América Latina e do Caribe, Brasília.

www.worldbank.org (15 March 2000, 12 April 2001, 18 July 2001).

World Bank (1995) *Children: School or Work? Brazil Country Assistance Strategy*, Washington, World Bank.

World Bank (2000) *The World Bank and Children*, Washington, World Bank Social Protection Human Development Network.

Young, M.E. (1998) 'Policy Implications of Early Childhood Development Programmes', *Nutrition, Health and Child Development*, Washington, Pan American Health Organization/World Bank.

Zeitlin, M. (1990) 'My Child is my Crown: Yoruba Parental Theories and Practices in Early Childhood', in S. Harkness and C. Super (eds) (1996) *Parents Cultural Belief Systems: Their Origin, Expressions and Consequences*, New York, Guilford Press, pp. 496–531.

Professionalism and professionalisation

Chapter 13

Misplacing the teacher?
New Zealand early childhood teachers and early childhood education policy reforms, 1984–96

Judith Duncan

Source: *J. Duncan, Contemporary Issues in Early Childhood, 5(2), 160–177, 2004.*

Abstract

Early childhood care and education services in New Zealand have experienced major policy reforms since 1984. Life history interviews were carried out over a two-year period to obtain insight into the impact of the major reforms on the lives of eight kindergarten teachers. This article looks at the teachers' own perception of the changes and how they often felt 'overtaken' or 'misplaced' within the reforms. The teachers' stories are positioned within an environment of competing discourses about education, where newly established discourses worked to relocate or misplace the teachers.

Introduction

Throughout the 1980s and 1990s the early childhood sector along with the compulsory education sector in New Zealand were involved in periods of tumultuous change. In this study I talked with eight kindergarten teachers about their perceptions of these changes in their day-to-day lives teaching within the New Zealand Free Kindergarten Service (Duncan, 2001a).[1]

This article discusses the eight New Zealand kindergarten teachers' sense of being 'smothered', 'overtaken', and 'misplaced' by all the changes and reforms coming down on them during the times of New Zealand's educational reform in the 1980s and early 1990s. The teachers' interviews illustrate these feelings in the context of policy implementation delivered from both government and local employers. They also demonstrate how the wider social and economic changes occurring in New Zealand at the same time added to this sense of being 'overtaken' and 'misplaced' by politics and top-down decision making.

The teachers were all experienced head teachers (or had been head teachers), who were able to reflect on their teaching years before the changes in 1984 and who were both willing and able to articulate their experiences in an interview context. The New Zealand early childhood world is a small one, and, as I myself had been a kindergarten teacher for some time, I knew all the teachers before approaching them to participate in this study. The eight teachers were based in the lower half of the South Island of New Zealand. This was due to geographical convenience for myself as the researcher. Each teacher was interviewed twice, once in late 1994 and again, early in 1996. The first interview took the form of a life (history) focused interview. This is a combined methodology, which brings the strengths of life history (which encompasses a person's life) alongside an analysis of a specified situation (in this case the experiences of being a kindergarten teacher at particular times of policy change). The second interview two years later had a twofold objective. Firstly, I wanted the teachers to be able to reflect on the initial analysis of their previous interview as set out in my proposed theoretical framework. Secondly, I wished to update the teachers' life stories, incorporating the changes and developments in their personal and professional lives since the first interview. Thus, this study was able to track the changes in both the personal and the professional lives of the teachers. This article discusses one aspect of their professional teaching experiences (see Duncan, 1999, 2001a, b, 2002, for other aspects of this doctoral study).

The New Zealand kindergarten service

I chose to research the impact of the early childhood education reforms on those within the kindergarten service, not only because I had been a kindergarten teacher myself, but also because the Free Kindergarten Service is unique, both in New Zealand and internationally, in its historical development, its philosophies, and its style of provision. The New Zealand Free Kindergartens (hereafter referred to as kindergartens and the kindergarten service) were the largest providers of early childhood education in New Zealand. They have only recently been surpassed by the provision of childcare centres (Ministry of Education, 2000). Kindergartens are administered by kindergarten associations. These associations operate as 'umbrella' organisations, responsible for managing the individual kindergartens in their region or area 'in accordance with their philosophies and Government requirements' (Education Review Office, 1997, p. 11).

A key philosophy of the kindergarten service has always been to maintain an accessible, high-quality, early childhood care and education service. The three key elements that support this philosophy are:

• fees are not charged for attendance, although substantial fundraising and voluntary donations are required;

- trained and qualified teachers are employed and supported by a professional team of senior teachers;[2]
- parents and caregivers are involved in the running and management of the service, from the level of parent committees in each individual kindergarten through to association level.

The New Zealand education reform context

Many commentators reflect that the years of the Fourth New Zealand Labour Government (1984–90) were the heyday for early childhood services (Meade, 1990; Smith, 1991; Wells, 1991; May, 1993). Gains were made across the whole sector and policies appeared to support and encourage quality in and accessibility to early childhood centres. The years 1987–90 were the period when policy and legislation began to address the pro-early childhood rhetoric of the 1984 Labour Government. This occurred alongside the general restructuring of educational administration in New Zealand. The Picot Report, *Administering for Excellence* (Taskforce to Review Education Administration, 1988), was the first overview of educational administration in New Zealand that included in its brief the issues involved in the early childhood sector. The pre-election promises of the Government led to a separate and concurrent review of the early childhood sector (May, 1990, p. 103). This review was undertaken by the Early Childhood Care and Education Working Group (1988). The Picot Report, however, was not a foreign or alien document for early childhood education, as it contained many aspects that were already consistent with practices in the early childhood sector: 'particularly the idea of a partnership between parent/employer/community groups and the government, where the main role of the government was to be one of ensuring standards and of bulk funding the different services/programmes/agencies' (May, 1990, p. 103). With the release of the Picot Report, the Early Childhood Care and Education Working Group then attempted to adapt the model to the early childhood sector in a way that would serve the needs of the sector and incorporate early childhood education into the bigger education picture. The resultant report, *Education To Be More* (1988), became referred to as the Meade Report, after the chair of the committee, Anne Meade.

The Meade Report was revolutionary in its holistic view of early childhood education and the key role Government should play in it. The Report made it clear that early childhood education was not only about providing good quality education for the very young child, but it was also about supporting women and Māori cultural survival (Early Childhood Care and Education Working Group, 1988). The language of the report and the integration of early childhood education within the reforms of the school sector indicated, to those encouraged by the direction of the Report, that early childhood education was no longer on the fringe. The Report was also clear on the role that Government had historically played in the early childhood sector and set out its current and future roles. This Report was to have far-reaching implications for the entire childhood sector, not least the free kindergartens.

At the time of the Meade Report, kindergarten services, compared to the other early childhood services, were receiving the greatest amount of the Government funding. For this reason commentators have referred to the kindergartens as the 'flagship of government support for New Zealand early childhood education' (Wylie, 1992, p. 2). Wylie identified how the historical level of Government support had meant that access to kindergarten had been 'free'. Parents had never been expected to pay fees, although they were asked for donations and expected to assist in fundraising.

The resultant *Before Five* document, the Government response to the Meade Report (Lange, 1988a), had substantial and important discursive differences from the Meade Report. As will be seen, the changes outlined in the document indicated particular philosophies that were not in keeping with the intent of the Meade Report and the politics of the early childhood sector itself. Within weeks of taking over office from the Labour party in 1990, the New Zealand National Government undermined all the very recent gains that had been made in early childhood education. Firstly, newly created quality guidelines were replaced by a document entitled the *Statement of Desirable Objectives and Practices,* released on 14 December 1990 and now commonly referred to as DOPs (Ministry of Education, 1990). These guidelines immediately removed the necessity for higher than minimum licensing requirements. Not only did this have the effect of lowering standards and mechanisms for monitoring quality, but many people who had already been working hard towards the higher standards were immediately alienated. Smith *et al.* (1994) argued that the commitment to higher quality over and above the minimum standard was lost and 'in effect the only requirement is to meet minimum standards for licensing' (p. 3).

In the years from 1984 to 1996, which were the focus of this study, the teachers experienced the constant shifts of the education policy discourses and their resultant discursive practices. When the teachers were interviewed they were able to reflect on both the positive and negative consequences of these years.

Discourse

In examining the teachers' experiences within this context I turned to the ideas of Foucault and, in particular, his use of discourse. Foucault identified discourses historically as the specific ways of speaking knowledge and truth, i.e. what it is possible to speak at any given moment, who can speak, and with what authority (Foucault, 1970, 1971, 1980). Discourses then act as sets of rules and behaviours. In this way discourses are powerful and are:

> practices that systematically form the objects of which they speak ...
> Discourses are not about objects, they do not identify objects, they

constitute them and in the practices of doing so conceal their own invention.

(Foucault, 1974, cited in Ball, 1990, p. 2)

Thus, for Foucault, discourses do not merely reflect what already exists but they actually work to create reality. These discourses (and their resultant discursive practices) appear often as the 'taken-for-granted' ways in society (Weedon, 1987; Gavey, 1989). Individuals act on the basis of their ideas of how the world should be. Within discursive fields (i.e. the arenas, institutions, or organisations where discourses are occurring) complex negotiations and struggles between the various discourses occur over the meanings to be given 'truth' status and to be incorporated into outcomes, such as state policy (Yeatman, 1990).

Discourses surrounding the general early childhood sector reforms have had particular contradictory consequences for the kindergarten service. Policy documents may contain differing discourses and discursive practices throughout the various processes of their conception, consultation, construction, delivery and final implementation. Commentators and writers looking at the education reforms (and the wider restructuring) within New Zealand that occurred in the 1980s and 1990s have described how the discourses of neo-liberalism were contrasted with social equity and community participatory discourses within policy and their resultant discursive practices (May, 1990; Middleton, 1993). The consequences of the changes brought about by the *Before Five* document placed the kindergarten service in a vulnerable and contradictory position in comparison to the rest of the early childhood sector, i.e. the flagship was downsized (Wylie, 1992; May, 1999). What are striking in the eight kindergarten teachers' accounts are the differences between the outcomes within the kindergarten service and the stated policy intentions at the time of the construction and initial delivery of the reforms. Beginning with the Meade Report, the discourses surrounding quality, accessibility, affordability, and cultural survival inspired the whole early childhood sector. While the changes between the Meade Report and the resulting Government White Paper, *Before Five*, signalled key discursive differences between the two documents (Wells, 1991; Mitchell & Noonan, 1994; Mitchell, 1997), the teachers were firmly positioned within the Meade Report's recommendations. The teachers felt this Report would improve their teaching experiences and reflected their beliefs about early childhood education to society in general, i.e. the Meade Report was compatible with their existing discourses and discursive practices.

The eight kindergarten teachers in this study provided numerous examples through their stories of where the funding and management practices, which were introduced to meet the wider early childhood sector changes, worked to lower standards in kindergartens. A key example here was the changes in funding arrangements. The kindergarten service, now not the only childhood service to receive Government funding or support, had to face capped funding while the other early childhood services caught up with its level of funding (Lange, 1988). In times of increased fiscal investment this would be fine, but in a climate of restraint, where many more had access to less, new financial constraints and stresses arose. Neo-liberal and New Right discourses presented problematic discursive practices for the kindergarten teachers. Such discourses draw on beliefs that: individuals are fundamentally concerned with the pursuit of self-interest and in maximising individual gain; there should be no regulation and restriction in the market place; commodification of almost everything is not only possible but desirable; and choice and competition are the way to ensure efficiency, maximum use of resources, and accountability. While Fitzsimons et al (1999) argue that neo-liberalism has become a form of governmental rationality, which has worked to silence alternative discourses, the kindergarten teachers' stories offer an alternative view.[3]

Being 'overtaken' and 'misplaced': the teachers' experiences

Looking at the education changes overall, both Elizabeth and Maggie discussed how the outcomes of all the changes contradicted the original intentions of the Meade Report and other early childhood research recommendations:

> *Elizabeth*: Some things are good things to deal with and some aren't … '84, '85 were definitely good things to live with [*laugh*]. And then it kind of went down [*laugh*]. But, you know, I mean the Meade Report came out and everybody thought, 'This is great. This is something positive. This is going to lift the standard of education. 'That's what it's s'posed to do and I'm sure that's what everyone wanted it to do. But, the reality is that because they had that one-to-15 minimum [teacher–child ratio] in there … us who are in our one-to-13 are having pressure put [on] us to meet the one-to-15 or otherwise you're going to lose a teacher, or 45/45 rolls … To me that is just totally against what *Education to Be More* is all about. I mean those were minimum standards. I mean minimum is something that, you know, you have to meet but you should be trying to make better, as far as I'm concerned. Whilst … it was a good concept to get everybody, you know, all early childhood reaching some sort of a standard – it's a shame that it's been used to pull … standards down. [*pause*]

> *Maggie*: Our education system is crumbling. That's dreadfully sad. So that reform [bulk funding], if you wanted to call it [a reform], to me is a real black area – real black day in New Zealand. I can't see why they can't see it's failed everywhere else in the world. So why are we doing it? … We're in the situation of possibly losing a teacher because we can't stuff 44 children in. They're not there to stuff and even if we did have them to stuff – 44 three-years-old – you know, Lillian Katz, who was here relatively recently stated categorically that large group size is not

conducive to good learning. The Roper Report[4], '86 was it? '86? has been filed in the too-hard basket. That working party[5] that had to re-convene three times with three different groups of people until they said things that the Government wanted, you know. All those so-called reforms are all the negative side. There's been good stuff for accountability – the charters, the uniformity of conditions of services and protection for children. All that's good, you know. The ethics committees that are being set up about child abuse legislation et cetera. That's all good stuff you know. So it has been good but the bad is the bulk funding which has starred above everything bad and I just see the rot spreading, which is a shame.

The pace of change, which is often referred to in other reviews of the political and education changes during the 1980 and 1990s, was a significant factor in the eight kindergarten teachers' feelings of having been 'overtaken':

> *Maggie*: I look at it now and I feel this oppression ... Like as a kid when you're playing with cushions – pillow fights – and you're the one at the bottom. All the pillows are on top. You know, that awful feeling of not being able to get out. That's the feeling I get when I read some of my stuff here ... 'cause that smothered feeling came to me. That's how I felt about it – like I was being smothered or that there was no fresh air around.

One new policy or directive had hardly arrived when the next one appeared. This meant that, even when the change may have been seen to have been a good one on reflection sometime later, for example *Te Whāriki* the New Zealand early childhood curriculum (Ministry of Education, 1996), at the time it was resisted due to the timing of its arrival. The pace and timing, combined with the procedures for introducing or implementing the change, created the context for whether the change was perceived by the teachers to be a good thing to get involved in, or added to their feelings of despair and low morale. Maggie's experiences with the draft of *Te Whāriki* demonstrated this. Maggie described how receiving the document became the final straw, using the children's story *Who Sank the Boat?* (Allen, 1982) to draw an analogy. In this children's picture book, while it is the combined weight of all the animals in the boat which ultimately sank the boat, it is on the arrival of the mouse in the boat – 'the last to get in and the lightest of all. Could it be him?' – that the boat sinks:

> *Maggie*: Looking back at it I think, 'Well, yeah, okay, all those things were going on. But I wasn't in control of them'. They were coming through the mailbox in their pieces of paper by the truckload [*pause*]. And I remember getting so upset about things ... So I don't think that there was ever anything wrong with the document and nothing wrong with the staff or anything. I just think it wasn't presented very well and everybody panicked basically. Others just put it to one side. Put it in the top drawer

and thought, 'Well, no, I won't look at that this century'. ... So I just think it was bad timing. So I think perhaps it was bad timing that people just thought, 'Oh no' ... and I think that was just another thing, you know, like the wee mouse in the boat, you know, 'Who Sank the Boat?' [*pause*] and I think perhaps that was the bit that came along that tipped the edge.

So, despite the professional development packages that were put in place to support the introduction of *Te Whāriki* the experiences of the teachers demonstrated that the timing added to the stress of the teachers and worked against the acceptance and implementation of the curriculum.

The ongoing creation and the volume of policies that kindergartens were expected to have, and continually update, was an ongoing issue for several of the teachers. Maggie reflected on the original introduction of the *Early Childhood Management Handbook* (Ministry of Education, 1989)[6] as one example of the mishandling of new policies in timing, volume and management of change:

> *Maggie*: The wonderful purple book got everybody all a flutter. We all got a very expensive little book and then we all went to untold meetings. Untold meetings. And then they replaced the whole purple book with four typewritten pages. I've never gotten over that [*pause*]. So, I mean, it just made you realise how futile the whole thing was anyway really. I couldn't believe it, you know. We've still got that purple book. We use the folder.

The introduction of the *Desirable Objective and Practices* (Ministry of Education, 1990) – which are the four replacement pages just mentioned – led to a plethora of policy writing in individual centres. For kindergarten's there are centre-based policies and association-based policies as well as national guidelines and legislative standards. The sheer volume of policies overtook both the parents and the teachers in both the construction and the understanding of them, as Elizabeth's policy poster demonstrated:

> *Elizabeth*: Oh you should ssseee it! You should see it! We've a got a folder full of policies and we have to have a lot of them, probably 80% of them, on display for our parents. So I've got this big poster on the wall with policies sticking out of it all over [*pause*]. No parent's ever been near it, but anyway [*laugh*]. ... Things that are management have to have policies. Heaps of different things. Then there's other, I suppose, there's other people who come in, like EEO,[7] where they [the association] had to formulate an EEO policy. Health and safety policy. I mean, that was another workshop. Health and safety – OHS 1 and OHS 2s[8] – and you just think, 'Oh, good grief' [*pause*]. It's just those sorts of things. Once they're all on board – it's just that it's all been going on the last two years really that they've been

doing these policies and there seems to be a constant flow of draft policies for comment or policies that are already done or policies up for review. You know, every week something comes through the letterbox and you think, 'Oh dear, I hope I'm not supposed to know all of these' [*laugh*]. I know I don't. I've got them in the folder. If I need them I know where they are [*laugh*].

The introduction in 1989 of the new minimum standards for all early childhood centres became another source of stress for teachers and parents. While the kindergarten teachers could see the positive aspects of some of the improvements in their kindergarten, they and their committees were overtaken by the changes they had to make due to the political and bureaucratic mismanagement of the implementation and direction of the standards – all tasks that they felt were taking them away from the work they wanted to do with the children. However, at one level, the improved health and safety requirements introduced with the new standards were seen as a positive move:

> *Margaret*: So I can see a lot of the reforms and things that have come into place are good, you know. I'm thinking of [*pause*] ... the standards of the buildings and things like that. Just for an example, it's fair enough that they had to be a certain standard too. What a load of rubbish we thought it was, when it all first came in. We thought, 'Oh heavens, Here goes!' – all the things that we had to do. But the committee just worked away. That was what was expected. So away they went and, you know, sort of achieved one step at a time and, oh, it was good [*pause*]. It was good and I think of things like the fences for instance. I mean the tiny wee, wee low fences [we had] ... I mean we'd never had any major hassles with them but how much more secure really it is to be childproof and for the children to not to be able to escape [*pause*]. And like I remember you telling me about that glass episode.[9] I mean the hundreds of dollars that cost us [to replace all the windows with safety glass] 'cause all our windows were low and I mean rather than have the bars across we opted for the whole [replacement].

However, committees and teachers were quickly overtaken by the physical tasks of raising enough money to make the necessary changes within the tight time frame given to gain licenses and thus be eligible for continued Government funding (as set out in *The Education {Early Childhood Centres} Regulations*, 1990 (New Zealand Government, 1990)). The changes often necessitated a large amount of physical work on buildings and playgrounds, and, while changes such as fencing, gates, and safety glass in windows made 'good sense', many of the other changes were perceived by the teachers and their committees as unnecessary or irrelevant to their centre, taking money and effort away from the more pressing and necessary maintenance and improvements of the kindergarten. For Elizabeth, Nikki, and Margaret, who were in a relatively new purpose-built building, the changes were particularly puzzling:

> *Elizabeth*: The minimum standards was a [*pause*] mm [*pause*] that was a great have. I mean, we were in a 10-year-old purpose-built building which had been built for 40 children and, you know, all of a sudden we didn't have enough toilets for goodness sake [*pause*]. Well, you know, we had enough toilets for 40 children the day before, but now we haven't got enough toilets [*pause*]. It was really annoying. You just thought, 'This is ridiculous'. So we had to change it so that the adults' toilet could be used as one of the children's toilets. So we got all that organised and then they said 'Oh no, you only need three toilets'. Oh shivers, you know, and nappy changing tables. I mean [*!*] … We had to reglaze all our windows.

> Thirteen hundred dollars it cost us to reglaze our windows. Only one of which had ever been broken and that was because some drunk threw a beet bottle through it one Saturday night [*laugh*]. So, you know, just, it was just all those things you thought [*!*]. We worked out, we spent about 6000 dollars getting our purpose-built 10-year-old building up to minimum standards … It was an exercise in time-wasting as far as I was concerned.

> *Nikki*: They [the minimum standards] probably caused a lot of hassles financially for a lot of centres. We were lucky 'cause we were reasonably new and most of it was already up to scratch but things, like for a new kindergarten that had only been up for five years, we were altering sink units and replumbing. Just seemed crazy. Just crazy. Why was it any different to what we've been doing before? We weren't going to take any younger children so what difference did it make? [*pause*]. Just seemed too financial. It was just a lot of money going out when it could be used for the children rather than for the building … it was just a waste of money. I think the whole business really has been a waste of money.

Centralised requirements had overtaken the teachers' and parents' more pressing concerns for their kindergartens. The committees were often left financially disadvantaged and disillusoned. In Margaret's case for example, her committee had worked quickly to meet the standards and it had cost them several thousand dollars to do just that. They had finished the tasks when the new Government in 1990 'watered down' the requirements, thereby making many of the changes unnecessary.

Margaret, Elizabeth, Nikki, and Maggie were concerned about the new management, administration, and employer expectations for associations, particularly with the introduction of bulk funding. They discussed the potential use and misuse of funds, especially for associations who may not have the expertise to manage such large sums of money; the increased workload, which was acting as a deterrent for new members to join associations and for the balance of power in older established associations to change; and the new necessity to pay officials in the associations to carry out the tasks – the monies being taken out of the bulk fund for this purpose. Elizabeth summed up the issues:

> *Elizabeth*: I mean the old associates are always a bit of fly in the ointment but I think, if the bulk funding was gone, that added power would be gone and the added workload on them would be gone and hopefully that would mean that more people would become involved rather that at the moment they have terrible getting people on the association because it's a huge commitment. It really is. I don't envy them at all ... I mean you do wonder what they get out of it. Why they do it? Why they would ever want to do it? [*laugh*]

All eight teachers also observed how the 'position' which was expected of parents within the changed administrative structures contrasted with the actual outcomes for parents. One of the objectives of the *Before Five* document (paralleling *Tomorrow's Schools* [Lange, 1988b]) was to involve parents more in the management and governance of early childhood centres. Historically, however, the kindergarten service had always had a high level of parental involvement in its management, both at association level and at committee level in individual kindergartens (particularly with regard to fundraising and maintenance). Interestingly, the education changes requiring increased involvement and responsibility in the management of the kindergarten, the changed funding arrangements, and the resulting increased workloads for parent volunteers all occurred at a time when there were fewer volunteers available (Early Childhood Education Project, 2000). This has resulted in a discrepancy between what was envisaged in the *Before Five* document and what subsequently became possible. Throughout the teachers' stories, problems due to the lack of available and willing parents were apparent at both association and committee levels. At the kindergarten committee level, the turnover of parents and the effort involved in filling a committee with willing parents had become an increased stress for the teachers and placed the teachers in a new position within their kindergartens.

Lynne found that a combination of factors made the concept of parental management, rather that just involvement, an unworkable model for her kindergarten. Firstly, social changes, such as the age group of the children starting at the kindergarten, meant that the children were not attending for as long, so the parents did not have the same time commitment to the kindergarten. Secondly, employment changes, particularly for women, meant that more mothers were in paid employment and also there were fewer parents from one-income families who could financially afford the extra costs associated with voluntary work, such as travelling costs. Thirdly, the increasing level of voluntary work required at many levels from Plunket[10] through to schools often meant that parents had either experienced the processes already and had their fair share (were burnt out already) or were already committed elsewhere. Fourthly, the lack of training and support for the role of management, when combined with the increased accountability and responsibility for management decisions, left the parents feeling 'out of their depth' and 'unsupported'. All these factors led to a difficult position for a head teacher, who was expected to work with parent committees in order to keep the kindergarten functioning:

> *Lynne*: Two years ago you [would] have [a] committee that would stick around for a couple of years – the core members. Now, because the families are getting smaller and there's bigger gaps between each child, someone might come and stand on a committee for a year. But then rather than staying for their second and third child they'll have a year or two off and then come back on when that next child comes on. So you lose all continuity. So I find that basically you're turning over a complete committee every 12 months virtually and … another new thing that's happening is people will now leave when the child leaves and moves to school; whereas before they'd always serve a year, so now they turn over every year. But then usually have another turnover halfway through the year so whereas you might start off with 10 you'd maybe lose five of those by July. You'd limp to the end of the year, lose everyone else and start afresh so there's no continuity whatsoever so the teachers' workload is [*pause*] just quadrupled overnight.

Discussion

Tracing policy change in education without listening to those it affects the most only gives us one side of the story. While numerous policy analyses have helped highlight the intention and some of the 'hidden' agendas behind policy documents and their construction (Lauder, 1987, 1990, 1991, 1993; Lauder *et al.*, 1988, Codd, 1989, 1990a, 1990b, 1992, 1999; Codd *et al.*, 1990a, b; Marshall & Peters, 1990; Peters & Marshall, 1990; Codd & Gordon, 1991; Peters, 1993; Lauder *et al.*, 1994; Peters *et al.*, 1994; Codd & Sullivan, 1997; Olssen & Morris Matthews, 1997; Lauder *et al.*, 1999), it is when we listen to the accounts of those who deal with the realities of implementing these policies that we can begin to see a fuller picture. This article has presented the 'insider' stories, which contrast with the 'outsider' or 'official' versions of the changes to the kindergarten service over the past two decades. The teacher in this study talked in terms of reform and change in the kindergarten service, from the social and economic changes which had dramatically altered the cultural context within which they worked, through to the latest changes arriving in their mailboxes.

Feelings of being 'overtaken' and 'misplaced' within the reforms were the experiences described by the teachers in this study. As discussed, the teachers and parents had been working within contradictory discursive positions since 1988 with the introduction of the *Before Five* document and the resulting legislative and funding changes. While the intent of the *Before Five* document was to improve standards across the early childhood sector, the teachers argued that it had worked to drag down kindergarten standards. Likewise, the teachers who positioned themselves to be involved in the wider organisational side of teaching found that, while they had a better understanding of the issues and were in a position to work actively for teachers, it placed them in positions of conflict with their employer associations and often the other staff. Parents were offered conflicting positions also. On the one hand, they were being encouraged to be involved (indeed legislated to be involved) but, on the other, the wider economic and social changes which occurred in New Zealand during this time left many parents in positions where this had become impossible.

As I have described earlier in this article, the gains for the early childhood sector over the period of study (1984–96) can be seen as reflection of the uneasy contradiction between the New Right economic philosophy and broader social justice goals. An outcome of this was the contradictory and competing discourses which surrounded both the introduction of the early childhood reforms and the resultant outcomes – policies, practices, and political changes. The teachers in this study were committed to the philosophy of kindergarten as being places for all children, irrespective of the parents' ability to pay, and as being community resources, with the role of the kindergarten teacher being to educate and care for the children as well as to support families and communities. These discourses set the teacher in an oppositional position to a kindergarten service where managerial and decentralised administration had become the focus as part of the neo-liberal changes. The energy, resources, and, simply the time taken out of each day of the teachers meant that the changes driven from above left the teachers feeling 'overtaken' and 'misplaced' in their work by the reforms and the processes of decision making and implementation.

Conclusion

The concept of discourse has been used here to demonstrate how conflicting discourses positioned the teachers in different ways. Through the teachers' stories of their experiences between 1984 and 1996 it can be seen that the dominant discourses, which contained key neo-liberal ideas, were so encompassing and the discursive practices so all-consuming that the teachers felt 'misplaced' in their service and 'overtaken' in their work.

What does this all mean for the year 2004? In New Zealand we have a Labour Government once again, which has articulated its support for early childhood services and provisions. It also has dedicated resources and a 10-year plan (*Pathways to the Future: Ngā Huarahi Arataki. A 10-year Strategic Plan for Early Childhood Education 2002–2012*, Ministry of Education, 2002) to improve the participation levels and the quality of our early childhood services. While the feeling within the early childhood sector is one of optimism, I feel that the messages from the teachers in the 1990s is a cautionary one. Early childhood 'won against the odds' in 1984 and it did so again in 2000. Now, with 2004 an election year, the political discourses could shift dramatically once more with any change of Government. Thus, the experiences of the contradictory discourses and discursive outcomes experienced by the teachers in this study can add to our understanding of the attempts to bring about change in the future and to continue to provide quality early childhood experiences for children and families.

Notes

1 The word 'free' in the name indicates that the kindergarten is open to all, irrespective of ethnicity and/or class, rather that being free of fees or charges to attend. It is worthy to note, however, the many of the kindergarten associations have recently removed the word 'free' from their names as they have begun to increase the charges for attendance at their kindergartens (Mitchell, 2001).

2 The senior teacher in the kindergarten service is a management position as well as a professional support position. Since 2000 professional support has also been provided by other professional support providers, such as Colleges of Education and Early Childhood Development, in addition to or in place of the senior teacher support team.

3 The transcript quotes that are included in this article are those that most succinctly and clearly articulate the current discussion, and the eight respondents' accounts have not been drawn upon equally. Nevertheless, all teachers voiced very similar concepts and the quotes chosen may be considered a valid representation of the views offered by all those interviewed.

4 The Roper Report (1987) was named after the chair of the Committee of Inquiry into Violence, Sir Clinton Roper. This Report was to the Minister of Justice and contained recommendations for reducing the incidences of violence and violent crime in New Zealand. The recommendations that Maggie is referring to are: 'That there be an immediate increase in the length of training for kindergarten teachers and childcare workers; that there be equal status for teachers in the total field of education; that realistic teacher/child ratios be provided in centres and kindergartens; and that adequate and equitable funding of early childhood services be provided'. (New Zealand Committee of Inquiry into Violence, 1987, p. 20).

5 Maggie is referring to the Early Childhood Advisory Committee, a working group

and early childhood training advisory group, which had been set up by the Qualifications Authority but in 1994 was 'sacked' and replaced. The reason given for
its replacement was 'because the members could not agree after two years what
qualifications should be developed' (Wellington [Press Association], 1994).

6 This Handbook arrived in a purple folder and thus became known by a range of
titles, all referring to the colour purple. For further discussion see Farquhar (1991).
7 EEO – Equal Employment Opportunity (New Zealand legislation).
8 OHS 1 and OHS 2 refer to Occupational Health and Safety requirements, which
all workplaces must demonstrate for their employees and clients, customers, or
users of their services under New Zealand legislation.
9 Margaret is referring to a teaching incident of mine in the mid 1980s, when a
child at kindergarten where I was head teacher ran into a sliding glass door and
received extensive facial injuries from the shattered glass.
10 The New Zealand Plunket Society is New Zealand's leading provider of child
and family health services for children from birth to five years old. 'Plunket supports families with young children by providing appropriate clinical and support
programmes and educational activities. They are the only non-profit organisation
in New Zealand to provide these facilities to New Zealand families' (taken from
New Zealand Plunket Society website: www.plunket.org.nz).

Correspondence

Judith Duncan, Children's Issues Centre, University of Otago, PO Box 56,
Dunedin, New Zealand (judith.duncan@stonebow.otago.ac.nz).

References

Allen, P. (1982) *Who Sank the Boat?* Melbourne: Thomas Nelson Australia.
Ball, S. J. (1990) *Foucault and Education: disciplines and knowledge.* London: Routledge.
Codd, J. (1989) Evaluating Tomorrow's Schools: accountability or control? *Delta*, 41,
pp. 3–11.
Codd, J. (1990a) Policy Documents and the Official Discourse of the State, in J. Codd,
R. Harker & R. Nash (Eds) *Political Issues in New Zealand Education*, pp. 133–149.
Palmerston North: Dunmore Press.
Codd, J. (1990b) Educational Policy and the Crisis of the New Zealand State, in
S. Middleton, J. Codd & A. Jones (Eds) *New Zealand Education Policy Today: critical
perspectives*, pp. 191–205. Wellington: Allen & Unwin.
Codd, J. (1999) Educational Reform, Accountability and the Culture of Distrust,
New Zealand Journal of Educational Studies, 34(1), pp. 44–54.
Codd, J. & Gordon, L. (1991) School Charters: the contractualist state and education
policy, *New Zealand Journal of Educational Studies*, 26(1), pp. 21–34.
Codd, J., Gordon, L. & Harker, R. (1990a) Education and the Role of the State:
devolution and control post-Picot, in H. Lauder & C. Wylie (Eds) *Towards Successful
Schooling*, pp. 15–33. London: Falmer Press.
Codd, J., Harker, R. & Nash, R. (1990b) Education, Politics and the Economic Crisis,
in J. Codd, R. Harker & R. Nash (Eds) *Political Issues in New Zealand Education*,
pp. 7–21. Palmerston North: Dunmore Press.

Codd, J. & Sullivan, K. (1997) Quality Assurance and Audit in New Zealand Universities: a review and case study, *New Zealand Annual Review of Education*, 6 (1996), pp. 29–50.

Codd, J. A. (1992) Contractualism, Contestability and Choice: capturing the language of educational reform in New Zealand, Australian Association for Research in Education/ New Zealand Association for Research in Education conference paper, Deakin University, 22–26 November.

Duncan, J. (1999) New Zealand Kindergarten Teachers and Sexual Abuse Protection Policies, *Teaching and Teacher Education*, 15(3), pp. 243–252.

Duncan, J. (2001a) Restructuring Lives: kindergarten teachers and the education reforms, 1984–1996, unpublished PhD thesis, University of Otago.

Duncan, J. (2001b) Taking the Life out of What You Do. Kindergarten Teachers Talk Education Changes: 1984–1996, *New Zealand Research in Early Childhood Education*, 4, pp. 103–124.

Duncan, J. (2002) Like Crabs in a Bucket: kindergarten teachers talk changes, 1984–1996, *New Zealand Journal of Educational Studies*, 37(2), pp. 141–157.

Early Childhood Care and Education Working Group (1988) *Education To Be More*. Wellington: Early Childhood Care and Education Working Group.

Early Childhood Education Project (2000) *The Workload of Volunteers in Early Childhood Services*. Wellington: New Zealand Educational Institute.

Education Review Office (1997) *What Counts as Quality in Kindergartens (Education Evaluation Report No. 1)*. Wellington: Education Review Office.

Farquhar, S.-E. (1991) A 'Purple People-eater' or Quality Assurance Mechanism? The 1989/90 Early Childhood Centre Charter Requirements, in M. Gold, L. Foote & A. Smith (Eds) *Proceedings of the Fifth Early Childhood Convention*, pp. 526–540. Dunedin: Fifth Early Childhood Convention Committee, University of Otago.

Fitzsimons, P., Peters, M. & Roberts, P. (1999) Economics and the Educational Policy Process in New Zealand, *New Zealand Journal of Educational Studies*, 34(1), pp. 35–44.

Foucault, M. (1970) *The Order of Things: an archaeology of the human sciences*. London: Routledge.

Foucault, M. (1971) Orders of Discourse, *Social Science Information*, 10(2), pp. 7–30.

Foucault, M. (1980) *The History of Sexuality*. New York: Pantheon Books.

Gavey, N. (1989) Feminist Poststucturalism and Discourse Analysis: contributions to feminist psychology, *Psychology of Women Quarterly*, 13, pp. 459–475.

Lange, D. R. H. (1988a) *Before Five: early childhood care and education in New Zealand*. Wellington: Ministry of Education.

Lange, D. R. H. (1988b) *Tomorrow's Schools: the reform of education administration in New Zealand*. Wellington: Ministry of Education.

Lauder, H. (1987) The New Right and Educational Policy in New Zealand, *New Zeland Journal of Educational Studies*, 22(1), pp. 3–23.

Lauder, H. (1990) The New Right Revolution and Education in New Zealand, in S. Middleton, J. Codd & A. Jones (Eds) *New Zealand Education Policy Today*, pp. 1–26. Wellington: Allen & Unwin.

Lauder, H. (1991) *Tomorrow's Education, Tomorrow's Economy*. Wellington: New Zealand Council of Trade Unions.

Lauder, H. (1993) *Democracy, the Economy and the Marketisation of Education*, Wellington: Victoria University Press.

Lauder, H., Hughes, D., Waslander, S., Thrupp, M., McGlinn, J., Newtons, S., & Dupuis, A. (1994) *The Creation of Market Competition for Education in New Zealand: an empirical analysis of New Zealand secondary school market, 1990–1993 (Phase One)*. Auckland: The Smithfield Project.

Lauder, H., Hughes, D., & Watson, S. (1999) The Introduction of Educational Markets in New Zealand: questions and consequences, *New Zealand Journal of Education Studies*, 34(1), pp. 85–98.

Lauder, H., Middleton, S., Boston, J. & Wylie, C. (1988) The Third Wave: a critique of the New Zealand Treasury's report on education, *New Zealand Journal of Education Studies*, 23(1), pp. 15–35.

Marshal, J. & Peters, M. (1990) The Insertion of 'New Right' Thinking into Education: an example from New Zealand, *Journal of Education Policy*, 5(2), pp. 143–156.

May, H. (1990) Growth and Change in the Early Childhood Services: a story of political conservatism, growth and constraint, in S. Middleton, J. Codd & A. Jones (Eds) *New Zealand Education Policy Today*, pp. 94–109. Wellington: Allen & Unwin.

May, H. (1993) *When Women's Rights Have Come to Stay, Oh Who Will Rock the Cradle?* Hamilton: Department of Early Childhood, Waikato University.

May, H. (1999) The Price of Partnership: the Before Five decade, *New Zealand Journal of Educational Studies*, 34(1), pp. 18–27.

Meade, A. (1990) Women and Young Children Gain a Foot in the Door, *Women's Studies Journal* [New Zealand], 6(1–2), pp. 96–110.

Middleton, S. (1993) *Educating Feminists: life histories and pedagogy*. New York: Teachers College Press.

Ministry of Education (1989) *Early Childhood Management Handbook*. Wellington: Government Print.

Ministry of Education (1990) *Early Childhood Education Charter Guidelines: a statement of desirable objectives and practices*. Wellington: Ministry of Education.

Ministry of Education (1996) *Te Whāriki: early childhood curriculum. He Whāriki Mātauranga mo ngū Mokopuna o Aotearoa*. Wellington: Learning Media.

Ministry of Education (2000) *Education Statistics News Sheet: July 1999 early childhood statistics*. Wellington: Ministry of Education.

Ministry of Education (2002) *Pathways to the Future: Ngū Huarahi Arataki. A 10-year Strategic Plan for Early Childhood Education 2002–2012*. Wellington: Learning Media.

Mitchell, L. (1997) Influencing Policy Change through Collective Action, unpublished manuscript.

Mitchell, L. (2001) *Bulk Funding of New Zealand's Early Childhood Services: an analysis of the impact*. Wellington: New Zealand Council for Educational Research.

Mitchell, L. & Noonan, R. (1994) Early Childhood Education: the New Zealand family, New Zealand Family Rights and Responsibilities symposium paper, Auckland, 14–16 October.

New Zealand Committee of Inquiry into Violence (1987) *Report of Ministerial Committee of Inquiry into Violence*. Wellington: New Zealand Government.

New Zealand Government (1990) *The Education (Early Years Centres) Regulations 1990*. Wellington: New Zealand Government.

Olssen, M. & Morris Matthews, K. (1997) *Education Policy in New Zealand*. Palmerston North: Dunmore Press.

Peters, M. (1993) Postmodernity and Neo-liberalism: restructuring education in

Aotearoa, *Delta*, 47, pp. 47–60.

Peters, M. & Marshall, J. (1990) Children of Rogernomics: the New Right, individualism and the culture of narcissism, *Sites*, 21 (Spring), pp. 74–191.

Peters, M., Marshall, J. & Massey, L. (1994) Recent Educational Reforms in Aotearoa, in E. Coxen, K. Jenkins, J. Marshall & L. Massey (Eds) *The Politics of Learning and Teaching in Aotearoa/New Zealand*, pp. 251–272. Palmerston North: Dunmore Press.

Smith, A. B. (1991) Early Childhood Educare in New Zealand: a case study of change, unpublished paper, University of Otago.

Smith, A.B., Hubbard, P.M., Ford, V.E. & White, E.J. (1994) Staff Working Conditions, Training and Job Satisfaction in Infant Childcare Centres: relationships with quality, New Zealand Association for Research in Education conference paper, Christchurch, 1–4 Decemeber.

Taskforce to Review Education Administration (1988) *Administering for Excellence: effective administration in education*. Wellington: Taskforce to Review Education Administration.

Weedon, C. (1987) *Feminist Practice and Poststructuralist theory*. Oxford: Blackwell.

Wellington (Press Association) (11 July 1994) Sacked Early Childhood Education Groups Replaced, *Otago Daily Times*.

Wells, C. (1991) The Impact of Change – against the odds, in M. Gold, I. Foote & A. B. Smith (Eds) *Fifth Early Childhood Convention*, pp. 115–127. Dunedin: Fifth Early Childhood Convention.

Wylie, C. (1992) *First Impressions: the initial impact of salary bulk funding on New Zealand kindergartens*. Wellington: New Zealand Council for Educational Research.

Yeatman, A. (1990) *Bureaucrats, Technocrats, Femocrats*. Sydney: Allen & Unwin.

Chapter 14

Professionalism and performativity

The feminist challenge facing early years practitioners

Jayne Osgood

Source: *J. Osgood, Early Years, 26(2), 187–199, 2006.*

Abstract

In this discussion paper, I seek to understand the complex interaction between notions of 'professionalism' and gendered identity constructions against the backdrop of increased state regulation and demands for performativity in the early years. I seek to explore the ways in which 'teacher professionalism' is constructed by government and how this transcends into a 'discourse of derision', which then becomes a subtle, yet powerful, means of controlling this occupational group. I conclude by presenting an alternative feminist conceptual framework for assessing the gendered nature of identity formation, and as an opportunity to consider the role agency can play when seeking to resist/renegotiate the rapid and powerful policy reform agenda in the early years.

Introduction

In recent years early childhood education and care in the UK has been subject to significant reform and the way in which it is governed and regulated has been significantly restructured. As Forrester (2000, p. 133) asserts, in general, education is now 'steered through the simultaneous centralisation of content and direction, and the decentralisation and devolution of responsibility to individual institutions'. As with other public services, the English government has placed a more central social and economic emphasis upon performance and public accountability in education.

Nearly two decades ago, teachers in the compulsory sector were subject to new managerialist centralising and decentralising reforms, under the Conservative government, with the introduction of the Education Reform Act 1988. The Act signalled a new era in the way in which schools were organised and teachers regulated. This was characterised by measures such as Local Management of Schools and a compulsory National Curriculum, and league tables were introduced to chart and make public the relative success of schools in a competitive education market place. The New Labour government has persisted in implementing further new managerialist measures in compulsory schooling to heighten managerial professionalism through greater accountability, efficiency and performativity (Sachs, 2001). However, until relatively recently the early years education sector seemed safe from the terrors of performativity (Ball, 2003). Yet, as a consequence of the National Childcare Strategy introduced in 1998, early childhood education and care providers have experienced increasing steerage from the state. Like school-teachers, early years practitioners now have to wrestle with the demands for accountability, attainment targets, a compulsory early years curriculum and standardised approaches to their practice. All of which mark a sharp movement towards centralised control and prescription, which poses a potential threat to professional autonomy and morale (Mahony & Hextall, 2000). Whilst I want to acknowledge the distinctions between teachers in the compulsory school system and early years practitioners, I also wish to highlight similarities and commonalities of the effects policy reform can have upon an occupational group comprised of individuals who are wrestling with their own collective identities and a commitment to 'being professional' in their work (Helsby, 1995).

The proletarianisation thesis

Changes in education policy have been accompanied by ongoing debates within the sociology of education regarding consequences for teachers' work and their identity. Some commentators argue that decentralisation and devolution of responsibility have empowered teachers and enhanced their professionalism (Nias *et al.*, 1992; Nias, 1999), whilst others suggest that teaching has become routinised and deskilled (Ozga & Lawn, 1981; Maguire & Ball, 1994; Ozga, 1995, 2000; Avis, 2003). I would argue that new managerialist policy reforms mean that teachers' autonomy has greatly reduced as a consequence of more directive approaches to curriculum and assessment. I support the 'proletarianisation thesis' posited by Ozga amongst others, which asserts that, as a consequence of policy reform, teachers have experienced an intensification of workload with an emphasis on technical competence and performativity. Within this thesis a paradox exists where centralising reforms have been presented as giving greater freedom but actually act to de-regulate and then re-regulate or, as Du Gay (1996) terms it, a process of 'controlled de-control'. Within this context teachers are represented and encouraged to think of themselves as enterprising neo-liberal professionals (Walkerdine, 2003), yet they are managed according to an ideology of professionalism which has the effect of de-and then re-professionalising them. The proletarianisation thesis has flourished for a considerable time and has been developed and extended by various commentators, it has also been challenged for being overly deterministic. By emphasising a structural explanation, a social constructionist account of 'teacher professionalism' is denied and an opportunity to engage with debates around personal agency become limited (Mahony & Hextall, 2000). Nevertheless, I would suggest that understanding structural changes at the level of policy reform and the use of education as a mechanism to alter society is key to the debate. Furthermore, the concept of 'professionalism' to control an occupational group is vital to aid an understanding of 'professional identity' in the early years.

With respect to the interplay between structure and agency, Giddens (1979) offers a useful approach. He presents the relationship between individual agency (in this case, early years practitioners and their values, occupational aims and professional ambitions) and social structure (the institution, pupils and parents, local education authorities, the Department for Education and Skills) as a 'duality' whereby they are mutually interdependent. In essence, Giddens suggests that it is not necessarily the case that individuals simply react to managerialist initiatives imposed upon them, but that they are actively involved in reproducing, interpreting and transforming policy through individual action or agency. But I would suggest that this overstates the case as it presupposes the individual agency of a group of practitioners is sufficiently homogeneous, unified and mobilised and that practitioners have sufficient belief in themselves as 'professionals' to challenge top-down policy implementation. In research I have undertaken with early years practitioners, I identified a prevailing 'passive resistance' (Osgood, 2004) wherein practitioners are overtly opposed to masculinist,[1] new managerialist policy reforms that encourage competitive, entrepreneurial individualism, yet feel powerless to resist. The concept of 'passive resistance' resonates with ideas around 'technicians of behaviour' who become 'bodies that are docile and capable' (Foucault, 1988). Louise Morley (referenced by Ball, 2003) develops this idea further in referring to a 'form of ventriloquism' when discussing the ways in which teachers engage with policy. In essence, this concept represents teachers as seeming to embody or perform a given policy intention, but they do not believe in it or feel able to resist it. Whilst I believe agency is vitally important when considering the relationship between policy imposition, identity construction and competing definitions of professionalism, I also recognise the tensions that exist between structure and agency and the power of certain discourses to become convincing and oppressive discursive truths.

Bowe et al. (1992) argue that government policy can be considered both text and discourse, and government seeks to create a 'correct reading' or promote certain discursive truths, in this instance, around an appropriate form of professionalism. Ozga (1995, p. 27) stresses the importance of understanding the cultural and historical specificity of professionalism and goes on to argue that 'managerialism works with the fissiparous character of the occupation and against public sector collective identities'. Further to this, I would argue that dominant (government) discourses in teacher professionalism assert particular realities and priorities that are in stark polarity to those of practitioners. Sinclair (1996, p. 232) usefully states that the way:

> people locate themselves in relation to certain discourses reflects the socially sanctioned dominance of certain ideologies and subjugation of others. Because discourses vary in their authority, at one particular time one discourse, such as managerialism or market approach seems 'natural' while another struggles to find expression in the way experience is described.

I argue that the 'naturalness' of the New Right conceptualisation of professionalism in the UK has become embedded in the rhetoric of state agencies, including the newly formed Sure Start Unit, which is the national agency with responsibility for governing early education and childcare (Osgood, 2005). Gee *et al.* (1996, pp. 19–21) describe the investment governments make into establishing and seeking to instil discursive truths:

> The new capitalism puts a great deal of faith in creating goals, core values, a vision, a culture – whatever one wants to call it (we would call it creating a Discourse) and communicating it to workers ... [it] is now quite open about the need to socialise people into 'communities of practice' that position people to be certain kinds of people. They now realise that they are in the business of creating and sustaining Discourses.

It is to this prevailing, hegemonic government discourse of practitioner professionalism that I now wish to turn (Figure 14.1).

The dichotomy I construct above draws attention to the masculinist undertones of new managerialism and the economic rationale behind policy reform in the early years. The New Labour government has stated its intention for early years practitioners to operate in entrepreneurial ways through its drive to encourage practitioners to adopt commercial approaches to the

Government discourse	Discourse of derision
• Enterprising	• Indolent
• Accountable	• Untrustworthy
• Competitive	• Unambitious
• Rational	• Intuitive
• Credentialised	• Under-qualified
• Individualistic	• Reliant
• Transparent	• Opaque

Figure 14.1 Discourses.

management of provision (Sure Start Unit, 2004). As I have argued elsewhere (Osgood, 2004, 2005), the new managerialist discourse places an emphasis on competition, performativity and rationality, an emphasis that is considered inappropriate by practitioners. The government focus on developing individualistic and entrepreneurial skills akin to those found in corporations, which tend to be defined as 'lean, mean, aggressive and rational' (Acker, 1992), is unbefitting in the overwhelmingly female-dominated context of early childhood education and care, where emotional labour is undertaken and the work characterised by an ethic of care (Yelland, 1998). Moyles (2001, p. 81) highlights a number of tensions that exist between constructions of professionalism and the emotional nature of working in the early years:

> it seems impossible to work effectively with very young children without the deep and sound commitment signified by the use of words like 'passionate'. Yet this very symbolisation gives a particular emotional slant to the work of early childhood practitioners which can work ... against them in their everyday roles and practices, bringing into question what constitutes professionalism and what being a 'teacher' means.

It is widely acknowledged that the nature of early years work demands strong feelings towards protecting and supporting children and engaging empathetically with a child's wider family and community (Katz, 1995). A body of contemporary research has established that feelings and emotions are acceptable, even desirable, as part of educational thinking and practice; for example, Freire's (1999) *Pedagogy of the heart*, Claxton's (1999) extensive references to 'intuitive practice' and the proposition by Edwards *et al.* (1998) that to operate emotionally equates to deep-level, higher-order thinking. In the early years concepts of caring and emotional labour are connected with discourses of nature, ethics and mothering (Vogt, 2002). Furthermore, Nias (1999) highlights the importance of personal investment, commitment, motivation related to gender and a culture of care characterised by affectivity, altruism, self-sacrifice and over-conscientiousness. I would suggest that the combination of these factors acts as a powerful self-regulatory mechanism. Yet, a counter 'discourse of derision' (Ball, 1990), such as that outlined above, illustrates the way in which such characteristics are denigrated and dismissed as unprofessional and in need of reform. The new managerialist construction of 'professionalism' values masculinised attributes which run counter to the beliefs and practices of early years practitioners, and this poses a very real threat to the professional integrity that practitioners cling on to, or as Ball (2003, p. 223) states:

> beliefs are no longer important, it is output that counts. Beliefs are part of an older, increasingly displaced discourse. Teachers (of the old order) seek

to hold onto knowledges about themselves which diverge from prevailing categories. These are now seen, in Foucault's terms, as 'knowledges inadequate to their task ... naïve knowledges ... disqualified knowledges' [Foucault, 1988, pp. 81–2]. A new kind of teacher, new kinds of knowledges are called upon by educational reform – a teacher who can maximise performance, set aside irrelevant principles.

I would argue that the 'terrors of performativity' to which Ball alludes are starting to be felt by early years practitioners as the rate and pace of policy reform in the early years intensifies (Osgood, 2004, 2005). The increased demands to demonstrate competence mean that professional judgement is subordinated to the requirements of performativity, and what is produced is the 'form of ventriloquism' referred to earlier, or what Butler (1990) argues is 'enacted fantasy', wherein practitioners feel compelled to cynically comply to the demands of performativity.

The increased state regulation and top-down policy prescription represents a direct challenge to 'professionalism from within'. The necessarily collaborative and collegial working relationships that are characteristic of the early years are threatened by 'discourses of individualisation' (Reay, 1998). Practitioners are rated according to an external set of criteria, which Ball (2003) argues has the effect of making practitioners 'ontologically insecure'. The (passionate) commitment practitioners have towards their work, the children they care for and educate, and the communities in which they are located, serve to motivate practitioners to provide good quality; but the 'Childcare Challenge', as New Labour perceive it, is that this good practice is not measurable and practitioners are afforded too much autonomy, so to embody hegemonic professionalism practitioners must succumb to the demands of performativity through 'mechanisms of projection' (Bernstein, 2000).

Is resistance possible? The role of agency

In an attempt to theorise an alternative reading of 'professionalism' in the early years I wish to apply a feminist lens to the concept or a 'counter hegemony', which Weiler (1988, p. 52) defines as: 'the creation of a self-conscious analysis of a situation and the development of collective practices and organisation that can oppose the hegemony of the existing order and begin to build the base for a new understanding and transformation'.

Whilst feminism must necessarily be understood as an umbrella term that incorporates many different, and often opposing perspectives, I would argue that a common set of unifying themes remain. Francis (2001) points to four central tenets which unite diverse feminist perspectives: a concern with gender; a perception of women as generally disadvantaged in gender relations; a perception of this gender inequity as problematic; and a consequent aim to emancipatory reform. She illustrates the problematic interplay between feminism as a modernist 'grand narrative', agency as an ability to proactively make decisions and resist oppression, and poststructuralist theories which promote the idea of power through discourses wherein the individual lacks agency. However, by drawing on the work of Mills (1997) and Jones (1997), Francis (2001, p. 166) resolves this tension by illustrating a 'new agency' perspective of the self, which incorporates both deterministic structural arguments and human agency. She argues that as well as positioning ourselves and others through discourse, we are simultaneously being positioned by others, and that such positioning is beyond our control, so that:

> the self incorporates both contradiction and consistency; is constructed by the self and by others; and has agency but is also determined by discursive and material forces. This account is flexible, able to incorporate the contradictory and complex nature of human interaction and power relations.

I believe that Francis's model of 'new agency' offers a useful and insightful framework to aid an understanding of the positioning of early years practitioners in a policy reform context and to reflect upon the highly problematic and politicised construction of the notion of 'professionalism' in the early years. In research I have undertaken (Osgood & Stone, 2002; Osgood, 2003), early years practitioners have articulated strong opinions and presented themselves in accordance with the characteristics outlined below in what I consider to be one possible model of 'counter hegemony' (see Figure 14.2).

As an example of the salience of the above model, I would draw attention to discussions I have had with practitioners about the (in)appropriateness of entrepreneurialism in the management of early years settings. Providers persistently drew upon discourses around 'non-competitive collaboration', 'altruism', 'community spirit', and 'voluntary self sacrifice', leading me to argue that a counterdiscourse existed which could be used to effectively oppose the dominant construction of professionalism as business orientated (Osgood, 2004). I acknowledge that my own subject position as a feminist researcher means that I apply certain constructions of self and reality to the research

Feminist discourse

- Innovative
- Autonomous
- Collaborative
- Reflexive
- Wise/experienced
- Collective

Figure 14.2 Feminist discourse.

process, and, as such, I present only one version of many possible 'truths' when seeking to understand the positionality and experiences of early years practitioners within a policy context. With this in mind, I want to propose that an alternative reading of 'professionalism' can be gained from applying a feminist framework.

As I have outlined, the masculinist, new managerialist project of de-and re-professionalising early years practitioners relies upon the dissemination and enculturation of certain discursive truths. I want to present an alternative reading informed by opinions and experiences of early years practitioners from research I have undertaken. In this discussion, I argue that an alternative set of 'truths' about what it means to be 'professional' in early childhood education and care has salience and value in this debate. I have argued that an ethic of care and emotional labour are cornerstones to practitioners' understanding of themselves, and that these qualities are denigrated in dominant discourses of professionalism. However, I believe that creating an alternative conception of 'professionalism', one that acknowledges the unique nature and complexity of educating and caring for young children, holds the possibility of providing a means of resisting an imposed and inappropriate definition. So where we see early years practitioners positioned in a discourse of derision when the hegemonic government construction of 'professionalism' is applied, a counter positioning is possible when we seek to define 'professionalism from within' using a feminist framework. But such a project is not without challenges. In a struggle to redefine and develop a form of professionalism early years practitioners find themselves in a situation where their expert knowledge is vulnerable to challenge.

Sachs (2001) argues that 'professional identity' is used to refer to a set of externally ascribed attributes that are used to differentiate. But applying Francis's (2001) model enables us to understand professional identity as a negotiated, shifting and ambiguous entity mediated by personal experience and beliefs and values about what it means to be a practitioner and the type of practitioner an individual aspires to be.

Moyles (2001) argues that to establish professionalism early years practitioners are required to exercise reflection, high levels of professional knowledge, self-esteem and self-confidence, which she argues many early years, female practitioners lack. This view is supported by others (Noddings, 1993; Claxton, 1999), who suggest that female practitioners are convinced that they are too emotional and powerless against (male) authority and are insecure about their professional status, and distrust and underestimate their own professional insights. Or, as Weiler (1988, p. 89) argues, 'it is the internalisation of male hegemony that leads women to devalue their own worth'. Therein lies the challenge, to construct a viable alternative construction of professionalism, which encapsulates and maintains an ethic of care and, at the same time, is infused with pride, confidence and self-belief.

Being reflexive and the role of (continuing) professional development

Helsby (1995) draws a useful distinction between 'being professional' and 'behaving professionally'; she illuminates a dichotomy between a range of characteristics associated with the favoured position supposedly occupied by 'professionals' – pay, status and autonomy and those which relate to personal and behavioural characteristics – dedication, commitment, highly skilled practice. Whilst some commentators have argued for the pursuit of the former set of characteristics to achieve professionalisation (Hoyle, 2001), the latter set of characteristics represents 'professionalism' and reliance upon self-reflection and an altruistic concern to improve practice. If it is accepted that the notion of professionalism is socially constructed, then the role practitioners play in that construction and the ways in which they accept or resist external control must be understood.

Hughes and Menmuir (2002) are amongst many to highlight the importance of depth of knowledge and reflection on practice as the key to professionalism in the early years. Increased participation in education and training that encourages greater reflexivity is certainly one approach to heightening professionalism, although I would wish to stress the importance of engaging in professional development activities that enable greater self-awareness and engender improved self-confidence rather than the pursuit of training to merely satisfy demands for more credentialised practitioners (Reay, 2001). I have seen clear evidence of the fervour and determination with which practitioners engage in education and training to improve their practice and gain in professional confidence (Osgood & Stone, 2002; Osgood, 2003, 2005). Yet, I have argued elsewhere (Osgood, 2005) that, for many practitioners, their gendered and classed identities mean that (re)entering the education arena to pursue further and higher levels of study is often costly in an emotional as well as financial sense. So, whilst pursuing education to improve professional identity is clearly valuable, the personal investment required should not be underestimated. Also the content and delivery of such activity should enable practitioners to build upon their expert knowledge and include space for critical reflection not just of themselves as professionals, but of the social and political context within which they work. I would argue that professional development should be seen as building upon practitioners' existing experiential professional wisdom. Goodfellow (2004, p. 68), in promoting the documentation of professional practice through the use of portfolios, stresses the fact that:

> professional practice draws upon our theoretical/professional knowledge as we engage in decision-making within our everyday practices. It is important to address hidden qualities and dimensions of our professional practice if we are to improve our way of being professional.

In the pursuit of professionalism through development activities and reflexivity, space to retain integrity, an ethic of care and 'feminine' attributes offer an alternative to the technical performance of competencies as embodied within the new managerialist version of 'professionalism'. Or, as Feldman (1997, p. 758) articulates:

> the wise practitioner is one who can draw upon and add to a wide set of knowledge, can use that knowledge and professional experience to deliberate about and reflect upon practice, and one who can act wisely within educational situations by relying on a growing and deepening understanding of what it means to teach and be a teacher.

I would propose that the 'educational situations' to which Feldman (1997) refers should not be confined to childcare settings, but should extend to raising questions and challenging the policy context and content of government directives. Dale (1981) identifies the importance of professional confidence to enable practitioners to impose their own professional interpretations of government policy, and to balance its demands against other professional priorities and to exploit what remains of their 'licensed autonomy'. Education and training should not be confined to a demonstration of practical competence, but provide a meaningful opportunity for critical reflection on how practitioners are being positioned and the ways in which they can actively position themselves in competing and alternative discourses of professionalism.

In a range of feminists' writings about the dilemmas caused by relativism and postmodern theory (Maynard, 1994; Jones, 1997; Francis, 1999, 2002; Hey, 1999; The London Feminist Salon Collective, 2004), the importance of conceptualising solidarity as well as difference in the interests of social justice is a recurring issue. This is perhaps most lucidly asserted by Hey (1999), who states concerns to: 'reinstate the possibility of collective or at least collaborative or co-operative "action" in contrast to a withdrawal from taking any responsibility for anybody on the post-modern grounds that nobody can claim to speak about anybody or about anything' (quoted in Francis, 2001, p. 165).

It is this concern for solidarity and collective action that I wish to focus upon in the context of the creation and negotiation of shared professional identities. Through a feminist lens the notion of professionalism can rest upon a shared collective identity to act as a form of resistance to top-down policy imposition to achieve emancipatory ends. In the UK, early years education and childcare comprises a diverse range of settings, from state-run nurseries and integrated centres to voluntary-sector day nurseries and playgroups and privately owned, for-profit nurseries. Despite the myriad differences and distinctions in the range of provision available, and within the early education and childcare workforce itself in terms of social class and 'race', I still maintain that a common set of values exists and that the effects of policy are felt in similar ways (Osgood, 2004, 2005). Whilst various settings differ in organisation and ethos, the practitioners within them share a commitment to providing quality^2 services for the children and parents they serve.

I would argue that there are significant and undeniable obstacles to solidarity. Not least the recent and massive expansion in early childhood education and childcare services (Brannen & Moss, 2003); but also the fragmentary way in which different providers coexist; the increasing policy demands to become more competitively individualistic; and the absence of a unified collective mouthpiece in the form of a professional body or union. Yet research I have undertaken with practitioners indicates that there is, at the very least, a willingness to share a collective commitment. Practitioners from across the early years workforce articulate their concern to improve the quality of service provided, to share ideas and to resist seemingly unwelcome and inappropriate policies (Osgood, 2004). From a feminist perspective I would argue that practitioners should be mindful of the opportunities that a collective approach could offer to critically appraise, and where necessary collectively resist, government diktats that threaten their professionalism, in similar fashion to the ways teachers have mobilised in the past (Forrester, 2000). As Weiler (1988, p. 51) asserts 'for women, who are so often excluded from the public sphere, the question of whether resistance can lead to change if it is only expressed in individual critique or private opposition is a very real one'.

Conclusion

I have tried to demonstrate how the application of an alternative model of 'professionalism', using a feminist framework and the concept of a 'new agency', might offer practitioners an opportunity to collectively reposition themselves, and resist hegemonic new managerialist discourses. Throughout the paper the central argument has been that professionalism is socially constructed, and that whilst early years practitioners may 'fail' to embody the hegemonic form of professionalism they can (and do) represent an alternative form. I go on to argue that if early years practitioners grasp the possibilities to construct (in the public consciousness) a viable alternative version of professionalism (one which rests upon professional pride and reflection), then 'professionalism' might come to be understood as something different.

The approach that I propose does not seek to dismiss the power inherent within policy discourses to assert derisory judgements about professionalism in the early years, which then all too readily become convincing discursive truths amongst a wider audience – an audience that includes those who make use of childcare services (Vincent & Ball, 2001). Rather, I believe that whilst the current policy context in which early childhood education and care is situated is both exciting and challenging, it remains imperative that practitioners rise to the challenge of critically reflecting upon how they are positioned and how they seek to position themselves and to construct their professional identities.

Notes

1 New managerialism/neoliberalism has been reflexively and progressively theorised as masculinist within the feminist academic community. Key proponents of this position include Walkerdine (2003), Reay (1998) and Francis (2001), amongst others. The central argument I present in this paper is from a feminist poststructuralist position, from which I endeavour to demonstrate the theorisation behind the conflation of new managerialism/neoliberalism and a masculinist project of professionalism. By presenting my own subjective position throughout the paper, in the poststructuralist (feminist) tradition, I acknowledge that my presentation of ideas is only one of many possibilities.
2 'Quality' like 'professionalism' is a highly contentious, socially constructed concept. Hence 'quality' as a concept is open to myriad interpretations dependent upon for whom, and for what purposes and in what context, a meaning is being sought. It is beyond the scope of this paper to engage in a debate around the issue of 'quality'. However, I acknowledge that to state that practitioners share a commitment to 'quality' is problematic. For the purposes of this discussion my intention is to focus attention upon the shared, collective commitment to quality rather than a precise definition or deconstruction of 'quality' as a concept.

References

Acker, J. (1992) Gendered organisational theory, in: A. J. Mills & P. Tancred (Eds) *Gendering organizational analysis* (London, Sage), 248–60.

Avis, J. (2003) Re-thinking trust in a performative culture: the case of education, *Journal of Education Policy*, 18(3), 315–332.

Ball, S. (1990) *Politics and policy making in education: explorations in policy sociology* (London, Routledge).

Ball, S. (2003) The teacher's soul and the terrors of performativity, *Journal of Education Policy*, 18(2), 215–228.

Bernstein, B. (2000) Official knowledge and pedagogic identities: the politics of recontextualising, in: S. Ball (Ed.) *The sociology of education: major themes* (London, RoutledgeFalmer).

Bowe, R., Ball, S. & Gold, A. (1992) *Reforming education and changing schools: case studies in policy sociology* (London, Routledge).

Brannen, J. & Moss, P. (Eds) (2003) *Rethinking children's care* (Buckingham, Open University Press).

Butler, J. (1990) *Gender trouble: feminism and the subversion of identity* (London, Routledge).

Claxton, G. (1999) The anatomy of intuition, in: T. Atkinson & G. Claxton (Eds) *The intuitive practitioner: on the value of not always knowing what one is doing* (Buckingham, Open University Press).

Dale, R. (1981) Education and the capitalist state, in: M. Apple (Ed.) *Economic and cultural reproduction in education* (London, Routledge & Kegan Paul).

Du Gay, P. (1996) *Consumption and identity at work* (London, Sage).

Edwards, C., Gandini, L. & Forman, G. (1998) *The hundred languages of children: the Reggio Emilia approach to early childhood education* (Norwood, NJ, Ablex).

Feldman, A. (1997) Varieties of wisdom in practice of teachers, *Teaching and Teacher Education*, 13(7), 757–773.

Forrester, G. (2000) Professional autonomy versus managerial control: the experience of teachers in an English primary school, *International Studies in Sociology of Education*, 10(2), 133–151.

Foucault, M. (1988) *Politics, philosophy, culture: interviews and other writings 1977–1984* (London, Routledge).

Francis, B. (1998) Modernist reductionism or post-structuralist relativism—can we move on? An evaluation of the arguments in relation to feminist educational research, *Gender and Education*, 11(4), 381–393.

Francis, B. (2001) Commonality and difference? Attempts to escape from theoretical dualisms in emancipatory research in education, *International Studies in Sociology of Education*, 11(2), 157–172.

Francis, B. (2002) Relativism, realism and feminism—an analysis of some theoretical tensions in research on gender identity, *Journal of Gender Studies*, 11(1), 39–54.

Francis, B. & Archer, L., for the London Feminist Salon Collective (2004) The problematisation of agency in post-modern theory: as feminist educational researchers where do we go from here? *Gender and Education*, 16(2), 25–33.

Friere, P. (1999) *Pedagogy of the heart* (New York, Continuum).

Gee, J. P., Hull, G. & Lankshear, C. (1996) *The new work order: behind the language of the new capitalism* (Sydney, Allen & Unwin).

Giddens, A. (1979) *Central problems in social theory: action, structure and contradiction social analysis* (Berkeley, CA, University of California Press).

Goodfellow, J. (2004) Documenting professional practice through the use of a professional portfolio, *Early Years*, 24(1), 63–74.

Helsby, G. (1995) Teachers' construction of professionalism in England in the 1990s, *Journal of Education for Teaching*, 21(3), 317–332.

Hey, V. (1999) Troubling the auto/biography of the questions: re/thinking rapport and the politics of social class in feminist participant observation paper presented at *Gender & Education 2nd International Conference*, University of Warwick, 29–31 April.

Hoyle, E. (2001) Teaching: prestige, status and esteem, *Educational Management and Administration*, 29(2), 139–152.

Hughes, A. & Menmuir, J. (2002) Being a student on a part-time Early Years degree, *Early Years*, 22(2), 147–161.

Jones, A. (1997) Teaching post-structuralist feminist theory in education: student resistances, *Gender and Education*, 9, 261–269.

Katz, L. (1995) *Talks with teachers of young children* (Norwood, NJ, Ablex).

Maguire, M. & Ball, B. (1994) Discourses of educational reform in the UK and the USA and the work of teachers, *British Journal of In-service Education*, 20(1), 5–16.

Mahony, P. & Hextall, I. (2000) *Reconstructing teaching* (London, Routledge Falmer).

Maynard, M. (1994) Race, gender and the concept of difference in feminist thought, in: H. Afshar & M. Maynard (Eds) *The 'dynamics' of race* (London, Taylor & Francis).

Moyles, J. (2001) Passion, paradox and professionalism in early years education, *Early Years*, 21(2), 81–95.

Nias, J. (1999) *Primary teaching as a culture of care* (London, Paul Chapman).

Nias, J., Southworth, G. & Campbell, P. (1992) *Whole school curriculum development in the primary school* (London, Falmer Press).

Noddings, N. (1993) Caring: a feminist perspective, in: K. A. Strike & P. L. Ternasky (Eds) *Ethics for professionals in education: perspectives in preparation and practice* (New York, Teachers College Press), 43–53.

Osgood, J. (2003) *Developing the business skills of childcare professionals: an evaluation of the business support programmes* (London, DfES).

Osgood, J. (2004) Time to get down to business? The responses of early years practitioners to entrepreneurial approaches to professionalism, *Journal of Early Childhood Research*, 2(1), 5–24.

Osgood, J. (2005) Who cares? The classed nature of childcare, *Gender and Education*, 17(3), 289–303.

Osgood, J. & Stone, V. (2002) *Assessing the business skills of early years, childcare and playwork providers* (London, DfES).

Ozga, J. (1995) Deskilling a profession: professionalism, deprofessionalisation and the new managerialism, in: H. Busher & R. Saran (Eds) *Managing teachers as professionals in schools* (London, Kogan Page).

Ozga, J. (2000) *Policy research in educational settings: contested terrain* (Milton Keynes, Open University Press).

Ozga, J. & Lawn, M. (1981) *Teachers, professionalism and class* (Lewes, Falmer Press).

Reay, D. (1998) Rethinking social class: qualitative perspectives on class and gender, *Sociology*, 32(2), 259–275.

Reay, D. (2001) Finding or losing yourself? Working-class relationships to education, *Journal of Education Policy*, 16(4), 333–346.

Sachs, J. (2001) Teacher professional identity: competing discourses, competing outcomes, *Journal of Education Policy*, 16(2), 149–161.

Sinclair, A. (1996) Leadership in administration: rediscovering a lost discourse, in: P. Weller & G. Davis (Eds) *New ideas, better government* (Sydney, Allen & Unwin).

Sure Start Unit (2004) *Working in childcare, early years and playwork*. Available online at: http:// www.childcarecareers.gov.uk (accessed 1 April 2004).

Vincent, C. & Ball, S. (2001) A market in love? Choosing pre-school childcare, *British Educational Research Journal*, 27(5), 633–651.

Vogt, F. (2002) A caring teacher: explorations into primary school teachers' professional identity and ethic of care, *Gender and Education*, 14(3), 251–264.

Walkerdine, V. (2003) Reclassifying upward mobility: femininity and the neo-liberal subject, *Gender and Education*, 15(3), 237–248.

Weiler, K. (1988) *Women teaching for change: gender, class and power* (New York, Bergin and Garvey Publishers).

Yelland, N. (Ed.) (1998) *Gender in early childhood* (London, RoutledgeFalmer).

Theme V

Research methods: Agency and voice

Chapter 15

Critical reflections on the experiences of a male early childhood worker

Jennifer Sumsion

Source: *J. Sumsion, Gender and Education, 11(4), 455–468, 1999.*

Abstract

This article presents a narrative account of one man's experiences during his decade of employment as an early childhood worker. This account is juxtaposed with reflections from feminist and pro-feminist critical perspectives on the reactions, incidents and events he encountered. Tensions between risks and rewards, perceptions of power and powerlessness, and personal and political contexts are explored. These tensions highlight the pervasiveness of hegemonic conceptions of masculinity, and how they constrain gender reform.

Introduction

The experiences of women who venture into traditionally male occupations and professions, and their consequent risk of encountering 'hostile male environments and harassment' (Kenway, 1997, p. 5) have been well documented (e.g. Spencer & Podmore, 1987; Abrams, 1993; Chetkovich, 1997; Davies-Netzley, 1998). Relatively little appears to be known, however, about the experiences of men moving into traditionally 'female' work environments, or about the rewards or risks entailed (Williams, 1992). In particular, scant attention has been paid to the men who chose to become professional carers and educators of young children.

Moreover, most of what *has* been written about male early childhood workers lacks an empirical basis, or is informed by limited theoretical analysis. Apart from a few noticeable exceptions (e.g. Skelton, 1991, 1994; Murray, 1996), there has been little attempt to interpret men's experiences in early childhood education from a critical perspective. This article draws on discourses of masculinity to highlight some of the tensions men may experience when their career choice challenges social, cultural, political and institutional norms.

Some feminists argue that focusing on men can deflect attention from the continuing inequalities between men and women (Skelton, 1991; Kenway, 1997). In particular, they point out that the 'competing victim syndrome' (Cox [1995], cited by Kenway, 1997), characterising aspects of the 'men's rights' and 'mythopoetic' men's movements, does little to overcome structural gender-based inequalities (Collinson & Hearn, 1994; Schwalbe, 1996; Connell, 1997; Mills, 1997; Messner, 1998). While sympathetic to these concerns, like McLean (1997), I argue that gender reform also involves developing 'sophisticated and empathetic understandings of men's experiences of masculinity in a variety of different contexts' (p. 61). As McLean points out, 'if we can identify the costs to men implicit in … gender inequality, then men may start to see that there are good reasons for them to join with women in seeking change' (p. 62). The purpose of this article is to document one man's experience of masculinity within the context of early childhood education and to identify some of the costs involved.

Theoretical perspective

An underlying premise is that the active engagement of males in the nurturing of young children challenges conventional perceptions of masculinity and so has the potential to contribute to gender reform (Williams, 1995; Murray, 1996). Here, masculinity is seen as a 'social construction about what it means to be male in certain times and certain places' (Kenway, 1995, p. 61). These constructions change over time and according to context and dominant discourses (Connell, 1995; Kenway, 1995). I adopt the term 'hegemonic masculinity' (Connell, 1995) to refer to the socially dominant form of masculinity in a specific time and context, but like Connell and Kenway, recognise the co-existence of competing or alternative masculinities. Following Kenway (1995), I also argue that an individual's masculine identity is formed by the intersection of his biography with the 'discourses of masculinity'(p. 62) of the social settings through which he moves. An understanding of an individual's biography, therefore, is integral to understanding his masculine identity.

Narrative is well suited to portraying and interpreting human experiences (Connelly & Clandinin, 1990; Polkinghorne, 1995). Typically, we impose a narrative structure to organise our images and experiences. Likewise, we 'hear and understand in narratives' (Gudmundsdottir, 1996, p. 291). Thus, narratives contribute some degree of shared meaning, despite widely differing life experiences and circumstances (Gudmundsdottir, 1996). As critics argue, however, narrative can become imbued with unwarranted authenticity (Pringle, 1995; Hargreaves, 1996; Phillips, 1997). In this article, I balance the personal and the political by juxtaposing excerpts from one male early childhood worker's professional biography with critical reflections on the experiences he encountered and his responses to these experiences.

Context

James (a pseudonym), a 33 year-old Anglo-Australian male, is married with two young daughters, aged 2 and 3 years. He has almost completed a 4-year Bachelor of Education (Early Childhood) degree, by part-time study through distance education. His previous qualifications include a 3-year Diploma of Teaching (Early Childhood) and a 2-year Certificate of Child Care Studies from a College of Technical and Further Education (TAFE). From 1986 to 1997, James was employed as a childcare worker in a heavily industrialised regional city in New South Wales, Australia. This city has a long and continuing history of institutionalised paedophilia. From 1994 to 1997, James was the director of a 40-place long daycare centre, catering for children aged from birth to 5 years. In this capacity, he had overall responsibility for the day-to-day running of the programme and the 10 staff employed within the centre. In 1996–97, James participated in a study of the experiences of males enrolled in early childhood teacher education programmes (Sumsion & Lubimowski, 1998). The present article is drawn from this larger study.

Method

The narrative excerpts referred to are taken from a series of three in-depth interviews held over 19 months from April 1996 to November 1997. The first two interviews were conducted by a male research assistant. The third interview took place after James contacted me to talk about an incident that he found particularly distressing.

The purpose of the first two interviews was to identify and explore formative experiences, pivotal events and critical incidents in James's 10 years as an early childhood professional. In the third and final interview, James focused primarily on the lead up to, and aftermath of, a specific incident, which precipitated his decision to leave the profession. Interviews were between 90 minutes and 2 hours in duration and were held in James's workplace. They were audio-taped and transcribed and transcripts returned to James, who confirmed their authenticity (Lincoln & Guba, 1985).

Concerns have been raised about the potential difficulties associated with women interviewing men. Laws (1990), for example, found it difficult to establish rapport with her male interviewees; while Williams & Heikes (1993) warn of the possibility of a 'social desirability bias' (p. 285) that could lead the interviewee to present what he perceives will be a socially sanctioned account of his experiences. In both studies, however, these researchers found that their concerns were not insurmountable.

In the present study, developing rapport did not appear difficult, perhaps in part because James and I were already acquainted. (We had met several years ago, when he was studying for his Diploma of Teaching, and had maintained intermittent contact since.) Moreover, analysis of the transcripts of his three interviews indicated little discrepancy between his responses to a male and female interviewer. I found, however, that when strong emotions surfaced for James, particularly as he talked about painful events, Stanko's (1994) reservations about women interviewing men resonated with me.

Commenting on her experiences of interviewing men who have been the victims of violence, Stanko (1994) concluded:

> The major disadvantage, for me, is that I do not have the personal resources to tap into my own experiences to explore what men say about violence. I am not a man, and do not have the accumulated and gendered knowledge against which to balance what men are saying and sharing about their lives. This work, I suspect, will have to be done by men.

In some ways, her implicit assumption that, for research about sensitive issues to be authentic, researchers need to be of the same gender as interviewees is contentious. Given that the dynamics of social class, race, and political and personal agendas are also influential in the research process (Phoenix, 1994), in effect, it would mean that researchers would only be equipped to work with participants of similar backgrounds and persuasions to their own – a limitation which seems likely to inhibit the emergence of new perspectives and understandings. Her concern is a timely reminder, though, that it is impossible to 'neutralize the social nature of interpretation' (Holland & Ramazanoglu, 1994, p. 133).

It was important, therefore, to minimise the risk of misinterpretation when constructing James's story. The use of in-depth interviews and narrative representation, and a commitment to sharing with James drafts of manuscripts arising from the project, as well as interview transcripts, were particularly helpful in clarifying issues and checking interpretations. Making explicit the processes of interpretation, and construction of the narrative was also essential. In brief, this involved noting the main themes that emerged as James recalled and reflected on formative experiences and events. Incidents representative of these themes were identified. Those incidents that had the potential to provide both an understanding of the personal context of James's experiences as well as a basis for considering broader sociocultural-political issues were portrayed in the following narrative. James's description of these incidents forms the basis of the narrative.

Throughout these processes of interpretation and construction I was conscious of many issues of trust and power and, as Glucksmann (1994) writes, of the need 'to draw the difficult line between interpreting the data in terms of its relevance to ... [my] research questions as opposed to twisting it in a way that amounts to a misrepresentation of what was said' (p. 163). In the interview context, differentials in power seemed minimal, as James and I met as professionals of equal standing in our respective work communities. As a researcher, though, I had considerably more power than James when interpreting and representing the data. My decision to adopt a critical orientation, with which James had little theoretical familiarity, privileged a feminist and pro-feminist perspective, over a non-critical, experientialist perspective.

Personal, theoretical and critical reflections

In the narrative that follows, the text in italics represents James's voice; the critical reflections following each fragment represent my voice. This device enables the inter-weaving of the personal, the theoretical and the critical. The narrative begins with James reflecting on his choice of occupation. He commented:

The Decision

I had a good job as a maintenance officer. It paid really good money and at the end of the week it was $500 in the hand. That was years ago and I don't even earn that now. But there had to be something more to life than getting up in the morning just for the money. I needed to take something home each day 'inside'. I needed to be able to make a difference to someone's life. If I did, maybe I could make the world a better place.

Reactions

My great grandfather was a miner, my grandfather was a miner, my father is a miner and my brother is a miner, so you can imagine my mother's disappointment. My father was fairly supportive, but as far as everyone else was concerned, it was 'James's just another normal red-blooded bloke. So why the hell is he doing this? Maybe there is something not quite right after all'.

For James, becoming an early childhood worker represented an attempt to explore alternatives to the hegemonic masculinity privileged in the working-class environment in which he had always lived. His career choice violated his community's expectations of masculinity which, in relation to work, emphasised providing financially for dependants through manual labour or mechanical or technical competence – in short, by having a 'man's' job. These expectations were held within a broader context of 'compulsory heterosexuality' (Connell, 1995, p. 103). James's decision to pursue 'women's' work, therefore, raised immediate doubts about his sexuality. Although aware that rejecting traditional male employment options to work with young children involved risks, he anticipated that the rewards would more than compensate. As the following excerpts illustrate, however, the reality proved otherwise.

The wedding ring

I was the first male to enrol at the TAFE {in James's home city}. I was treated like a novelty – asked out continuously and lots of sexual references. There was quite a bit of harassment, really. Playful slapping on the bum and all that sort of stuff. I didn't like it at all. I didn't feel that I should be treated like that just because I was male. I took it all on the chin but I got to the point where I got so sick and tired of it that I started wearing a wedding ring – to provide the illusion that I was married and therefore unattainable, and also to show that I wasn't gay. {James emphasised that he was not homophobic but that the community in which he lived and worked was extremely so.}

Practicum placements

I had some trouble on placements. When I did a family daycare placement I got a phone call after the first day … 'Oh, James. My husband doesn't like the idea that you're here. You'll have to find somewhere else'. I found that very hard to cope with.

There were some difficulties with pracs at university, too. The same sort of reaction from parents – the raised eyebrows, the shaking of heads. I can cope to a certain degree when somebody is quite prejudiced and they're verbal about it. You know how to react – you know what to say and you know how to come to terms with that, internally. But the passive prejudice is like a subtle sort of sabotage.

Each of these excerpts reflects widely held assumptions about masculinity. Essentially, each defines masculinity in terms of sexuality. The first suggests a perception of males as non-discriminating 'playboys' and sexual adventurers. The second focuses on men as sexual predators and competitors, while the third constructs men as potential abusers of sexual power.

These constructions of masculinity intersect with connotations of nurturing and teaching young children as a quintessentially female role (Steedman, 1988; Acker, 1995; Steinberg, 1996). This confluence leads to assumptions that 'men who want to work with young children must have a tendency towards paedophilia' (Skelton, 1991, p. 285). Murray (1996) puts it more bluntly: 'When men choose to do child care work, they become suspect' (p. 368). The relatively low pay and status, and lack of other socially acceptable rewards for men who choose to work in childcare fuel these inherent suspicions. James's attempts to explore an alternative to the mainstream hegemonic masculinity, therefore, took place in a context that precluded acceptance of males working in a professional capacity to care for young children. This fundamental schism between community perceptions of masculinities and the 'maternal imagery' (Acker, 1995, p. 23) that surrounds early childhood education created many tensions.

The 'wedding ring' incident exemplifies some of these tensions. It also supports Kanter's (1977) claim that 'token' participants in gender-segregated occupations, regardless of sex, are likely to encounter unwelcome attention, stereotyping and marginalisation. Resorting to a wedding ring to deter unwanted sexual advances resonates with the harassment experienced by many women in traditionally male occupational enclaves (Benokraitis, 1997; Kenway, 1997). A later excerpt from James's narrative suggests, however, that his token status may also have worked to his advantage, unlike the experience of most women in male-dominated professions (Williams, 1995). To James, however, the cumulative effect of these incidents contributed to a sense of vulnerability, which is encapsulated in the following excerpt.

Differences

I enjoyed university. I enjoyed the study and I enjoyed the people. But – and this is really important but it's hard to verbalise – in my heart of hearts I knew that I was different. With a lot of people in Early Childhood, there are common threads and I don't think I shared those same threads. Child sexual assault was coming much more to the fore. So much so, that I kept a file of articles about it. It was an issue for me. It wasn't an issue for any of the girls {fellow students}because it didn't relate to them. But I knew that it was something that could relate to me. Once, there was an opportunity for the male students to get together with a male lecturer and bare our souls. We didn't have a great deal of time to talk but we shared something, and each of us kind of appreciated that. And it seemed to create a kind of bond between us.

In comparison to their female counterparts, males enrolled in early childhood education pre-service programmes are more likely to be mature age students and to have broader life experiences (Sumsion & Lubimowski, 1998). In this extract, though, James alludes to a more fundamental difference. For women, early childhood teaching is a socially sanctioned career choice; for men, it is not. Increasingly, this realisation became the interpretative frame though which James made sense of his professional experiences.

During his pre-service programme, James welcomed the opportunity to establish bonds with his male peers. After graduation, though, he became increasingly apprehensive about associating with male colleagues, because of the possibility of inadvertently associating with paedophiles. In his words, 'I know that I am all right but I can't know for sure about *them*'. His fear militated against his seeking solidarity with other men to work collectively for change, and precluded him from finding a forum in which he could address his anxieties and feelings of isolation. Without collective effort towards reform, there seemed little scope to exert 'social leverage' (Connell, 1995, p. 141) for greater acceptance of men in early childhood education. Nevertheless, despite its oppressive nature, hegemonic masculinity and its patriarchal structures conferred on James certain career advantages, as illustrated in the following.

Career advancement

After I finished my diploma I took a 'second teacher's' job, a new role that the organisation was introducing. Because it was a brand new concept, there were no role models and no support networks. Before, I had just been one of the childcare workers and I found it hard moving into a more managerial type position. It was a step up and there were a lot more expectations. I really needed someone to nurture me and give me confidence. The director was quite nurturing with the other staff, but I think she felt that, with me, she had to be really quite aggressive. I think she had a really hard time coming to terms with the fact that I was male. Maybe that was because of her perception of men, generally.

And I think that I probably got her 'off-side' because of my insecurity. I made quite a few mistakes in that way. So I can't say that it was a really pleasant time. But it was exciting and challenging. It was hard, though, because of the expectations placed on you. Because you're a male, to be considered half as good {as females}, you have to try twice as hard. Sometimes I get really sick of trying so hard.

James's rapid promotion exemplifies the 'glass escalator' effect which advances the careers of many men in traditionally female professions, enabling them to rise quickly to higher paid and higher status positions (Acker, 1990; Williams, 1995; Isaacs & Poole, 1996; Murray, 1996). As organisational cultures tend to favour hegemonic masculine norms, even in female-dominated professions, the traditional gender hierarchy tends to be reproduced (Williams, 1995). These structural advantages favouring men might account for what James perceived as resentment on behalf of the female director. Alternatively, her resentment could reflect the stereotyped gender beliefs and expectations of some female early childhood workers, and their subsequent difficulty in 'accepting the commitment and capacities of their [male] colleagues' (Clyde, 1995, p. 14). James's focus on his personal context, rather than on broader sociocultural and political influences, encouraged a perception that males in early childhood education are disadvantaged by their gender. The following extract explores this perception further.

Celebrating men

I've never been a very pessimistic sort of person and I still had that feeling of wanting to be a champion for men's rights. You hear all the time that 'Women can do anything!' but there's nobody standing up saying 'Hey, men can do anything, too'. Children get shaped and moulded very young in life. One of the reasons that I was in early childhood was to demonstrate to children that you should never be limited by your sex in your career choice. By being here, I was saying to the children 'You can be whatever you want to. Find something that fulfils you totally'.

And I think that men do have a very special quality about them. I suppose that, really, it's just that they are males going into an all female setting. I think they help make it a really well rounded environment. I've seen some children respond to me in a completely different way to how they respond to female staff. I've introduced activities, such as carpentry and handyperson activities, that should have been included but that some female staff never think of including. So yeah, I think that men bring a richness to the environment.

James's comments suggest a lack of awareness of the complexity of gender dynamics and gender reform. His frustration at the constraints and costs of hegemonic masculinity blinds him to its patriarchal dividends (Connell, 1995). Essentially, he overlooks the power, choice and opportunities conferred on men, as a group. His failure to distinguish his personal circumstances from the broader socio-political context, and his tendency to attribute male oppression to feminism could limit his potential contribution to gender reform. Conceivably, it could also attract him to reactionary 'men's rights' movements, discredited by many pro-feminist men (e.g. Connell, 1997; Mills, 1997).

His perceptions of the contribution of male early childhood workers also reveal some inconsistency. On the one hand, he contends that the presence of male role models contributes 'to the breakdown of destructive gender stereo-types' (Williams, 1995, p. 153) that perpetuate current inequities and continue to limit perceived career options. Yet, at the same time, he draws on stereotyped gender roles to argue that men contribute traditional male characteristics, interests and expertise and that these enhance early childhood learning environments. While James seemed to enter early childhood education with the implicit intent of subverting hegemonic masculine norms, he seems to have little understanding of how hegemonic masculinity continued to constrain his thinking.

The following extract is from the third interview with James, and concerns the incident that prompted him to contact me with the request that we meet. The event described in this excerpt was pivotal in James's decision, a few months later, to leave the early childhood field.

The ticking bomb

I love my job but the cost of being male in early childhood is enormous. There are so many aspersions cast on your sexuality and there is so much day-to-day prejudice. I've had people phone anonymously and call me a 'rock spider' {paedophile}. I've had new parents come through the door and say, 'I'd like to meet the director'. I say,

'Hi, my name is James and I'm the director. Can I help you?' – and they've just turned around and walked straight out.

It's like sitting on a time bomb which is ticking away – the accusation will come sooner or later. It's not a case of if it's going to happen; it's a case of when it's going to happen. I honestly believe that.

When you're single, you don't really worry. You think 'If I ever got accused {of child sexual abuse}, I'll know that it's not true. Yeah, some mud will stick, but it would only be words'. I thought that if anything happened, I would take it on the chin and fight it to the hilt. I used to think that I was invincible, that I was a bit of a champion for men, that I was providing an example for men. I was invited to open days {at schools and career markets} and I'd encourage boys and young men to consider a career in child care. It was like 'Go on! You can do it!'

But when you get married, it hurts more people. I've got a wife and two children now and I don't want to drag them through a child sexual assault allegation. I couldn't live with that. I couldn't live with my wife being put through it and I certainly couldn't put my children at risk. I love my children dearly and if anything happened to them, I would want blood. So I can see how people would naturally jump to the wrong conclusions. I couldn't stand somebody thinking that about me. I couldn't take it at all.

A few weeks ago, there was a reference in the newspaper to concerns about a male working in a local early childhood programme. It wasn't a direct accusation, but there were questions raised. Panic set in. My wife and I did a quick count of all the males we knew in the region and came up with seven men. But as far as the parents of many of the children in my centre, I am the ONLY male they know in early childhood. Anyway, it turned out that the report should have read that 'Pre-school aged children had been assaulted by a relative of the family'. But it shows how inaccurate reporting puts a cloud over your head. One night, soon afterwards, the words 'James Straffe is a paedophile' were spray painted on the walls of the centre. I just 'dropped the ball'.

This excerpt provides some insight into the covert and overt discrimination encountered by men who flout the norms of hegemonic masculinity. It also highlights the current globalised moral panic about paedophilia and the inflammatory contribution of the mass media (Glaser, 1998). As Kenway (1995) argues, 'the mass media offer multiple messages about what it means to be male, but some messages are much stronger than others. Given the sweep of their influence ... mass media versions of masculinities exercise an authority of some force' (p. 61). This excerpt indicates that this agency is not necessarily exercised responsibly.

Although the vast majority of perpetrators of child sexual abuse are family members, relatives, caregivers in some capacity, or family acquaintances (Pringle, 1995; Glaser, 1998), this does not justify assumptions that men who choose to be involved with children have a propensity to abuse. Other than being male, no identifiable characteristics distinguish perpetrators of child sexual abuse from the remainder of the population (Pringle, 1995; Glaser, 1998). Indeed, the implicit assumption that men who choose to work professionally with young children do so because of opportunities for abuse sits uncomfortably with findings of male aggression – in general, that men with the most traditional gender attitudes are more likely to violate against women and children (Howard & Hollander, 1997). As it seems unlikely that men with highly traditional gender attitudes will seek a career in early childhood education, it could be argued that, proportionately, male early childhood workers are less likely to sexually abuse children than the male population, as a whole.

The last excerpt is also interesting for its metaphorical language, which inadvertently illustrates the centrality of aggression to hegemonic masculinity (Howard & Hollander, 1997). Despite James's intent to work towards subverting conventional masculine norms by becoming an early childhood worker, he retains the hegemonic assumption that his role as defender of his wife and children justifies aggression. Simultaneously, he anticipates that as his career choice in many respects violates social norms, the outcome will inevitably involve violence. Although he dreads becoming a victim of this (emotional) violence, he implicitly condones its use.

The aftermath

I really hate the person who did this {the spray painting}. Hate is a strong word but when they did that, they took something away from me that I didn't think anyone could. They broke something inside me that now interferes with the way that I relate to children.

Before, it would be nothing for children to come up to me and there would be all this warmth and empathy. But now I just feel like holding them all at arm's length and saying 'Don't come near me. Don't touch me. Just stay away from me'. I've always had a close relationship with them. And on my first day back {after a period of stress-related leave, which James was eventually granted after a considerable struggle}, because they hadn't seen me for 6 weeks, they wanted to be all over me. They were jumping and screaming and touching me. And I just couldn't cope with it. I had to lock myself away in the office.

Even with my own kids, before, it would have been nothing for us to jump into the bath together and things like that. And I said to my wife 'I know this sounds silly, but ...' And she said, 'You are these children's father! You're not to talk like that! You're not to feel like that!' But it's really hard, you know. Because when you're in that mode of thinking 8 hours a day and then you've got your own children to go home to, well, it's like you're still wanting to protect yourself. There were never any closed doors in our house, but there are now.

Something feels broken inside. And the most worrying thing is that I don't want to fix it. Because if I hold them at a distance there is less chance that anything like that could ever happen again. I knew this would happen. I knew that it was inevitable.

Two paradoxes are evident in this final excerpt. First, James was attracted to early childhood education because he perceived it offered opportunities for emotional closeness and fulfilment. Yet his attempts to transcend the emotional impoverishment of conventional hegemonic masculinities ultimately resulted in emotional withdrawal. Bathriek & Kaufman (1998) contend that while relinquishing some of the privileges of hegemonic masculinities can make men more emotionally vulnerable, the feeling of not being in control creates possibilities of closer, more rewarding relationships and a greater sense of connectedness with others. For James, however, this was not the case.

Second, men's growing involvement in the care of their own children is widely assumed to hold promise for loosening some of the constraints of hegemonic masculinity (Hood, 1993; Coltrane, 1996; Brandth & Kvande, 1998). These writers argue that a greater emphasis on nurturing capacities, and valuing of the caring role, may lead to the participation of more men in the 'caring professions', a gradual disassociation of masculinity with aggression, and an erosion of patriarchal attitudes and structures. In James's case, though, his commitment to his own children accentuated his perceptions of the risks his role as a professional carer of young children entailed, and was a catalyst for his departure from the field.

Discussion

James's narrative highlights the need to hear more from men in caring professions if we are to further our understanding of the complexities of gender reform. His story points to the pervasiveness of hegemonic structures which perpetuate the paucity of men in early childhood education and similar professions (Pringle, 1995). It also illustrates the considerable emotional distress and turmoil which can accompany attempts to 'remake' conventional masculinities (Connell, 1995). Yet, at the same time, it demonstrates the need for caution and critical reflection as we listen to 'the voices of men defining the reality of the worlds around them' (Pringle, 1995, p. 9). Otherwise, as James's story shows, in the midst of personal anguish it is easy to lose sight of broader political contexts.

If we accept that greater involvement of men in the nurturing of young children has considerable potential to challenge conventional constructions of masculinity (Hearn, 1987; Connell, 1995; Murray, 1996), then we need to consider how men like James might be retained in early childhood education and assisted to become agents of gender reform. As Connell argues, and as James's narrative indicates, rejecting the constraints of the dominant masculinity requires a great deal of commitment in the face of derision, hostility and suspicion. It also calls for considerable insight into one's actions, as well as into influences perpetuating hegemonic structures. Moreover, Connell asserts, the emotional distress that challenging and attempting to transform these structures can entail makes reform unlikely if left to individuals. Collective action, he contends, is more likely to succeed, especially if it focuses on precipitating change from multiple bases and strategic pressure points. The following discussion focuses on three possibilities: (i) forming professional and parental alliances; (ii) making use of the mass media; and (iii) reconceptualising the organisational and professional culture of early childhood education.

Forming professional and parental alliances

I use the term *professional and parental alliances* to refer to the formation of networks of parents and early childhood professionals to explore perceptions of masculinity, and how these might be reshaped in 'more positive and creative ways' (Pringle, 1995, p. 181). Assuming an atmosphere of trust is established, these networks could provide a supportive space for exploring alternative masculinities and new gender identities. This is likely to involve deconstructing the stereotypes, costs and privileges of conventional masculinities; identifying how these stereotypes and inequities are perpetuated; and how they might be eroded and transformed. Promoting images of masculinity characterised by qualities such as emotional openness, mutual caring and respectful interdependence would be a key priority (Pringle, 1995). Parental advocacy for greater involvement of males in the care and education of young children could become a powerful strategy for challenging community attitudes and legitimising the involvement of males.

Making use of the mass media

To be effective, advocates will have to address community concerns about child sexual abuse. They will need to acknowledge 'the incidence and severity of male violence' (MacCormack, 1996, p. 17), but simultaneously emphasise that 'most men, like most women, commit little aggressive violence' (Howard & Hollander, 1997, p. 136). In other words, they will recognise community concerns about 'the interrelationships of masculinity, sexuality and violence' (Skelton, 1994, p. 87), but challenge the community's acceptance of its inevitability. To do this effectively, advocacy efforts must harness the power of the media in order to portray images of masculinity centred on interconnectedness and caring, rather than on power and violence. Evidence that media images are reflecting the growing tendency of many men to become more involved in caring for their own children suggests that this is potentially fertile ground for change (Hearn, 1987; Connell, 1995).

Reconceptualising the organisational and professional culture of early childhood education

Reconceptualising the professional and organisational culture of early childhood education – that is, the 'shared symbols, language, practices ("how we do things around here") and deeply embedded beliefs and values' (Newman, 1995, p. 11) – could also assist gender reform. Steinberg (1996) urges early childhood educators to 'deconstruct the gender context that has insidiously shaped the field' (p. 35). In particular, she refers to the seemingly unquestioned assumptions amongst many early childhood professionals that the ethic of caring characterising the profession is inevitably linked with female gender roles and perpetuates the 'maternal model' of early childhood educator (p. 34). With its emphasis on caring relationships, the early childhood profession may have overlooked the social and political contexts in which these relationships develop (Acker, 1995). Without a critical awareness, it will be difficult for early childhood educators to understand the ways in which gender is socially constructed. Focusing on the experiences of men in childcare could assist in raising awareness of gender issues and provide a useful starting point for deconstructing gender stereotypes (Murray, 1996).

As part of this process of reconceptualisation, gendered practices and policies should also be reconsidered. For example, as Skelton (1994) points out, it is inappropriate to rely on men to construct 'their own frameworks in which to work "safely" with children' (p. 87). Explicit and transparent protective measures are a right of all early childhood workers, regardless of gender. Pringle (1995) advises maintaining a constant alertness to the possibility of abuse, avoiding situations and actions that could conceivably be misinterpreted as abusive, and minimising physical contact with children. Such measures, however, seem likely to perpetuate the negative expectations and climate of suspicion that has characterised men's involvement in early childhood education.

A better alternative may be to emphasise the importance of providing safe and respectful environments for children and adults alike, and to involve parents and early childhood professionals in developing guidelines appropriate to particular contexts. Such guidelines would need to protect young children; support the right of adults, regardless of gender, to work with them; acknowledge community concerns about child sexual abuse; recognise the constraints of early childhood settings; and take account of the potential impact of such guidelines on children, early childhood workers and their colleagues (Skelton, 1994). Resolving these tensions, especially without resorting to simplistic and inappropriate solutions, will be challenging, but essential if early childhood education is to take a more proactive role in gender reform.

Support mechanisms for those unjustly accused of child sexual abuse would also be needed. These would include recognition of the enormity of the impact of such accusations, and access to counselling services and support groups. An appropriate benchmark might be the types of support supposedly extended to victims of sexual assault. Provisions such as these would need to be informed by an awareness of the pervasiveness of hegemonic perceptions of masculinity and the difficulties involved in challenging these perceptions.

To date, most of the literature concerning early childhood education has shown little understanding of these issues. Take, for example, the implicit assumptions that early childhood professionals are necessarily female. References to what James called the 'ticking bomb' are conspicuously absent, even though they figure prominently in the few existing accounts of other male early childhood professionals. Just as contemporary conceptualisations of women's career stages and professional development needs (e.g. Poole & Langan-Fox, 1997) take account of many women's interrupted participation in the workforce due to family responsibilities, it seems timely to consider the impact of gender influences on men's participation in early childhood education and other traditionally 'female' professions.

Conclusion

This article is not intended as a representative portrayal of the experiences of male early childhood workers. Nevertheless, focusing on one man's experiences and the tensions that led to his eventual departure from the field highlights the pervasiveness, contradictions and complexities of hegemonic masculinity and their constraints on gender reform. The participation of men in childcare appears to offer potential leverage for reform. The challenges faced by James, however, suggest that collective action, rather than relying on the actions of individuals alone, will be needed for this potential to be realised.

Success in increasing the number of men in childcare would, in turn, raise many questions of gender politics. Would the involvement of more men, for example, raise the status of the childcare profession, and elevate nurturing and other roles traditionally seen as feminine, and therefore traditionally undervalued? Or would the glass escalator effect advantage male early childhood workers at the expense of their female colleagues, and perpetuate gender inequalities? Might men attracted to childcare be committed to exploring alternative masculinities, and if so, would this encourage boys to do likewise – and invite female early childhood workers and girls to explore alternative femininities? Or would a greater influx of men simply reinforce hegemonic conceptions of masculinity and femininity? There are many unknowns, many potential gains and risks to the involvement of more males in professional childcare. James's narrative alerts us to some of the possibilities.

Acknowledgements

I wish to thank James for sharing his experiences so candidly. I am also grateful to Gary Lubimovski, research assistant. This article benefited from the detailed and constructive critique of earlier drafts by two anonymous reviewers.

References

Abrams, R. (1993) *Woman in a Man's World, Pioneering Career Women of the Twentieth Century* (London, Methuen).

Acker, J. (1990) Hierarchies, jobs, bodies: a theory of gendered organizations, *Gender & Society*, 4, pp. 139–158.

Acker, S. (1995) Carry on caring: the work of women teachers, *British Journal of Sociology of Education*, 16, pp. 21–36.

Bathriek, D. & Kaufman, G. (1998) Male privilege and male violence, *Journal of the Medical Association of Georgia*, 87, pp. 45–47.

Benokraitis, N. (1997) *Subtle Sexism, Current Practices and Prospects for Change* (Thousand Oaks, CA, Sage).

Brandth, B. & Kvande, E. (1998) Masculinity and child care: the reconstruction of fathering, *Sociological Review*, 46, pp. 293–311.

Chetkovitch, C. (1997) *Real Heat, Gender and Race in the Urban Fire Service* (London, Rutgers University Press).

Clyde, M. (1995) Is early childhood a man's world? Paper presented at the *Sixth Early Childhood Convention*, Auckland.

Collinson, D. & Hearn, J. (1994) Naming men as men: implications for work, organization and management, *Gender, Work and Organization*, 1, pp. 2–19.

Coltrane, S. (1996) *Family Man, Fatherhood, Housework, and Gender Equity* (New York, Oxford University Press).

Connell, R. (1995) *Masculinities* (Sydney, Allen & Unwin).

Connell, R. (1997) Men, masculinities and feminism, *Social Alternatives*, 16, pp. 7–10.

Connelly, M. & Clandinin, J. (1990) Stories of experience and narrative inquiry, *Educational Researcher*, 19, pp. 2–14.

Davies-Netzley, S.A. (1998) Women above the glass ceiling: perceptions on corporate mobility and strategies for success, *Gender & Society*, 12, pp. 339–355.

Glaser, B. (1998) Psychiatry and paedophilia: a major public health issue, *Australian and New Zealand Journal of Psychiatry*, 32, pp. 162–167.

Glucksmann, M. (1994) The work of knowledge and the knowledge of women's work, in: M. Maynard & J. Purvis (Eds) *Researching Women's Lives from a Feminist Perspective* (London, Taylor & Francis).

Gudmundsdottir, S. (1996) The teller, the tale and the one being told: the narrative nature of the research interview, *Curriculum Inquiry*, 26, pp. 293–306.

Hargreaves, A. (1996) Revisiting voice, *Educational Researcher*, 25, pp. 12–19.

Hearn, J. (1987) *The Gender of Oppression* (Worcester, Wheatsheaf Books).

Holland, J. & Ramazanoglu, C. (1994) Power and interpretation in researching young women's sexuality, in: M. Maynard & J. Purvis (Eds) *Researching Women's Lives from a Feminist Perspective*, pp. 125–148 (London, Taylor & Francis).

Hood, J. (Ed.) (1993) *Men, Work, and Family* (Newbury Park, CA, Sage).

Howard, J.& Hollander, J. (1997) *Gendered Situations, Gendered Selves, a Gender Lens on Social Psychology* (London, Sage).

Isaacs, D. & Poole, M. (1996) Being a man and becoming a nurse: three men's stories, *Journal of Gender Studies*, 5, pp. 39–47.

Kanter, R. (1977) *Men and Women of the Corporation* (New York, Basic Books).

Kenway, J. (1995) Masculinities in schools: under siege, on the defensive and under reconstruction? *Discourse*, 16, pp. 59–79.

Kenway, J. (1997) Boy's education in the context of gender reform, *Curriculum Perspectives*, 17, pp. 57–61.

Laws, S. (1990) *Issues of Blood, the Politics of Menstruation* (London, Macmillan).

Lincoln, Y. & Guba, E. (1985) *Naturalistic Inquiry* (BeverlyHills, CA, Sage).

MacCormack, T. (1996) Looking at male violence, *Canadian Journal of Counselling*, 30, pp. 17–30.

McLean, C. (1997) Engaging with boys' experiences of masculinity: implications for gender reform in schools, *Curriculum Perspectives*, 17, pp. 61–64.

Messner, M. (1998) The limits of the 'male sex role': an analysis of the men's liberation and men rights movements' discourse, *Gender & Society*, 12, pp. 255–276.

Mills, M. (1997) Wild men: looking back and lashing out, *Social Alternatives*, 16, pp. 11–14.

Murray, S. (1996) 'We all love Charles': men in child care and the social construction of gender, *Gender & Society*, 10, pp. 368–385.

Newman, J. (1995) Gender and cultural change, in: C. Itzin & J. Ewman (Eds) *Gender, Culture and Organizational Change, Putting Theory into Practice* (London, Routledge).

Phillips, D.C. (1997) Telling the truth about stories, *Teaching and Teacher Education*, 13, pp. 101–109.

Phoenix, A. (1994) Gender and 'race' in the research process, in: M. Maynard & J. Purvis (Eds) *Researching Women's Lives from a Feminist Perspective* (London, Taylor & Francis).

Polkinghorne, D. (1995) Narrative configuration in qualitative analysis, *Qualitative Studies in Education*, 8, pp. 5–23.

Poole, M. & Langan-Fox, J. (1997) *Australian Women and Careers, Psychological and Contextual Influences over the Life Course* (Melbourne, Cambridge University Press).

Pringle, K. (1995) *Men, Masculinities & Social Welfare* (London, UCL Press).

Schwalbe, M. (1996) *Unlocking the Iron Cage: the men's movement, gender politics, and American culture* (New York, Oxford University Press).

Skelton, C. (1991) A study of the career perspectives of male teachers of young children, *Gender and Education*, 3, pp. 279–289.

Skelton, C. (1994) Sex, male teachers and young children, *Gender and Education*, 6, pp. 87–93.

Spencer, A. & Podmore, D. (Eds) (1987) *In a Man's World: essays on women in male dominated professions* (London, Tavistock).

Stanko, E. (1994) Dancing with denial: researching women and questioning men, in: M. Maynard & J. Purvis (Eds) *Researching Women's Lives from a Feminist Perspective* (London, Taylor & Francis).

Steedman, C. (1988) 'The mother made conscious': the historical development of a primary school pedagogy, in: M. Woodhead & A. McGrath (Eds) *Family, School and Society* (Milton Keynes, Open University Press).

Steinberg, S. (1996) Early childhood as a gendered construction, *Journal of Curriculum Theorizing*, 12, pp. 33–36.

Sumsion, J. & Lubimowski, G. (1998) Male early childhood teachers' hopes, fears and aspirations, *Australian Research in Early Childhood Education*, 5, pp. 70–81.

Williams, C. (1992) The glass escalator: hidden advantages for men in the 'female' professions, *Social Problems*, 39, pp. 253–267.

Williams, C. & Heikes, J. (1993) The importance of researcher's gender in the in-depth interview: evidence from two case studies of male nurses, *Gender & Society*, 7, pp. 280–291.

Williams, C. (1995) *Still a Man's World: men who do women's work* (Berkeley, CA, University of California Press).

Chapter 16

Building social capital in early childhood education and care

An Australian study

Ann Farrell, Collette Tayler and Lee Tennent

Source: *A. Farrell, C. Tayler and L. Tennent, British Educational Research Journal, 30(5), 623–632, 2004.*

Abstract

Mounting research evidence demonstrates that effective 'early childhood education and care' (ECEC) has short-term and longer-term social and educational benefits for children and families. An allied body of evidence attests to the contribution of social capital (i.e. social networks and relationships based on trust) to such benefits. The research reported in this article bridges these two bodies of evidence by researching the social capital of children, their families and community members in the context of a state-wide initiative (in Queensland, Australia) of integrated early childhood and family hubs. Drawn conceptually from the sociology of childhood, a methodological feature of the research is a broadened focus on children, not just adults, as reliable informants of their own everyday experience in ECEC. Some 138 children (aged 4–8 years) in urban and rural/remote localities in Queensland participated in research conversations about their social experience in and beyond ECEC. Children's social capital was found to be higher in the urban community than in the rural community, highlighting the potential of child and family hubs to strengthen children's social capital in those communities with few social facilities.

Mounting research evidence demonstrates that effective 'early childhood education and care' (ECEC) has short-term and long-term social and educational benefits for children and families (Ball, 1994; Schweinhart & Weikert, 1997; McCain & Mustard, 1999; Pascal *et al.*, 1999; Organization for Economic Cooperation and Development [OECD], 2001; Sylva *et al.*, 2003). An allied body of evidence attests to the contribution of social capital (i.e. social relations and networks based on trust and reciprocity) to such benefits (Furstenberg & Hughes, 1995; Runyon *et al.*, 1998; Stone, 2001). The research reported in this article is part of a larger study that bridges and advances these two bodies of evidence by researching the social capital of young children, their families and community members in the context of a state-wide initiative (in Queensland, Australia) of integrated early childhood and family hubs (Tayler *et al.*, 2002; Tennent *et al.*, 2002; Farrell *et al.*, 2003). This ongoing research is funded by the Australian Research Council, while preliminary research received funding and/or in-kind support from the Commonwealth Department of Family and Community Services, Education Queensland, Queensland Department of Families, Queensland Health, Commission for Children and Young People, Crèche & Kindergarten Association of Queensland and Queensland University of Technology. The research questions posed within the larger study are:

- What are the perspectives of stakeholders (i.e. children, parents, hub personnel and service providers) on the child and family hubs?
- What is the impact of the hubs on child, family and community outcomes?
- What factors facilitate and hinder hub development in local communities?

In light of the first of these questions, this article deals with a subset of the child data with respect to their views on social capital.

Our construct of social capital includes micro-social individual behaviour and macro-social structural factors, thus setting 'social relationships, social interactions and social networks in context' (Morrow, 2001, p. 4). A conceptual and methodological distinction of our research drawn from the sociology of children is its broadened focus on children, not just adults, as reliable informants of their own everyday experience (James & Prout, 1997; Mayall, 2003). Children in our research are seen, therefore, as active social agents, who construct and shape the social structures and processes of their lives (Clark *et al.*, 2003).

Social capital, however, is a highly contested theoretical construct (Fine, 1999; Foley & Edwards, 1999; Gamarnikov & Green, 1999; Hawe & Shiell, 2000). Conceptualizations range from Bourdieu's (1986, 1993) sociological account of different, yet interrelated, forms of capital (social, economic, cultural and symbolic) to Putnam's (1993, 2000) popularist notion of social and community networks and civic engagement based on norms of cooperation, reciprocity and mutual trust.

Social capital, nonetheless, has been championed by Australia's Commonwealth Department of Family and Community Services (2000) as one of five key determinants of social and family well-being. Its rationale is that communities high in social capital (evidenced by dense and complex social relationships, helpful information networks, clear-cut norms and perceptions of stability) have significantly higher levels of well-being than communities with limited social capital (evidenced by alienation, fragmentation, loneliness, intolerance and vulnerability (Coleman, 1988; Fegan & Bowes, 1999; Jack & Jordan, 1999).

While social capital may be championed by government and its agencies (as is the case of Australia), its rigorous description, measurement and analysis can prove challenging. Moreover, measurement instruments such as those used by Putnam (1993) in the USA and Stone and Hughes (2000) in Australia are characteristically applied to adults as community members and citizens, with little scope for inclusion of children's accounts of their own social experience. A notable exception is Morrow's (2001) British work on children's accounts of their experience of neighbourhood.

So our research sought to listen to children as key stakeholders in ECEC services, as 'social and cultural actors' (Woodhead & Faulkner, 2000, p. 31), whose accounts should underpin the nature of, and future directions in, the provision of such services.

Methodology

Participants were 138 children (aged 4–8 years) from four schools, two each in rural and urban localities. The rural hub was developed around two state primary schools of 100 students in a remote region of Far North Queensland, and servicing a community of predominantly Australians of European background. Prior to the development of the hub, community facil-ities for children and families in one locality comprised the school only, with one community lacking even a post office or public store. The urban sites (in metropolitan Brisbane), however, were more heterogeneous (in ethnicity, race and language), with access to a range of social and health services, albeit fragmented.

Children were invited to engage in informal conversations with a trained practitioner-researcher within the familiar context of the regular classroom of the hub community. The conversations were approximately 30 minutes in duration and conducted in the naturalistic environs of the classroom. Ethical clearance was given by the University Human Research Ethics Committee and children and parents gave their informed voluntary consent to participate. Conversations were based on six dimensions of social capital (adapted, with permission, from Onyx & Bullen, 1997):

- participation in community activities;
- neighbourhood connections;
- family and friend connections;
- proactivity in a social context;
- feelings of trust and safety; and
- tolerance of diversity.

In addition, as per previous studies by Evans and Fuller (1998) and Farrell *et al.* (2002a), children were asked the following questions about their pre-school or school life in informal conversations with teachers:

- Why do you come here?
- What do you like about coming here?
- What don't you like about coming here?

Children were also asked:

- If a new person comes here, what would they need to know to be happy?

These questions provided children with the opportunity to disclose additional perspectives on their social experience and to demonstrate 'alternate' perspective-taking, as in the case of providing advice to a newcomer.

Quantitative data were coded and analysed using *SPSS for Windows* with frequency statistics used to identify patterns among the responses, while open-ended responses underwent thematic analysis to generate discursive themes within the data set. This latter analytic approach identifies the actual categories that participants – in this case, children – use to 'make sense of people and events' (Silverman, 1998, p. 88). Such analysis searches for the categories that the children themselves introduce as they describe their everyday social worlds. The value of this analytic approach is 'that it can uncover and formulate functions which practices facilitate, yet which are, or were, unrecognised or unappreciated by members' (Heap, 1990, p. 47). Thus, it makes visible the ordinary and everyday experiences of children (Silverman, 2001).

Findings

Table 16.1 shows children's responses to the social capital items. More than twice as many urban children compared to rural children were found to be members of clubs or groups, while rural children were marginally less likely than urban children to visit friends, relatives or neighbours very often. Rural children were marginally less likely to agree that they would help a friend with schoolwork (one child explaining this as 'cheating') and substantially less likely to agree that they liked being with people who were different from them. The only difference, according to the four different age groups, was an increase over the years in children's club or group membership.

Why do you come here?

There were no ascertainable differences between the responses of rural and urban children as to why they believed they came to the facility. As Table 16.2 indicates, a clear majority of pre-school children believed that they came to

Table 16.1 Percentage responses to social capital items (according to locality and year level)

	Location		Grade			
	Rural (n = 42)	Urban (n = 96)	Pre-school	Year 1	Year 2	Year 3
Are you in any clubs or groups?	17	36	11.8	27.3	27.5	58.1
Do you visit friends or relatives very often?	67	77	73.5	72.7	67.5	83.9
Do you get to visit neighbours very often?	50	68	61.8	57.6	57.5	51.6
Do you trust most people?	62	94	76.5	69.7	57.5	61.3
Do you feel safe living in this area?	93	93	91.2	100.0	90.0	93.5
Would you pick up other people's rubbish in the playground?	93	99	88.2	90.9	97.5	93.5
If a friend was having difficulty with schoolwork would you help them out?	86	99	94.1	100.0	97.5	87.1
Do you like being with people who are different to you (like from another country)?	48	90	84.8	75.8	67.5	80.6

Table 16.2 Responses to 'Why do you come here?'

	Age group			
	Pre-school %	Year 1 %	Year 2 %	Year 3 %
I like it	59.3	36.4	30.5	4.0
Practical issues (live close by/siblings come/Mum & Dad make me)	18.5	45.5	24.9	32.2
It's a good/the best school/nice teachers	0.0	0.0	11.1	39.3
We learn	3.7	30.3	47.2	25.0
To make friends	0.0	0.0	8.3	17.9

pre-school simply because they liked it. Among Year 1 children, practical issues such as proximity of the school or choices made by parents dominated responses, whereas in Year 2, 'to learn' became the primary reason. By Year 3, children's responses focused on attributes of their school and possibility of friendship.

Table 16.3 Responses to 'What do you like about coming here?'

| | Age group | | | |
	Pre-school %	Year 1 %	Year 2 %	Year 3 %
Being/playing with others	25.0	25.7	54.5	40.0
Learning/work/literacy/numeracy/computers	46.9	65.7	21.2	24.0
Outdoor games/facilities	28.1	17.1	39.4	24.0
Construction, making things	40.1	8.6	6.1	4.0
Play/playing/playtime	6.2	17.1	9.1	2.0
Symbolic/pretend play	18.7	2.8	0.0	0.0

What do you like about coming here?

As Table 16.3 demonstrates, children's responses varied according to their age group, with the most enjoyable aspects of school, for pre-school and Year 1 children, being learning activities. Construction activities and symbolic play were notably popular among pre-schoolers, while among Year 2 and 3 children, being or playing with friends was the most liked aspect of coming to school.

What don't you like about coming here?

Regardless of their age, children's responses focused on the unpleasant behaviours of others (see Table 16.4). Many children referred to instances of what they labelled as 'bullying', often at the hands of peers, as negative experiences.

What would a new person need to know in order to be happy here?

Table 16.5 illustrates the most common types of advice that children thought they might offer a newcomer, with the number and complexity of suggestions increasing with the age of the respondent. More than other groups,

Table 16.4 Responses to 'What don't you like about coming here?'

| | Age group | | | |
	Pre-school %	Year 1 %	Year 2 %	Year 3 %
Bullying/upsetting behaviour	71.4	74.1	52.6	52.2
Specific subjects/activities	14.3	14.8	15.8	4.3
Boring/nothing to do	0.0	11.1	5.3	8.7

Table 16.5 Responses to 'What advice would you give to a newcomer?'

| | Age group | | | |
	Pre-school %	Year 1 %	Year 2 %	Year 3 %
That I'll play with them/help teach them	42.8	56.7	68.6	32.0
Where things are	10.7	51.3	40.0	71.4
Rules/routines	3.6	13.5	14.3	28.0
How to behave	28.6	18.9	14.3	12.0
Other's names	0.0	10.8	22.8	24.0

pre-schoolers recommended newcomers be aware of behavioural expectations and, with the exception of Year 3 children, the most common response across the sample was: an offer of friendship or help with doing things. The older children were more concerned than were the younger children that newcomers know where things are and comply with rules.

Discussion

Such findings indicated that, according to Onyx and Bullen's (1997) measure, children's social capital was higher in the urban community than in the rural community. In relation to individual dimensions, it was encouraging that the majority of children in both the rural and the urban communities agreed that they felt safe. Rural children were half as likely to be involved in clubs, and marginally less likely to visit friends, relatives or neighbours. Many in the rural community lived some distance from people and facilities, so, for these children, school offered the sole or primary opportunity for socialization outside the immediate family. This has important implications for the social capital potential of child and family hubs within rural communities, where hitherto the school was the primary facility for socialization outside the family.

Children in the urban community were marginally more likely to agree that they trusted most people but nearly twice as likely to agree that they liked being with people who were different from them. It is probable that this acceptance of others stems from the ethnic diversity that characterizes the urban locality. Similar exposure to other cultures through increased socialization or increased awareness (potentially developed in the hub) may help to increase rural children's exposure to and respect for people who are different from them.

It was clear from the open-ended questions (e.g. What do you like about being here?), that most children across the two communities enjoyed their school life. Indeed, more than half of the pre-school children interviewed believed that the reason they attended pre-school was *because* they liked it so much. This enjoyment is especially important given that positive experiences within ECEC can contribute to children's well-being. Findings suggest that, in order to best facilitate positive experiences, children's changing needs and interests need to be considered (for example, pre-schoolers' enjoyment of pretend play and construction activities). Socializing and making friends appeared to become more salient in the upper years, at a time when children's relationships outside of the home may assume greater importance. These older children were also more likely to comment that they were members of clubs or groups. Overall, there was enjoyment of learning, socialization, playing outdoors and an appreciation of things unique to individual settings. This is consistent with findings by Sheridan and Samuelson (2001), who also noted a preference for outdoor play in Swedish pre-school children.

Children's emerging enjoyment of learning, friendships and physical activity were tempered, however, by less pleasant experiences. Almost three-quarters of pre-school and Year 1 children and more than half of Year 2 and Year 3 children in both localities referred to acts of verbal or physical aggression by other children as a source of unhappiness. Acts of aggression were also a 'least favourite' activity among day care children in an earlier study by Armstrong and Sugawara (1989) and one of five aspects of nursery school that children in Evans and Fuller's (1998) study disliked. Accounts of the adverse social behaviour that some children label as bullying should be of concern to policy makers and practitioners given its potentially harmful emotional and physical effects (Homel, 1998; Farrell, 1999). As Evans and Fuller (1998) noted, such reports call for 'vigilance by practitioners to ensure that children's rights not to endure such experiences are met' (p. 73).

One of the enduring challenges for children was adapting to the new ECEC environment. Thus, it is important for policy makers and practitioners to understand what factors facilitate a smooth and effective transition for these children and thereby enhance their social capital. In relation to advice for newcomers, pre-school, Year 1 and Year 2 children focused on emotional support and assistance with tasks. Year 3 children, on the other hand, were primarily concerned with pragmatic issues such as time, place, rules, routines and people's names. This emerging awareness of the social geography and daily routines of school life corroborated earlier research on children's competent awareness of the institution's social geography (Farrell et al., 2002a, b). Such evidence demonstrates the need for further methodological innovation to uncover, in greater depth, other aspects of the social geography of children's worlds, within the hub services and extending to the broader community in which the hub operates.

Thus, this work highlights the conceptual merit of piloting and refining the methodological and analytic use of children's views of social capital, rarely considered in interdepartmental and cross-sectoral planning of services of this nature and magnitude. That children express their views on issues that concern them and affect their everyday lives is central to the provision of integrated health, care and education services for families and children. In this way, children are validated stakeholders in ECEC, who, in Australia, have hitherto not been listened to in social capital research. A challenge for this research field is for practitioners and policy makers to promote the social dimensions of communities within and beyond ECEC that stand to enhance social capital and, in turn, contribute to the well-being of young children, their families and communities.

References

Armstrong, J. & Sugawara, A. I. (1989) Children's perceptions of their day care experiences, *Early Child Development and Care*, 49, 1–15.

Ball, C. (1994) *Start right: the importance of early learning* (London, RSA Report).

Bourdieu, P. (1986) On the family as a realized category, *Theory, Culture & Society*, 13(3), 19–26.

Bourdieu, P. (1993) *Sociology in question* (London, Sage).

Clark, A., McQuail, S. & Moss, P. (2003) *Exploring the field of listening to and consulting with young children* (London, Department for Education and Skills).

Coleman, J. S. (1988) Social capital in the creation of human capital, *American Journal of Sociology*, 94, 94–120.

Commonwealth Department of Family and Community Services (2000) *Indicators of social and family functioning* (Canberra, ACT, Australian Commonwealth Government).

Evans, P. & Fuller, M. (1998) Children's perceptions of their nursery education, *International Journal of Early Years Education*, 6(1), 59–74.

Farrell, A. (1999) Bullying: a case for early intervention, *Australian and New Zealand Journal of Law and Education*, 4(1), 40–46.

Farrell, A., Tayler, C, Tennent, L. & Gahan, D. (2002a) Listening to children: a study of child and family services, *Early Years*, 22(1), 27–38.

Farrell, A., Tayler, C. & Tennent, L. (2002b) Early childhood services: what can children tell us? *Australian Journal of Early Childhood*, 27(3), 12–18.

Farrell, A., Tayler, C. & Tennent, L. (2003) Social capital and early childhood education, *Perspectives on Educational Leadership*, 13(7), 1–2.

Fegan, M. & Bowes, J. (1999) Isolation in rural, remote and urban communities, in: J. M. Bowes & A. Hayes (Eds) *Children, families, and communities. Contexts and consequences* (Melbourne, Oxford University Press), 115–135.

Fine, B. (1999) The developmental state is dead—long live social capital? *Development and Change*, 30, 1–19.

Foley, M. & Edwards, B. (1999) Is it time to disinvest in social capital? *Journal of Public Policy*, 19(2), 141–173.

Furstenberg, F. R. & Hughes, M. E. (1995) Social capital and successful development among at-risk youth, *Journal of Marriage and the Family*, 57, 580–592.

Gamarnikov, E. & Green, A. (1999) The third way and social capital: education action zones and a new agenda for education, parents and community? *International Studies in Sociology of Education*, 9(1), 3–22.

Hawe, P. & Shiell, P. (2000) Social capital and health promotion: a review, *Social Science and Medicine*, 51, 871–885.

Heap, J. (1999) Applied ethnomethodology, *Human Studies*, 13, 39–72.

Homel, R. (1998) *A report for the National Campaign against Violence and Crime and the National Crime Strategy* (Canberra, ACT, Developmental Crime Prevention Consortium).

Jack, G. & Jordan, B. (1999) Social capital and child welfare, *Children and Society*, 13, 242–256.

James, A. & Prout, A. (Eds) (1997) *Constructing and reconstructing childhood. Contemporary issues in the sociological study of childhood* (London, Falmer Press).

Mayall, B. (2003) *Sociologies of childhood and educational thinking* (London, Institute of Education).

McCain, M. & Mustard, F. (1999) *Reversing the brain-drain. The Early Years Study* (Toronto, Children's Secretariat). Available online at: http://www.childsec.gov.on.ca.

Morrow, V. (2001) *Networks and neighbourhood: children's and young people's perspectives* (London, NHS Health Development Agency).

Onyx, J. & Bullen, P. (1997) *Measuring social capital in five communities* (Sydney, University of Technology).

Organization for Economic Cooperation and Development (OECD) (2001) *Starting strong. Early education and care. Report on an OECD Thematic Review* (Paris, OECD).

Pascal, C., Bertram, T., Gasper, M., Mould, C, Ramsden, F. & Saunders, M. (1999) *Research to inform the early excellence centres' pilot program* (Worcester, Centre for Research in Early Childhood).

Putnam, R. (1993) *Making democracy work. Civic traditions in modern Italy* (Princeton, NJ, Princeton University Press).

Putnam, R. (2000) *Bowling alone: the collapse and revival of American community* (New York, Simon & Schuster).

Runyan, D. K., Hunter, W. M., Socolar, R. *et al.* (1998) Children who prosper in unfavourable environments: the relationship to social capital, *Pediatrics*, 101(1), 12–18.

Schweinhart, L. J. & Weikert, D. P. (1997) *Lasting differences: the High/Scope Preschool Curriculum Comparison Study through Age 23* (Ypsilanti, MI, High/Scope Press).

Sheridan, S. & Samuelsson, I. P. (2001) Children's conceptions of participation and influence in preschool: a perspective on pedagogical quality, *Contemporary Issues in Early Childhood*, 2(2), 169–194.

Silverman, D. (1998) *Harvey Sacks: social science and conversation analysis* (Cambridge, Polity Press).

Silverman, D. (2001) *Interpreting qualitative data* (2nd edn) (London, Sage).

Stone, W. (2001) *Measuring social capital. Towards a theoretically informed measurement framework for researching social capital in family and community life* (Melbourne, Australian Institute of Family Studies).

Stone, W. & Hughes, J. (2000) What role for social capital in family policy? *Family Matters*, 56, 20–28.

Sylva, K., Siraj-Blatchford, I. & Taggart, B. (2003) *Assessing quality in the early years* (Stoke on Trent, Trentham Books).

Tayler, C, Tennent, L., Farrell, A. & Gahan, D. (2002) Use and integration of early childhood services: insights from an inner city community, *Journal of Australian Research in Early Childhood Education*, 9(1), 113–123.

Tennent, L., Tayler, C. & Farrell, A. (2002) Integrated service hubs: potential outcomes for children and communities, *Australian Association for Educational Research Conference Proceedings*, Brisbane, 1–5 December. Available online at: http:www.aare.edu.au.index.htm. TEN02259 (accessed 1 November 2003).

Woodhead, M. & Faulkner, D. (2000) Subjects, objects or participants? in: P. Christensen & A. James (Eds) *Research with children. Perspectives and practices* (London, Falmer Press), 9–33.

Chapter 17

Gendered childhoods
A cross-disciplinary overview

Heather Montgomery

Source: *H. Montgomery, Gender and Education, 17(5), 471–482, 2005.*

Abstract

The last three decades have seen the emergence of a new discipline of childhood studies, made up of contributions from sociology, anthropology and cultural studies, challenging previous studies of children based on paradigms from psychology and education. This new discipline has revolutionized the study of children and demanded that they be looked as important subjects in their own right. Tensions remain, however, between studies of gender and those of generation, and the importance of the latter has sometimes been overlooked as researchers concentrate on childhood as an age related experience and not a gendered one. This article looks at how this has come about and the ways in which the study of these two aspects of children's lives needs to be better integrated.

Children are pygmies among giants, ignorant among the knowledgeable, wordless among the articulate. … And to the adults, children everywhere represent something weak and helpless, in need of protection, supervision, training, models, skills, beliefs, education.

(Mead & Wolfenstein, 1955, p. 7)

Introduction

The last decade has seen an upsurge of interest in childhood studies and a re-examination of the ways in which children and their lives have been understood and analyzed within the social sciences. Anthropology, sociology and cultural studies all now have thriving sub-disciplines which focus primarily on children and which have challenged the dominant paradigms that developmental psychology and education have traditionally brought to the study of children.

While this new interest is very welcome, and long overdue, it has also raised problems of inter-disciplinarity and although there is a great deal of work in many fields, researchers rarely talk across disciplinary boundaries or are aware of developments in fields outside their own. As an anthropologist working on the ways that anthropologists have written about children, I have become aware of the gaps that exist in the discourse between educationalists, sociologists and anthropologists and the ways in which anthropologists have focused on certain aspects of children's lives while delegating other facets to other disciplines. In doing so, certain features of children's lives have fallen through the disciplinary gaps and remained under-theorized. Nowhere is this more obvious than in the theoretical interplay between studies of women and studies of children which have, at times, appeared mutually antagonistic with children being seen either as a problematic aspect of women's gender roles, or by those interested in child-centred research, as a distinct category of people often unconnected to their carers.

This article will be in three parts. The first will look briefly at how the conceptual and practical relationship between women and children has been viewed by sociologists and educationalists, a debate in which anthropologists have played little part. It will then turn to how anthropologists have understood children in the past and the roles that children have played in ethnographic monographs and in anthropological theory, including a brief examination of the more recent field of child-centred anthropology and the insights this has brought to the study of children. The final part will look specifically at the role of gender in children's lives, focusing on the ways that girls' labour has been routinely missed, ignored or mistaken for socialization. An article of this length cannot be comprehensive or cover all theorists, but by referring to certain key ethnographic monographs, I aim to pull out some central themes and argue for the need for more careful examinations of the role of gender in children's lives.

'The same lousy boat'

While children have been present, if marginal, in ethnographic monographs, in sociology, they have been more extensively politicized and their role as social subordinates discussed in much greater detail. Studies of children in sociology sprang directly out of the second wave feminism of the early 1970s, which acknowledged the shared political and social subordination of women and children, while questioning why women's lives were conceptually and practically tied to those of children. Feminist sociologists, while acknowledging that studies of women, by necessity, had to include studies of children, also saw the relationship between women and children as complex and possibly conflictual. Drawing on Marxist theories, and the work of Engels in particular, it was argued that women and children were equally subordinated under patriarchy, both taking on the role of an oppressed proletariat in the household. Yet, it was equally clear that women and children did not have the same interests and that while, in some circumstances, children and women might be allies, they could also be enemies, their interests inimical to each other. Shulamith Firestone, one of the first feminist writers to look specifically at children and childhood argued, that 'The heart of women's oppression is her childbearing and childrearing role' (1971, p. 79). Writers such as Firestone acknowledged the practical restraints that children put on women and argued convincingly that until children and their care were seen as a social rather than a maternal issue, women could not truly be liberated, and would remain in 'the same lousy boat' (1971, p. 102). Although Firestone, amongst others, recognized that children too were oppressed and in need of liberation, this liberation was less about their own needs and more of a way of freeing women from the confines of the home and of the drudgery of childbirth and childrearing.

The ideological uses of children and the construction of their needs has been a key theme in feminist sociology. As Denise Riley shows so clearly in *The war in the nursery* (1984), ideas about childhood and the demands of children cannot be seen as politically neutral. While Firestone saw women's childrearing as being at the heart of their oppression, Riley looked at the ways in which society reinforced this oppression by imposing a model of universal, unchanging biological needs into understandings of childhood so that ideas such as bonding or maternal attachment became seen as enduring and unchallengeable facts rather than the product of studies on particular children in particular circumstances. Other writers such as Caroline New and Miriam David (1985) drew on their own experiences of being mothers and their own issues with childcare in order to show that when it came to children, the personal *was* the political and that as long as children remained the primary responsibility of women, then feminist sociology could not disengage from studies of childhood.

The rise of feminist sociology in the 1970s politicized the role of children but it had little interest in them as subjects for research. An analysis of gender necessitated an analysis of childhood but not from the perspective of children themselves but through a particular lens which saw children as women's special responsibility and about which women would be the most reliable informants. As Ann Oakley argues:

> What happened was that the deconstruction of notions of 'the family', and the uncovering of biases in theoretical assumptions made about women, resulted in an emphasis on *women's* experiences of children rather than *children's* experiences of women (or of anything else). Children came to be represented as a *problem* to women. This reflected the political concerns within the women's movement to do with freeing women from compulsory motherhood and childcare work.
>
> (1994, p. 22)

It was only when academics began to focus directly on children as their primary unit of analysis that other power structures and other ways of understanding children began to be acknowledged. Oakley (1994) pointed out that while historically there were parallels in the social and political position of women and children, they did, in fact, have very different positions in society and that an understanding of women, even if it included work on children and childcare, was not adequate for analyzing children's lives. Judith Ennew (1986) argued that women and children had very different access to political, social and economic structures, both within the family and outside and therefore the assumption that they have the same agenda or that what was beneficial to women was also beneficial for children, was not necessarily true. Furthermore, she argued that while both women and children occupied subservient positions in relation to men, as adults, women wielded enormous, unchecked power over children and that this power could be abused.

This work has been enormously influential and has opened up the study of children as subjects of research in their own right rather than as part of women's experiences. However, tension between the study of women's and children's worlds continues. The rise of research which focuses directly on children's lives has meant that those who centre their work on children have pulled away from work done in gender studies. In 1994 Ann Oakley warned that, 'Because women's studies neglected *children*, there may be a contrary impulse among male academics studying children to neglect *gender*' (Oakley, 1994, p. 22). It is not just male academics however, who neglect gender in children's lives. While feminist sociologists have looked at the impact of children on women's lives and childhood studies specialists have looked at the role of adults in children's lives, and at children's own experiences, understandings and world views, discussions of gender have fallen through the gaps and there remains a marked reluctance in disciplines such as anthropology to study childhood as a gendered experience as well as an age related one.

Childhood at the margins

The specific study of children in anthropology has a much shorted history. Anthropologists have long pointed out the economic significance of children, their role in legitimating marriages and the implied economic contracts at marriage which assign children to one lineage or another. They have looked at the ways that adults have shaped children, both socially in order to make them full persons within their communities and physically through the use of corporal punishment or through practices designed to teach them bravery or how to cope with pain without fear. They have noted the presence of children in their studies of culture, and they have sometimes used them directly as informants to find out in more detail aspects of that culture. They have implicitly acknowledged the importance of age, gender or position in the family, and discussed the ways in which a firstborn child was dealt with differently from the youngest child (see Fortes, 1974). Until recently however, children have been marginal to anthropological theory, a backdrop to more mainstream concerns of kinship or political organization. Holistic studies of small-scale societies such as those pioneered by Malinowski (1922), Radcliffe-Browne (1933) or Firth (1936), inevitably acknowledged children and their role in the family but paid little attention to their economic contributions, their agency or their own understandings of their lives. For many such anthropologists, the study of a social phenomenon or a cultural group implied a process of socialization that everyone in that group has passed through. They made the assumption that adults were the finished product of this socialization process and therefore the best, and indeed only, source of information about the society. As Jean La Fontaine argued: 'In general, anthropology has retained an outdated view of children as raw material, unfinished specimens of the social beings whose ideas and behaviour are the proper subject matter for social science' (1986, p. 10).

North American anthropology appeared to show a keener interest in children, especially anthropologists such as Margaret Mead or Ruth Benedict or their followers in the culture and personality school. Drawing heavily on psychological theory, and Freudian theory in particular, they attempted to explain how a child, born without culture, and as a purely biological being was formed into a cultural one. Education was understood as the way in which children were brought up to know their proper role in society and it was a role they accepted without challenge. Margaret Mead argued in her most famous book, *Coming of age in Samoa*, that the study of Samoan girls was a 'tale of another way of life [which] is mainly concerned with education, with the process by which the baby, arrived cultureless upon the human scene, becomes a full-fledged adult member of his or her society' (Mead, 1928, p. 18). The culture and personality school paid particular attention as to how childcare practices such as weaning or discipline affected personalities and, as such, how they were key to understanding the collective culture of a society. However, while children were the locus of study, these anthropologists were not interested in children themselves but in the ways in which the bodily practices imposed on children affected future personality at both an individual and a national level. As Super and Harkness put it:

> ... although the focus of data collection in these studies may be childhood, the focus of theoretical interest is apt to be adulthood. It is almost as if the anthropologist were Freud talking to one of his women patients: the issue of concern is the functioning of the adult, not the life of the child.
>
> (Harkness & Super, 1983, p. 222)

Many of the above problems can be best illustrated by looking at the ways in which anthropologists have described socialization, and in particular, children's roles and understandings of it. Because children have tended to be seen as passive, empty bottles into which culture is gradually poured, attempts to describe the ways in which children grow up have either concentrated on the minutiae of daily routines or much more broadly on social structures such as age sets or initiation. The early years of childhood have often been overlooked because there seems to be comparatively little to say about them and no way of accessing these children as informants. Overt discipline, physical punishment or the sorts of duties children can be expected to carry out have all been commented on but there is often a tendency to view young children as relatively marginal to a society and as beings who acquire its habits and characteristics by a form of osmosis. From the earliest ethnographies which attempted to discuss all aspects of social life, children appear to be outside the main society, waiting patiently to be regarded as interesting only when they grow up. Indeed, in her pioneering study of Manus children in Papua New Guinea, Margaret Mead (1930) described an indifference to adult life and claimed that children had 'a dull, uninteresting child life, romping good-naturedly until they are tired, then lying inert and breathless until rested sufficiently to romp again' (1930, p. 14). Among a different community in Melanesia, the Lesu, Hortense Powdermaker made similar claims.

> As a whole, the children are in the background. They are given sufficient care to see that they do not fall into trouble, but they are not the centre of attention. For the most part they are onlookers and minor participants in the adult activities. It is in this that much of their education consists.
>   (Powdermaker, 1933, pp. 85–86)

Her view of Lesu children is interesting in this regard, not only because it shows up some of her assumptions about children and ways of childrearing, but it also helps to explain anthropologists' lack of interest in children. For both her and Mead, children are dull, marginal and largely separate from the adult world, and of little interest to adults in general and anthropologists in particular. Education, like socialization, was something that happened to children, that they had little awareness of, and little part in. It is also noticeable in the language of these monographs that 'the child' is represented without reference to gender or age. As children were of so little interest, even such fundamental differences between children were never analyzed. Although Mead and Powdermaker discuss the difference in duties and responsibilities for boys and girls, the idea of childhood as gendered experience is not examined. The child remained, as Judith Ennew put it 'that strange, ungendered isolate' (quoted in Oakley, 1994, p. 21).

It was not until the 1970s that children started to become of interest to anthropologists, not simply as passive beings who were socialized by others but as people in their own right. Charlotte Hardman (1973) and Enid Schildkrout (1978) published groundbreaking articles in which they claimed that children's lives were as worthy of study as any other section of society and, furthermore, that a focus on children could reveal aspects of social life not found in more conventional ethnographies. By the 1980s, others, most notably Allison James, Jean La Fontaine and Judith Ennew, challenged the notion that children were simply 'raw material' and began to show an interest in children both methodologically and ethnographically. As anthropology at this time had relatively little to say about children it is interesting to note how heavily these anthropologists had to draw on sociological and psychological theories for their analyses of children's role and status within society. This borrowing was somewhat selective however and the large literature on childcare policies mentioned previously did not figure. The focus of these anthropologists writing about children was on children's lives rather than childcare and children's effect on the lives of women. In this, they were joined by sociologists such as Jens Qvortup (1994), Alan Prout (James & Prout, 1997; James et al., 1998) and Chris Jenks (1992). Whatever the disciplinary background, those interested in working with children promoted 'child-centred' research, which involved conceptualizing children as social actors and agents, capable of participating in making sense of their own lives, and of describing and explaining their actions, motivations and meanings. It aimed to understand children's effects on adults and their communities, and concentrated on them as human beings rather than as 'human becomings'. Child-centred research removed the study of childhood from studies of socialization or enculturation, which, as Peter Gow observes:

> … necessarily imply that what children do is directed at the future goal of being a fully socialized or enculturated adult. Not only are these teleological views biologically unsustainable, they also significantly distort the manner in which the specificities of human ontogenies are already predicated on the complexities of human social relations.
>
> (Gow, 2001, p. 1)

Child-centred anthropology entailed bringing children in from the margins of anthropological literature, where references to them had previously been located, and placing them at the centre of research projects. Equally importantly, it challenged previous methodologies of finding out about children. A child-centred anthropology viewed children as the best informants of their own lives and worlds, and therefore insisted on the necessity of interviewing children directly and taking on board their subjectivities. Finally, those who promoted child-centred anthropology argued, alongside sociologists such as Ann Oakley, for the breakage of the conceptual link between women and children. Jean La Fontaine argued: 'the salient distinction on which family roles are based appears to be that of generation not gender' (1990, p. 187).

Studies of socialization in which children are seen as raw material are now rare and ethnographic accounts of children's lives routinely examine issues such as children's agency, techniques of research with children as well as the various competing and conflicting conceptualizations and constructions of childhood.

Notions of childhood have been deconstructed and visions of the child, as set out in international legislation, such as the UNCRC (United Nations Convention on the Rights of the Child), have provided much scope for analysis. It is unsurprising therefore that many of those who claim to be child-centred anthropologists have specialized in ethnographies of children in 'especially difficult circumstances', such as street children, refugee children, child soldiers or child prostitutes because it is these children who challenge the Western ideal of childhood as a safe, enclosed environment in which children are protected until the age of 18 from the adult concerns of work, sex, death and money. In attempting to get away from studies of children within the family, many anthropologists have turned to those outside the family who appear to exist either on their own or with other children away from adults and it is very noticeable that the most extensively studied category of children written about by anthropologists has been street children (see Ennew, 1994; Baker, 1998; Hecht, 1998; Burr, 2000; Panter-Brick, 2000, 2001). There have, of course, been anthropologists, especially those from Scandinavia (see Gullestad, 1984; Solberg, 1988) who have examined children's relationships and daily lives within families and recognized children's importance in social and community relationships. Equally many anthropologists who have worked in Britain such as Allison James (1993) or Anna Laerke (1998) have worked in schools. Nevertheless, studies of street children or child labourers have often dominated anthropological accounts of childhoods around the world and have often been used as vehicles to examine other ideas, for example the universal applicability of children's rights or the cultural politics of childhood (see the contributors to the volumes edited by Scheper-Hughes, 1998; or Stephens, 1995). Analysis of the lives of these children has yielded important theoretical insights, but it has also had the unintended effect of sidelining children's experiences of gender roles and understandings. There is surprisingly little systematic research on how children learn gender, how they understand it and negotiate it on a daily basis, even though this sort of study is well established in the study of adult women. There has been a backing away from an analysis of gender in the lives of children and other factors, such as location, profession or familial relationships have been given much greater prominence.

Gender socialization

As suggested previously, the emphasis on generation as the primary point of interest in the study of children has been important in that it has set up the study of children's lives as a legitimate, stand alone area but in doing so, it has sidelined gender. Studies of socialization, and indeed more holistic ethnographic studies, have assumed that gender is something that affects children intimately but which they do not negotiate or challenge. It is acknowledged but it remains under-analyzed. This is particularly true in discussions of the very important economic roles that young girls play in many societies and the ways that these roles are analyzed by anthropologists. There is often a conceptual blurring between education, socialization and economic activity so that children's agency is overlooked and their contribution to the household is only implicitly acknowledged. This, coupled with the tendency to play down women's economic significance (Oakley, 1985), has meant that discussions of girls' lives have been doubly blind to their role within the family and to the specific economic contributions they make to the economy; overlooked as both children and females. Many ethnographies take it as axiomatic that boys and girls are taught about their roles in society in different ways, but within many anthropological monographs these processes are viewed as unspoken, uncontested and unchallenged. The differences between boys and girls have been described, as have the ways in which divisions of labour often map onto divisions of space, so that girls are associated with the private sphere and women's activities whereas boys have a greater degree of physical freedom and learn to take their place in the public, male sphere (Miles, 1994). Isaac Schapera, for example, quotes a saying from his informants, the Kgatla of South Africa which states: 'A boy takes his law from the council place (i.e., his father), a girl takes her law from the compound (i.e., from her mother)' (1971, p. 226). However, children's own understandings of these processes are never asked and gender is often essentialized and downplayed; presented as a matter of fact rather than of negotiation. Yet the centrality of gender in children's lives is such that the very length of childhood may be determined by gender rather than chronological age, biological changes or socially recognized rites of passage. Napoleon Chagnon, for example, writes of the Yanamano (an Amerindian group living on the Brazilian/Venezuelan border):

> A girl's childhood ends sooner than a boy's. The game of playing house fades imperceptively into a constant responsibility to help mother. By the time a girl is ten years old or so, she has become an economic asset to the mother and spends a great deal of time working. Little boys, by contrast, spend hours playing among themselves and are able to prolong their childhood into their late teens if they so wish. By that time a girl has married, and may even have a child or two.
>
> (Chagnon, 1968, p. 85)

Anthropologists have, therefore, acknowledged that gender has a profound impact on children's lives and from the earliest ethnographies onwards have discussed at length how girls and boys have different roles and responsibilities within their families and communities and how these can be mapped both spatially and conceptually. Hortense Powdermaker, for example, discussed the very different childhoods of boys and girls, with girls being brought up to be helpful to their mothers at a much earlier age while boys were expected to be irresponsible (1933). Even in more contemporary accounts of children's lives, this assumption of unquestioned gender division, where girls are socially responsible at a much earlier age, remains an important feature. Annette Hamilton (1981) discusses at length the different roles and responsibilities of boys and girls among Australian Aborigines, and notes how girls are expected to do much more than boys, and also to take instructions from men in the same way that older women do, while there is less expectation on boys to be compliant and obedient. In other contexts too, the centrality of children's gender is stated as a fact so that, among the Fulani of West Africa, a girl is encouraged to look after younger siblings from the age of three or four, collect water and firewood and cook, and from the age of around six, is expected to pound grain, weave and sew while there is no such expectation for boys (Johnson, 2000). Such distinctions are usually taken for granted and based on adult observation and adult views, neither girls nor boys are asked about their work or their understandings of their gender.

What is a consistent feature of these studies is the continual downplaying of girls' work as a form of economic activity. It is interesting to note that while all the above authors (and indeed many others) note the earlier burden of responsibility for girls, they fail to point out the economic significance of girls' work and the important role they play in household economics, preferring instead to see it as socialization or education for the future. Until relatively recently, there was almost no acknowledgement of the economic function of children, their contribution to the household economy, or their ability to free up other members of the household to take on economic work, yet studies such as that carried out by Enid Schildkrout showed how crucial children are to both the economy and the social system. In her study of a Hausa community in Nigeria (1978), she showed how children's labour, in the form of their ability to carry out errands, and sell the goods their mothers made at home, enabled that community to enforce its strict purdah laws. As women could not leave the house, it was children who acted as go-betweens and enabled women to be economically productive without breaching social codes. This blindness to the work of children is shared by many. Olga Nieuwenhuys (1996) argues that anthropologists have often ignored the amount of hard and heavy work that children do and that by calling work on the family land or in the family home, socialization or play, they have not allowed themselves to see economic activity. It is also worth noting that girls themselves will also under value their own work. Pamela Reynolds, in her study of child labour in the Zambezi, watched a 14-year-old girl prepare a breakfast of porridge for herself and her younger brother, wash the plates from the previous night's meal and collect water twice from a source two kilometres away. Yet when questioned directly about what she had done that morning replied simply, 'Nothing' (Reynolds, 1991).

Those who have carried out detailed studies of children's time and activities have shown that children contribute a great deal to households in economic terms but that this may not be seen either by themselves or their parents as useful and productive labour, especially when those doing the labour are girls. What is missing from such studies is a discussion of gender roles and how children come to understand these roles and the duties associated with them. The category 'children' is often used to obscure the gendered roles that make boys' and girls' childhood so different. In Java, for example, parents claimed that children did not work, they just tended the ducks, cared for their younger siblings or collected firewood, even though these activities took up several hours a day (Hull, 1975). Adults associated work with the activities done to keep a family together and the responsibilities that came with family life. They looked on the children's work as a form of indulgence, wiling away the days watching ducks, without the pressures and duties that came with adulthood. However, it is not made explicit in such instances which children perform these tasks. Housework was specifically discounted as work (and it is probably safe to assume that girls undertook the majority of this) and many parents claimed that children who did not work as labourers outside the family were economically unproductive and a drain on household income rather than an addition. It was only when the children were older and began to be involved with waged labour that these parents began to see their children as actively contributing to the household and acknowledged the importance of their contribution. Boys were much more likely than girls to undertake waged labour outside the house and therefore less likely to be perceived as an economic burden on their parents. Such a study cries out for a greater analysis of children's gender roles – looking in detail at whether boys are working only when they are older or whether all children work from a young age but only when money is involved is it publicly acknowledged as work. We need much more information about how gender roles map onto children's lives and how they negotiate or challenge them.

In terms of the often hidden domestic labour done by girls, this inability to see girls' labour is especially obvious and while there are many studies of waged, and often exploitative, child labour (see Ennew, 1984; Blanchet, 1996; Berlan, 2004), studies of girls' domestic work are rare and the very real contribution of their labour is frequently unnoticed (although there are notable exceptions such as Ennew, 1993; Nieuwenhuys, 1994). This is especially noticeable in the case of childcare, the most common form of work that girls undertake. It is usual in large parts of Africa, Asia and Amazonia for girls to look after younger siblings or cousins at a very early age. Very rarely is this seen by them, their parents or anthropologists as work. Instead, it is assumed to be a useful preparation for their role as mothers later on as well as a way of easing their mother's burden and allowing her to be more productive (Wolf, 1972; Johnson, 2000). Yet the importance of children caring for other children is very real. Margaret Wolf, for example, comments on the fact that girls in rural Taiwan are disciplined much more harshly than their brothers because of the burdens of responsibility that they have. 'Obedience training comes earlier for girls than for boys, less by plan than by accident of role requirements. A child who must be responsible for another child's welfare cannot be allowed to disobey on whim' (1972, p. 79). Despite this, however, childcare is still discounted as productive labour. It is also very rare that this view is challenged or that children themselves are asked their opinions on what they do, although Margaret Mead does suggest that in Samoa, girls found looking after younger siblings boring and would rather not have done so (Feinberg, 1988). They saw it as a chore rather then their natural role or socialization for the future. Whether or not they saw it as an economic activity, as part of their 'natural' gender role (as Mead implied) or as an age related issue also needs examination but without detailed investigations into their understandings of their gender and the impact it had on their lives many such studies are frustratingly oblique.

Conclusion

Both anthropology and sociology are beginning to embrace the study of childhood and children's lives as mainstream concerns and there has been useful collaboration between the two disciplines in the emerging field of childhood studies. Within the new discipline however, there are certain gaps, most notably discussions of childhood as gendered and the impact of children as social and economic agents. While most sociologists and anthropologists have accepted the contribution of women to household economies, the economic role of girls is still under-studied and consequently under valued. There is still, all too frequently, an elision between socialization and economic activity and childcare by girls is routinely commented on without an acknowledgement of the contribution this plays in the home. It is a blindness shared by parents, children and academics and is based on Western assumptions about the essential economic passivity of the child. It is an area which demands much more research, as well as a conceptual shift in how we understand children, their role in the family and the expectations placed on them by their gender. While ideas about the essential economic incapacity of children are now being challenged, it is rare to find this in combination with the understandings that girls' experiences need to be placed within a conceptual matrix which includes both gender and generation. Only when these two shifts occur will girls' economic worth truly be taken into account. The new anthropology of children has succeeded in its insistence on the importance of age and generation but in doing so, gender has been pushed to the margins. The challenge for childhood studies now is to emphasize the importance of the inter-linkage between the study of generation and gender, to get rid of the notion of the 'strange, ungendered isolate' and replace it with a vision of a child as both a young person and a gendered one.

References

Baker, R. (1998) *Negotiating identities: a study of the lives of street children in Nepal.* Unpublished doctoral thesis, University of Durham.
Berlan, A. (2004) *Child labour in Ghana.* Unpublished doctoral thesis, University of Oxford.

Blanchet, T. (1996) *Lost innocence, stolen childhoods* (Dhaka, University of Dhaka Press).

Burr, R. (2000) *Understanding children's rights.* Unpublished Ph.D. thesis, Brunel University.

Chagnon, N. (1968) *Yanamamö: the fierce people* (New York, Holt, Rinehart & Winston).

Ennew, J. (1986) *Sexual exploitation of children* (Cambridge, Polity Press).

Ennew, J. (1993) Maids of all work, *New Internationalist,* February, 240, 12–13.

Ennew, J. (1994) *Street and working children* (London, Save the Children).

Feinberg, R. (1988) Margaret Mead and Samoa: coming of age in fact and fiction, *American Anthropologist,* 90(3), 656–663.

Firestone, S. (1971) *The dialectic of sex* (London, Jonathan Cape).

Firth, R. (1936) *We, the Tikopia* (London, George Allen & Unwin).

Fortes, M. (1974) The first born, *Journal of Child Psychology and Psychiatry,* 15, 81–104.

Gow, P. (2001) *What Piro children find interesting,* paper presented at the *Children in their Places Conference,* Brunel University, London, 21–23 June.

Gullestad, M. (1984) *Kitchen table society* (Oslo, Scandinavian University Press).

Hamilton, A. (1981) *Nature and nurture: aboriginal child-rearing in north-central Arnhem Land* (Canberra, Institute of Aboriginal Studies).

Hardman, C. (1973) Can there be an anthropology of childhood?, *JASO,* 4(1), 85–99.

Harkness, S. & Super, C. (1983) The cultural construction of child development, *Ethos,* 11(4), 221–231.

Hecht, T. (1998) *At home in the street: street children of northeast Brazil* (Cambridge, Cambridge University Press).

Hull, T. (1975) *Each child brings its own fortune.* Unpublished doctoral thesis, Australian National University.

James, A. (1993) *Childhood identities: self and social relationship in the experience of the child* (Edinburgh, Edinburgh University Press).

James, A. & Prout, A. (1997) *Constructing and reconstructing childhood: contemporary issues in the sociological study of childhood* (London, Falmer).

James, A., Jenks, C. & Prout, A. (1998) *Theorizing childhood* (Cambridge, Polity Press).

Jenks, C. (1992) *Childhood* (London, Routledge).

Johnson, M. (2000) The view from the *Wuro*: a guide to childrearing for Fulani parents, in: J. DeLoache & A. Gottlieb (Eds) *A world of babies. Imagined childcare guides for seven societies* (Cambridge, Cambridge University Press).

Laerke, A. (1998) By means of re-membering. Notes on a fieldwork with English children, *Anthropology Today,* 14(1), 3–7.

La Fontaine, J. (1986) An anthropological perspective on children, in: M. Richards & P. Light (Eds) *Children of social worlds* (Cambridge, Polity Press).

La Fontaine, J. (1990) *Child sexual abuse* (Cambridge, Polity Press).

Malinowski, B. (1922) *Argonauts of the Western Pacific* (London, Routledge).

Mead, M. (1928) *Coming of age in Samoa* (London, Pelican).

Mead, M. (1930) *Growing up in New Guinea* (New York, Morrow).

Mead, M. & Wolfenstein, M. (1955) *Childhood in contemporary cultures* (Chicago, University of Chicago Press).

Miles, A. (1994) Helping out at home: gender socialization, moral development and devil stories in Cuenca, Ecuador, *Ethos,* 22(2), 132–157.

New, C. & David, M. (1985) *For the children's sake: making childcare more than women's business* (Harmondsworth, Penguin).

Nieuwenhuys, O. (1994) *Children's lifeworlds. Gender, welfare and labour in the developing world* (London, Routledge).

Nieuwenhuys, O. (1996) The paradox of child labor and anthropology, *Annual Review of Anthropology,* 25, 237–251.

Oakley, A. (1985) *The sociology of housework* (Oxford, Blackwell).

Oakley, A. (1994) Women and children first and last: parallels and differences between children's and women's studies, in: B. Mayall (Ed.) *Children's childhoods: observed and experienced* (London, The Falmer Press).

Panter-Brick, C. (2000) Nobody's children? A reconsideration of child abandonment, in: C. Panter-Brick & M. Smith (Eds) *Abandoned children* (Cambridge, Cambridge University Press).

Panter-Brick, C. (2001). Street children and their peers: perspectives on homelessness, poverty, and health, in: H. Schwartzman (Ed.) *Children and anthropology: perspectives for the twenty-first century* (Westport, Bergin & Garvey).

Powdermaker, H. (1933) *Life in Lesu. The study of a Melanesian society in New Ireland* (London, Williams & Norgate).

Qvortrup, J. (1994) *Childhood matters: social theory practice and politics* (Aldershot, Avebury Press).

Radcliffe-Brown, A. R. (1933) *The Andaman islanders* (Cambridge, Cambridge University Press).

Reynolds, P. (1991) *Dance civet cat: child labour in the Zambezi Valley* (Harare, Baobab Books).

Riley, D. (1984) *The war in the nursery: theories of the child and the mother* (London, Virago).

Schapera, I. (1971) *Married life in an African tribe* (London, Pelican).

Scheper-Hughes, N. & Sargent, C. (1998) *Small wars. The cultural politics of childhood* (Berkeley, University of California Press).

Schildkrout, E. (1978) Roles of children in urban Kano, in: J. La Fontaine (Ed.) *Sex and age as principles of social differentiation* (London, Athlone Press).

Solberg, A. (1998) Negotiating childhood: changing constructions of age for Norwegian children, in: A. James & A. Prout (Eds) *Constructing and reconstructing childhood* (Basingstoke, Falmer Press).

Stephens, S. (1995) *Children and the politics of culture* (Princeton, Princeton University Press).

Wolf, M. (1972) *Women and the family in rural Taiwan* (Stanford, Stanford University Press).

Index

Page references in italics indicate an illustration, t following a page reference indicates a table

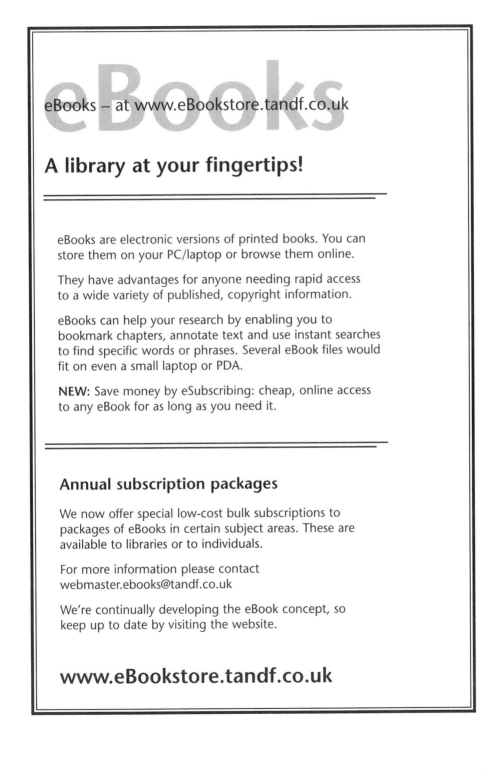

Nutrition: A Lifespan Approach

Simon Langley-Evans, BSc., Phd., RNutr.

Chair in Human Nutrition
School of Biosciences
University of Nottingham

WILEY-BLACKWELL

A John Wiley & Sons, Ltd., Publication

This edition first published 2009
© 2009 Simon Langley-Evans

Blackwell Publishing was acquired by John Wiley & Sons in February 2007. Blackwell's publishing programme has been merged with Wiley's global Scientific, Technical, and Medical business to form Wiley-Blackwell.

Registered office
John Wiley & Sons Ltd, The Atrium, Southern Gate, Chichester, West Sussex, PO19 8SQ, United Kingdom

Editorial offices
9600 Garsington Road, Oxford, OX4 2DQ, United Kingdom
2121 State Avenue, Ames, Iowa 50014-8300, USA

For details of our global editorial offices, for customer services and for information about how to apply for permission to reuse the copyright material in this book please see our website at www.wiley.com/wiley-blackwell.

The right of the author to be identified as the author of this work has been asserted in accordance with the Copyright, Designs and Patents Act 1988.

Library of Congress Cataloging-in-Publication Data

Langley-Evans, S. C.
    Nutrition : a lifespan approach / Simon Langley-Evans.
      p. ; cm.
    Includes bibliographical references and index.
    ISBN 978-1-4051-7878-5 (pbk. : alk. paper) 1. Nutrition–Textbooks.
I. Title.
    [DNLM: 1. Nutritional Requirements.   2. Diet.   3. Growth and Development–physiology.   4. Nutrition
Assessment.   5. Nutritive Value. QU 145 L283n 2009]
      QP141.L2 2009
      612.3–dc22

                                                                                        2008053122

A catalogue record for this book is available from the British Library.

Set in 10/12pt Minion by Aptara® Inc., New Delhi, India
Printed in Singapore

1   2009